The Historicity of International Politics

The past is constantly present, not least in the study of imperialism and imperial forms of power in international politics. This volume shows how historical trajectories have shaped international affairs covering a wide range of imperial and (post-)colonial settings in international politics, substantiating the claim that imperial and colonial legacies – and how they have transformed over time – are foundational to the historicity of international politics. It contributes to debates on the role of history in International Relations (IR) by combining theoretical arguments on the role of history through the concept of 'historicity' with concrete empirical analyses on a wide range of imperial and colonial legacies. This volume also advances interdisciplinary perspectives on this topic by fostering dialogue with Historical Sociology and Global History. It will interest scholars and advanced students of IR, historical sociology and global politics, especially those working on the history of international politics, and the legacies of colonialism and imperialism.

Klaus Schlichte is Professor of International Relations and World Society at the University of Bremen. His works, published in English and German leading political science journals, cover theories of political sociology, armed conflict and dynamics of state domination. He has carried out research in Germany, Senegal, Mali, Serbia, France and Uganda, and he has taught in the United States, France, Kyrgystan and Germany.

Stephan Stetter is Professor of International Politics and Conflict Studies at the University of the Bundeswehr Munich. His research, published in leading journals and with leading book publishers, addresses historical-sociological topics revolving around international politics, violent conflicts with a particular focus on the Middle East as well as EU foreign politics. He has carried out research in Israel, Palestine, Lebanon and the EU institutions in Brussels.

The Historicity of International Politics

Imperialism and the Presence of the Past

Edited by

Klaus Schlichte

University of Bremen

Stephan Stetter

University of the Bundeswehr Munich

CAMBRIDGE
UNIVERSITY PRESS

CAMBRIDGE
UNIVERSITY PRESS

Shaftesbury Road, Cambridge CB2 8EA, United Kingdom

One Liberty Plaza, 20th Floor, New York, NY 10006, USA

477 Williamstown Road, Port Melbourne, VIC 3207, Australia

314–321, 3rd Floor, Plot 3, Splendor Forum, Jasola District Centre, New Delhi – 110025, India

103 Penang Road, #05–06/07, Visioncrest Commercial, Singapore 238467

Cambridge University Press is part of Cambridge University Press & Assessment, a department of the University of Cambridge.

We share the University's mission to contribute to society through the pursuit of education, learning and research at the highest international levels of excellence.

www.cambridge.org
Information on this title: www.cambridge.org/9781009199056

DOI: 10.1017/9781009199100

First published 2023

A catalogue record for this publication is available from the British Library.

A Cataloging-in-Publication data record for this book is available from the Library of Congress

ISBN 978-1-009-19905-6 Hardback

Contents

Figures

Contributors

TOMOKO AKAMI is Associate Professor (Reader) in the College of Asia and the Pacific at the Australian National University. Her most recent research project is 'Towards a Globalised History of International Relations' (the Australian Research Council, 2020–2023). Her publications include *Internationalizing the Pacific* (2002), *Japan's News Propaganda and Reuters' News Empire in Northeast Asia* (2012), *Soft Power of Japan's Total War State* (2014) and 'Imperial Polities, Inter-colonialism, and the Shaping of Global Governing Norms', *The Journal of Global History*, 2017.

MATHIAS ALBERT is Professor of Political Science at the Faculty of Sociology of Bielefeld University. His current research interests are in the sociology and history of world politics, polar politics and science, and youth studies. His most recent books include *A Theory of World Politics* (Cambridge University Press, 2016), *What in the World? Understanding Global Social Change* (edited with T. Werron, Bristol University Press, 2021), *Envisioning the World. Mapping and Making the Global* (edited with S. Holtgreve, K. Preuß, transcript, 2021), *The Social Evolution of World Politics* (with H. Brunkhorst, I.B. Neumann and S. Stetter, transcript, 2023).

BENJAMIN DE CARVALHO is Research Professor at the Norwegian Institute of International Affairs (NUPI) in Oslo. His research focuses on the status, state formation and identity, sovereignty and the historical emergence of overseas empires. Recent publications include 'Everyday Sovereignty: International Experts, Brokers and Local Ownership in Peacebuilding Liberia' (with X. Guillaume and N. Schia), *European Journal of International Relations*, 2019, 'Moral Authority and Status in International Relations: Good States and the Social Dimension of Status Seeking' (with H. Leira, W. Wohlforth and I. B. Neumann), *Review of International Studies*, 2018 as well as 'The Making of the Political Subject: Subjects and Territory in the Formation of the State', *Theory & Society*, 2016.

JOËL GLASMAN is Professor of African History at the University of Bayreuth. His research focuses on the history of the post-colonial state, refugee regimes and humanitarianism. His last book analyses humanitarian statistics and the emergence of an international government of Africa: *Minimal Humanity: Humanitarianism and the Quantification of Human Needs* (Routledge, 2020).

JULIAN GO is Professor of Sociology at the University of Chicago. His recent books include *Global Historical Sociology* (edited with G. Lawson, Cambridge University Press, 2017) and *Postcolonial Thought and Social Theory* (Oxford University Press, 2016). His forthcoming book, *Policing Empires: Militarization and Race in Britain and America, 1829–Present* (Oxford University Press), explores the colonial origins of police militarization in the United States and England. It continues the theme of US empire in his earlier books, *Patterns of Empire: The British and American Empires, 1688 to the Present* (Cambridge University Press, 2011) and *American Empire and the Politics of Meaning* (Duke University Press, 2008).

TERESA KOLOMA BECK is Professor of Sociology at Helmut Schmidt University in Hamburg. Her research focuses on everyday life in the borderlands of global modernity. Recent key publications are 'Violent Conflictition: Armed Conflicts and Global Competition for Attention and Legitimacy' (with T. Werron), *International Journal of Politics, Culture, and Society*, 2018, and 'Welterzeugung: Gewaltsoziologie als kritische Gesellschaftstheorie', *Zeitschrift für Theoretische Soziologie*, 2019.

GEORGE LAWSON is Professor of International Relations at the Australian National University. His work focuses on the relationship between international relations and history, with a particular focus on global historical sociology. His most recent books are *On Revolutions* (co-authored with C. Beck, M. Bukovansky, E. Chenoweth, S. Nepstad and D. Ritter, Oxford University Press, 2022), *Anatomies of Revolution* (Cambridge University Press, 2019) and *Global Historical Sociology* (edited with J. Go, Cambridge University Press, 2017).

HALVARD LEIRA is Research Professor at NUPI in Oslo. His research falls mainly under the heading of Historical International Relations, with an emphasis on conceptual history, diplomacy and foreign policy. His latest publications include *The Sea and International Relations* (edited with B. de Carvalho, Manchester University Press, 2022), *The Routledge Handbook of Historical International Relations* (edited with B. de Carvalho and J. Costa Lopez, Routledge, 2021) and 'The Emergence of Foreign Policy', *International Studies Quarterly*, 2019.

THOMAS MÜLLER is Postdoctoral Researcher at Bielefeld University. His main research interests are great power politics, the interplay of hierarchies and the politics of quantification in world politics. In his PhD thesis, he traced the history of the allocation of special rights and duties to the group of great powers. In the Collaborative Research Centre 1288 'Practices of Comparing' at Bielefeld University, he currently co-leads a project that studies how state and non-state actors produce and use knowledge on the distribution of power in world politics. His most recent articles have been published in the *Review of International Studies*, *Global Society* and the *European Journal of International Security*.

IVER B. NEUMANN is Director at The Fridtjof Nansen Institute, Norway. His research focuses on states systems. His latest books are *The Steppe Tradition in International Relations: Russians, Turks and European State-Building 4000 BCE–2018 CE* (with E. Wigen, Cambridge University Press, 2018) and *Concepts of International Relations, for Students and Other Smarties* (University of Michigan Press, 2019), *The Social Evolution of World Politics* (with M. Albert, H. Brunkhorst and S. Stetter, transcript, 2023).

KLAUS SCHLICHTE is Professor for International Relations and World Society at the University of Bremen. His research areas are state formation, internationalized rule and political violence in a historical sociology perspective. His books in English language are *Extended Experience: The Political Anthropology of Internationalized Politics* (edited with S. Biecker, Rowman & Littlefield, 2021), *In the Shadow of Violence: The Politics of Armed Groups* (Campus Verlag and Chicago University Press, 2009) and *The Dynamics of States: The Formation and Crisis of State Domination* (ed., Ashgate, 2005).

DANIEL SPEICH CHASSÉ is Professor of Global History at the University of Lucerne. His research focuses on the history of knowledge in international relations. He has published an influential German-language monograph on the invention of the gross domestic product, namely *Erfindung des Bruttosozialprodukts* (Vandenhoeck & Ruprecht, 2013) and several articles on the historical unfolding of comparative statistics of nations since the late eighteenth century. The latest contribution is 'In Search of a Global Centre of Calculation: The Washington Statistical Conferences of 1947', in W. Steinmetz (ed.), *The Force of Comparison: A New Perspective on Modern European History and the Contemporary World* (Berghahn, 2019).

GEORGE STEINMETZ is the Charles Tilly Collegiate Professor of Sociology in the Department of Sociology at the University of Michigan and a Corresponding Member of the Centre de Sociologie Européenne, Paris. He is a social theorist and a historical sociologist of colonial history, the history of social science, social and sociological theory. His most recent publications are: *The Colonial Origins of Modern Social Thought: French Sociology and the Overseas Empire* (Princeton University Press, 2023) and *The Social Sciences in the Looking-Glass: Studies in the Production of Knowledge* (with D. Fassin, Duke University Press, 2023).

STEPHAN STETTER is Professor of International Politics and Conflict Studies at the University of the Bundeswehr Munich. His research focuses on theories of politics in global modernity, world society theory and international politics, as well as Middle East politics and society. His recent books are *Middle East Christianity: Local Practices, World Societal Entanglements* (edited with M. Moussa Nabo, Palgrave, 2018) and *Modern Subjectivities in World Society: Global Structures and Local Practices* (edited with D. Jung, Palgrave, 2018), *The Social Evolution of World Politics* (with M. Albert, H. Brunkhorst and I.B. Neumann, transcript, 2023).

ANNA VLACHOPOULOU is Lecturer of Southeastern Europe at the Ludwig-Maximilian University Munich, specializing in the history of the Ottoman Balkans. Among her key publications are *Revolution auf der Morea: Die Peloponnes während der zweiten Turkokratie (1715–1821)* (De Gruyter Oldenbourg, 2017) and 'Osmanische Eliten in Südosteuropa: Konkurrenzen, Kooperationen, Konflikte, am Beispiel der Peloponnes', in I. Zelepos and K. Roth (eds.), *Klientelismus in Südosteuropa* (Peter Lang, 2018).

EINAR WIGEN is Professor of Turkish Studies at the University of Oslo, where he works on political legitimacy and imperial legacies in Turkey, the Ottoman Empire and the wider Turkic world. He is the author of *State of Translation: Turkey in Interlingual Relations* (University of Michigan Press, 2018) and *The Steppe Tradition in International Relations: Russians, Turks, and European State Building, 4000 BCE–2017 CE* (with I. B. Neumann, Cambridge University Press, 2018).

AYŞE ZARAKOL is Professor of International Relations at the University of Cambridge and a Fellow at Emmanuel College. Her research is at the intersection of IR and historical sociology, focusing on East–West relations in the international system, history and future of world order(s), conceptualizations of modernity and sovereignty, rising and declining powers, and Turkish politics in a comparative perspective. She is the author of *After Defeat: How the East Learned to Live with the West* (Cambridge University Press, 2011) and the editor of the prize-winning *Hierarchies in World Politics* (Cambridge University Press, 2017). Her most recent book, *Before the West: the Rise and Fall of Eastern World Orders*, which advances an alternative global history for IR to rethink the concepts of sovereignty, order and decline, was published in 2022 by Cambridge University Press.

Acknowledgements

The journey towards the publication of this volume started in the city of Duisburg, back in 2015, where the idea of this book originally emerged when we both had (successfully) run for the chairmanship of the IR section of the German Political Science Association. As one of our 'election promises', we suggested to gather a group of internationally renowned colleagues in order to explore the imperial underpinnings of international politics, and the role of historicity in international politics, more generally speaking. Our journey then took us to several destinations in Germany where we have held inspiring author conferences with the contributors summoned in this volume. These conferences were held in the very south of Germany, namely in Bayrischzell, Bavarian Alps and the very north of the country in Bremerhaven, North Sea. We are grateful for financial (the University of Bremen and the University of the Bundeswehr Munich) and logistical support, not least by Stephan's student assistants David Frank and Alexander Heinze. Gunnar Bantz helped us to create the index. Many thanks also to John Haslam, Tobias Ginsberg and Shivani Nallana from Cambridge University Press our copy-editor Vishal Thuyavan and Thirumangai Thamizhmani from Lumina Datamatics for shepherding us through the publication process and to the two anonymous reviewers for their insightful comments that have helped in strengthening the arguments in this volume. The final product now rolls out to the world from Cambridge in England, and we hope to not have only formally delivered on our election promise: our hope is to not only have brought such a book on the market but hopefully to inspire in the discipline and beyond more conceptual and empirical work on the entanglements between imperialism, historicity and international politics.

Introduction

1 The Presence of the Past

Imperialism and Modes of Historicity in International Politics

Klaus Schlichte and Stephan Stetter[1]

1 Introduction

What does it mean to say that international politics has a history? To us, this seems to be one of the most fundamental questions that can be asked in the discipline of International Relations (IR). In this book, we suggest that drawing from the concept of historicity – and ensuing modes of historicity – can provide fruitful answers to this question, while studying imperial politics and their afterlives provides promising empirical 'flesh' for such conceptual debates.

This focus on history – or, more specifically, on the concept of historicity and on imperial formations – is in our view important not least due to the discipline's widely acknowledged theoretical crisis stemming inter alia from the largely ahistorical set-up of its core theories (Buzan & Little, 2001; Dunne et al., 2013). As the work by historian Herbert Lüthy – who taught at the universities of Zurich and Basel and from whom we have borrowed the notion of *the presence of the past* – shows IR is not alone amongst academic disciplines in this ahistoricism. Thus, in his 1967 essay 'History as Self-Reflection' (*Geschichte als Selbstbesinnung*), Lüthy (1967: 28) forcefully argues that there is an encompassing, yet unfortunate trend in European philosophy since early modernity of ignoring history, amounting to 'the bankruptcy of ahistorical political philosophy'. This is also the bankruptcy of much IR theorizing, not surprising given its Eurocentric underpinnings (Hobson, 2012). Thus, for much of its history as an academic discipline, wide segments of IR had neglected historical analysis both as an empirical point of reference and as a fundamental element of theorizing. Fortunately, though, the last few years have witnessed a growing interest in history in parts of IR,

[1] We wish to thank Lisa Gaufman and Alex Veit, as well as all contributors to this book, for comments on earlier versions of this chapter. We also profited a lot from the helpful and stimulating comments by the two anonymous reviewers.

in particular through a highly dynamic research field coined historical sociology of IR (HSIR; starting with Hobdon & Hobson, 2002; Lawson, 2006; Hobson & Lawson, 2008; for an overview, cf. de Carvalho et al., 2021). This is a research field with which also this volume self-identifies, wishing to contribute and further develop debates in HSIR by bringing in the concept of historicity.[2] The critique levelled against core IR theories – such as liberalism, realism, regime theory and social constructivism – by the HSIR shows some overlaps with other fields of research across the social sciences and humanities that study the effects of history on global political relations. Thus, post-colonial perspectives, Global History and Global Historical Sociology, to mention the most prominent examples, are research fields that share with the HSIR an interest in how history shapes the world we live in. A focus on history includes, crucially, the question how history appears differently depending on from where it is studied. For example, scholarship under the banner of 'Global IR' and post-colonialism pleas to pay much greater attention to the intellectual traditions and concrete political perspectives from the Global South, many of them shaped by historical experiences. We should note here that we see most conceptual complementarity between the HSIR, on the one hand, and Historical Sociology (e.g. Steinmetz, 2014; Go & Lawson, 2017), and Global History (e.g. Osterhammel, 2009, 2016; Bayly, 2016), on the other. This will also be reflected in the structure of this book that brings in studies on the historicity-imperialism nexus that, while attempting to be interdisciplinary from the outset, departs from IR (Part I of the book), Historical Sociology (Part II) and Global History (Part III).

We do not claim that these research fields are the same and will highlight in the following text what distinguishes our approach – situated in and further contributing to HSIR perspectives – from post-colonialism and Global IR but also from Global History (there are most overlaps of our approach, and the HSIR at large, with Historical Sociology). Yet, what all these different perspectives have in common is that they

[2] See Section 2 for a detailed overview on this literature. It is beyond the scope of this introduction to make judgements about IR literature in other languages than English. Such an analysis would be part of a truly global history of IR as a discipline. Suffice here to say that to our knowledge, both in France and in Germany, there is a continuous tradition of IR scholarship stressing the historical dimension of international politics. In the German context, though, this historical orientation was somewhat lost by a self-proclaimed 'internationalization' of German IR and an increasing dominance of regime and governance theories and liberal 'constructivism' with its well-known ahistoric presentism. As far as English-language IR is concerned, and the niches historically interested scholarship has maintained therein in the HSIR and beyond, see the remainder of this chapter.

underline, explicitly or implicitly, that the historical dimension of international politics ought not to be ignored, neither in IR theorizing nor in empirically inclined studies of international politics. While, thus, departing from this joined assumption, we develop in this chapter and the book at large a novel conceptual angle on this topic rooted in the HSIR (and Historical Sociology as well as Global History). Doing so, we will draw extensively from continental European scholarship so far less familiar to a readership from the Anglosphere, namely a research angle based on the concept of historicity (or *Geschichtlichkeit*) – which we develop from the writings of historians and philosophers like Herbert Lüthy, William Sewell, Jürgen Osterhammel, Fernand Braudel and Hans-Georg Gadamer (see Section 3). Historicity then is the core concept of this book. Historicity allows us to not only trace and theorize the presence of the past in international politics but, generally speaking, enables us to take into account the broader temporal dimension of international politics at large.

The core idea about historicity – which we break up further in the following text in this chapter into six specific modes of historicity studied throughout the various chapters of this book – is that the past is not over. Instead, the past is constantly enacted and constructed in the present. As Lüthy (1967: 23) explains, the past ought to take centre stage for two reasons. Firstly, because studying social and political relations, at least in global modernity, is about integrating into our conceptual vocabulary the fundamental notion of 'world history', that is, situated positionalities. This is an argument shared by Global IR and post-colonialism. Secondly, and most fundamentally, this is because the past generates the very present and the future(s) we (will) live in. As Lüthy (1967: 37) notes succinctly, all the '"un-dealt past" is today present as a present-un-dealt'. In other words, the political struggles, cleavages and conflicts of our contemporary era is a temporal extension, into the presence, of re-enacted and therefore un-dealt pasts. This past is present in languages, in concepts, in mental maps, in practices and materiality, in the social habitus of political and administrative personnel, and even in the very logics of what international politics is meant to be. Historicity can, in sum, be defined as the historically formed infrastructures, specific semantics and multi-layered temporalities of social contexts within and between which political action takes place. History, from that perspective, is not something from a by-gone point of time but the 'function of its respective presence' (Lüthy 1967: 34). As such, the past also extends into the future. To paraphrase Lüthy (1967: 32) once more here, it is one of the gravest methodological errors to consider the past 'over-and-out', and likewise the future as something undetermined and 'free'. Historicity is our conceptual contribution to a debate unfolding in HSIR and related academic fields that all show that history is so much more than to 'only' look back. And if there is a need for a handy definition, then we would suggest to view historicity as the unity of past, present and future, mediated and enacted through invocations of specific dimensions of the past, which allow to make sense of the present and conceive of the future.

Further below in this chapter, we will identify on that basis six different modes of historicity, which then also guide the analysis in the various contributions to this volume. These modes of historicity (see Section 4) are (1) the role of history in shaping reality, (2) the centrality of complex temporalities, (3) the paramount importance of the temporality of observers, (4) the necessity to interpret contexts, (5) the significance of sedimented forms of power and domination and (6) change through non-linear pathways. Building on this concept of historicity, we aim to show what is in store, theoretically and empirically, when looking at international politics as a social realm with a historical dimension that is not gone by, but constantly present: in sum, the presence of the past.

Our argument about historicity is of course not restricted to present times. In other epochs, politics have had their historical imprint as well. But these days, we see a particular urgency to discuss the history of IR more thoroughly. One reason is the return to imperial motives and the invocation of former imperial grandeur that many observers ascribe, for example, to Russia's and Turkey's foreign policy. The analysis of the historicity of foreign policy is, in our view, all the more needed in order to disentangle legitimization strategies of post-imperial politics. Historicity is thus not calling for accepting whatever historical arguments are made. It means to understand and to explain how historical claims appear in foreign policy discourses and practices, for example, in Russian president's Vladimir Putin (2021) rather imperial-style essay on Ukraine's historical (and, for him, of course future) relationship with Russia. A second argument of urgency can well be studied when looking at the EU. Thus, some scholars have portrayed its interventionist roles since the early 2000s as those of an 'empire in denial' (Chandler, 2006), while others, quite to the contrary, miss a more assertive stance of the EU that should live up more to what it allegedly already is: namely an empire, as amongst others political theorist Münkler (2006) claims. In our view, accepting the historicity of IR will enable us to be much more reflective about the repercussions of such bold statements.

We proceed in this chapter as follows. In Section 2, we make the case why looking at imperialism – the cross-cutting theme addressed in every chapter in this book – is a particularly fruitful way for both tracing the role of history in international politics and making use of the concept of historicity. Section 3 then delineates our argument – based on the HSIR with some continental European flavour – from other approaches in IR that focus on history, in general, and imperial and colonial underpinnings of international politics, in specific. This applies not only to post-colonial studies but also to the recent move towards 'Global IR', to studies of empires and to the historical perspectives prominent in the English School. We are sympathetic to these approaches but think that an HSIR and in particular a more systematic recourse to the concept of historicity overcomes some of the conceptual and empirical limitations of these other research traditions. In Section 4, we will then lay out in greater detail the main contours of the concept of historicity and how this can be linked to the study of imperialism in international politics, past and present. At the end of this chapter, in Section 5, we will briefly present the core arguments of the other contributions to this volume, and will outline what consequences historical thinking, and the recognition of historicity, has in our view for the development of methods and theory building in IR. The chapters in this book, while all engaging with the concept of historicity and while all drawing from research on international politics inspired by the HSIR, Global History and Historical Sociology, depart from three distinct disciplinary angles: Part I of the book (Chapters 2–7) as well as Ayşe Zarakol's conclusion (Chapter 14) are written mainly from historically oriented IR perspectives, whereas Parts II and III of the book bring in interdisciplinary perspectives shaped by Historical Sociology (Chapters 8–10) and Global History (Chapters 11–13).

2 Imperialism in the Past and Its Presence in International Politics

History, as should be clear by now, is not just about generating more and more data in the form of empirical 'facts' one should know. And it also is not only about showing how contemporary structures and events of international politics – think of trade, diplomacy and war – originally formed. What has to be added here, and where the concept of historicity comes in, is understanding that the past is present in international politics in a much more fundamental way. We will address this historical grounding of international politics throughout this book on the basis of a cross-cutting thematic issue addressed in every chapter, namely the imperial and colonial past and present of international politics. This choice is based on the centrality which imperial/colonial imprints have for international politics on several levels – thus underlining both the academic and the policy-related urgency of engaging in a much more focused manner with imperialism and its afterlives in the context of historically informed IR. Several aspects have to be considered here.

Firstly, and contrary to IR's widespread statism, it is only for the last sixty years or so that one can reasonably talk about an international system consisting of nation-states. Yet, most mainstream IR theories start from the implicit but mythical assumption that international politics always, or at least since 1648 or 1919, has been shaped by states (Carvalho et al., 2011) – and this while in fact empires, and not states, had been the dominant actors in international arenas for centuries. As the contributions to this book show, the shadows of empires continue to be a powerful undercurrent of international politics until today (cf. Halperin & Palan, 2015). Strangely, none of the so-called core IR theories has taken this sufficiently into account. Thus, empires – and in that context imperialism and colonialism – have only recently gained greater traction in the discipline, mainly thanks to the contribution of postcolonial perspectives and the HSIR. The chapters by de Carvalho and Leira as well as Wigen and Neumann offer an alternative perspective, namely one that widens the focus on forgotten origins and actor constellations – and their legacies – for international order, for example, privateering (de Carvalho & Leira) and steppe-nomadic empires (Wigen & Neumann).

Secondly, West European nation-states – including France and Great Britain – are often perceived, both in scholarship and in public discourse, as centuries-old entities. Yet, during most of their modern history, some of them were first and foremost empires, consisting of highly diverse populations and based on authoritarian relations between the metropolitan centre and the peripheries. These empires, like other actors, waged wars of subjugation and violently repressed opposition. They institutionalized legal inequality between citizens and subjects (Mamdani, 1996), while enforcing modernization by drawing from forced labour, resettlement and land expropriation. They were, in short, 'imperial republics' (Aron, 1973). These features, and not their state characteristics, shaped the way they engaged in international politics too. For example, their imperial past has been the hotbed of the very institutionalized racism that can be considered a structural feature of domestic and international politics until today (cf. Arendt, [1951] 1976: chap. 7; Vitalis, 2000).

A third insight concerns the 'liberal' ordering of the international system that is seen endangered today by the rise of 'populism' or even outright authoritarianism. While populism is certainly a destabilizing factor both in many domestic contexts and internationally, such a concern ignores that for most people on the planet, international order (or domestic order as in the US) was for most of the time never really liberal (cf. Mehta, 1997; Vitalis, 2000). The history of individual global mobility, or rather immobility, is perhaps the most evident indicator of the persistence of different and often illiberal legal spheres, many of them imperially induced, that distinguish between carriers of specific passports (many of them Western) and the rest.

Finally, the imperial past is present as an interpretive frame of international politics. For example, in most if not all formerly colonized arenas, Western interventions tend to be read until today through the lens of the colonial and imperial past. Intervening powers too follow imperial scripts, as in the case of French interventions in West Africa (Schlichte, 1998). Russia's relations to its 'near abroad' (Isachenko, 2019)[3] or the debate about Germany's hegemonic role in Europe (cf. Markovits et al., 1996) and the EU's attempts to shape its neighbourhood (Del Sarto, 2016; Forsberg & Haukkala, 2018) point to similar dynamics. Or imperial pasts can be invoked in memory cultures as Vlachopoulou and Stetter discuss in this book with a view to the battle of Kosovo and the status of Jerusalem. In short, in international politics, the Global South is often perceived as a security problem (Bilgin, 2010), while interventions in various formats by mainly but not exclusively the West are portrayed as a cure. Moreover, in that context, mainstream IR theories tend to overlook and under-theorize the agency of the East and South (Hobson, 2007), for example, in the 'politics of extraversion' (Bayart, 2000; cf. Glasman and Schlichte's chapter in this volume).

Looking at IR at large, addressing such imperial imprints must still be viewed as a challenge to a disciplinary hegemony that for long has rather ignored and suppressed history, in general, and imperial dynamics, in specific. We, thus, consider this book as a continuation of a growing research stream in IR that emphasizes the historical dimension of international politics and its imperial imprints. While the current state of research in historically oriented IR is comprehensively presented in de Carvalho et al. (2021), we would only wish to mention here that we see the beginning of a systematic interest in this topic in Hobden and Hobson's plea for a historical sociology of international relations published

[3] Note that this text was finalized in January 2022. We see the war of Russia against Ukraine that started a few weeks later, as well as the ensuing debate on this war, as a pertinent case for the general argument of this book. We have deliberately decided not to include hasty passages on our interpretation of this specific war into this chapter or the book at large – trusting that solid, historically and sociologically grounded studies on this topic speaking to the overall theme of 'historicity' will be published by us, our authors in this volume or others in the years to come.

back in 2002 (for more on the HSIR, see Section 3).[4] This can also be read as some form of convergence of research in Global History, Historical Sociology and historically oriented IR – the three main conceptual perspectives represented in the various contributions of this book too. For our argument about historicity, Hobson and Lawson (2008) mark a decisive turning point. This is because they made a powerful plea for a 'historicist historical sociology' as a middle way between radical historicism and ahistoric positivism. Bringing in imperialism then was an almost natural offspring therefrom. Thus, as Hobson (2012) has shown a few years later, this suppression of history is closely linked to an underlying Eurocentrism in Western international theory throughout the modern era, in both its imperialist and anti-imperialist traditions. Studies of disciplinary history and intellectual history are therefore an important strand in literatures that challenge ahistoric disciplinary traditions. This applies, for example, to Rosenboim (2017) and Bell's (2007) studies on the imperial backgrounds of ideas about global order, or to Bayly's (2016) work on the role of imperial imaginations, frontier zones and interventionist politics. Vitalis's (2000, 2015) analysis of the hidden history of racism and African-American internationalism and Bell's (2019) edited volume about the neglected long-term effects of imperial expansion on the notion of global justice are equally important contributions that underline the new interest in formative effects of imperial history for international politics. Contributions of particular relevance here are furthermore the studies by Bartelson (1995) and Walker (1993), which address the genealogy of the international system and the history of ideas in that context. This also includes Bartelson's (2017) study on the evolution of the concept of war. Carvalho et al.'s (2021) edited book offers, as highlighted earlier, an excellent overview on core facets of historical IR, including discussions on the role of empires. The works by Branch (2014) on the history of cartography and by Nexon (2009) on state formation within composite political structures in European history are highly informative for our analysis of contemporary dynamics of political domination too – as is, finally, Halperin and Palan's (2015) edited book that addresses the manifold legacies of empires – both Western and non-Western, formal and informal (such as the US) – in today's world.

A major outflow from this growing interest in history and patterns of domination in global politics have been publications inspired by

[4] We restrict ourselves here to IR in English-speaking contexts. Interestingly, both in German and in French IR, similar tendencies emerged around the same time (cf. Bayart, 1996; Bayart, 1996; Siegelberg & Schlichte, 2000). In the German-language context, the notion of historicity of international politics, which we highlight in this book, has recently been suggested also by Hoppe (2021).

historical-sociological thinking. This is not a single church but relates to a broad range of studies. Some of them are firmly anchored in specific theoretical tradition, such as Marxism and critical theory. Rosenberg's (2006) concept of 'global uneven and combined development', inspired theoretically by Leon Trotsky, stands out here (cf. Anievas & Matin, 2016) – and sheds light on how a combination of economic, technological and political factors has allowed the West to dominate international politics. Anievas and Nişancıoğlu (2015) have in that context highlighted the global origins of capitalism as a major underlying force of international politics. The racist underpinnings of international order shaped by a 'global colour line' is central here too (Anievas & Nişancıoğlu, 2015), as are studies of global hierarchies and of an auto-orientalism of (former) non-Western empires such as Japan, post-Ottoman Turkey and post-Soviet Russia (Zarakol, 2010, 2017). Important here is also research on historically generated frames that shape the perception of actors in contemporary politics. A good example here is Autesserre's (2010) work on the role of frames in the context of international peacebuilding and how such frames sustain the reification of imaginaries of an allegedly secure but threatened West versus a perception of an insecure and dangerous South.

This short overview, in sum, offers manifold reasons why studying historicity through the prism of imperial underpinnings of international politics is in our view a highly promising way forward. In many ways, the turn to the HSIR has been crucial for a much greater empirical and theoretical consideration of hierarchies and imperial legacies in IR. As one reviewer for this book argued (and we apologize to all feather vertebrates and ornithologists here), this focus on imperialism kills two birds with one stone: we develop the concept of historicity, while placing it in a burgeoning non-Eurocentric literature on the imperial past and its extension into the present. We do not limit ourselves here to a pure post-colonial analysis, which is in our view all too often haunted by politicized and rather schematic dichotomies between an alleged all-powerful West and an allegedly constantly marginalized Global South. Instead, we ground this analysis firmly in an HSIR – which in our view is conceptually more nuanced than most post-colonial scholarship – thereby wishing to contribute to both literatures on imperialism/colonialism and debates on the role of history in international politics more generally speaking. We will further develop this argument by discussing in greater detail in the following section core literatures in IR and beyond on the role of history in international politics, in general, and the past and present of imperial imprints of international politics, in specific.

3 History and the Imperial Condition: An Overview on Debates in IR

3.1 Historical Lenses in IR and the Main Contours of Historical Sociologies of IR

As highlighted above, scholars from many corners of the IR universe have, over the course of the last two decades, criticized the state of the discipline when it comes to (the lack of) taking 'history' into account. There is no need to recapture here in detail the entire spectrum of research in historically oriented IR scholarship (cf. de Carvalho et al., 2021). But a few comments are useful, not least because we see our own approach firmly placed within this school of HSIR (Hobden & Hobson, 2002; Hobson & Lawson, 2008; Hobson, 2012; Go & Lawson, 2017). We wish to direct attention in this chapter in particular on what 'historical' and 'sociologies' in an HSIR implies. Firstly, highlighting the role of history has triggered fascinating IR research (e.g. Buzan & Lawson, 2015; Albert, 2016) that extends the usually 'temperalocentrist' outlook of IR scholarship on more or less post–World War II international politics, to a much wider research project that includes crucially a focus on the formative effects of the nineteenth century and the global entanglements during that period also studied, but less theorized, by Global History, for the contemporary global political system – or even extends to studies that cover much longer time-periods, even taking into perspective early human civilizations and the international relations they entertained (Buzan & Little, 2000; Neumann & Wigen, 2018). When we say sociological here we basically have two main dimensions in mind. This is firstly, a systematic perspective on how social change and transformations (e.g. revolutions and technological changes) affect international politics, for example, the various societal changes during the nineteenth century, such as industrialization and the emergence of mass societies (cf. Buzan & Lawson, 2015). Secondly, then, a sociologically informed perspective sheds light on social and political power as well as the exercise of domination (*Herrschaft*). This is a perspective that not only underpins the turn of some IR scholarship to the study of hierarchies and domination but also struggles over social positions across various (international) fields. We firmly think that such a sociologically informed view on power in international politics offers a much richer theoretical and empirical perspective on international politics, both past and present, than the still popular but in our view quite meagre concept of anarchy.

Against the background of this steadily growing scholarship in the field of the HSIR that subscribes to the relevance of history and a sociologically informed perspective on power and domination, it appears to us as not accidental that we witness in that context a simultaneously growing interest in post-colonial and imperial imprints of international politics. This allows also overcoming a tendency in much IR theorizing to uncritically mimic (Western) government perspectives without much distance to the language used, the methods employed or the problems addressed. This deficit has, of course, been scrutinized from different angles that share a joint approach in challenging mainstream statist as well as Eurocentric perspectives. This includes the feminist critique of IR (Weber, 1999; Tickner, 2001, 2006; Sjöberg, 2012), pleas for an ethnography of IR (Vrasti, 2008; Biecker & Schlichte, 2021), critical security studies (Booth, 2005; Hansen, 2013) and a more general move towards 'Critical IR' (cf. Linklater, 1990; Siegelberg, 1994; Schlichte, 2005; Bayart, 2008; Weber, 2014; Koddenbrock, 2015; Anderl & Wallmaier, 2018).

In addition to such approaches, we consider it particularly noteworthy that, from angles different to an HSIR, scholarship in other branches of IR has also (re-)discovered history as a central concept to address theoretical and empirical deficits in the discipline. While these historically oriented perspectives in IR address manifold issues, one of the key research foci has been the renewed interest in the imperial and colonial past, and how this past shapes contemporary affairs. Without getting into detail here, it is important to understand that this interest is renewed in the sense that there are traditions in IR that had highlighted long ago that colonialism and European imperialism are constitutive parts of international politics. We think here in particular of world systems theory and *dependencia* theory. Currently, we see – apart from the HSIR – two other very prominent debates at the forefront of the contestation of established IR theory through historical lenses that address imperial underpinnings. These are post-colonial studies and the plea for 'Global IR'. We add to this a discussion of the English school's perspective on history and IR. In order to further situate the HSIR – and in particular our own approach and the concept of historicity (which we will outline in detail in the next section) – we will now offer a short overview on how imperialism/colonialism is discussed in post-colonialism, Global IR and the English School, while highlighting also where we see shortcomings of these approaches that an HSIR based on the concept of historicity in our view helps overcoming.

3.2 *The Post-colonial Critique of IR and Its Limits*

For more than twenty years now, the post-colonial critique of social science theorizing, including IR, has questioned 'Eurocentrism' and its rationalization as theory. Chakrabarthy (2000) has powerfully made this point. Ever since, it has become more and more accepted that modernity, understood in its idealized version in liberal social and political theory, is a fundamentally contested concept if not purely ideological. The second major criticism by post-colonial studies pertains to the silenced dark side of modernity. Not only is the violent past of colonialism ignored in many social theories, but it even lives on in binary oppositions that delineate an idealized liberal, modern and democratic West or North from an allegedly violent, undemocratic and traditional South or East. Paramount here is, of course, Said's (1978) analysis of 'Orientalism' as a discursive pattern that reifies the Middle East as a backward and savage region in opposition to a self-proclaimed civilized Western Europe. Since then, the genesis of this imaginary has been developed in great detail by analyses of the history of political ideas (e.g. Todorov, 1989), of the history of Africa (e.g. Mudimbe, 1988; Mbembe, 2000, 2013) and the Balkans (Todorova, 1997).

Over the last twenty years, post-colonial studies – but also studies on connected histories owing to a sociological tradition (Bhambra, 2007) – have emphasized the pertinent role of the colonial past for the structure of our current international system (Darby, 2004; Seth, 2011). This scholarship has made an important contribution to a better understanding of global imperial entanglements including the historical linkages between the colonized in anti-colonial struggles, as in Shilliam's (2015) work on the Pacific region. Key studies in the field have focused on specific aspects of international politics, globalization and post-colonialism, such as in Barkawi's (2005) study of war or Jabri's (2012) analysis of post-colonial subjects, but also in studies relating to the interstices between globalization and post-colonial order (Krishna, 2008; Persaud & Sajed, 2018). It should be noted though that notwithstanding its many merits, post-colonialism also comes with some problems. By often presenting binaries, post-colonialism at times cannot adequately account for the huge differences, over time and space, between different colonial and post-colonial settings, nor for the differences between different *situations coloniales* (Balandier, [1951] 1952) and post-colonial situations (Smouts, 2007), including hybrid identities and connected histories. Moreover, neither colonial nor post-colonial time is linear. There is a great variation in terms of speed, rhythms and conjunctions. As has been highlighted (Cooper, 1991; Bayart & Bertrand, 2006), post-colonial studies – many times driven by a highly politicized yet conceptually simplistic impulse – often neglect the historicity of the highly diverse historical forms of colonialism, the forms of accommodation and adaptation as well as the importance of intermediary rule. Our argument about historicity is exactly about these differences. While we agree that the historical imprint of empires and colonialism is all-too often ignored in IR, we find it implausible that history and its weight is reduced to the history of colonialism. Such a position could, for example, not adequately deal with empires that were not 'colonial' or at least Western in the usual sense, like the Russian/Soviet empire or Ottoman rule. Both were mainly political projects, even though they there were not void of a 'civilizational mission' (cf. Laurence, 2009: 78–80). Furthermore, other important varieties of historicity are ignored in most post-colonial perspectives. This applies, for example, to the realm of post-socialist settings, ranging from East Germany to the Chinese border. But even cases like state formation in Liberia, Thailand or Ethiopia can hardly be subsumed under a post-colonial framework.

There is no doubt, in our view, that there is a persistent fundamental antagonism in global politics and that this has been rightly highlighted by post-colonial studies, drawing inspiration from the classical anti-colonial writings of Césaire (1955), Fanon (1952, 1961), and Du Bois (1944). This is an antagonism between an Orientalizing West, the powerhouse of international politics, and an Orientalized Global South in which various strategies of adopting and resisting Western dominance have shaped foreign and domestic policies during the last two centuries at least (see with a view to Afghanistan the chapter by Koloma Beck). Post-colonialism has thereby shown that there is a deep-seated global mentality that attributes rationality and security to the West, while non-Western conflicts, states and people are regularly constructed as security problems that need to be regulated, developed and controlled (Li, 2007; Jabri, 2012). In current IR debates such reflections have then been taken up by scholars, for example in critical security studies, that see a continuity of this binary thinking in the way that interventions and the 'war on terror' play out. The South then is a constitutive Other – the colony in the past, failed states, organized crime and transnational terrorism today – that shapes the self-understanding and self-assertion of 'the West' (Bilgin, 2010).

The core argument in post-colonial thought in IR is that such perceptions of Self and Other in international politics go hand in hand with deeply entrenched power asymmetries. As mentioned above, Hobson (2012) has shown that this suppression of history is closely linked to an underlying Eurocentrism in Western international theory throughout the modern era, in both its imperialist and anti-imperialist traditions. Such studies of disciplinary history and intellectual history are therefore another important strand in the literature that allows detecting this formative role of history. Mentalities that emerged in colonial and imperial times persist, even if in modified form, and these mentalities have real-world consequences, leading to the current post-colonial condition that endures even decades after the formal demise of most formal colonial systems. One can think here of the underlying security imperative of international peace-building in Central Africa (Autesserre, 2010; Veit, 2010), in Afghanistan (Owen, 2015) and the Middle East (Stetter, 2008). Many researchers have rightfully highlighted that international security is fundamentally shaped by an underlying binary structure that juxtaposes a global or Western order that needs to be protected, and threats to this order that stem from insecurity that is constructed as ontologically inherent to the Global South. It was noted how this affects immigration policies (Bigo, 2002) as well as the merger of development and security policies (Duffield, 2001). Terrorism, poverty, violence, migration, corruption, ethno-national conflicts, failed statehood and other dynamics are constructed as a problem of the Global South and not as phenomena that result from the unevenness and power asymmetries of international politics. This re-inscribes the past in the present insofar as such bifurcated trajectories have been part and parcel of classical colonial ways of securing 'order' in colonized territories (see also the chapter by Go in this volume).

In other words, the complex ways through which global power asymmetries and hierarchies contribute to such insecurities is the blind spot of many academic and policy-related discussions on global threats such as state failure, transnational terrorism and organized crime. It is an interesting and frustrating observation that such a Eurocentric view that obscures imperialism and hierarchies also undergirds most of the canonical IR theories, for example in Waltz and Wendt, as Hobson (2012) elaborates in his landmark book on *The Eurocentric Conception of World Politics*. Yet, and notwithstanding the merits of post-colonial approaches, we are sceptical of some of the fundamental assumptions that shape the analytic and normative agenda of post-colonial scholarship. Two problems stand out in our view. The first is that post-colonialism depends analytically speaking on the assumption of a fundamental binary between the colonized and the colonizers. In combination with the politicized impulses in parts of post-colonial scholarship, this has not only nurtured a neglect of non-Western forms of colonialism, but also fostered an all-too schematic dichotomization between colonizers and colonized that ignores notions of hybridity, connectivity as well as the quite diverse forms of (post-)colonial encounters studied for example in the Historical Sociology of imperialism (Steinmetz, 2007). Secondly, then, post-colonial scholarship often tends to underestimate the complexities as well as the productive dimension of power (e.g. what Foucault terms the power of the marginalized or what Bourdieu refers to when studying power struggles in social fields; for an alternative take based on Balandier see the chapter by Speich Chassé on the emergence of the notion of the 'Third World').

3.3 Global IR and Theories of Empire

The second stream of critical contributions is more recent but not less interesting for the theoretical development in IR. Almost twenty years after historians turned to Global History, the plea for the globalization of IR has reached this discipline as well. Here, the call is to de-centre theories and concepts that are criticized as being largely based on European history, Greek-Roman antiquity, and on political concepts from the US (Acharya, 2014). The alternative focus is to focus on international relations (theory) from around the world (Tickner & Wæver, 2009), although Global IR lacks – in contrast to an HSIR – a clear conceptual perspective, unless one considers the call for diversity and de-centring theory as such (for a de-centring of IR theory based on a historically informed perspective see the chapter by Akami in this book). By highlighting, for example, the role of transnational religious communal beliefs like the *umma* (cf. Shani, 2008), and other traditions of international political thinking in non-Western regions and intellectual spheres (Bilgin, 2008), a multitude of contending perspectives comes into focus. The goal then is to overcome imaginations of a world in which all good things allegedly derive from the 'developed' North and are just adopted elsewhere, as for example, liberal diffusion theory holds (Börzel & Risse, 2012). That this is a construction is shown by Speich Chassé and Akami in this volume. Halperin and Palan (2015) have shown that the juxtaposition of a developed North and an underdeveloped South is itself a legacy of empires at work.

While arguably post-colonial theory and the project of 'Global IR' are the most prominent fields of study in IR that today highlight the centrality of imperialism and colonialism, one should also mention theories of empire here. Or better: the theory of a global, neo-liberal empire with the US as its hub, as this has been studied by Hardt and Negri (2000) as well as, even though in a different manner, by Strange (1988). It also figures somewhat in Rosenberg's (2006) conceptualization of global politics around the idea of 'global uneven and combined development'. Ikenberry (2001) – and Mazower (2013) in the field of Global History – has linked this discussion on empire to the institutional structure of international politics. According to this perspective, what we see in the context of the UN – and precursors such as the League of Nations and the

Concert of Europe – can be described as ingrained inequality based on institutional rules established by the leading imperial power of the time, such as Britain in the nineteenth century and the 1920s and the US in the 1940s (see the chapter by Müller in this volume).

We consider these studies very useful but think that they can be enriched through a more systematic consideration of how the complex set-up of global modernity impacts on imperialism and its afterlives. This is where the sociological dimension of the HSIR comes in again. Central in the study of empire from such a perspective has then been in particular the work by Steinmetz (2007, 2014, this volume). Debates in the Historical Sociology of empire have, for example, shown that the formation of nation-states in Europe cannot be separated from imperial expansion and 'imperial cultures' (Blanchard & Lemaire, 2004), that erected moral codes of superiority and inferiority, including labour and gender relations (Stoler, 1997), and produced categories like castes and tribes in the colonies which became organizing principles even in daily life (Cooper & Stoler, 1997: 5). From a disciplinary angle it has then been observed that the social sciences throughout the West have been part of these cultural projects too (Steinmetz, 2013), as they introduced a division of labour between sociology (for the West) and anthropology (for the rest). The long-lasting effects can be seen today, as this is probably one of the reasons why so many fields of social sciences ignore non-Western regions and their experiences in theory-building and empirical research – a tendency hopefully gradually eroding not least through attempts to decolonize theory-building by integrating intellectual traditions from the Global South (and the non-English-speaking world in the West too; Mignolo & Walsh, 2015; Derichs, 2017). Historians have also shown that imperial powers always tried to universalize their own particularity, producing counter-movements in the form of nationalist attempts of emancipation (Laurence, 2009: 236). This too is not just an affair of the past, as traces of imperial attitudes connected with a habitus of civilizational superiority can be found not only in Western colonialism but to take a concrete example, also in contemporary German discourse about Poland (cf. Conrad, 2014).

3.4 *The English School and Related Approaches*

A final exception from the ahistoric nature of core IR theories is the English School. Due to its overarching core concept of 'international society', the English school has an in-built interest in understanding how, historically, this society had formed and great power relations therein play out.

This also includes the issue of how non-Western outsiders – such as Japan, China and the Ottoman Empire – tried to become accepted members of international society (Buzan, 2018). The British committee on the theory of international politics, out of which the School formed, owed much to the contribution of historians, like Herbert Butterfield, but also IR scholars highly sensitive to the role of history and trained in historical study. Aalberts (2010) recaps the centrality of history in the work of Manning (1962). A key contribution in the English School context has been Buzan's (2004) discussion of how the central institutional parameter of international society, which he refers to as primary institutions, emerged and changed in historical time. This includes primary institutions such as diplomacy, war, balance of power, trade and human rights. The notion of primary institutions bears resemblance to Reus-Smit's (1999) historical focus on the foundational institutions of different international societies in human history, while Dunne and Reus-Smit (2017) discuss change in the context of globalizing effects in international society.

Yet an explicit reference to imperialism and colonialism has only recently and half-heartedly appeared in the English School and has so far not been systematically integrated into broader English School thinking and it is here that we see some in-built limitations of the English School fully engaging with an HSIR – arguably resulting from its state-based bias ingrained in the concept of international society. The fact that imperial legacies are an important component is though part of Buzan's (2014) discussion of the so-called 'standard of civilization' – pertaining to the broader impact of colonial institutions for modern international politics to which Keene (2002) has pointed and which can, more generally speaking, been studied in the context of theories of hierarchy in international politics, as in the work by Zarakol (2017). A particularly important contribution – beyond the English School – has been made by Philips and Sharman (2015) who have shown – closely linked to an argument about heterogeneity that also figures strongly in our book – that notwithstanding the paramount importance of global interconnectedness and pervasive hierarchies, international order is to a large degree characterized by enduring diversity and complex power constellations (cf. Philips & Reus-Smit, 2020). Buzan and Lawson (2015) have, finally, highlighted the centrality of colonial and imperial centre-periphery relations in the nineteenth century for the way international society got consolidated in this period, while others such as Gonzalez-Pelaez (2009) have linked the English School concept of international society to the study of non-Western regional international societies, such as the Middle East.

4 Temporality and the Concept of Historicity

4.1 Starting Points

As discussed in the previous section, post-colonial criticism, the plea for a 'Global IR', insights from Global History in IR-literature and the historical elements in the English School have rendered the topic of history more central to current IR debates and are perspectives that provide important additions to an HSIR. In this section, we want to push the debate yet another step forward by asking a fundamental question: What does it now mean theoretically when we conceive of international politics having a history? This leads us to our core argument, namely that introducing the concept of historicity (see our arguments on Lüthy in Section 1) and modes of historicity not only enriches other historical sociologies of IR – but also offers in our view conceptual perspectives that are often neglected in scholarship from post-colonial, Global IR and English School perspectives, but can and should certainly be brought in dialogue with them.

Of course, several answers to the question what it means theoretically when conceiving of international politics having a history can be imagined (for a discussion on scales and levels in a theory of history in IR see the chapter by Albert). A first one would perhaps stress that the past is an *Eldorado* of empirical evidence. In a sense, what we call international politics belongs, after all, to the past – as actually any empirical object is, at the moment of study, already a thing of the past. The history of international politics in that sense is just a host of data points, it is the deeds and 'facts' of what historiography has filtered and reconstructed from sources left over or handed-down from whatever earlier past, be it days or centuries. This is perhaps the understanding of history that prevails in general opinion, and it is also dominant in mainstream IR. History is data about past events.

A second answer would be closer to what historians usually stress vis-à-vis an often all to brisk attitude in the social sciences which often treat all centuries and eras alike, paying only little attention to differences between historical times. History in this second meaning is a statement against universal claims, sweeping theses and law-like propositions. Historians would stress that international politics in different regions and at different historical times works quite differently, that even the term 'international' is an expression of a particular time and does not make much sense universally throughout history. This second position contradicts thus the first view as it rejects the notion of a homogeneous historical space and stresses particularities and differences instead.

In this section, we will build on this objection by (global) historians and present our major theoretical tenets of what it means when we acknowledge 'historicity' as a fundamental trait in the study of international politics. For that end, we build on the structuralist understanding of Fernand Braudel, the reflections of William H. Sewell on temporality, and on Jürgen Osterhammel's approach to global history and link this with the philosophical work on hermeneutics by Hans Georg Gadamer and, finally, the study of *Geschichtlichkeit* in the work of Lüthy (1969), which we had already introduced in detail earlier in this chapter. As highlighted in the beginning of this chapter, the core idea about historicity is that the past is not really over. Instead, it is present in its constant re-construction based on countless material, practical and discursive instances of international politics, including theories of international politics. In all these instances, we find traces of the past and its structuring effects.

We see these arguments in particular in line with the move towards a 'global historical sociology' (cf. Chapters 8 and 10 in this volume), a position that we feel closest to and that complements other studies in the tradition of an HSIR referred to above, from Hobden and Hobson (2002) to Carvalho et al. (2021). This line of reasoning we suggest here runs as follows: moving beyond the tradition of 'international history',[5] global history has emerged as a prolific field of historical research attempting to leave behind methodological nationalism and Eurocentric concept formation. It looks at flows and global-local entanglements instead of taking legal, institutional, or any other boundaries and fixed structures as starting points. We need, global historians argue, to look instead at formations, slow or quick, as well as on emergence and processes. Doing this does not deny that structures matter. It would in fact mean to identify the *longue durée* of institutions understood as the outcome of social conflicts and to look at asymmetries and differences, in order to see what changes take place and in what temporal rhythm.[6] Furthermore, historians usually show a strong reluctance to strive for abstract generalizations, probably because they are aware of much more variety of social and political forms than the average IR scholar looking at post–World War II and Western shaped events and structures.

[5] International History is the state-centred tradition in which historians have used to work on questions of international politics prior to the turn towards global history. Not unlike diplomatic history, an almost forgotten early paradigm in IR, it overlaps with studies in IR of scholars such as for example Schroeder (1994, 1997).

[6] We should acknowledge that there are different temporalities, different speeds of action and of change, often in the same time-space as expressed in Ernst Bloch's notion of the 'simultaneity of the non-simultaneous' (*Gleichzeitigkeit des Ungleichzeitigen* (cf. Bloch, 1932).

Historians share this extended experience with social anthropologists as they too encounter often fundamentally different social and political logics at work.

4.2 Temporality in Global History

We are inspired, as far as the title of this book is concerned, by the writings of historian Herbert Lüthy (1918–2002). His path-breaking collection of essays from 1967 'In the Presence of the Past' (*In Gegenwart der Geschichte*) outlines the fundamental ideas that have today become a generally accepted understanding of historiography: History as such is by-gone forever and untraceable. What we call history are only the fragments that we know of it, based on sources that are interpreted by us in the light of the present time. And yet, this present time is itself a historical product. Any statement on the past is thus both historically impregnated and shaped by the preoccupations of our present time. Both dimensions render interpretations of a given social context inherently difficult and challenging. Moreover, academic analyses become a very demanding intellectual activity, as 'historical rights' are so often invoked for legitimizing specific political projects. Based on Lüthy, a number of additional arguments by (global) historians appear to us as crucial for understanding better why the present and the past are actually inseparable.

Jürgen Osterhammel can be seen as one of the most prominent authors of global history, a field of research that took off in the late 1990s and has become one of the most dynamic fields of contemporary history writing. In his landmark study on the nineteenth century, Osterhammel (2009) gives a rather structuralist account of the changes he considers, like later on Buzan and Lawson (2015), to be fundamental in shaping the modern world, for example, industrialization and changes in technology. He makes a strong plea for overcoming the distinction between historiography as a merely descriptive science, while sociology (and one might add IR here) is conceived as a science of the generalizable. Global history as the history of entanglements and embeddedness draws from a plurality of approaches and a 'controlled eclecticism' (Osterhammel, 2016: 27). While comparative in nature, it focuses on fluidity, flows and liquidity of movements and change, as well as on processes and networks that leave old 'national' and 'regional' history writing behind. Instead, Global History focuses on all sorts of global-local entanglements (Osterhammel, 2016: 38). Osterhammel furthermore raised the question, in what language, and with the help of which concepts these changes can be studied without suppressing too much diversity, conjunctures and contradictions. This leads him to the notion of temporality, which is closely linked to the concept of historicity. His plea here is to take into account that changes take place in different temporal scales, a theoretical challenge though that neither sociology nor global history has so far sufficiently addressed (Osterhammel, 2016: 41).

Osterhammel follows up on a problem here that another prominent historian with theoretical outlook, Sewell (2005), had also highlighted with regard to the relationship between history and the social sciences. Sewell too wants to overcome the stereotype of history as ideographic versus sociology as a nomothetic science. He also pays particular attention to the question of temporality. Time, as Sewell sees it, is infateful and irreversible, it is replete with sequences, with contingent outcomes and with punctuating events. Even stronger is his claim that temporal heterogeneity, a point he shares with Osterhammel, implies causal heterogeneity – the search for universal laws and probably even decontextualized mechanisms so widespread in IR is in vain. In different historical times – and due to the non-simultaneity of different contexts, to paraphrase Bloch (1932) – there are different temporal rhythms. Events can obviously change causal logics – the defeat of the French nobility, for example, changed the rules of the game of French politics, and by extension of the 'international game'. Contexts differ not only, they change, and this may create different causal pathways. Contextualization is therefore mandatory (Sewell, 2005: 10).

In addition to this, Sewell argues against an overtly structuralist understanding of history and prefers a concept of 'eventful history', in which stubborn durability goes hand in hand with sudden breaks. Path-dependencies are not more important than temporally heterogeneous causalities and global contingencies (Sewell, 2005: 102), and good causal narratives matter in his view as much as mathematical formalization and statistical calculation. The aim of comparisons is then not to establish causal laws but to theorize and explain historical developments in each case (Sewell, 2005: 121). As Sewell maintains, 'the epic quest of sociology for laws is illusory' (Sewell, 2005: 110). With his emphasis on the idea of 'eventful history', Sewell is explicitly critical of one of the hallmark contributions to the theory of history, namely Fernand Braudel's concept of the *longue durée*. One could, and we would, however, read the two authors discussed above as mere comments to Braudel's attempt to create the ground for a theory of history that would not need teleological ideas but would neither end up in a simple collection of unconnected stories.

Braudel distinguishes three levels of temporality that mark any context. The first is the layer of events and of news that constitutes most of what we call political history. It is the 'the most treacherous', we 'hardly see its flame' (Braudel, 1969: 45) and we can only judge its importance if we assess its impacts on the two other layers. The second then is the layer of cycles and conjunctures, the movements of prices, trends and slow changes that historians can observe and discern as changing patterns. The third layer is reached when changes become 'secular tendencies', when they become structures that matter for several generations, as we find them in modes of production, in settlement patterns, religious beliefs and infrastructures. It is only in long, diachronic comparisons that the *longue durée* becomes visible. But in order to understand a context, the identification and the constant reference to the *longue durée* as a baseline is mandatory since the assessment of the causal weight of events and trends is impossible without taking into account this core of the historical formation of social contexts, including political ones.

4.3 Modes of Historicity and the Study of Imperialism

Drawing from these insights derived from writings on temporality in Lüthy, Sewell, Osterhammel and Braudel, the concept of historicity thus relates to the historically formed infrastructures, specific semantics and multi-layered temporalities of social contexts within and between which political action takes place. Historicity, thus understood, matters for IR on the following six modes that describes the various modes of historicity that allow to conceptualize the ways the imperial past is inscribed in the presence of international politics and that are discussed in greater detail in the subsequent chapters. We develop these modes in particular by linking them to elements of the philosophy of Hans-Georg Gadamer.

Firstly, and most centrally, history shapes. It shapes not only infrastructures and other material dimensions, but also – as all chapters in this book show – our modes of thinking (or, as de Carvalho and Leira explain, our modes of forgetting), our schemes of perception and evaluation. Even our language is historically formed in contexts. Historical experiences are therefore stored in languages, as well as in concepts and in the rules regulating their usage. Historicity means, in the words of Gadamer, that the authority of the past (*Autorität des Überkommenen*) exerts power over our actions and behaviour: 'The reality of customs, for example, is and will remain to a large extent valid due to the validity of origin (*Herkommen*) and transmission (*Überlieferung*)' (Gadamer, 1990: 285). This can be well exemplified when looking at the history of imperialism and how imperialism shapes international politics and dominant IR approaches. This is basically a Foucauldian argument on genealogy, based on power-knowledge nexuses: In that context, it is noteworthy that a genealogy of IR was for a long time unwritten.[7] In recent critical contributions on this largely neglected topic, such as in Hobson (2012), and in earlier seminal work by Bartelson (1995) or Walker (1993), the power-knowledge nexus of mainstream IR, its imbrication in 'real' politics, became quite apparent. Thus, realism is a theoretical understanding that is taught in military academies around the globe, it serves as a legitimizing discourse for foreign policy staff and countless state employees around the world. Liberal IR theory, on the other hand, is hard to be disconnected from a political process of internationalization and globalization, be it by think tanks, private foundations and, as a quite well-studied case, the EU or international organizations (see the chapter by George Lawson on a different take on the colonial origins and legacies of international organizations). Critical approaches to IR are usually based on experiences with oppositional social movements and non-governmental organizations in Western societies and the Global South. They represent a power-knowledge nexus that operates around oppositional reflexes, rather than entrenched power hierarchies. To delve into the genealogy of theoretical schools reveals their historicity, as all theories come from somewhere, are formed and shaped in particular settings and in particular historical times – and tend to serve specific interests. Beyond the power-knowledge nexus, our argument about historicity applies as well to practices and ideas that form international relations as a concrete social realm. There are famous and very visible cases of foreign policy that cannot be explained without reference to 'historical reasons'. France's numerous interventions in its former African colonies, a practice continuing until today, can only be explained by referring to the political habitus of the French political class in which the former colonies are not just any countries but a specific realm of action (cf. Schlichte, 1998; Powell, 2017). Similar observations can be made about Russia's foreign policy towards its neighbours (Toal, 2017), about Germany's 'drive to the East' (*Drang nach Osten*) or the resented interferences of US foreign policy in Latin America, and, finally, with a view to intervention practices of Middle Eastern states vis-à-vis each other (Halliday, 2005). The historicity of foreign policy has not remained unnoticed, but in our view, it has theoretically been hidden by superficial categorizations as 'historical reasons' or 'geopolitical interest', or, as in liberal constructivism, as 'norms' or 'ideas' that matter (e.g. Checkel, 1999). When attention

[7] The most comprehensive attempt, not confined to IR in a narrow disciplinary understanding, is Heinz Gollwitzer's two volumes on 'Geschichte des weltpolitischen Denkens' (1972/1982). Much less comprehensive but closer to the present is the work by Knutsen (2016).

is paid to the historicity of these relations, seemingly irrational or even pathologic behaviour of governments, popular attitudes or single leaders' actions become, all of sudden, in a sociological sense, comprehensible.

Secondly, history unfolds in complex temporalities (see, e.g., the chapters by Lawson, Müller, Glasman/Schlichte, Wigen/Neumann and Albert from an IR perspective, or Koloma Beck and Go from a Historical Sociology perspective, as well as Speich Chassé and Vlachopoulou/Stetter from Global History viewpoints). Teleological understandings of history are nice narratives, but historically flawed. Francis Fukuyama's conservative Hegelian attempt in 1989 to declare the 'end of history' was probably a late version of a long-standing tradition to see history as a linear process with a *telos*, one that also figured in Wendt's (2003) notion of the world state. Building on the notions of temporality identified above, we are also cautioning against an understanding of a smooth flow of a homogeneous time, stressing instead discontinuities, ruptures and turning points. Often, coincidence matters more than strict causalities. These convulsions of big events, sudden ruptures, contrasted by long stagnation and stable institutional settings create a *temps mondial* (Laïdi, 1999) of its own. The temporalities of imperialism are complex and diverse, too. As the contributions in this volume show, the imperial experience consists of different stories. Thus, imperial experiences have not been all of the same kind, they adhere to diverse *temps mondial*. There are huge differences both in the global historical timing of when empires were erected, and when their forms of subordination developed as different forms of domination emerged, depending largely on local conditions. The duration of empires differs enormously and so do the political consequences that endure until the present time. The impact of colonial rule was, for example, much stronger in the settler colony of South Africa than amongst nomads in the Sahara (e.g. Dayak, 1992; Bourgeot, 1994). The speed and form of conquest created differences as did the length and depth of population control. In some instances, these might have been quick and disruptive experiences, eventful histories in the sense of Sewell, in others rather slow encroachments and incremental changes of livelihoods. This alone is a reason to abstain from sweeping statements about colonial rule across continents and centuries. And that is why Bayart and Bertrand (2006) have asked: 'Of which colonial heritage are we talking?'

Thirdly, history is linked to the observer. Historicity is not only a quality of the observed but of the observer too. The long history of hermeneutics as the art of reconstructing meaning has taught us that interpretation requires a connection of the interpreter to the interpreted texts and artefacts. While all academic disciplines strife for some kind of objectivity in their observations, interpretations are heavily dependent on the historicity of the observer (see here particularly the chapters by Steinmetz, Koloma Beck and Akami as well as the conclusion by Zarakol). 'Human beings in history' (Gadamer, 1990: 145) is an expression for the insight that epistemological positions cannot be detached from historical settings as history is not only present but that 'we ourselves stand in it' (Gadamer, 1990: 203). It is these differences that account, presumably, for a lot of controversy about imperial past and its impact on the presence both in the political realm and also in academic debates. The historicity of the observer, the observer's cultural upbringing, historical experiences and lifeworlds render viewpoints more or less convincing. So far, only a rather marginal methodological school in IR, namely the ethnographic debate about the positionality of authors addresses this head-on (cf. Vrasti, 2008; Biecker & Schlichte, 2021). This observer-dependence nevertheless plays a great role in the study of colonial rule and imperialism. Imperial experiences still have an impact on political debates, creating far-reaching contestation also within academia. Anthropology was perhaps the first discipline to critically address its own history because scholars became increasingly attentive to experiences untold and voices unheard. This new attention played, for example, into the scandal when French president Nicolas Sarkozy stated in Dakar in 2007 that colonialism was an inevitable and benign civilizing endeavour. It created an outcry not only in West Africa but also among French intellectuals. Ongoing discussions about the restitution of artefacts from museums in London, Paris and Berlin, or the dispute over colonial monuments are litmus tests of how diverse the views on the colonial pasts are. As several contributions in this volume show, the imperial past still is a golden age in the eye of some and a dark age in the eyes of other observers.

Fourthly, historicity highlights the need for interpretation. As we have argued, historicity is not a 'fact' that can be directly observed and is uncontested.[8] Indeed, a lot of political discourse in any setting is about the interpretation of history (see here, e.g., the chapters by Glasman/Schlichte, Wigen/Neumann as well as by Akami, Speich Chassé and Vlachopoulou/Stetter). When scholars agree that history matters it does not mean that they agree on what exactly this means for a particular subject. Basically, the discipline of history has its critical role here as its discussions are attempts to develop contests about the plausibility of different interpretations, including the methods on how such plausibility can be

[8] While there is some overlap of our position with historical institutionalism (cf. Fioretos, 2011; Rixen et al., 2016), institutionalism has so far not sufficiently taken into account historicity as an interpretivist prerequisite.

established, what a sufficient number of sources is for what kind of statement and how to weigh plausibility. Political science, in particular when trusting too much in formal discussions about causality or 'grand theory', has so far underestimated the weight of these operations for our self-understanding and for appropriate ways of dealing with the past and its presence. What can be learned here from historians is perhaps that a first prerequisite for a decent interpretation is a deep knowledge of contexts (even of 'forgotten' ones as de Carvalho and Leira show in their chapter on the entanglements between imperialism and privateering). Not the formal elegance of a mathematical model or the parsimonious purity of theories is the ultimate measure for the quality of an explanation but how much of the context has been taken into account since language, views of actors across political arenas, and other historically relevant features matter most for interpretive explanations. This expertise will of course not replace the rigid force of logical thinking. However, it is not just complementary but necessary as any form ultimately is empty if it has no historical content. The essential point of our argument here is that without an engagement with the past, a decent interpretation of politics – such as the imperial underpinnings of international politics – is not possible. Even when coming from a behaviouralist tradition, interpretation will depend on earlier experiences. Nowadays, an understanding of social sciences prevails that follows Max Weber's famous definition of social action, according to which both observable behaviour and subjective meaning of social actors have to be part of any explanation. If we take this view a step further by asking what makes a good interpretation, we can follow the hermeneutical argument that any part can only be understood well in its relation to the whole (cf. Gadamer, 1959). To delve into the history of political action, of political structures and institutions would then mean also to think about relatedness, of insertions into broader settings, both temporal and spatial. It is this *mise en relation* that renders the particularities and specificities of a given social contexts, such as imperial dynamics in international politics, visible.

Fifthly, studying the presence of the past in international politics is always also an analysis of power (see here, although another running theme in almost all chapters, in particular, the chapters by Lawson, Müller, de Carvalho/Leira as well as by Steinmetz, Koloma Beck and Go and Zarakol's conclusion). With this argument, we want to insist on the particular value of studies in IR that acknowledge the historicity of its subjects. This does not mean that the future is determined by the weight of the past, nor should we infer from this that the future of IR lies exclusively in studying the past. But it means that a lot of power relations, and in particular those that we often take for granted or do not even notice, such as post-colonial hierarchies, become only visible when we study the past and the stories of how things came into being. To identify such meanings, however, needs critical discussion of competing interpretations. This interpretive struggle about history is of course a power phenomenon too (see also the arguments by Zarakol in the concluding chapter). This applies to political institutions, apparatuses and arenas, but it also applies to the way we think and argue. The debate about 'decolonizing' social sciences and popular knowledge is basically about this. Political history is particularly well suited for making this point. The historicity of political domination is mostly unobserved and not immediately visible. Most of what Weber calls legitimate orders and what is infrastructural power for Mann (1984) are such unobserved, sedimented rules of *longue durée*. That states have territorial boundaries, that governments make decisions, that there is a legal difference between citizens and non–citizens, all these are legitimate conceptions, yet they are historically produced. The study of orders, of the rules of world, and of international politics at large needs thus to a large extent be focused on the detection of sedimented forms as parts of domination, of power that has become so deeply engrained that it usually even elapses attention and is difficult to get addressed. In contrast to these sediments of international politics that become visible through the prism of the concept of historicity, there is perhaps a general exaggeration of power in many IR theories that aim to detect a conscious and deliberate will, as if domination would mostly consist of conscious acts of acknowledgement and deliberation, and as if all actors involved had clear visions of reasons of validity. Historicity can thus serve as a panacea against overly rationalist interpretations that view actors as kind of all-knowing, all-powerful Gods and ignore the very historical formations, which have become so taken for granted that they are no longer visible. Thorough historical analysis reveals that contractual understandings of the state and of international organizations are often not adequate to re-construct the processes of their historical formation (cf. Migdal, 2001; Bliesemann de Guevara, 2012; Mazower, 2013).

Finally, to accept the historicity of international politics does not imply a belief in historical determinism. Change is not impossible and it is also observable, as all chapters in this book explain by tracing continuities and discontinuities between erstwhile 'high imperialism' and contemporary ramifications of imperial rule. In the history of any context, there is ample evidence for Sewell's 'eventful history' and of evolution of the social world, including international politics (cf. Alnert et al. 2023, Adler, 2019). The formation of states, the trajectory of each single state as a historical institutional formation as well as the formation and change of international institutions, and the international system as such, including colonialism and imperialism, is full of punctuating events creating particular meanings, strong long-lasting effects on mentalities or even path-dependencies. Neither is historicity an idea about the course of history. Immanuel Kant's statement that without a constituting idea, history would just be a 'sad haphazard' (*trostloses Ungefähr*; Kant, 1973: 6) remains certainly relevant. Historicity is not such a constituting idea of history it just means that the past has structuring effects, that the past is present in it as past experiences are ingrained in institutional forms, in mentalities, in notions and concepts used in language, and in schemes of perception and evaluation. It is an argument about the complex temporal nature of present-day politics – not a statement about what history is an ontological sense. The emphasis we put on historicity as a fundamental quality of international politics does therefore not imply that – in the sense of historicism – epochs or 'cultures' are mutually incomprehensible. And it also does not mean that there is one unique direction built in within history. Countering such too simplistic perspectives, our focus on historicity as well as various chapters in this book stress instead analytics based on the coexistence of multiple temporalities.

5 Conclusion and Overview on Chapters

Based on what we have outlined above, the aim of our endeavour to insert more historical thinking into IR is not just an argument that more attention should be paid to historical underpinnings of present-day politics. The conceptual ideas which we have developed above can well linked to current debates in the HSIR and other (still limited) contributions in IR and beyond on international politics, discussed in Section 3, that take note of the fundamental ways in which history shapes the present of international politics. If our argument about historicity is taken seriously, it has major consequences for methodology and theory. We see three potential core questions for the study of such consequences stemming from the concept of historicity and its application to the study of international politics based on the modes of historicity outlined above and further studied in the various chapters of this book.

Firstly, what is structure? And what is process? In the works of Niklas Luhmann as well as in Weber's methodological pieces, or in the writings by Norbert Elias, Hannah Arendt and Michel Foucault, all structures are finally viewed as outcomes of long-term processes. What all these authors have in common is a way of thinking about processes in a complex and differentiated manner. Instead of looking for formulas that can causally explain outcomes that have in fact very different historical trajectories, IR informed by the concept of historicity should rather look at conflicting and overlapping temporalities, as well as at mutual constitution, emerging interdependencies, variation and stabilization, translations and adaptations.

Secondly, do we cherish descriptions enough? Similar causes might not have the same outcomes, nor do similar outcomes necessarily have the same causes. While looking for regularities, assessing the causal weight of events or structural conditions are core tasks of research, the analysis of single cases and the open, small-N-comparison[9] should be given more room in the study of international politics and it should be held in higher esteem. Studies in historical sociology and global history prove the productiveness of open research designs in such investigations. Neither Weber's sociology of religions, nor Foucault's analysis of governmentality, Luhmann's theory of world society, or Arendt's theory of totalitarian rule would have ever seen daylight if comparativism based on stylish formalism had been the benchmark. This also means that the devaluation of descriptions as 'only' descriptive should be rejected. Anyone who has ever attempted to deliver the first description of a social or political topic, using up-to-standard methods including triangulation and different genres of sources, will confirm that this can be much more challenging than running logistical regressions.

Thirdly, when should big concepts and grand theory come in? With a view to theory building, our argument suggests to leave the usual deductivism inherent to liberal 'constructivism'[10] behind us. The dichotomous language that tends to pathologize non-Western forms of politics – failed vs. strong states, corrupt vs. accountable regimes, traditional vs. modern societies, etc. – is a hindrance for understanding how both domestic and international politics really work. All too often, basic vocabulary constitutes 'governance objects' without reflection (Allan, 2017). We suggest following an advice by Weber that is dear to historians too: concepts are the result of investigations and not necessarily their starting point. Only after a thorough study of empirical phenomena, including their historical dimension, should we suggest concepts (*Begriffe*), as Weber has demonstrated with a view to concepts such as capitalism, patrimonialism, charismatic domination and others.

[9] With this expression, we refer to comparisons that do not follow J. S. Mill's logic of dependent and independent variable designs, but comparisons that look simply for similarities and differences, an approach very common in the study of history, but marginalized in political science (cf. Swedberg, 2014).

[10] We assume that closer inspection would show that so-called 'liberal constructivism' in IR is actually not so constructivist but rather a reformulation of pre-existing liberal IR theory. Liberal 'constructivism' does not at all share seminal constructivist positions like a decentred subject, double contingency and observer dependency. Instead, it stresses the role of norms, ideas and identities.

With this volume, we do not want to answer all questions about the historicity of international relations and imperialism, nor about the historicity of the academic discipline that investigates this, that is IR. We rather plea for a more self-enlightened practice within the discipline and for paying much greater attention to topics like colonialism and imperialism, and their enduring imprint on international politics, that ahistoric scholarship all too often discards. The contributions collected in this volume provide theoretical and empirical insights into the presence of the past in international relations, in general, and these imperial underpinnings, in specific. Studying this deep impact of history on IR, and the different modes of historicity at play needs, in our view, to be a multidisciplinary exercise from the outset. That is why we bring together a balanced number of perspectives on this topic from historically oriented IR (Chapters 2–7 and 14) as well as from global historical sociology (Chapters 8–10) and global history (Chapters 11–13). While engaging with the modes of historicity outlined above the contributions to this volume move beyond a mere reiteration of the points discussed in this chapter. Each of them highlights, devoted to a particular thematic issue, how the imperial past matters and how it shapes the present.

We commence this book with a collection of six contributions from IR scholars (Part I: IR contributions). *George Lawson* studies in his chapter the close relationship between colonialism and international organizations. This chapter charts three stages in this relationship since the early nineteenth century: firstly, the use of international organizations as a means of coordinating imperialism and containing or, preferably, preventing inter-imperial conflict; secondly, the global expansion of international organizations as a means of stratifying polities initially via a 'standard of civilization' and, later, through quotients of modernization/development; and thirdly, the use of international organizations as a means for carrying out various forms of interventionism. Taken together, these three stages mark a shift from a limited realm of international organization to a virtually universal condition of international administration. If international organizations were born in the formal inequalities of power that marked world politics during the nineteenth century and the first half of the twentieth century, in contemporary world politics, these inequalities have been reconfigured, rearticulated and redistributed. In this way, more than any other lie traces of the colonial past in the present of world politics.

This is followed by *Thomas Müller's* exploration of the co-evolution of colonial hierarchies and collective hegemony. Collective hegemony, the chapter shows, denotes institutionalized arrangements through which a select group of powerful states steers world politics. Examples are the

Concert of Europe, the UN Security Council and the G7. Collective hegemony is usually analysed in IR as the establishment of institutionalized hierarchies in a society of sovereign, equal states. Yet, most of its history unfolded in an international society pervaded by colonial hierarchies. The chapter argues that decolonization – that is, discontinuities in colonial hierarchies – resulted in an increased level of contestation and delegitimation of collective hegemony but that it nevertheless persisted. It analyses three episodes of discourses about collective hegemony – the Second Hague Conference in 1907, the rise of the Non-aligned Movement during the Cold War and the current UN Security Council reform – to show that formerly colonized states have been the prime actors in the contestation of collective hegemony. By relying on path-dependencies in formal institutions as well as informal institutions, the powerful states were nonetheless able to continue their collective hegemony. The presence of the colonial past thus manifests in more contestation and a persistent, but changed, practice of collective hegemony.

Joël Glasman and *Klaus Schlichte* challenge the prevalent notion of statehood in Africa in much IR scholarship as being 'imported', 'weak' and 'corrupted'. The chapter argues that this dominant perspective lacks an attention for the historicity of political rule, and it offers a historically sensitive perspective on African statehood. Through a cross-reading of the Ugandan and Cameroonian trajectory of welfare services, it shows how the construction of the state shaped the present. The chapter highlights four main features of the contemporary state and traces their roots in the history of integration into international politics since the colonial period: States are internationalized structures of domination, they are bifurcated, they work through discharge, and they partly avoid the kind of bureaucratic knowledge that is associated with modern governmentality. All four features have long historical roots going back at least to the colonial period. Ultimately, the chapter argues that one cannot understand current welfare systems without a careful analysis of the specific historical trajectory of the state.

This analysis is followed by a chapter written by *Benjamin de Carvalho* and *Halvard Leira* who propose to focus away from units, anchoring instead IR analysis of the *longue durée* in international institutions. The chapter does so by focusing on privateering, and how this institution developed in and around processes of trade, imperial expansion and state formation over a period of more than 600 years. Privateering played an important role in the making and breaking of empires, and thus in the establishment of many of the macro-structures of the present. It is argued that privateering is perhaps most obviously present through its absence, and that the central way, which connects the privateering past with our present is that of forgetting. This amnesia, in turn, has helped normalizing the idea of a modern state with a monopoly on legitimate violence as well as the oceans as a global common under the control of benign hegemons. The focus on privateering allows scholarship to question not only periodization and its aims, but also the extent to which the past still informs how we handle current problems and how the forgetting of privateering is central to how states and oceans are conceived of today.

Iver B. Neumann and *Einar Wigen* then show how today's Eurasia has remnants of a number of imperial traditions. One of these hails from the Eurasian steppe, long inhabited by nomads. Beginning with the Xiongnu 209 BCE, nomadic empires rose and fell north of the boundaries of Chinese, Persian and Byzantine civilizations. The last and greatest of these were the Mongol empires, which lasted into the eighteenth-century CE. By dominating the entire steppe and conquering all the main sedentary civilizations immediately beyond it, Chinggis Khan's Mongol empire and its offshoots left remnants across Eurasia. The first part of the chapter outlines how these empires emerged and functioned. The second part discusses where the core groups of human beings that made up the Mongol empire ended up after its fall. The third part discusses the social remnants of this tradition as it is to be found primarily in Afghanistan and the rest of central Asia, but also to some degree in Turkey and Russia.

The final chapter from an IR perspective comes from *Mathias Albert* and highlights some of the key insights to be gained from aligning IR more closely with elaborated notions of history. For that purpose, it explores the contemporary system of world politics by looking at it through the lenses of this system's (anti-) Napoleonic past and the remnants of the structure of the Holy Roman Empire. It seeks to provide a methodological input into contemporary debates about global historical sociology by demonstrating how stories and historical trajectories that unfold from a singular event leave their traces. In this sense, the chapter deliberately explores the structures of the colonial 'within' what is a Europe-centred system of world politics in the early nineteenth century. Firstly, it explores a period of turmoil that was re-stabilized in the Congress of Vienna that established a system that arguably paved the way for another century or so of the incorporation of large parts of the non-European world into the spheres of authority of European colonial empires and powers. Secondly, it argues that the formal demise of the Holy Roman Empire can, among many other things, also be seen as the final establishment of the 'Westphalian' principle of exclusive territorial sovereignty as the norm for organizing political authority in the system of world politics, then established globally through colonial practices.

The second part of the book then presents chapters on international politics and the role of imperialism coming from three scholars working in Global Historical Sociology (Part II) and from three scholars from Global History (Part III). From a sociological perspective, the chapter by *George Steinmetz* looks at the sociology of empires and colonies. It starts from the observation that when compared with other social sciences scholarship in IR may in the end have little difficulty in seeing the world as a place of present-day empires and a palimpsest of past ones. For others, seeing the world through the filter of colonialism and imperialism requires a kind of *Gestalt* switch. Empire seems to be invisible and hidden, not omnipresent, in the US as in Europe. This chapter surveys the afterlives of empire with a focus on Europe and the US. Based on research across Europe and America, it sketches the various ways in which present social life is permeated with colonial and imperial ideas, tropes, images, practices, and ruins. The main focus is Europe, the metropole of the world's greatest modern colonial empires. The chapter also touches on imperial afterlives in the former European colonies and the United States. The problem of imperial afterlives has to be posed somewhat differently in the American case, where empire cannot yet be spoken of entirely in the past tense. Yet European colonialism and American imperialism have been connected in ways that give a special salience to the problem of imperial afterlives. Anti-imperialist and anticolonial ideas have circulated back and forth across the Atlantic. The chapter finally discusses current practices as they relate to imperial afterlives.

This chapter is followed by an analysis by *Teresa Koloma Beck* who draws on Frantz Fanon and his sociology of colonial society. In this Fanonian reconstruction, socio-spatial particularities play a central role: the colony is described as a world divided in two, in which colonizers and colonized are kept apart from each other, and in which the border between them is produced and defended by securitized infrastructures and discourses. In most former colonies such enforced racial or ethnic segregation has become a thing of the past. Yet, the socio-spatial arrangements described by Fanon re-emerge in contemporary zones of conflict, where they are recreated as security measures intended to separate the protagonists of international peace and development from the threats posed by contentious local populations. Based on ethnographic field research in Kabul, this chapter analytically pursues these structural resemblances. The aim, however, is not to make a (cheap) argument about the neo-colonial character of global humanitarianism, but to investigate the significance of this observation for a sociology of world society.

In the next chapter, *Julian Go* then addresses the colonial origins of policing in the US and the UK. Thus, the so-called 'civil police', which originated in London and then spread to the US and the rest of the world, has been a crucial institution for maintaining the international order. This is because the civil police, unlike the army, is a coercive regime meant for 'citizens' rather than 'foreigners' or 'subjects'. The civil police regulates 'domestic' space, while the military is oriented to 'foreign' or 'international' space. This chapter examines the origins of this important institution in the United Kingdom and the United States and reveals its colonial genealogy. The first civil police, the London Metropolitan Police, founded in the nineteenth century, was modelled after a colonial counter-insurgency force, the Irish Constabulary. In the United States, the civil police was initially modelled after the London police but later, in the early twentieth century, appropriated a series of techniques and tactics from America's colonial regime in the Philippines. The strategic operation of both civil police institutions has been to draw upon the colonial site while covering up its colonial counter-insurgency and militaristic origins.

The book then continues with three perspectives inspired by Global History. This section commences with a chapter by *Tomoko Akami* on the colonial genealogies of IR in Japan. The chapter argues that the notion of the 'International' became 'a-colonial,' in which process, the formation of the discipline of IR played a significant role. The chapter examines the parallel processes of making the field of study of IR at the International Studies Conference (ISC) and in Japan in the 1920s–1950s, and unearths the 'Colonial' in this process. In particular, it reveals the element of colonial policy studies in the latter process in Japan, which can be traced back to the 1900s, and examines its complex meaning for emerging area studies and international economy in the 1940s–1950s. The chapter suggests that a similar process can be revealed in the genealogies of IR in other countries, and argues that recognizing and reintegrating colonial policy studies as constitutive of the discipline of IR will be a critical step towards making the knowledge of the 'International' global, and will allow us to examine the roles and meanings of neglected actors and complex interactions among them in modern international relations.

This is followed by a chapter by *Daniel Speich Chassé* on the notion of the 'Third World'. This chapter focuses on the discursive formation of the 'Third World' as a singular phenomenon, which was epistemologically rooted in quantitative economic expertise. It takes up some notions originally coined by the French sociologist Georges Balandier in order to better understand major shifts in global political communication. The core argument is that, firstly, decolonization and the end of most formal empires in the 1950s and the 1960s lead to conceptual confusion and that, secondly, economic knowledge production through macroeconomic statistics helped solve this impasse. The background story is the history of quantitative (i.e. statistical) economic knowledge. It recalls the relative (un-)importance of quantitative economic knowledge in imperial practice before roughly the 1950s. This stands in a stark contrast to the way in which economists post-1945 gained an almost 'imperial' position in stabilizing global expertise on socio-economic inequality and difference in the emerging world society. Most certainly, the 'Third World' never only was an effect of theory but rather a political concept uniting relatively poor nation states across the world in their struggle against material post-colonial dominance.

In the subsequent chapter, *Anna Vlachopoulou* and *Stephan Stetter* explore how the historical experience of imperial politics has shaped the memory cultures in Ottoman and post-Ottoman spaces, in particular in relation to the Myth of Kosovo and the status of Jerusalem. The imperial experiences in this realm should be understood as 'double' ones, counting both the transformation of the Ottoman Empire during the long nineteenth century that led to a growing self-understanding of the Ottoman Empire as a modern imperial and quasi-colonial power, and the ever-growing influence of European (imperial) powers in Ottoman realms that resulted in some regions in the replacement of the Ottoman administration by a European Colonial regime. Analysing the case studies of the memory cultures surrounding the myth of the Battle of Kosovo (Albania/Serbia) and of the status of Jerusalem (Israel/Palestine), this chapter traces how these memory cultures changed over time, how they interplayed with imperialist politics in the respective region and how memory cultures were used (and abused) by the respective nation state following the time of empires.

The book ends with a conclusion by *Ayşe Zarakol* who asks why, if the arguments in favour of historicism are so compelling, historicism has such relative difficulty in gaining a strong foothold in IR, even after decades of the historical turn. The chapter focuses on the structural constraints historicism faces in IR and highlights IR's particular American origins as a discipline (as well as the continued domination of US standards in the evaluation of IR scholarship globally) as a major explaining factor. It also argues that this will not be solved automatically as American influence in the discipline and the world decreases. Approaches to IR hailing from other parts of the world have their own motivations to reject historicism even as they seem to care more about history than US-based approaches. Historicism, Zarakol explains, needs to be realistic about the obstacles it faces.

In the light of the contributions to this book, we can now arrive at conclusions about what it means to say that international politics has a history. In a nutshell, it means thoroughly engaging with the concept of historicity and we suggest in this book doing so on the basis of specific modes of historicity. We have started our introduction with this question, and we hope to now have shed some light on how we aim to address this question throughout this book. The concept of historicity is core to our argument here, namely that not only international politics but also the intellectual debate about international politics, which fundamentally includes the discipline of IR, bear the traces of the past each and every moment. We think that this insight about the constant presence of the past can help us to replace often reified concepts like 'identity' or 'culture' that are often used as shortcuts for avoiding engaging with the role of history in international politics. And we are convinced that embracing historicity as a core concept for IR will lead to innovation both methodologically and theoretically.

As far as methodological consequences are concerned, historicity is clearly implying resorting to interpretivist methods. Historicity as a structural feature of politics reveals the limits of formalization in research methods. While, of course, all phenomena can be compared in one way or the other, we caution against simplistic equations of 'like units'. Logics of explanation that build on the behaviouralist tradition, and refrain from any interpretation of contexts, are ill-suited for the study of historical phenomena. For example, sixty years of research aiming to find law-like propositions to explain warfare have in our view failed. That does not mean that scientific logics of explanation are of no use at all. Clearly, research that strives for detecting regularities continues to be a worthwhile and necessary endeavour. But – echoing Weber's methodological approach – embedding such observations of regularities within an interpretive frame of analysis that hinges on understanding subjective meanings ascribed by social actors are the indispensable part of any form of explanation in the social sciences (Weber, [1913] 2012).

If this is the core methodological consequence from what we have argued throughout this chapter, then our main conclusion is not more, but also not less, than to require from IR scholarship to read more about history. We suggest by turning more to Global History and Historical Sociology and fostering the dialogue of these research strands with a historically oriented IR. We are also convinced that greater attention to the past will not only produce better insights into the present. We also think that this will have a beneficial effect for theory-building in IR. Thus, our argument about historicity applies as well to theories. The theories we work with are time-bound too. That there is a historical imprint, stemming from the era of colonial imperialism, impacting our understanding of international politics is the core argument of post-colonial scholarship. What we suggest to do now is to take this critical self-reflection a step further: to specify – on the basis of the modes of historicity presented above – which concrete historical experiences generate the truth conditions from which specific theories, including post-colonialism, result.

References

Aalberts, T. E. (2010). Playing the Game of Sovereign States: Charles Manning's Constructivism avant-la-lettre, *European Journal of International Relations*, 16(2), 247–68.

Acharya, A. (2014). Global International Relations (IR) and Regional Worlds: A New Agenda for International Studies, *International Studies Quarterly*, 58(4), 647–59.

Adler, E. (2019). *World Ordering: A Social Theory of Cognitive Evolution*, Cambridge: Cambridge University Press.

Albert, M. (2016). *A Theory of World Politics*, Cambridge: Cambridge University Press.

Albert, M., Brunkhorst, H., Neumann, I.B. & Stetter, S. (2023). *The Social Evolution of World Politics*, Bielefeld: transcript.

Allan, B. (2017). From Subjects to Objects: Knowledge in International Relations Theory, *European Journal of International Relations*, 24(4), 841–64.

Anderl, F. & Wallmeier, P. (2018). Modi der Kritik des Internationalen Regierens: Ein Plädoyer für immanente Kritik, *Zeitschrift für Internationale Beziehungen*, 25(1), 65–89.

Anievas, A. & Kamran, M. (eds.). (2016). *Historical Sociology and World History: Uneven and Combined Development over the Longue Duree*, Lanham: Rowman & Littlefield.

Anievas, A. & Nişancıoğlu, K. (2015). *How the West Came to Rule the Geopolitical Origins of Capitalism*, London: Pluto Press.

Arendt, H. [1951] (1976). *The Origins of Totalitarianism*, San Diego: Harcourt.

Aron, R. (1973). *République impériale: Les Etats-Unis dans le monde, 1945–1972*, Paris: Calmann-Lévy.

Autesserre, S. (2010). *The Trouble with the Congo: Local Violence and the Failure of International Peacebuilding*, Cambridge: Cambridge University Press.

Balandier, G. [1951] (1952). The Fact of Colonialism: A Theoretical Approach, *Cross Currents*, 2(4), 10–31.

Barkawi, T. (2005). *Globalization and War*, Lanham: Rowman & Littlefield.

Bartelson, J. (2017). *War in International Thought*, Cambridge: Cambridge University Press.

Bartelson, J. (1995). *A Genealogy of Sovereignty*, Cambridge: Cambridge University Press.

Bayart, J.-F. (2008). *Global Subjects: A Political Critique of Globalization*, London: Polity.

Bayart, J.-F. (2000). Africa in the World: A History of Extraversion, *African Affairs*, 99(395), 217–67.

Bayart, J.-F. (1996). L'historicité de l'Etat importé, in J.-F. Bayart (ed.). *La reinvention du capitalisme. Les trajectorie du politique*, 11–39, Paris: Karthala.

Bayart, J.-F. & Bertrand, R. (2006). De quel legs colonial parle-t-on? *Esprit* (12), 1–27.

Bayly, M. (2016). *Taming the Imperial Imagination: Colonial Knowledge, International Relations, and the Anglo-Afghan Encounter, 1808–1878*, Cambridge: Cambridge University Press.

Bell, D. (ed.). (2019). *Empire, Race and Global Justice*, Cambridge: Cambridge University Press.

Bell, D. (2007). *The Idea of Greater Britain: Empire and the Future of World Order, 1860–1900*, Princeton: Princeton University Press.

Bhambra, G. (2007). *Rethinking Modernity: Postcolonialism and the Sociological Imagination*, Houndmills: Palgrave.

Biecker, S. & Schlichte, K. (2021). *Extended Experience: The Political Anthropology of Internationalized Politics*, Lanham: Rowman & Littlefield.

Bigo, D. (2002). Security and Immigration: Toward a Critique of the Governmentality of Unease, *Alternatives*, 27(1), 63–92.

Bilgin, P. (2010). The 'Western-Centrism' of Security Studies: 'Blind Spot' or Constitutive Practice?, *Security Dialogue*, 41(6), 615–22.

Bilgin, P. (2008). Thinking Past 'Western IR', *Third World Quarterly*, 29(1), 5–23.

Blanchard, P. & Lemaire, S. (2004). *Culture Imperial, 1931–1961: Les colonies au cœur e la République*, Paris: Editions Autrement.

Bliesemann de Guevara, B. (ed.). (2012). *Statebuilding and State-Formation: The Political Sociology of Intervention*, New York: Routledge.

Bloch, E. (1932). *Erbschaft dieser Zeit*, Frankfurt: Suhrkamp.

Booth, K. (2005). *Critical Security Studies and World Politics*, London: Lynne Rienner.

Börzel, T. A. & Risse, T. (2012). From Europeanisation to Diffusion, *West European Politics*, 35(1), 1–19.

Bourgeot, A. (1994). Révoltes et rébellions en pays touareg, *Afrique contemporaine*, 170, 3–19.

Branch, J. (2014). *The Cartographic State*, Cambridge: Cambridge University Press.

Braudel, F. (1969). Histoire et sciences sociales: la longue durée, in F. Braudel (ed.), *Ecrits sur l'histoire*, 41–83, Paris: Flammarion.

Buzan, B. (2018). China's Rise in English School Perspective, *International Relations of the Asia-Pacific*, 18(3), 449–76.

Buzan, B. (2014). The 'Standard of Civilisation' as an English School Concept, *Millennium: Journal of International Studies*, 42(3), 576–94.

Buzan, B. (2004). *From International to World Society? English School Theory and the Social Structure of Globalisation*, Cambridge: Cambridge University Press.

Buzan, B. & Lawson, G. (2015). *The Global Transformation: History, Modernity, and the Making of International Order*, Cambridge: Cambridge University Press.

Buzan, B. & Little, R. (2001). Why International Relations Has Failed as an Intellectual Project and What to Do About It, *Millennium*, 30(1), 19–39.

Buzan, B. & Little, R. (2000). *International Systems in World History: Remaking the Study of International Relations*, Oxford: Oxford University Press.
Carvalho, B., Leira, H. & Hobson, J. M. (2011). The Big Bangs of IR: The Myths That Your Teachers Still Tell You About 1648 and 1919, *Millennium*, 39(3), 735–58.
Carvalho, B., Lopez, Julia C. & Leira, H. (eds.). (2021). *Routledge Handbook of Historical International Relations*, London: Routledge.
Césaire, A. [1955] (2004). *Discours sur le colonialisme*, Paris: Présence Africaine.
Chakrabarthy, D. (2000). *Provincializing Europe: Postcolonial Thought and Historical Difference*, Princeton: Princeton University Press.
Chandler, D. (2006). *Empire in Denial: The Politics of State-Building*, London: Pluto Press.
Checkel, J. (1999). Norms, Institutions, and National Identity in Contemporary Europe, *International Studies Quarterly*, 43(1), 83–114.
Conrad, S. (2014). Internal Colonialism in Germany: Culture Wars, Germanification of the Soil, and the Global Market Imaginery, in B. Naranch & G. Eley (eds.). *German Colonialism in a Global Age*, 246–64, Durham: Duke University Press.
Cooper, F. (1991). *Colonialism in Question: Theory, Knowledge, History*, Berkeley: University of California Press.
Cooper, F. & Stoler, A. L. (eds.). (1997). *Tensions of Empire: Colonial Cultures in a Bourgeois World*, Berkeley: University of California Press.
Darby, P. (2004). Pursuing the Political: A Postcolonial Rethinking of International Relations, *Millennium: Journal of International Studies*, 33(1), 1–32.
Dayak, M. (1992). *Touareg, la tragédie*, Paris: Lattès.
Del Sarto, R. A. (2016). Normative Empire Europe: The European Union, Its Borderlands, and the 'Arab Spring', *Journal of Common Market Studies*, 54(2), 215–32.
Derichs, C. (2017). *Knowledge Production, Area Studies and Global Cooperation*, London: Routledge.
Du Bois, W. (1944). Prospect of a World without Race Conflict, in M. Weinberg (ed.). *William Du Bois: A Reader*, New York: Harper & Row.
Duffield, M. (2001). *Global Governance and New Wars: The Merging of Development and Security*, London: Zed Books.
Dunne, T., Hansen, L. & Wight, C. (2013). The End of International Relations Theory? *European Journal of International Relations*, 19(3), 405–25.
Dunne, T. & Reus-Smit, C. (eds.). (2017). *The Globalization of International Society*, Oxford: Oxford University Press.
Fanon, F. (1961). *Les damnes de la terre*, Paris: Maspero.
Fanon, F. (1952). *Peau noire, masques blancs*, Paris: Seuil.
Fioretos, O. (2011). Historical Institutionalism in International Relations, *International Organization*, 65(3), 367–99.
Forsberg, T. & Haukkala, H. (2018). An Empire without an Emperor? The EU and Its Eastern Neighbourhood, in R. Heiskala & J. Aro (eds.). *Policy Design in the European Union*, New York: Palgrave.
Gadamer, H.-G. (1990). *Gesammelte Werke*, Tübingen: Mohr.

Gadamer, H.-G. (1959). Vom Zirkel des Verstehens, in H.-G. Gadamer (ed.). *Gesammelte Werke*, 57–65, Tübingen: Mohr.

Go, J. & Lawson, G. (eds.). (2017). *Global Historical Sociology*, Cambridge: Cambridge University Press.

Gollwitzer, H. (1972/1982). *Geschichte des weltpolitischen Denkens,* Göttingen: Vandenhoeck and Ruprecht.

Gonzalez-Pelaez, A. (2009). The Primary Institutions of the Middle Eastern Regional Interstate Society, in B. Buzan & A. Gonzalez-Pelaez (eds.). *International Society and the Middle East: English School Theory at the Regional Level*, 92–116, New York: Palgrave.

Halliday, F. (2005). *The Middle East in International Relations: Power, Politics and Ideology*, Cambridge: Cambridge University Press.

Halperin, S. & Palan, R. (2015). Introduction. Legacies of Empire, in S. Halperin & R. Palan (eds.). *Legacies of Empire*, 1–24, Cambridge: Cambridge University Press.

Hansen, L. (2013). The End of International Relations Theory? *European Journal of International Relations*, 19(3), 405–25.

Hardt, M. & Negri, A. (2000). *Empire,* Cambridge: Harvard University Press.

Hobden, S. & Hobson, J. (eds.). (2002). *Historical Sociology of International Relations*, Cambridge: Cambridge University Press.

Hobson, J. M. (2012). *The Eurocentric Conception of World Politics: Western International Theory, 1760–2010*, New York: Cambridge University Press.

Hobson, J. M. (2007). Is Critical Theory Always for the White West and of Western Imperialism? Beyond Westphalia towards a Post-Racist Critical IR, *Review of International Studies*, 93 (S1), 91–116.

Hobson, J. & Lawson, G. (2008). What Is History in International Relations? *Millennium: Journal of International Studies*, 37(2), 415–35.

Hoppe, S. (2021). Internationale historische Soziologie und historische Sozialwissenschaft in den deutschen und anglo-amerikanischen IB: Zur Relevanz einer Paralleldebatte für die Außenpolitikforschung, *Zeitschrift für Internationale Beziehungen*, 28(1), 1–35.

Ikenberry, G. J. (2001). *After Victory: Institutions, Strategic Restraint, and the Rebuilding of Order after Major Wars*, Princeton: Princeton University Press.

Isachenko, D. (2019). Coordination and Control in Russia's Foreign Policy: Travails of Putin's Curators in the Near Abroad. *Third World Quarterly*, Online first.

Jabri, V. (2012). *The Postcolonial Subject: Claiming Politics/Governing Others in Late Modernity*, London: Routledge.

Kant, I. [1784] (1973). Idee zu einer allgemeinen Geschichte in weltbürgerlicher Absicht, in I. Kant (ed.), *Kleinere Schriften zur Geschichtsphilosophie, Ethik und Politik*, 3–20, Hamburg: Meiner.

Keene, E. (2002). *Beyond the Anarchical Society: Grotius, Colonialism and Order in World Politics*, Cambridge: Cambridge University Press.

Knutsen, T. (2016). *A History of International Relations Theory*, Manchester: Manchester University Press.

Koddenbrock, K. (2015). Strategies of Critique in International Relations: From Foucault and Latour towards Marx, *European Journal of International Relations*, 21(2), 243–66.

Krishna, S. (2008). *Globalization and Postcolonialism: Hegemony and Resistance in the Twenty-First Century*, Lanham: Rowman & Littlefield.
Laïdi, Z. (1999). *Le temps mondial*, Bruxelles: Editions Complexes.
Laurence, H. (2009). *L'empire et ses ennemis*, Paris: Seuil.
Lawson, G. (2006). The Promise of Historical Sociology in International Relations, *International Studies Review*, 8(3), 397–423.
Li, T. M. (2007). *The Will to Improve: Governmentality, Development and the Practice of Politics*, Durham: Duke University Press.
Linklater, A. (1990). *Beyond Realism and Marxism: Critical Theory and International Relations*, Houndmills: Macmillan.
Lüthy, H. (1967). *In Gegenwart der Geschichte*, Köln: Kiepenheuer & Witsch.
Mamdani, M. (1996). *Citizen and Subject: Contemporary Africa and the Legacy of Late Colonialism*, Princeton: Princeton University Press.
Mann, M. (1984). The Autonomous Power of the State: Its Origins, Mechanisms and Results, *European Journal of Sociology*, 25(2), 185–213.
Manning, C. A. W. (1962). *The Nature of International Society*, London: Palgrave.
Markovits, A. S., Reich, S. & Westermann, F. (1996). Germany: Hegemonic Power and Economic Gain?, *Review of International Political Economy*, 3(4), 698–727.
Mazower, M. (2013). *Governing the World: The History of an Idea*, London: Penguin.
Mbembe, A. (2013). *Critique de la raison nègre*, Paris: La Découverte.
Mbembe, A. (2000). *De la postcolonie: Essai sur l'imagination politique dans l'Afrique contemporaine*, Paris: Karthala.
Mehta, U. S. (1997). Liberal Strategies of Exclusion, in F. Cooper & A. L. Stoler (eds.). *Tensions of Empire: Colonial Cultures in a Bourgeois World*, 59–86, Berkeley: University of California Press.
Migdal, J. S. (2001). *States in Societies: Studying How States and Societies Transform and Constitute One Another*, Cambridge: Cambridge University Press.
Mignolo, W. D. & Walsh, C. E. (2015). *On Decoloniality: Concepts, Analytics, Praxis*, Durham: Duke University Press.
Mudimbe, V.-Y. (1988). *The Invention of Africa: Gnosis, Philosophy and the Order of Knowledge*, Bloomington: Indiana University Press.
Münkler, H. (2006). *Imperien: Die Logik der Weltherrschaft. Vom Alten Rom bis zu den Vereinigten Staaten*, Reinbek: Rowohlt.
Neumann, I. B. & Wigen, E. (2018). *The Steppe Tradition in International Relations: Russians, Turks and European State Building 4000 BCE-2017 CE*, Cambridge: Cambridge University Press.
Nexon, D. H. (2009). *The Struggle for Power in Early Modern Europe: Religious Conflict, Dynastic Empires & International Change*, Princeton: Princeton University Press.
Osterhammel, J. (2016). Global History and Historical Sociology, in J. Belich, J. Darwin, M. Frenz & C. Wickham (eds.). *The Prospect of Global History*, 23–46, Oxford: Oxford University Press.
Osterhammel, J. (2009). *Die Verwandlung der Welt: Eine Geschichte des 19. Jahrhunderts*, München: Beck.
Owen, J. (2015). *Fail: Why the US Lost the War in Afghanistan*, Fayetteville: Blacksmith.

Persaud, R. & Sajed, A. (eds.). (2018). *Race, Gender, and Culture in International Relations: Postcolonial Perspectives*, New York: Routledge.

Philips, A. & Reus-Smit, C. (eds.). (2020). *Culture and Order in World Politics*, Cambridge: Cambridge University Press.

Philips, A. & Sharman, J. C. (2015). *International Order in Diversity: War, Trade and Rule in the Indian Ocean*, Cambridge: Cambridge University Press.

Powell, N. (2017). Battling Instability? The Recurring Logic of French Military Interventions in Africa, *African Security*, 10(1), 42–72.

Putin, V. (2021). *On the Historical Unity of Russians and Ukrainians*, Moscow: Kremlin.

Reus-Smit, C. (1999). *The Moral Purpose of the State: Culture, Social Identity, and Institutional Rationality in International Relations*, Princeton: Princeton University Press.

Rixen, T, Viola, L. & Zürn, M. (eds.). (2016). *Historical Institutionalism and International Relations: Explaining Institutional Development in World Politics*, Oxford: Oxford University Press.

Rosenberg, J. (2006). Why Is There No International Political Sociology? *European Journal of International Relations*, 12(3), 307–40.

Rosenboim, O. (2017). *The Emergence of Globalism: Visions of World Order in Britain and the United States, 1939–1950*, Princeton: Princeton University Press.

Said, E. (1978). *Orientalism*, New York: Pantheon Books.

Schlichte, K. (ed.). (2005). *Dynamics of States: The Emergence and Crisis of State Domination Outside the OECD*, Aldershot: Ashgate.

Schlichte, K. (1998). La Françafrique: Postkolonialer Habitus und Klientelismus in der französischen Afrikapolitik, *Zeitschrift für Internationale Beziehungen*, 5(2), 309–43.

Schroeder, P. W. (1997). History and International Relations Theory: Not Use or Abuse, but Fit or Misfit, *International Security*, 22(1), 64–74.

Schroeder, P. W. (1994). *The Transformation of European Politics, 1763–1848*, Oxford: Clarendon Press.

Seth, S. (2011). Postcolonial Theory and the Critique of International Relations, *Millennium: Journal of International Studies*, 40(1), 167–83.

Sewell, W. H. (2005). *Logics of History: Social Theory and Social Transformation*, Chicago: Chicago University Press.

Shani, G. (2008). Toward a Post-Western IR: The Umma, Khalsa Panth, and Critical International Relations Theory, *International Studies Review*, 10, 722–34.

Shilliam, R. (2015). *The Black Pacific: Anti-colonial Struggles and Oceanic Connections*, London: Bloomsbury.

Siegelberg, J. (1994). *Kapitalismus und Krieg: Eine Theorie des Krieges in der Weltgesellschaft*, Hamburg: LIT Verlag.

Siegelberg, J. & Schlichte, K. (eds.). (2000). *Strukturwandel internationaler Beziehungen. Zum Verhältnis von Staat und internationalem System seit dem Westfälischen Frieden*, Opladen: Westdeutscher Verlag.

Sjoberg, L. (2012). Gender, Structure, and War: What Waltz Couldn't See, *International Theory*, 4(1), 1–38.

Smouts, M.-C. (ed.). (2007). *La situation post-coloniale: Les postcolonial studies dans le débat français*, Paris: Presse de Science Po.
Steinmetz, G. (2014). The Sociology of Empires, Colonies, and Postcolonialism, *Annual Review of Sociology*, 40(1), 77–103.
Steinmetz, G. (ed.). (2013). *Sociology and Empire: The Imperial Entanglements of a Discipline*. Durham: Duke University Press.
Steinmetz, G. (2007). *The Devil's Handwriting: Procoloniality and the German Colonial State in Qingdao, Samoa, and Southwest Africa*, Chicago: Chicago University Press.
Stetter, S. (2008). *World Society and the Middle East: Reconstructions in Regional Politics*, Houndsmill: Palgrave.
Stoler, A. (1997). Sexual Affronts and Racial Frontiers: European Identities and the Cultural Politics of Exclusion in Colonial Southeast Asia, in F. Cooper & A. L. Stoler (eds.). *Tensions of Empire: Colonial Cultures in a Bourgeois World*, 198–237, Berkeley: University of California Press.
Strange, S. (1988). The Future of the American Empire, *Journal of International Affairs*, 42(1), 1–17.
Swedberg, R. (2014). *The Art of Social Theory*, Princeton: Princeton University Press.
Tickner, J. (2006). Feminism Meets International Relations: Some Methodological Issues, in A. A. Brooke, M. Stern & J. True (eds.). *Feminist Methodologies for International Relations*, 19–41, Cambridge: Cambridge University Press.
Tickner, A. (2001). *Gendering World Politics: Issues and Approaches in the Post-Cold War Era*, New York: Columbia University Press.
Tickner, A. & Wæver, O. (eds.). (2009). *International Relations Scholarship Around the World*, London: Routledge.
Toal, G. (2017). *Near Abroad: Putin, the West and the Contest over Ukraine and the Caucasus*, Oxford: Oxford University Press.
Todorov, T. (1989). *Nous et les autres: La réflexion française sur la diversité humaine*, Paris: Seuil.
Todorova, M. (1997). *Imagining the Balkans*, Oxford: Oxford University Press.
Veit, A. (2010). *Intervention as Indirect Rule: Civil War and State Building in the Democratic Republic of Congo*, Frankfurt: Campus Verlag and Chicago University Press.
Vitalis, R. (2015). *White World Order, Black Power Politics: The Birth of American International Relations*, Ithaca: Cornell University Press.
Vitalis, R. (2000). The Graceful and the Generous Liberal Gesture: Making Racism Visible in American International Relations, *Millenium*, 29(2), 331–56.
Vrasti, W. (2008). The Strange Case of Ethnography and International Relations, *Millenium*, 37(3), 279–301.
Walker, R. B. J. (1993). *Inside/Outside: International Relations as Political Theory*, Cambridge: Cambridge University Press.
Weber, C. (2014). *International Relations Theory: A Critical Introduction*, London: Routledge.
Weber, C. (1999). IR: The Resurrection or New Frontiers of Incorporation, *European Journal of International Relations*, 5(4), 435–50.

Weber, M. [1913] (2012). On Some Categories of Interpretive Sociology, in H. Bruun & S. Whimster (eds.). *Max Weber: Collected Methodological Writings*, 273–301, London: Routledge.

Wendt, A. (2003). Why a World State Is Inevitable, *European Journal of International Relations*, 9(4), 491–542.

Zarakol, A. (ed.). (2017). *Hierarchies in World Politics*, Cambridge: Cambridge University Press.

Zarakol, A. (2010). *After Defeat: How the East Learned to Live with the West*, Cambridge: Cambridge University Press.

Part I

The Imperial Past and Present in International Politics and IR

2 The Colonial Origins – and Legacies – of International Organizations

George Lawson

1 Introduction

This chapter argues that international organizations in particular, and forms of international administration in general, owe core aspects of their origins, development and legacies to colonialism. It builds on the claim made in the Introduction that history shapes international relations: its main dynamics, principal institutions, key forms of legitimation and more. The origins of modern international organizations lie primarily in the nineteenth century, particularly the last quarter of the century, when the 'new imperialism' was at its zenith. Since then, the relationship between colonialism and international organizations has taken many forms. Yet, during this period as a whole, the presence of the colonial past has been central to how international organizations have been established and sustained.

The origins of international organizations lie in regional formations, like the Concert of Europe, that sought to prevent or contain conflict between polities that were simultaneously empires and nation-states. The Concert seeded the notion of 'legalised hegemony': 'the realisation through legal forms of great power prerogatives' (Simpson, 2004: x). This seed germinated successfully over subsequent years. Legalized hegemony meant recognizing both equality between imperial nation-states and inequality between them and other polities. From the Concert on, 'dual authority' has been at the heart of international organizations, driven in large part by colonialism. This forms the backdrop to three subsequent stages in the relationship between colonialism and international organizations: first, the establishment of technical forums, such as the Universal Postal Union (UPU), which were set up in order to coordinate inter-imperial activities; the emergence of international movements (such as Bandung), some of which morphed into organizations (such as the G77), which sought to weaken or supplant colonialism; and finally, the emergence in the contemporary world of forms of international administration that act as vehicles of extensive interventionism, particularly in the Global South. In the aftermath of decolonization, the power asymmetries, legitimating rationales and forms of intervention that were sustained by colonialism have shifted in locus, while retaining a core logic of interventionism. In the contemporary world, sites of international administration are one of the principal means through which practices of intervention are authorized.

This narrative demonstrates not just the many ways in which history shapes international dynamics, but also the salience of modes of historicity associated with 'complex temporalities', power differentials and non-linear pathways (Schlichte & Stetter, this volume). Indeed, there are three main 'modes' through which the presence of the colonial past can be found in contemporary global governance. First, the shift from colonialism to less explicit sites of international hierarchy has seen a *reconfiguration* in the ways that 'dual authority' works. The regulation of inter-imperial rivalry and the maintenance of imperial hierarchies has been replaced by more 'neutral' rationales: the management of great power relations and the fostering of international order. This reconfiguration has, in turn, witnessed the *rearticulation* of international hierarchies: imperial-nation states have been reconceptualized as 'advanced' states; imperial 'tutelage' has morphed into a concern for 'development' and so on. Finally, as the disparities of power that enabled a handful of largely white, Western states to engender a highly unequal international order has weakened, so power has been *redistributed* from international organizations to diverse forms of international administration ranging from the G20 to the Asian Infrastructure Investment Bank. The roots of this redistribution are deep. But the form they have taken in the contemporary world speaks to a multi-scalar order in which forms of rule are widely dispersed, but deeply embedded. Here can be found the most explicit way in which modes of historicity contribute to our understanding of international organizations. As history has shaped their development, it has done so in ways that have their roots in shifting geometries of power. This chapter represents an attempt to unpack this complex story.

2 International Order as Imperial Order

As noted above, the origins of modern international organizations are often said to lie in the nineteenth century Concert of Europe (e.g. Mitzen, 2013). In many ways, the Concert represented a 'de-globalisation' of world politics (Osterhammel, 2014: 473), a turning away from the 'world crisis' (Bayly, 2004: 147) of the late eighteenth and early nineteenth centuries in favour of a reckoning with intra-European politics. Along with the 1823 Monroe Doctrine, the Concert served to compartmentalize world politics into regional spheres of influence. What is often left out of this story is the co-implication of the Concert with the emergence of modern imperialism. Between 1814 and 1849, the size of Britain's empire in India increased by over two-thirds (Hobsbawm, 1962: 136). During this period, Britain accumulated a series of staging posts in the Mediterranean (e.g. Cyprus), Africa (e.g. Cape Town), the Middle East (e.g. Aden) and Asia (e.g. Singapore). In the early 1830s, Leopold von Ranke was already warning that Britain was a 'colossal world power'. By 1840, the British navy possessed almost as many ships as the rest of Europe put together (Hobsbawm, 1962: 135). The mid-century Opium Wars required China to cede Hong Kong to the British, pay an indemnity for starting the conflict, open up five new treaty ports and guarantee extraterritorial rights for British nationals. Such developments help to explain why Britain sought to maintain a European peace – its interests were increasingly measured on a global scale.

These dynamics were not confined to Britain. At the time the Concert was being established, nearly three-quarters of the world's population lived in large, fragmented, ethnically mixed agrarian empires. The late eighteenth and early nineteenth centuries were periods of wide-ranging contestation, pitching advocates of constitutions and representative government on one side of the barricades, and those defending dynasticism and imperial rule on the other. During the middle part of the nineteenth century, France sought to extend its power in the Middle East and the Americas, most notably in Algeria and Mexico. Between 1810 and 1870, the US carried out seventy-one territorial annexations and military interventions (Go, 2011: 39). During the course of the century as a whole, the US became both a continental empire, seizing territory from Native Americans, the Spanish and the Mexicans, and an overseas empire, extending its authority over Cuba, Nicaragua, the Dominican Republic, Haiti, Hawaii, Puerto Rico, Guam, the Philippines, Samoa and the Virgin Islands. A range of other settler states also became colonial powers in their own right, including Australia and New Zealand in the Pacific. Japan constructed an empire in East Asia, while Russian expansionism accelerated both southwards to Uzbekistan, Kazakhstan and Turkmenistan, and eastwards to Sakhalin and Vladivostok.

Imperial expansion was met by contestation and civil strife. The mid-century Taiping Rebellion in China mobilized over one million combatants and spread to an area the size of France and Germany combined (Meier, 2012: 89). The American Civil War mobilized half of all white male Americans, of which a third lost their lives; the direct costs of the war are estimated at $6.6 billion (Belich, 2009: 331). The 1864–1870 war between Paraguay and the 'Triple Alliance' of Argentina, the Empire of Brazil and Uruguay stands as the bloodiest conflict ever to have taken place in Latin America; Paraguay alone lost two-thirds of its adult male population. Violent wars of national independence in Germany, Italy, Mexico and elsewhere added to the death toll; so too did the ethnic nationalist conflicts that took place in the Balkans and Caucuses. The break-up of maritime Atlantic empires, imperial expansion (by Russia) and contraction (in the case of the Ottomans) in Eurasia, as well as independence struggles in many parts of the world added up to a 'world in turmoil' (Geyer & Bright, 1996: 622).

The origins of modern international organizations, therefore, run in parallel to a 'global transformation' in which imperialism and related dynamics generated a single, if highly differentiated, world of competing empires (Buzan & Lawson, 2015). And imperial expansion was met by contestation from below. This analysis generates two points. First, amidst this turmoil was the formalization of a privileged role for a new category of 'great powers', which were to underpin a system of 'collective hegemony' (see Müller, this volume). Rather than associating international order with a 'ranking of powers' based on precedence, title and position, this period saw a shift towards the 'grading of powers' based on power capabilities (Keene, 2013). Great powers saw themselves and were recognized by others as having, managerial responsibility for international order. All of these great powers were imperial nation-states. This helped to formalize the system of legalized hegemony in which imperial nation-states recognized a reciprocal right of sovereignty and non-intervention between each other, but only between each other (Simpson, 2004).

Second was the emergence of the 'standard of civilization', which served as the basis for discriminating between unequal sovereigns. The standard of civilization stratified polities not just by power capability, but also by culture, race, religion and relative 'modernity'. Western imperial-states were 'civilized', next came 'barbarians' (understood as those, often Asian, peoples who lacked certain cultural and/or material features of modernity), and finally 'savages', a term usually reserved for 'darker' peoples who were thought to lack the necessary racial and 'civilisational' characteristics that constituted 'modern' societies (Gong, 1984; Anghie, 2004; Suzuki, 2009; Millennium, 2014). Those considered to be deficient became 'quasi-sovereign' – part or all of their governance was transferred to the 'wardship' of an imperial power (Grovogui, 1996: 79–81). If some international agreements, such as the Geneva Convention and its successor conventions at The Hague in 1899 and 1907, imposed limits on war, this was only for conflicts fought between 'civilized' polities. In conflicts between 'civilized' states, these conventions banned bullets that flattened in the body (building on an earlier agreement on the non-use of so-called 'dum dum' bullets at the 1868 St. Petersburg Conference), bombing from various kinds of aircraft, and the use of gases as weapons. They also restricted the deployment of mines and torpedoes. But codification of the laws of war distinguished 'privileged belligerents' (inhabitants of the 'civilized' world) from 'unprivileged belligerents' (those who lived outside this zone). Privileged belligerents were subject to rules that determined the scope of legitimate violence, not least that it should be discriminate and proportional. Unprivileged combatants were considered to be outside such rules – violence in 'uncivilized' spaces took place without these legal restrictions (Anghie, 2004: 241–42; cf. Mantilla, 2020).

The early history of international organizations, therefore, was closely bound up with 'dual authority'. Many of the first international organizations, including the Concert, were intended to – and did – restrain conflict between imperial nation-states within Europe. At the same time, outside Europe, there was no 'long peace'; rather, there was something more akin to a continuous war. Between 1803 and 1901, Britain alone was involved in fifty major colonial wars. Colonialism extended the reach of great powers with a scale and intensity that was unprecedented in world history. Because the stratification of international order between 'greater' and 'lesser' powers instituted in the Concert coincided with the imperial expansion of Western power, European hierarchy operated on a global scale, buttressed by a 'standard of civilization' that divided the world into civilized, barbarian and savage peoples. International organizations maintained intra-regional peace, while simultaneously stratifying global order in a world of empires.

3 International (or Inter-Imperial) Organizations

The notion of dual authority that underpinned the Concert became, over time, a standard operating procedure. The British diplomat, Webster (1919), wrote a widely circulated study of the Congress in his role as secretary to the military section of the British delegation at the Paris Peace Conference. One of the architects of the League of Nations, Jan Smuts, self-consciously borrowed from the experience of the Concert in designing a governing council in which the Great Powers served as permanent members. The formation of a permanent group of five Great Powers (the P5) within the United Nations (UN) Security Council and the granting to these power of vetoes was a deliberate attempt to replicate the hierarchical management system of the great powers that had been instituted in the Concert. Both Churchill and Roosevelt saw the

Concert as the precedent for a system of global trusteeship under the jurisdiction of the Great Powers (Mazower, 2012: 196). The Concert was the first, but hardly the last, instance of the ways in which imperial nation-states took on the title of great powers and established a directorate over key areas of world politics (on imperial legacies, see Steinmetz, this volume).[1]

During the second half of the nineteenth century, imperialism helped to foster demands for further coordination and standardization, hence the functions of many international organizations that emerged during this period: the International Telecommunications Union (1865), the UPU (1874) and the International Bureau of Weights and Measures (1875). The UPU, for example, responded to the need for interoperability within and between empires. By 1875, six million letters per year were being sent between Britain and the United States, a threefold increase from figures just twenty years earlier (Belich, 2009: 122). From the 1860s onwards, international organizations multiplied rapidly. By 1913, there were forty-five, establishing the foundations for the more ambitious developments that followed the First World War. The Hague Peace Conferences founded the Permanent Court of Arbitration as a dispute settlement mechanism, and paved the way for the Permanent Court of International Justice (PCIJ) that was part of the Versailles Treaties in 1919.

If the leading actors within these international organizations were Western imperial nation-states, during the second half of the nineteenth century, membership expanded to include significant numbers of non-Western countries, including some still under colonial rule. These developments coincided with the emergence of prominent anti-colonial movements: the Indian National Congress was formed in 1885, and the African National Congress in 1912. In 1920, Marcus Garvey's Universal Negro Improvement Association issued its *Declaration of the Rights of the Negro Peoples of the World*, which called for a general 'awakening of race consciousness'. A Congress of Oppressed Nationalities met in Brussels in 1927, while anti-colonial movements from Syria to Ethiopia fought

[1] This assessment comes with a cautionary note. The Concert had less scope and reach than its successors: it had no permanent secretariat, no enduring bureaucracy, no enforcement mechanism and no general guarantee. Nor did it create standing legal organizations. To the contrary, the Concert was strongest when it was based around the personal connections forged by a transnational elite who shared a common background, culture and worldview; it weakened when these actors were replaced by abstract committees and professional diplomats (Jarrett, 2013). In this sense, the Concert was in many ways a period piece – a set of practices that belonged to an era of conservative, aristocratic authority. It was an elite syndicate rather than a deeply embedded governance structure.

sustained insurgencies against imperial powers. 'First peoples' such as the Maori, Kikuyu and Nisga'a petitioned the British crown to end the unequal privileges afforded to white settlers, while Indians living in southern and eastern Africa lobbied international organizations for equal treatment within imperial spaces.

Despite these entreaties, the inter-war years largely maintained colonial-era practices, classifying territories on the basis of their 'primitive' (usually racial) quotient (Mazower, 2012: 166–67; also see Akami, this volume). At the 1919 Versailles Conference, a Japanese attempt to be accepted as racial equals was rejected by Western powers. Of the forty-eight states that sent delegates to the League of Nations, only four were from Asia (including the Raj) and none were from the Middle East. After the Second World War, Western states sought to maintain the system of dual authority within international organizations. Indeed, legalized hegemony formed the backdrop to a range of debates that took place during the early years of the UN: the make-up of the Security Council; the formation of a Trusteeship Council to monitor readiness for self-determination; and the adjudication of responsibility between metropolitan powers and local authorities over human rights provisions. Perhaps the main innovation was the grouping together of a number of inter-governmental organizations within a single framework, a process that began with the League and extended by the UN. As well as having a Council and an Assembly, the League incorporated a Permanent Secretariat divided into a number of sections, including the Social Section, headed by the British feminist Rachel Crowdy, which led high-profile campaigns against slavery, the opium trade and the trafficking of women and children. The League handed over to the UN most of its associated bureaucracies, such as the International Labour Organization, the PCIJ, which became the International Court of Justice, the Health Organization, which became the World Health Organization, and the International Commission on Intellectual Cooperation, which became the United Nations Educational, Scientific and Cultural Organization.

Outside the UN system were dynamics that spoke to deeper shifts in world politics – decolonization strengthened demands by former colonized peoples for plenipotentiary status within international society. During the 1950s and 1960s, the UN General Assembly filled with new states from Africa, the Middle East and Asia. Between 1940 and 1980, eighty-one colonies and four quasi-colonies became independent states (Abernathy, 2000: 133). By 2000, two-thirds of the non-European member states of the United Nations had once been governed by European powers: thirty-seven of these states had experienced more than 250 years of European rule and sixty of them had at least 100 years of colonial rule (Abernathy, 2000: 12). The General Assembly became the expression of the now universal institution of sovereign equality.

The influx of former colonies into the UN reaffirmed the sentiments expressed by earlier anti-colonial movements. In 1946, the UN passed a motion condemning racial discrimination in South Africa; thereafter, this vote became an annual event. The 1947 Asian Relations Conference in Delhi formed part of a broader pan-Asian movement that both built on earlier developments (such as the inter-war Pan-Asian People's Conferences in Nagasaki and Shanghai), and acted as the forerunner to the ambitious agenda initiated at the Bandung conference in April 1955, in which twenty-nine African and Asian states met to condemn colonialism and seek a diminution of great power influence in favour of universal, egalitarian principles of self-determination. In 1960, the UN General Assembly passed Resolution 1514 – 'Declaration on the Granting of Independence to Colonial Countries and People' – advocating a more or less unconditional right of self-determination. In 1965, the General Assembly backed the Convention on the Elimination of all Forms of Racial Discrimination. The force of positive international law in the twentieth century was wielded to rectify the inequalities it had facilitated during the nineteenth century.

Such changes also affected issues of political economy, leading to the development of the World Food Programme (1961), the G77 group of 'underdeveloped' states (1967), the UN Conference on Trade and Development (1964) and related proposals for a New International Economic Order (1974). This south-south cooperation was the forerunner to a range of contemporary developments, from the emergence of the G20 to China's Belt and Road initiative. Crucial to unravelling these dynamics is the relationship between two apparently contradictory dynamics: the first hierarchical, the latter egalitarian. As noted above, beginning with the Concert of Europe, world politics was home to an oligarchic management system. Yet, the Concert also sought to represent small states and statelets – if Poland was partitioned, the independence of Belgium, Switzerland and Luxemburg was assured. The League also sought to balance hierarchy (in the Council) and egalitarianism (in the Assembly). In the UN, the influence of the P5 was meant to be at least partly offset by ten rotating members of the Security Council who did not hold vetoes, but who could make things uncomfortable for the great powers. As outlined in Teresa Koloma Beck's chapter, colonialism generated a dual international order, one that ranged from legal status to the make-up of international organizations.

4 From Intervention to Interventionism

The origins and evolution of international organizations are, therefore, characterized by dual authority: imperial-nation states were tied together horizontally, while a vertical point of demarcation was drawn between 'greater' and 'lesser' powers. The superior power capabilities and status held by the great powers meant that they were granted special rights (e.g. over intervention) and responsibilities (such as a duty to maintain international order). Indeed, a core aspect of the definition of great powers was that they were able to carry out interventions but were themselves secure from them.

The inter-war years began to see the reconfiguration and rearticulation of these rights and responsibilities. The mandate system, which was first applied to the colonies of the defeated Central Powers, Germany and the Ottoman Empire, was a formula for replacing empires without either annexing their colonies or granting them independence. Along with the trusteeship principle, which embodied the idea that 'political power should be exercised for the benefit of those persons who are subject to it' (Bain, 2003: 50–52), the mandate system rested on a 'sacred trust' of 'uplift' towards 'backwards peoples' who were 'not yet' ready for self-rule (Pedersen, 2015: 4). If this was meant to represent a new, more humane imperialism, the reality was different. Of fourteen mandates, only one state (Iraq) became independent and, even then, it was a conspicuously shallow independence – Iraq provided major concessions to Britain, including jurisdiction over its airfields and oil fields (Sluga & Clavin, 2017). Resistance to trusteeship was common, most notably in southwest Africa, Syria, Western Samoa, Iraq and Ethiopia. The students, it seems, did not want to learn from their tutors.

Anti-imperial revolts intensified after the Second World War. So too did other challenges to Western hegemony. The Japanese, despite being defeated, broke the myth of white power in Asia through their conquests of American, British, French and Dutch territories early in the war. This was reinforced, and magnified, by experiences of fascism, which discredited both racism and any pretence that Europe represented a superior 'standard of civilization'. Over time, international order shifted from a three-tiered colonial order regulated by divided sovereignty to a global order grounded on the principle of sovereign equality (Reus-Smit, 2013). Rather than disappearing, status inequalities were reconfigured and rearticulated. Most notably, the package of colonialism, human inequality/racism, the 'standard of civilization' and divided sovereignty was rearticulated as a package of sovereign equality, self-determination, and human equality/anti-racism. Accompanying self-determination was a strengthened notion of human rights, which gave practical form to human equality and anti-racism (Clark, 2007: 131–51). The new norm of human equality was embedded in the Charter of the United Nations and most visibly expressed in the 1948 Universal Declaration of Human Rights, which made individual human beings 'rights holders on their own behalf'. Human rights were also embodied in many UN Conventions and Committees, as they were in a number of regional bodies.

Although the formal stratification represented by the 'standard of civilization' had been discredited, the colonial construction of non-Europeans as being at a lower stage of development within a single model of civilization was reconfigured rather than overturned. The colonial obligation of the metropolitan powers to 'uplift' the natives shifted into an obligation on the part of the rich world to 'assist' in the 'development' and 'modernization' of the 'Third World' (Zarakol, 2011; also see Chapters 8 and 11 in this volume). Development drew legitimacy from both a sense of obligation by the former colonial powers (now 'advanced' states) and a sense of prerogative by post-colonial ('developing') states. It also drew legitimacy from its synergies with the redistributive dimensions of the human rights and human security regimes with their emphasis on rights to adequate nutrition, clean water, shelter, education and more. For Western policy makers, development also had the benefit of preserving market advantages by providing investment opportunities for firms, shoring up compliant elites and, perhaps most importantly, helping to curtail the spread of communism. After 1945, the 'development project' became a universal goal, albeit one attended by considerable uncertainties and disagreements over how it was to be realized.

Crucial to the reconfiguring and rearticulation of international organizations were practices of intervention. On the one hand, during the nineteenth century, intervention was a tool through which imperial-nation states sought to manage intra-elite competition and forestall challenges from below. In this way, intervention maintained a form of sovereignty that limited forms of political expression considered threatening to incumbent elites. Such conceptions were central to interventions carried out by the Austro-Hungarian Empire in Naples in 1821, the French in Spain in 1823 and the Prussians in Bavaria and Baden in 1849. On the other hand, intervention became associated with a family of practices, including blockades and sanctions, which were responsible for the coercive restructuring of 'other' societies. Intervention was a means through which to transform 'backward' places, whether this backwardness was conceived as a deficient economy, an illegitimate polity, or an uncivilized culture (Lawson & Tardelli, 2013).

Once again, the rationale for, and meaning of, intervention was reconfigured and rearticulated during the Cold War, when both the United States and the Soviet Union used intervention as a means of extending their sphere of influence and maintaining the balance between them. In practice, this entailed 'intervention within the blocs, non-intervention between them, and a tenuous non-intervention outside them' (Vincent, 1974: 353). Morgenthau (1967), amongst others, stressed the need for the superpowers to prop up newly decolonized states given the weakness of indigenous governance structures. The provision of military and economic aid created ties of inequality that the provider could exploit by either supplying or withdrawing aid, thus dramatically influencing local political developments. At the same time, local elites often invited external aid as a means by which to counter domestic rivals and implement development projects. The US justified its frequent interventions in the interests of preserving the global correlation of forces, as, for example, in the 'domino' metaphor used to legitimize its intervention in Vietnam. For their part, the Soviets limited the sovereignty of satellite states and intervened to maintain the homogeneity of their bloc, while intervening in a range of polities in the 'Third World', from Afghanistan to Ethiopia. Given the frequency of interventions by both superpowers, the Cold War in the Third World was akin to a clash between two 'regimes of global intervention' (Westad, 2005).

As contemporary debates around Afghanistan, Crimea and Syria illustrate, military intervention remains a contentious subject. The onset of a wave of humanitarian, usually multilateral, interventions after the collapse of the Soviet Union prompted considerable work on the 'ought' of intervention (cf. Wheeler, 2000; Weiss, 2007; Orford, 2011). At times, this work contextualized contemporary debates by reaching back to instances of intervention claimed to have been carried out for humanitarian motives or to have had humanitarian outcomes: the British campaign against the slave trade; William Gladstone's lobbying for action in the face of the 'Bulgarian horrors'; or India's intervention in East Pakistan (later Bangladesh) (cf. Wheeler, 2000). However, these debates often missed the ways in which the character of intervention was being reconstructed. In the post-Cold War world, both public and private actors 'intervened' in polities around the world to such an extent as to coercively reshape state–society relations without resorting to military force (Duffield, 2007; Hameiri, 2010). As the practice of intervention evolved, it became more expansive, shifting from a discrete practice reserved for the great powers to one that was permanent in form and universal in aspiration. To some extent, intervention shifted from overt methods of coercive restructuring towards 'everyday' forms of 'interventionism' (Williams, 2013).

Some aspects of the nineteenth century 'right to intervene' remain central to the governance of the contemporary world, most notably in the obligations of the UN Security Council to uphold international order and, following the agreement on the Responsibility to Protect, to intervene in order to halt genocide, ethnic cleansing, war crimes and crimes against humanity. There are two factors, however, that mitigate these obligations. First is the uncertain implementation by the Security Council of their role in guaranteeing international peace and security, including via the Responsibility to Protect. In 2011, the Security Council authorized the use of force for human protection purposes against the wishes of a functioning state (Libya) for the first time. However, five states (Brazil, China, Russia, India and Germany) abstained from the vote. Further disagreements over the scope of Responsibility to Protect in relation to Syria and the Cote d'Ivoire demonstrated the difficulties of turning agreement on principles into decisive action. The US retreat from Afghanistan in 2021 sounded, perhaps, the death knell of this practice.

Second is the increasingly decentred character of contemporary global order (Buzan & Lawson, 2014). The rise of China is the contemporary standard bearer for this process, but outside the West it was Japan that first made this leap. Japan's defeat of Russia in 1904–1905 signalled for the first time in the modern era the rise of a non-white, non-Western state. Many other states – the 'Asian Tigers', Turkey, Indonesia, Brazil, and more – subsequently followed suit. As a result, the period of Western hegemony, which lasted from the middle of the nineteenth century to the first quarter of the twenty-first century, is coming to an end. A more decentred international environment means that it is difficult for any single power, or cluster of powers, to dominate international affairs. This trend is likely to continue – the core of global society is becoming bigger and less Western. And it can be observed in a range of dynamics, from patterns of trade to security alliances. As noted in the Introduction to this book, history is shaped in significant measure by power asymmetries. As power shifts in locus in the contemporary world, so too will practices around intervention. If the system of great powers that first claimed the right to intervene was closely tied to Western ideas and practices, in a world in which Western power no longer serves as the fulcrum of international order, it is not axiomatic that comparable views of intervention will be sustained, particularly when emerging powers have spent many years struggling for non-intervention to be recognized in *de facto* as well as *de jure* terms (Lawson & Tardelli, 2013).

The power preponderance that enabled Western imperial nation-states to overwhelm most parts of the world during the nineteenth century is, therefore, receding as modernity expands. This points to a more dispersed global distribution of power, one in which a myriad of forms of international administration play a major role. In recent years, banking, securities, insurance, accounting, auditing, corporate governance, insolvency, creditor rights and money laundering have become subject to international standards by bodies ranging from the G20 to the Financial Stability Board. Such a regulatory environment marks a redistribution of power from Western-controlled international organizations to a multilayered spectrum of international administration. Here, once again, can be found the 'complex temporalities' that accompany world historical development.

As noted in the previous section, in the nineteenth and twentieth centuries, inequalities between polities were sanctioned through the denial of competence to non-Western, non-white, non-Christian, non-'modern' peoples. These polities were the wards of imperial-nation states that retained the right to intervene in order to correct 'deficiencies' in practices, institutions and cosmologies. In the contemporary world, however, a redistribution of global power has gone hand-in-hand with the denial of any fundamental source of difference between peoples around the world. Rather, inequality is seen, at least in formal circles, as the result of temporary conditions: deficient institutions, weak governance, poor leadership, a corrupt ruling elite and so on.[2] This means that there are no longer formal barriers to intervention. Rather, the claims of present-day advocates of intervention are universal. As the former Secretary General of the UN, Annan (2012: 13), put it: 'if the UN truly was to reflect a humanity that cared more, not less, for the suffering in its midst, and would do more, and not less, to end it, the organization has to be an agent of intervention in every sphere of human security.'

Kofi Annan's remarks speak to a world in which boundaries of inside-outside, no longer resting on the standard of civilization or constrained by norms of sovereign territoriality, are dissolved. Rather, the bundling of territoriality with rights of reciprocal sovereignty is being replaced by a fluid notion of sovereignty that is contingent on meeting standards of human protection. This is an important reformulation of the sovereignty norm. Rather than sovereignty being associated with the *control* of a territory, it is now seen as a *responsibility* that comes into force when states pass a certain 'yardstick' (Orford, 2011). Forms of international administration, including international courts, territorial mandates and

[2] 'Formal' is doing a lot of work here. Even a passing familiarity with the US withdrawal from Afghanistan in August 2021 makes clear the ongoing potency of imperial-era modalities in contemporary debates around intervention.

peacekeeping forces are the mechanisms through which an international apparatus takes on the functions of nation-states, particularly in the Global South. The UN is now the second largest deployer of troops in the world (after the US); in 2021, the organization maintained nearly 100,000 uniformed personnel from over 100 countries. All UN peacekeeping operations are taking place in the Global South, the vast majority of them in Africa. At the same time, peacekeeping operations are assuming increasingly expansive roles – of the forty-nine UN-mandated peacekeeping operations undertaken between 1989 and 2011, thirty-four contained a commitment to state-building (Dodge, 2013: 1192). The power inequality that sustained dual authority and made the sovereignty of 'lesser' polities dependent on the actions of great powers, has not disappeared, but is being redistributed to forms of international administration. The majority of UN troops deployed in the contemporary world come from Asia and Africa. The UN High Commissioner for Refugees has the power to set up camps, and make life and death decisions, without recourse to consultation with the UN's member states. The World Bank dictates the content and direction of global development programs. In this way, international organizations fix meanings, establish rules and transmit norms around the international realm (Barnett & Finnemore, 2004).

The redistribution of intervention from a tool of great power privilege to one administered 'neutrally' by international organizations is important for two reasons. First, interventions carried out by trans-scalar forms of international administration are claimed to represent not just the views of some members of international society, but global society as a whole. Second, and linked, this means that interventionism is becoming, if anything, *more* widespread. One aspect of this is increasing numbers of south-south interventions, whether under the auspices of regional international organizations or conducted directly by states. Since the end of the Cold War, the African Union (AU) has intervened in Darfur (2003, 2008), Burundi (2003–2004) and Somalia (2007–present); the Economic Community of West African States (ECOWAS) has intervened in Liberia (1990), Sierra Leone (1997), Guinea-Bissau (1999), Ivory Coast (2003) and Mali (2013); and the Gulf Cooperation Council has intervened in Bahrain (2011) and blockaded Qatar (2017–2018). Since 2011, several Middle Eastern states have intervened in Libya, Yemen and Syria. Meanwhile, China has steadily increased its contributions to UN peacekeeping operations and missions. States throughout the Global South are increasingly following in the footsteps of Western states, which have long used not just military power, but also aid, think-tanks, foundations, universities and forms of media as ways of spreading

Western norms, ideas and practices. Tools that were once the preserve of Western imperial powers are becoming increasingly universalized.

5 Conclusion

The relationship between colonialism and international organizations is, therefore, a close one. This chapter has charted three stages in this relationship since the early nineteenth century that highlight different modes of historicity at play: first, the use of international organizations as a means of coordinating imperialism and containing or, preferably, preventing inter-imperial conflict; second, the global expansion of international organizations as a means of stratifying polities initially via the 'standard of civilization' and, later, through quotients of modernization/ development; and third, the use of international organizations as a means for various forms of interventionism. Taken together, these three stages mark a shift from a limited realm of international organization to a virtually universal condition of international administration. Over the past two centuries, the rationale and competences of international organizations have been reconfigured, rearticulated and redistributed.

Narrating the history of international organizations in this way helps to address the ways in which 'colonial history is written into our present' (Schlichte & Stetter, this volume). It is often said that the modern world has seen a shift from a world of empires to a world of nation-states (e.g. Wimmer, 2013). In two ways, this narrative is less clear-cut than it appears. First, the polities that forged international order in the nineteenth and twentieth centuries were both empires and nation-states – they were imperial-nation states. As such, there is not always a hard-and-fast distinction between these political forms. Second, decolonization did not mark the sharp replacement of empires with nation-states – there was no political 'big bang' in this respect. Rather, as this chapter has shown, in many ways, the more important shift was the reconfiguration, rearticulation and redistribution of power from international organizations to various forms of international administration. Today, these forms of international administration are highly interventionist, particularly in the Global South.

In the contemporary world, there is a complex architecture of global governance that includes international organizations, financial institutions, non-governmental organizations, corporate actors and more. This multi-layered system has redistributed rationalities of rule, fracturing international administration, while simultaneously deepening it. At times, this rationality of rule is formal and explicit, as seen in the compounds that house – and separate – 'internationals' from domestic populations in parts of the Global South (see the chapter by Koloma Beck). At other times, it exists behind the scenes, in the sinews of global politics, as in the quiet funding of programmes by foundations, think-tanks and similar entities that are intended to create a homogeneous, yet cosmopolitan, elite capable of providing an interchangeable pool of personnel within international organizations. International organizations were born in the formal inequalities of power that marked world politics during the nineteenth century and the first half of the twentieth century. Today, these inequalities have been reconfigured, rearticulated and redistributed. In this way, more than any other lie traces of the colonial past in the present of world politics.

References

Abernathy, D. B. (2000). *The Dynamics of Global Dominance*, New Haven: Yale University Press.

Anghie, A. (2004). *Imperialism, Sovereignty and the Making of International Law*, Cambridge: Cambridge University Press.

Annan, K. (2012). *Interventions: A Life in War and Peace*, London: Allen Lane.

Armstrong, D., Lloyd, L. & Redmond, J. (2004). *International Organization in World Politics*, Basingstoke: Palgrave Macmillan.

Bain, W. (2003). *Between Anarchy and Society: Trusteeship and the Obligations of Power*, Oxford: Oxford University Press.

Barnett, M. & Finnemore, M. (2004). *Rules for the World: International Organizations in Global Politics*, Ithaca, NY: Cornell University Press.

Bayly, C. A. (2004). *The Birth of the Modern World, 1780–1914*, Oxford: Blackwell Publishing.

Belich, J. (2009). *Replenishing the Earth: The Settler Revolution and the Rise of the Anglo-World, 1783–1939*, New York: Oxford University Press.

Buzan, B. & Lawson, G. (2014). Capitalism and the Emergent World Order, *International Affairs*, 90(1), 71–91.

Buzan, B. & Lawson, G. (2015). *The Global Transformation: History, Modernity and the Making of International Relations*, Cambridge: Cambridge University Press.

Clark, I. (2007). *International Legitimacy and World Society*, Oxford: Oxford University Press.

Dodge, T. (2013). Intervention and Dreams of Exogeneous Statebuilding: The Application of Liberal Peacebuilding in Afghanistan and Iraq, *Review of International Studies*, 39(5), 1189–212.

Duffield, M. (2007). *Development, Security and Unending War: Governing the World of Peoples*, Cambridge: Polity.

Geyer, M. & Bright, C. (1996). Global Violence and Nationalizing Wars in Eurasia and the Americas, *Comparative Studies in Society and History*, 38(4), 619–57.

Go, J. (2011). *Patterns of Empire*, Cambridge: Cambridge University Press.

Gong, G. W. (1984). *The Standard of 'Civilization' in International Society*, Oxford: Clarendon Press.
Grovogui, S. (1996). *Sovereigns, Quasi Sovereigns, and Africans*, Minneapolis: University of Minnesota Press.
Hameiri, S. (2010). *Regulating Statehood: State Building and the Transformation of the Global Order*, London: Palgrave Macmillan.
Hobsbawm, E. (1962). *The Age of Revolution, 1789–1848*, London: Abacus.
Jarrett, M. (2013). *The Congress of Vienna and Its Legacy*, London: I. B. Tauris.
Keene, E. (2013). International Hierarchy and the Origins of the Modern Practice of Intervention, *Review of International Studies*, 29(5), 1077–90.
Lawson, G. & Tardelli, L. (2013). The Past, Present and the Future of Intervention, *Review of International Studies*, 39(5), 1233–53.
Mantilla, G. (2020). *Lawmaking under Pressure: International Humanitarian Law and Internal Armed Conflict*, Ithaca, NY: Cornell University Press.
Mazower, M. (2012). *Governing the World*, London: Allen Lane.
Meier, C. S. (2012). Leviathan 2.0, in E. S. Rosenberg (ed.). *A World Connecting, 1870–1945*, 29–282, Cambridge: Belknap.
Millennium (2014). Special Issue: The Standard of Civilization, *Millennium*, 42(3), 546–849.
Mitzen, J. (2013). *Power in Concert*, Chicago: University of Chicago Press.
Morgenthau, H. J. (1967). To Intervene or Not to Intervene, *Foreign Affairs*, 45(3), 425–36.
Orford, A. (2011). *International Authority and the Responsibility to Protect*, Cambridge: Cambridge University Press.
Osterhammel, J. (2014). *The Transformation of the World: A Global History of the Nineteenth Century*, Princeton: Princeton University Press.
Pedersen, S. (2015). *The Guardians: The League of Nations the Crisis of Empire*, Oxford: Oxford University Press.
Reus-Smit, C. (2013). *Individual Rights and the Making of the International System*, Cambridge: Cambridge University Press.
Simpson, G. (2004). *Great Powers and Outlaw States*, Cambridge: Cambridge University Press.
Sluga, G. & Clavin, P. (2017). *Internationalisms: A Twentieth Century History*, Cambridge: Cambridge University Press.
Suzuki, S. (2009). *Civilization and Empire*, London: Routledge.
Vincent, J. (1974). *Non-Intervention and International Order*, Princeton: Princeton University Press.
Webster, C. (1919). *The Congress of Vienna*, London: H. Milford.
Weiss, T. (2007). *Humanitarian Intervention*, Cambridge: Polity.
Westad, A. (2005). *The Global Cold War*, Cambridge: Cambridge University Press.
Wheeler, N. (2000). *Saving Strangers*, Oxford: Oxford University Press.
Williams, D. (2013). Development, Intervention and International Order, *Review of International Studies*, 39(5), 1213–31.
Wimmer, A. (2013). *Waves of War*, Cambridge: Cambridge University Press.
Zarakol, A. (2011). *After Defeat: How the East Learned to Live with the West*, Cambridge: Cambridge University Press.

3 Collective Hegemony after Decolonization
Persistence despite Delegitimation

Thomas Müller

1 Introduction

Collective hegemony has been a key feature of the governance practice of international society since the early nineteenth century. Collective hegemony can be defined as institutionalized arrangements through which a small group of powerful states collectively steers and regulates matters that affect international society as a whole.[1] The most prominent examples are the Concert of Europe in the nineteenth century as well as the Council of the League of Nations and the UN Security Council in the twentieth century. While these three governance institutions defined the group in the same way – as the group of great powers – collective hegemony has been based on various conceptions of this group. The G7 and G20 notably embody broader and more economic conceptions.

The history of collective hegemony is generally conceptualized and analysed as a deviation from the principle of sovereign equality that creates institutionalized forms of hierarchies (cf. Bull, 2002: 194–222; Simpson, 2004; Bukovansky et al., 2012). What makes this perspective problematic is that it treats international society as a society of equals in which the establishment of forms of collective hegemony introduces elements of institutionalized inequality. Yet, when the Concert of Europe, the League's Council and the UN Security Council were established, the cluster of sovereign, formally equal states formed but one strata of a broader stratified, colonial international society. While European imperialism is often in some way present in these studies – usually as a likewise problematic background narrative of the 'expansion' from a European to a global international society[2] – they nevertheless generally

[1] For recent studies of the history on collective hegemony in international society, cf. Simpson (2004), Badie (2013), Pouliot and Thérien (2015), and my own dissertation (Müller 2017) on which this chapter draws.

[2] Bull and Watson (1984) presented an 'expansion' narrative in which international society gradually becomes global through the admission of non-European states. By reducing international society to a society of states, this narrative downplays the stratified, colonial

trace the evolution of forms of collective hegemony without systematically analysing their co-evolution with other hierarchies such as notably colonial hierarchies.

The present chapter examines the modes of historicity underlying the co-evolution and interplay of collective hegemony and colonial hierarchies from the nineteenth century to the present. The colonial underpinnings of the governance architecture of international society have been emphasized by several authors (cf. Anghie, 2005; Mazower, 2009; Buzan & Lawson, 2015). There are indeed important *continuities* in the hierarchical structure and practice of international organizations as the chapter by Lawson in this volume shows. Yet, while intertwined, colonial hierarchies and collective hegemony were also two distinct hierarchical dimensions. This chapter highlights the effects of decolonization – that is, of discontinuities in colonial hierarchies – on the continuing practice of collective hegemony.[3] These effects correspond to the first mode of historicity highlighted by the editors in their introduction. The structuring effects of history are visible not only in national structures of domination (see the chapter by Glasman and Schlichte in this volume), but also in international ones: the presence of the colonial past affected collective hegemony through an increased level of contestation and delegitimation in the wake of two waves of decolonization which cumulatively, while not ending the practice of collective hegemony, changed the ways in which collective hegemony could and can be institutionalized and performed.

The chapter proceeds as follows. The first section frames the effects of decolonization on collective hegemony as an interplay of two types of hierarchies. The second section highlights why collective hegemony is usually studied in relation to the cluster of sovereign states: this cluster was the main focus of the governance activities of the various forms of collective hegemony which were only occasionally practiced for the colonial sphere. The third section then uses three episodes of discourses about collective hegemony – the Second Hague Conference in 1907, the rise of the Non-Aligned Movement and the current UN Security Council reform debate – to show how formerly colonized states were prime actors in the contestation of collective hegemony. Despite this increased level of contestation and delegitimation, the powerful states

nature nineteenth and twentieth centuries international society (Keene, 2014; Dunne & Reus-Smit, 2017).

[3] This chapter accordingly concentrates on the effects of decolonization on the governance practice of international society. It brackets the contestation of and struggles against the colonial powers that took place within the colonies. For a study of how anticolonial national movements influenced the international contestation of colonialism and great power dominance, cf. Mazower (2009: 149–89).

were able to continue to practice forms of collective hegemony due to formal path-dependencies and the reliance on informal variants. The final section briefly summarizes the main arguments and reflects on their implications.

2 The Co-evolution and Interplay of Two Hierarchical Dimensions

The research on hierarchies in IR has only recently begun to shift its analytical focus from the evolution of individual hierarchies – a focus that still dominates the research on collective hegemony – to the intersection and interplay of different types of hierarchies (cf. Keene, 2014; Zarakol, 2017). While international society features multiple hierarchies, the present chapter zooms in on the co-evolution and interplay of two hierarchical dimensions. The two dimensions feature different types of hierarchies, although both involve political relations of super- and subordination.

The first dimension consists in the various forms of collective hegemony that groups of powerful states have historically practiced. In the influential conceptualization of the English School (Bull, 1980: 194–222; Clark, 2011: 34–70), collective hegemony refers to more than simply a preponderance of power. It denotes a mode of governance in which (a) the group of most powerful states jointly acts together to perform certain governance functions relating to international society as a whole, with (b) the other members of international society empowering them to do so by granting them special privileges and rights.[4] While modifying the English School's conceptualization, more recent approaches retain and indeed foreground its central premise that collective hegemony is a form of legitimate political authority (Simpson, 2004: 67–76; Bukovansky et al., 2012: 4–5, 10, 69–77).[5] It represents a relation of political super- and subordination when and as long as the other states accept, at least tacitly, that the most powerful states have a privileged role in the governance of international society. The special rights are sometimes formally granted, as in the case of the League of Nations and the UN. It is, though, debatable whether all forms of collective hegemony involve the acceptance of a

[4] Following SFB 700 (2009: 4), this chapter understands 'governance' as institutionalized modes of social coordination that aim at generating general rules, tackling common problems and promoting common goals in and for a social group (in the present case: international society). In this perspective, governance can take both non-hierarchical as well as hierarchical forms.

[5] For a different conceptualization that stresses the oligarchic ambitions of the most powerful states rather than political authority, cf. Badie (2013).

limited right to rule, especially since informal forms such as the Concert of Europe or the G7 have never been formally consented to by international society as a whole.

The second hierarchical dimension comprises the various colonial hierarchies that have permeated international society and which, taken together, created a stratified political order consisting of different layers of polities. Colonial hierarchies are relations of super- and subordination in which one imperial power transforms conquered territories into one or more dependent political entities that are subordinate to it (Osterhammel, 2009a: 16). Colonial hierarchies are but one type of imperial hierarchies through which a superordinate polity imposes some forms of political and economic control over another polity or other polities. The European imperial powers, for instance, transformed some territories into colonies while establishing a system of unequal treaties with other polities without turning them into formal colonies. In the nineteenth and early twentieth centuries, the various colonial and imperial hierarchies were usually legitimized by European and Western powers with the 'standard of civilization'. In the logic of this standard, several layers of polities existed which differed in their degree of civilization and sovereignty, with full membership in international society being restricted to civilized, sovereign states according to the standard set by the European and Western powers (Anghie, 2005: 52–65; Bowden, 2009: 103–58).

These two hierarchical dimensions co-existed alongside each other for roughly 150 years in the nineteenth and twentieth centuries. Colonial hierarchies already existed before the emergence of institutionalized forms of collective hegemony with the establishment of the Concert of Europe in 1814–1815/1818. As the first wave of decolonization occurred in Latin America in the early nineteenth century, the institutionalized forms of collective hegemony always existed in a global international society in which some parts were already decolonized while others were still colonized. The co-evolution of the two hierarchical dimensions was thus characterized by complex temporalities, that is, the second mode of historicity identified by the editors. The institutionalized forms of collective hegemony then outlasted the formal end of colonial hierarchies with the final wave of decolonization after the Second World War.

The two hierarchical dimensions did not only overlap temporally but also in terms of their ruling class. They were distinct from each other insomuch as they were organized around different constellations of rulers and ruled and enacted through different practices of governance and domination. Whereas collective hegemony was (and is) characterized by a group of states governing over a group of formally sovereign states, colonial hierarchies involved one state subjugating one or several other polities and integrating them into its colonial empire. What intertwined the two hierarchical dimensions was the overlapping ruling class. The group of great powers practiced the key forms of collective hegemony. While not the only imperial powers, the great powers were also the key players in the colonial and imperial game. Moreover, the same factor enabled the great powers to dominate both hierarchies: their preponderance in political, military and economic power (cf. Buzan & Lawson, 2015).

The mode of historicity that most strongly shaped the co-evolution of the two hierarchical dimensions were the structuring effects of history. The following analysis traces how the demise of formal colonial hierarchies affected the practice of collective hegemony. As the analysis will show, the presence of the colonial past has been visible in both the progressive delegitimation and persistent practice of collective hegemony:

- Progressive delegitimation: The legitimacy of collective hegemony has been questioned from its very beginning. Formerly colonized and now sovereign states were the key actors contesting collective hegemony. The waves of decolonization cumulatively increased their number and political leverage in international society, thus contributing to the progressive delegitimation of collective hegemony.
- Persistent practice: The waves of decolonization did neither end the practice of collective hegemony nor erase the underlying power inequalities. Decolonization further undermined the legitimacy of collective hegemony but formal forms established during colonial times persisted. Moreover, the great powers offset the progressive delegitimation by relying on informal forms of collective hegemony that did not require formal consent from the formerly colonized states.

The element interlinking both modes are the politics of legitimation and delegitimation. Actors accept hierarchies for a mixture of motives ranging from coercion over an interest in the outcomes generated by the hierarchy to a belief in the legitimacy – that is, normative appropriateness – of the hierarchy (Hurd, 1999). To be stable and durable, hierarchies generally have to be considered to be legitimate by the relevant constituency of actors. The politics of legitimation and delegitimation denote the attempts by various actors to increase, maintain or contest the legitimacy of hierarchies and orders (Nullmeier et al., 2012: 23–28). For the analysis of the impact of decolonization, two observations made by Weber (1972: 123) in his discussion of legitimate rule are useful: variances in the legitimation of forms of rule can not only influence the durability but also the practice and design of these forms. And when the constellation of power overwhelmingly favours the rulers, then the rulers can sometimes dispense with the need to garner legitimacy among the ruled. In a nutshell, decolonization did not end, but nevertheless the practice of collective hegemony changed. As formal consent was now even harder to attain, decolonization essentially restricted the spectrum of possible forms of collective hegemony to informal variants.

3 Collective Hegemony in a Colonial International Society

In the roughly 150 years in which both hierarchical dimensions co-evolved, collective hegemony was institutionalized and practiced mainly through three governance institutions: the Concert of Europe from 1818 to 1914 (Sédouy, 2009; Schulz, 2012), the League's Council in the interwar period (Walters, 1969) and the UN Security Council after 1945 (Bosco, 2009). This section briefly outlines how these three forms of collective hegemony framed their spheres of governance. The great powers developed arrangements that delineated matters that they intended to govern collectively as a group from matters that were deemed to fall outside the collective purview of the group of great powers. The colonial powers were generally inclined to keep colonial issues in the latter category, thus creating a regime of separated governance spheres in which the forms of collective hegemony were primarily designed for the sphere of sovereign states but not for the colonial sphere.

The regime of separated spheres of governance was created by the Congress of Vienna in 1814–1815 and the subsequent practice of the Concert of Europe.[6] On Great Britain's insistence, the five great powers agreed to limit the scope of their collective governance activities to European matters. Given that colonial questions had been part of the previous great power settlement after the Seven Years' War, this arrangement amounted to a purposive de-globalization of the governance sphere of the Concert of Europe which decoupled it from the regulation of colonial affairs (Osterhammel, 2009b: 679–82). Until the 1870s, the collective governance practice was confined to what the Concert termed general European affairs, which it defined as matters threatening the peace and balance in Europe (which since the Congress of Paris in 1856 also included matters relating to the Ottoman Empire[7]).

In the 1880s, this decoupling ended when the great powers began to also react to and regulate certain colonial issues as a group. Among these

[6] The Concert of Europe consisted of five great powers: Austria, France, Great Britain, Prussia and Russia, with Italy becoming the sixth member in 1867.

[7] On the lasting effects of the Concert's policies regarding the Ottoman Empire, see the chapter by Vlachopoulou and Stetter in this volume.

collective activities were notably the Berlin Conference in 1884–1885 on colonial activities in Africa as well as the military intervention of the eight great powers – the six members of the Concert plus the USA and Japan – in China in 1900–1901. The geographical expansion happened through a bifurcation of the practice of collective hegemony. The six great powers continued to use the Concert of Europe for European matters while in parallel an enlarged concert format emerged for the governance of select colonial affairs, with varying additional participants besides the six European great powers (Müller, 2017: 249–61). That said, collective hegemony remained the exception rather than the rule in the colonial sphere, which continued to be foremost the product of competing colonial empires rather than the product of collective action by the group of great powers (Osterhammel, 2009b: 682).

Global forms of collective hegemony were then institutionalized with the League of Nations in 1919 and the UN in 1945. During the establishment of both institutions, colonial issues were raised in the negotiations and colonial powers sought to use the two institutions to preserve their empires (Mazower, 2009: 17). Similar to the Concert of Europe, the League's Council and the UN Security Council were nevertheless primarily designed for the governance of the sphere of sovereign states. The membership of the League and the UN consisted foremost of sovereign states. The League formally also admitted dominions and colonies, though in practice only several British dominions and one British colony, India, became members (cf. Walters, 1969: 43–44, 64–65).

Both the League and the UN were designed to govern select colonial territories, though attempts to place all colonial territories under the purview of the League and the UN failed due to opposition of major colonial powers such as France and Great Britain. The League of Nations created a Mandates System for the administration of territories formerly controlled by Germany and the Ottoman Empire (Anghie, 2005: 115–90; Pedersen, 2015). The UN's Trusteeship Council, in turn, oversaw the administration of so-called trust territories, most of which had formerly been mandate territories (Schlesinger, 2004: 79–80, 234–36).[8]

The establishment of the UN happened at a time when the colonial powers already faced considerable anti-colonial pressure. The UN Charter accordingly obliged all colonial powers to 'develop self-government' (which for the USA meant independence) in their dependent territories and tasked all colonial powers, and not just those powers administrating

[8] Besides the interests of colonial powers, an US interest in retaining strategic military bases acquired during the World War also played a role in the creation of the Trusteeship Council.

trust territories, to submit information on the development of their dependent territories to the UN (Pearson, 2017). Over time, the UN became a key forum for the further delegitimation of colonial hierarchies and the promotion of decolonization (cf. Mazower, 2009: 148–89).

4 Delegitimizing Forms of Collective Hegemony

In the politics of legitimation and delegitimation, the great powers have mainly pointed to their preponderant power, their greater contributions and their general interests as justifications for their claims to privileged positions and roles in the governance of international society (Simpson, 2004; Müller, 2017). Their colonial empires were usually not among the main justifications – and in this sense were apparently not regarded as a good legitimation for collective hegemony[9] – but were nevertheless sometimes invoked indirectly. During the negotiations on the design of the UN Security Council, for instance, Great Britain justified the veto with the argument that the five great powers 'represent probably more than half the population of the world, and account has to be taken of that fact', an argument that only worked when the populations of the British and French colonies were factored in (United Nations Information Organizations, 1945: 320).

That said, the interplay between the two hierarchical dimensions mattered significantly for the contestation and delegitimation of collective hegemony. While the legitimacy of these practices was 'constantly subject to challenge' (Bull, 1980: 438), formerly colonized states have been the main critics of forms of collective hegemony. The successive waves of decolonization contributed to their growing weight in the deliberations and thus made the contestation more pronounced over time. After overcoming one hierarchy dominated by the great powers (colonial rule), the decolonized states were reluctant to create new forms of hierarchies again dominated by the great powers (the institutionalized inequality embodied by forms of collective hegemony). The remainder of this section explores the effects of decolonization on the evolution of institutionalized forms of collective hegemony at three critical junctures: the Second Hague Conference in 1907, the emergence of the Non-Aligned Movement (NAM) and the current debate on the reform of the UN Security Council.

[9] This low salience as a justification for collective hegemony has to be distinguished from the salience of colonial empires as markers for great power status (which was arguably highest in the period of high imperialism and 'world power' discourses at the end of the nineteenth century).

4.1 The Rejection of Great Power Privileges at the Second Hague Conference

The Second Hague Conference in 1907, which was attended by forty-four states, arguably marked the first key episode in the contestation of collective hegemony (Simpson, 2004: 132–64; Becker Lorca, 2014: 158–68). Besides other proposals, the conference deliberated on two court projects – an international prize court and a court of arbitration – which envisaged special privileges for the group of great powers. The smaller powers criticized but ultimately accepted the proposal for the prize court. However, they rejected the more important proposal for the court of arbitration. Moreover, due to the lack of the necessary ratifications, the convention on the prize court never entered into force.

The Second Hague Conference has been described as a 'turning point in the international system' (Simpson, 2004: 135). In contrast to the First Hague Conference eight years earlier, a significant number of non-European states participated in the conference, including China, Japan as well as the Middle and South American states that had gained their sovereignty in the decolonization wave in the Americas in the early nineteenth century. In 1899, Mexico had been the only participant from South America. The conference thus featured a significant number of formerly colonized states and these states were the main opponents of the efforts of the great powers to establish for the first time formal, globalized forms of collective hegemony.

Interestingly, the initial, informally discussed proposals for both courts included conceptions of the group of privileged states that were broader than the group of great powers. For the court of arbitration, for instance, the USA, Great Britain and Germany proposed permanent seats for countries with more than thirty million inhabitants. Brazil advanced an alternative proposal with permanent seats for fifteen states, including itself, China, Mexico and the Ottoman Empire. These proposals were met with criticism by (smaller) European states, which disapproved of permanent seats for China and the Ottoman Empire (Davis, 1975: 264–66). In reaction to these European criticisms, the great powers refined their proposals and now reserved permanent seats solely for the eight great powers.

In the following formal discussions, Brazil led the opposition against the great powers' proposals. In his promotion of sovereign equality, the Brazilian delegate Barbosa also stressed the post-colonial status of South America, pointing out that the South American states were 'not tributary States' such as those which still existed 'in other parts of the world' (quoted in Scott, 1921: 646). They were sovereign states like those of the

'Old World' and would not consent to the 'hierarchy' implied by the proposal for the court of arbitration because, Barbosa argued, this hierarchy was incompatible with the equality of states, which was integral to the principle of sovereignty. Brazil's critique was shared by many other small states, especially – though not only – from South and Middle America (cf. Scott, 1920: 326–28). As the conference operated on a principle of near unanimity, this opposition prevented the adoption of the great powers' proposal for a court of arbitration.

The two court proposals failed due to the contestation by the Middle and South American states. Because of their opposition, no formal vote was tabled for the court of arbitration. The prize court, which was deliberated before the court of arbitration, was accepted by the conference with thirty-seven affirmative votes, with Brazil casting the sole negative vote (Scott, 1920: 168). But six states abstained and ten states deposited reservations arguing that the prize court violated the principle of sovereign equality. All ten countries were non-European and eight of them from Middle and South America.[10] There was thus a clear cleavage between European and non-European participants of the conference, with the latter being much more critical of the attempts of the powerful states to establish new forms of collective hegemony. Their opposition was based on a strong conception of sovereignty and absolute sovereign equality which was intended to shield these states from the unequal treaties and interventions that the imperial powers still practiced at that time in Africa and Asia (Becker Lorca, 2014: 158). The project of a court of arbitration – though less so the prize court – was seen as an attempt to legalize new gradations of sovereignty. As Barbosa put it, the Latin-American states were not coming to the Second Hague Conference to 'solemnly sign an act derogatory to their sovereignty' (quoted in Scott, 1921: 620).

4.2 Contestation by the NAM during the Cold War

The contestation of collective hegemony reached a new level in the Cold War. The decolonization wave in Asia and Africa was paralleled by a group formation process, in which many of the newly sovereign states organized themselves as the NAM in the 1950s and 1960s. The Bandung Conference in 1955 brought together states from Asia and Africa that shared the same political agenda of anticolonialism, self-determination and non-intervention by the powerful states of the Global North (Ballantyne

[10] The six countries abstaining were the Dominican Republic, Japan, Russia, Siam, Turkey and Venezuela. Reservations were deposited by Chile, China, Columbia, Cuba, Ecuador, Guatemala, Haiti, Persia, El Salvador and Uruguay (Scott, 1920: 166–68).

& Burton, 2012: 391–92; Acharya, 2014). The Belgrade Declaration, issued by the first Conference of Non-Aligned Countries in September 1961, then stressed that the world was in the middle of a 'transition from an old order based on domination to a new order based on cooperation between nations, founded on freedom, equality and social justice for the promotion of prosperity' (Non-Aligned Countries, 1961).

The NAM accordingly opposed the bipolar logic of the Cold War and attacked the existing structure of inequalities and privileges in the international system, demanding in particular an end to colonialism, a more equitable economic order and the 'democratization of international relations' understood as the assertion of the 'right of all countries to participate in international relations on an equal footing' (Non-Aligned Countries, 1970: 197). For the NAM, collective hegemony was no longer acceptable as a governance mode of international society. As the NAM put it in 1983, 'international relations have entered a phase where decision-making on issues of vital concern to all countries of the world can no longer be the prerogative of a small group of countries, however powerful they may be' (Non-Aligned Countries, 1983: 11).

It was thus again a group of decolonized states – this time more numerous and, additionally, also jointly acting as a formal group – that assumed the role of the main critic of the collective hegemony of the group of great powers. In parallel, the admission of the newly independent states into the UN transformed the UN General Assembly into a forum in which decolonized, developing countries formed the majority. The Asian and African states used this emerging majority to pass UN General Assembly resolutions that delegitimized and denounced colonial and racial hierarchies (cf. Getachew 2019: 71–106). They also created a special forum for their economic agenda with the United Nations Conference on Trade and Development established in 1964 (Kennedy, 2006: 125–26).

Nevertheless, the NAM did not achieve the democratization of international relations. The existing structures of collective hegemony – in particular the UN Security Council – persisted. The formal privileges of the five permanent members of the UN Security Council were not dismantled. The NAM, though, had some success in reforming the composition of the UN Security Council. In 1963, the great powers reluctantly accepted the demands of the African and Asian UN members for four additional seats for non-permanent members (Bosco 2009: 98–103). In 1971, furthermore, the communist and NAM members used their majority in the General Assembly to replace Taiwan with China as UN member and consequently also as permanent member of the Security Council (Bosco, 2009: 121–24).

What is more, new forms of collective hegemony emerged in the late 1960s and the 1970s. In important respects, however, the design of these new forms reflected the growing contestation of the practice of collective hegemony. The Non-Proliferation Treaty, concluded in 1968, created new formal privileges for the group of (five) great powers by making them the only legitimate holders of nuclear weapons. These privileges were nevertheless – importantly – framed as temporary rather than permanent in the bargain between great powers and non-great-powers, with the great powers pledging to work towards nuclear disarmament (Bukovansky et al. 2012: 93–118). The NPT was negotiated in the Eighteen Nation Committee on Disarmament, which had – on pressure of the NAM – replaced the previous Ten Nation Committee on Disarmament composed solely of states from the Global North. Seven of the eight new members of the Committee were associated with the NAM (Plesch, 2016: 1211–12). Moreover, while the NPT treaty implied a special duty of the great powers (to work towards disarmament), it did not create a special council composed of the great powers to deal with disarmament matters. Two of the five great powers – China and France – did not join the treaty during the Cold War. In line with the position of the NAM, China refused to participate in special conferences of the five nuclear powers on nuclear disarmament. In 1971, for instance, China argued that '[a]ll countries in the world, big or small, should be equal' and that nuclear disarmament, as a matter affecting all states, should not form a 'monopoly' of a 'few big Powers' but rather be 'discussed and settled' by all states (UN General Assembly, 1971: 2).

Moreover, the Western powers side-stepped the NAM's efforts to regulate the global economy through inclusive, multilateral formats such as the United Nations Conference on Trade and Development. They formed the Group of Seven (G7) consisting of Canada, France, Great Britain, Italy, Japan, the United States and West Germany. The G7 established a regular conference cycle through which its members coordinated – and still coordinate – their economic and political activities (Hajnal, 2007: 11–35, 65–83). While the G7's informal character was also due to its members' preference for a non-formal format, it arguably as well reflected their awareness that it was politically not possible to formalize their informally practiced role as the de facto steering committee for global economic and financial governance. If the G7 members had demanded a formal recognition of this special role, the other members of international society would not have consented to it, especially given the NAM's preference for democratic forms of economic and financial governance. The (partial) shift from the G7 to the G20 as steering committee in 2008 made this form of collective hegemony more inclusive, thus decreasing the level of contestation by co-opting rising powers as well as key middle powers into the club (Cooper & Pouliot, 2015: 345–47).

4.3 The UN Security Council Reform and the Persistence of Formal Privileges

The present legitimacy of the UN Security Council is ambivalent. On the one hand, the UN members formally consented to this form of collective hegemony when they became part of the UN, which gives it formal and procedural legitimacy. On the other hand, many UN members regard it as politically necessary rather than normatively desirable. Collective hegemony, after all, violates the demands for democratic, equality-based modes of governance for which the NAM continues to argue both outside and within the UN (Strydom, 2007: 15–30). Since the early 1990s, the UN has debated a reform of the Security Council without so far reaching an agreement on how to reform it.[11] The formal nature of the UN creates an institutional path-dependency. While a majority of the UN members, including particularly the NAM states, would prefer to abolish the double special privilege of permanent membership and veto power, this outcome is unrealistic. The UN Charter can only be amended by a two-thirds majority of all UN members including the current five permanent members, which however refuse to give up their privileges.

Because of this path-dependency, the proponents of a democratization of the Security Council face the dilemma of how to reconcile their demands with the continued existence of special privileges. This dilemma divides the NAM coalition. Notably, the African Union (AU) and the Uniting for Consensus (UfC) coalition argue for diverging solutions. The AU stresses that 'most of Africa was not represented' when the UN Security Council was formed in 1945 (UN General Assembly, 2005a: 2). While it would actually prefer the abolition of the special privileges, the AU nevertheless insists on two permanent seats with veto power for African states as the only way of securing an equal regional representation given the non-negotiability of these privileges. The UfC, in contrast, opposes the creation of new permanent seats, and instead proposes a new category of re-electable seats. As Canada put it in 2005, the UfC sees the 'Council of 1945 (…) as an anomaly to be accommodated, not as a model to be emulated' (UN General Assembly, 2005b: 2). In the view of the UfC, the addition of new permanent seats would increase rather

[11] For overviews over the reform debate, cf. Pouliot and Thérien (2015: 224–28) and Pouliot (2016: 154–89).

than decrease the existing inequalities. Pakistan, another UfC member, added that, unlike in 1945, 'today we do have a choice, and we will not choose to appoint six States with special privileges and stamp ourselves as second-class Members of the Organisation' (UN General Assembly, 2005c: 8). While both coalitions lament the inequalities created in 1945, the two coalitions thus differ on whether new permanent seats would reduce (AU) or increase (UfC) these inequalities.

These statements also illustrate a key narrative underpinning the negotiations. The present debate on the reform of the Security Council takes place in a 'different world' (UN, 2004: 10) than the world in which the UN Security Council was established. When describing the many changes that have occurred since 1945 the report of the High Level Panel published in 2004 prominently stressed that the process of 'decolonisation (…) transformed the United Nations' (UN, 2004: 10). The statements of the UN members likewise invoke this narrative of a changed world. States striving for permanent membership often point to a changed distribution of power.[12] In contrast, as the above examples highlight, groups such as the AU and the UfC instead emphasize the non-representation of many of the present-day UN members when the UN was established in 1945.

5 Conclusion

This chapter explored the colonial underpinnings of international order by examining the interplay of two hierarchical dimensions: forms of collective hegemony by groups of powerful states on the one hand and their colonial empires on the other hand. It showed that the main impact of the evolution of the colonial hierarchies on the evolution of the collective hegemony consisted in the delegitimizing effects of the decolonization waves of the early nineteenth century and the second half of the twentieth century. The chapter highlighted three aspects of this delegitimization. Firstly, decolonized states were more vocal critics of the collective hegemony than states without a colonial past. Secondly, these states did usually not directly invoke the colonial past but rather stressed the sovereignty that they had gained in the process of becoming independent and that they refused to give up again. They consequently argued against collective hegemony and for a mode of governance based on sovereign

[12] The distribution of power is usually invoked indirectly by arguing that states that make greater contributions to the UN and the Security Council should have better – that is, permanent – representation. See notably the proposal of the G4 group lobbying for permanent seats for Brazil, Germany, India and Japan (UN General Assembly, 2005d).

equality. Thirdly, despite the growing level of contestation by the majority of states in international society, the practice of collective hegemony has nevertheless persisted.

The persistence of forms of collective hegemony despite their delegitimation exemplifies the first mode of historicity, that is, the structuring effects of history. These effects are visible – as just described – in the dynamics of the debate about the (lack of) legitimacy of collective hegemony. The continuing practice of collective hegemony moreover underscores that decolonization dismantled some hierarchies that had emerged in the colonial era but not others (for the persistence of economic inequalities see the chapter by Speich Chassé in this volume). The analysis pointed to three mechanisms that account for the persistence of collective hegemony: the sidestepping of the smaller states' consent by the recourse to informal forms of collective hegemony, the co-optation of rising and middle powers and the resilience offered by path-dependency effects of formal forms of collective hegemony. As a result of the last mechanism, the setup of the UN Security Council still resembles more the power structures of the colonial world of 1945 than the composition, power structures and norms of present-day international society.

References

Acharya, A. (2014). Who Are the Norm Makers? The Asian-African Conference in Bandung and the Evolution of Norms, *Global Governance*, 20(3), 405–17.

Anghie, A. (2005). *Imperialism, Sovereignty and the Making of International Law*, Cambridge: Cambridge University Press.

Badie, B. (2013). *La diplomatie de connivence: Les dérives oligarchiques du système international*, Paris: La Découverte.

Ballantyne, T. & Burton, A. (2012). Imperien und Globalität, in E. S. Rosenberg (ed.). *Weltmärkte und Weltkriege*, 287–432, München: C.H. Beck.

Becker Lorca, A. (2014). *Mestizo International Law: A Global Intellectual History 1842–1933*, Cambridge: Cambridge University Press.

Bosco, D. L. (2009). *Five to Rule Them All: The Security Council and the Making of the Modern World*, New York: Oxford University Press.

Bowden, B. (2009). *The Empire of Civilization: The Evolution of an Idea*, Chicago: University of Chicago Press.

Bukovansky, M., Clark, I., Eckersley, R., Price, R. M., Reus-Smit, C. & Wheeler, N. (2012). *Special Responsibilities: Global Problems and American Power*, Cambridge: Cambridge University Press.

Bull, H. (1980). The Great Irresponsibles? The United States, the Soviet Union, and World Order, *International Journal*, 35(3), 437–47.

Bull, H. (2002). *The Anarchical Society: A Study of Order in World Politics*, Basingstoke: Palgrave.

Bull, H. & Watson, A. (eds.). (1984). *The Expansion of International Society*, Cambridge: Polity.

Buzan, B. & Lawson, G. (2015). *The Global Transformation: History, Modernity and the Making of International Relations*, Cambridge: Cambridge University Press.

Clark, I. (2011). *Hegemony in International Society*, Oxford: Oxford University Press.

Cooper, A. F. & Pouliot, V. (2015). How Much Is Global Governance Changing? The G20 as International Practice, *Cooperation and Conflict*, 50(3), 334–50.

Davis, C. D. (1975). *The United States and the Second Hague Peace Conference: American Diplomacy and International Organization 1899–1914*, Durham: Duke University Press.

Dunne, T. & Reus-Smit, C. (eds.). (2017). *The Globalization of International Society*, Oxford: Oxford University Press.

Getachew, A. (2019). *Worldmaking after Empire: The Rise and Fall of Self-Determination*, Princeton, NJ: Princeton University Press.

Hajnal, P. I. (2007). *The G8 System and the G20: Evolution, Role and Documentation*, Farnham: Ashgate.

Hurd, I. (1999). Legitimacy and Authority in International Politics, *International Organization*, 53(2), 379–408.

Keene, E. (2014). The Standard of 'Civilization', the Expansion Thesis and the 19th-century International Social Space, *Millennium*, 42(3), 651–73.

Kennedy, P. M. (2006). *The Parliament of Man: The Past, Present, and Future of the United Nations*, New York: Vintage Books.

Mazower, M. (2009). *No Enchanted Palace: The End of Empire and the Ideological Origins of the United Nations*, Princeton: Princeton University Press.

Müller, T. (2017). Governance by the Few in International Society: A History of the Institution of Great Powers (PhD Dissertation), Bielefeld: Bielefeld University.

Non-Aligned Countries. (1961). *Belgrade Declaration of Non-Aligned Countries*. Retrieved from http://cns.miis.edu/nam/documents/Official_Document/1st_Summit_FD_Belgrade_Declaration_1961.pdf (last accessed 1 March 2019).

Non-Aligned Countries. (1970). *Lusaka Declaration on Peace, Independence, Development, Co-operation and Democratisation of International Relations*, Lusaka. Retrieved from http://cns.miis.edu/nam/documents/Official_Document/3rd_Summit_FD_Lusaka_Declaration_1970.pdf (last accessed 1 March 2019).

Non-Aligned Countries. (1983). *Final Document of the Seventh Conference of Head of State or Government of Non-Aligned Countries*, held at New Delhi from 7 to 12 March 1983: A/38/132, S/15675. Retrieved from https://documents-dds-ny.un.org/doc/UNDOC/GEN/N83/085/56/pdf/N8308556.pdf?OpenElement (last accessed 1 March 2019).

Nullmeier, F., Geis, A. & Daase, C. (2012). Der Aufstieg der Legitimitätspolitik: Rechtfertigung und Kritik politisch-ökonomischer Ordnungen, in A. Geis, F. Nullmeier & C. Daase (eds.). *Der Aufstieg der Legitimitätspolitik: Rechtfertigung und Kritik politisch-ökonomischer Ordnungen*, 11–38, Baden-Baden: Nomos.

Osterhammel, J. (2009a). *Kolonialismus. Geschichte, Formen, Folgen*, München: C.H. Beck.

Osterhammel, J. (2009b). *Die Verwandlung der Welt: Eine Geschichte des 19. Jahrhunderts*, München: C.H. Beck.

Pearson, J. L. (2017). Defending Empire at the United Nations: The Politics of International Colonial Oversight in the Era of Decolonisation, *The Journal of Imperial and Commonwealth History*, 45(3), 525–49.

Pedersen, S. (2015). *The Guardians: The League of Nations and the Crisis of Empire*, Oxford: Oxford University Press.

Plesch, D. (2016). The South and Disarmament at the UN, *Third World Quarterly*, 37(7), 1203–18.

Pouliot, V. (2016). *International Pecking Orders: The Politics and Practice of Multilateral Diplomacy*, Cambridge: Cambridge University Press.

Pouliot, V. & Thérien, J.-P. (2015). The Politics of Inclusion: Changing Patterns in the Governance of International Security, *Review of International Studies*, 41(2), 211–37.

Schlesinger, S. C. (2004). *Act of Creation: The Founding of the United Nations*, Cambridge: Westview Press.

Schulz, M. (2012). 'Defenders of the Right?' Diplomatic Practice and International Law in the 19th Century, in L. Nuzzo & M. Vec (eds.). *Constructing International Law: The Birth of a Discipline*, 251–75, Frankfurt: Vittorio Klostermann.

Scott, J. B. (ed.). (1920). *The Proceedings of the Hague Peace Conferences: Translation of the Official Texts, The Conference of 1907*, Vol. I: Plenary Meetings of the Conference, New York: Oxford University Press.

Scott, J. B. (ed.). (1921). *The Proceedings of the Hague Peace Conferences: Translation of the Official Texts, The Conference of 1907*, Vol. II: Meetings of the First Commission, New York: Oxford University Press.

Sédouy, J.-A. (2009). *Le concert européen: aux origines de l'Europe*, Paris: Fayard.

SFB 700. (2009). Grundbegriffe der Governanceforschung: Ein Beitrag aus dem Teilprojekt A1, SFB-Governance Working Paper Series. Berlin.

Simpson, G. (2004). *Great Powers and Outlaw States: Unequal Sovereigns in the International Legal Order*, Cambridge: Cambridge University Press.

Strydom, H. (2007). The Non-Aligned Movement and the Reform of International Relations, *Max Planck Yearbook of United Nations Law*, 11, 1–46.

UN. (2004). *A More Secure World: Our Shared Responsibility*, New York: United Nations.

UN General Assembly. (1971). *Letter Dated 24 November 1971 from the Permanent Representative of China to the United Nations Addressed to the Secretary-General (A/8536 and S/10397)*, New York: United Nations.

UN General Assembly. (2005a). *Reform of the Security Council: Draft Resolution (A/59/L.67)*, New York: United Nations.

UN General Assembly. (2005b). *Official Records: Fifty-Ninth Session, 112nd Plenary Meeting (A/59/PV.112)*, New York: United Nations.

UN General Assembly. (2005c). *Official Records: Fifty-Ninth Session, 111st Plenary Meeting (A/59/PV.111)*, New York: United Nations.

UN General Assembly. (2005d). *Security Council Reform (A/59/L.64)*, New York: United Nations.

United Nations Information Organization. (ed.). (1945). *Documents of the United Nations Conference on International Organization, San Francisco, 1945*, Vol. XI: Commission III Security Council, London and New York: United Nations.
Walters, F. P. (1969). *A History of the League of Nations*, New York: Oxford University Press.
Weber, M. (1972). *Wirtschaft und Gesellschaft: Grundriss der verstehenden Soziologie*, Tübingen: J.C.B. Mohr.
Zarakol, A. (ed.). (2017). *Hierarchies in World Politics*, Cambridge: Cambridge University Press.

4 The Historicity of State Formation
Welfare Services in Uganda and Cameroon

Joël Glasman and Klaus Schlichte[1]

1 Introduction

In opposition to many themes of international relations, statehood in Africa is often seen in a colonial continuum. The African state is an alleged colonial 'import' (Badie, 1995). In this contribution, we want to argue in a different direction. Instead of discussing the usual suspects like boundaries, official languages, or formal institutions again, we want to use ideas from critical sociology to highlight features of state rule in two African countries that usually elapse the attention of IR scholars. We aim at criticizing mainstream IR, which in an ahistorical manner only identifies deficits of 'governance' in 'areas of limited statehood' (Krasner & Risse, 2014), controlled by 'corrupt elites' (Zartman, 1995). Taking the historicity of state seriously, we argue, brings to the fore that what is usually considered to be recent crisis, has it long roots in the past of how states have been formed. Each state, we argue, has its own historical trajectory and complex temporalities. And while we want to avoid essentializing 'the African state', we argue that both states' trajectories show a number of similarities (which however requires understanding and interpreting contexts, as Schlichte/Stetter have highlighted in the introduction, mode 4). These similarities tell us something about international politics and about state formation.

We will present the results of a structured comparison between Uganda and Cameroon. Both polities have their roots in the processes of submissions and integration into international politics, first in colonial times and then as independent states in liberal world market. There are four features of similarities that we want to highlight here. Our main

[1] Research of Klaus Schlichte for this chapter has been funded by the German Research Foundation (DFG, Deutsche Forschungsgemeinschaft) within the project 'Figurations of Internationalized Rule', co-directed with Jude Kagoro, and within the Collaborative Research Centre 'Global Dynamics of Social Policy' (CRC 1432), also funded by DFG. Research of Joël Glasman has been funded by the Cluster of Excellence at the University of Bayreuth, funded by the German Research Foundation (DFG) as part of its strategy of excellence (EXC 2052/1 – 390713894).

argument, and the first feature we want to highlight, is that African states are highly internationalized structures of domination (Schlichte, 2017). Their genesis as well as their current functioning is marked by a long history of outward orientation, at times even dependency. This core argument is based on a closer look on the fate of welfare state elements in both countries. Social policies in Uganda and in Cameroon were, as in other countries, part and result of the formation of the state. This formation of political domination was both highly internationalized from the outset and it led to a specific constellation that has had a lasting impact until present times. Corporations, mission societies and later NGOs, bilateral 'donors' and International Organisations (IOs) have played major roles in the design and provision of social services to answer the social question since the early colonial time (cf. Veit et al., 2017).

The internationalized structure of domination of African post-colonial states has been historically shaped and reinforced by further features that we want to highlight. The second feature is what Mamdani (1996) has characterized as legal bifurcation of colonial regimes, distinguishing 'citizens' from 'subjects'. While both Uganda and Cameroon are constitutional republics, sharp divides run through both between a small formal economy, a formal legal sphere and an affluent political class on the one hand, and large informal economy, popular forms of social control and a culture of eroding communalism on the other hand. These bifurcations are bridged by political systems in which patronage practices prevail, in all the diverse forms that are usually labelled 'corruption'. With regard to the modes of historicity distinguished in the introduction of this volume, we see this bifurcation as a case of complex temporality in which a colonially induced structure has been translated and survived decolonization (see the chapter by Koloma Beck in this volume).

The third feature in which we see a strong, even if not unchanged, 'tradition' from colonial patterns is the 'discharge of the state' (Hibou, 1999). It designates all those forms by which African states delegate functions to private or semi-private agencies without giving up final control of them. In Uganda and Cameroon, this can concern even the management of public investment, the production of security in urban spaces, or the provision of services in health and education. Instead of a contractual relationship between a 'society', on the one hand, and a state, on the other, the analysis of welfare in contemporary Uganda reveals a highly unequal relationship, at times even a disconnectedness between large segments of the population and the official sphere of state rule.

The fourth feature, 'power without knowledge' is one that implies a critique of the Foucauldian idea about power-knowledge nexus. Breckenridge (2008) has developed this argument referring to the nineteenth century colonial South Africa, but we see current continuities at work in our cases as well. By delegating functions and by their particular form of rule, many African states work without an established and far-reaching bureaucratic knowledge of their population – a term which would actually presuppose such knowledge and the respective governmentality (cf. Foucault, 2004). The internationalized structure of domination does not reduce African actors to mere objects of international processes. In fact, we see in both cases confirmed what other authors (Clapham, 1996; Bayart & Ellis, 2000) have stated about the aptness and artfulness of African politicians, entrepreneurs and other actors to bend and direct external forces in ways that are beneficial to them. This 'gate-keeper' function (Cooper, 2002) is perhaps an observation that helps us to derive new ideas about the mutual constitution of states and the international system also with regard to statehood elsewhere.

Our argument thus breaks with the conventional narrative on modern statehood. We focus on the relationship between statehood and welfare provision because, in conventional social theory, the emergence of the 'welfare state' in the mid-nineteenth century was a key moment in the genesis of modern statehood. The main consequence of the development of a welfare state, the narrative goes, did not lie in the immediate improvement of health or education, but in the reinforcement of state apparatus as well as in the formation of national societies. Welfare policies provided economic regulation, central governance and a new kind of bureaucracy. Welfare provisions enabled the surveillance of the urban poor, the capture of peripheral peasantry and the accumulation of a state knowledge over population. According to conventional theories, the provision of welfare was key in the emergence of modern statehood, for, at least in the European experience, welfare justified state intervention and the deployment of bureaucratic technologies like birth certificates, population registers, demography statistics, vulnerability maps, programme planification, etc. (cf. Hennock, 2007; Kuhnle & Sander, 2010).

An important effect of the emergence of the welfare state in Western Europe was the 'nationalization' of politics and societies (cf. Noiriel, 1996). State welfare was expected to produce the healthy workers, the tall soldiers and the literate subjects that the modern state needed. Through welfare services, the state thus produced a national society that did not precede the state. This is why social theory from Norbert Elias to Michel Foucault up to Pierre Bourdieu and many others has regarded welfare services – education, health, pensions, etc. – as constitutive elements of modern statehood.

However, the four features that we identify as a colonial legacy challenge conventional theory of the state by highlighting specific modes of historicity at play: the 'bifurcation' of the state, the 'discharge' of social services to private or semi-private actors, the lack of 'will to know' and the internationalization of politics are not mere signs of the 'failures' or 'limits' of statehood. Instead, they are integral parts of post-colonial statehood. This does not mean, however, that those features are mere colonial legacies and did not evolve after having gained independence. Our comparison shows that despite historical differences, low-level generalizations are possible. We argue here that we cannot understand the contemporary state in Uganda and Cameroon without a careful look at their colonial legacy, but we also highlight the fact that this legacy has been constantly reworked by the post-colonial state – to such an extent that independence (1960 for Cameroon, 1962 for Uganda) should not be seen as a clear-cut for welfare policy.

These histories of welfare in colonial and post-colonial Uganda and Cameroon will be told in three chapters each. In early colonial times (1880s–1930/1940s), into a second period of government of the late colonial period and early independence (1940s–1980s), and finally the neoliberal internationalized government that emerged since the early 1990s. This threefold distinction will structure the presentation of the two cases respectively.

2 Colonial and Post-colonial Welfare in Uganda

2.1 Initial Observations

On 8 November 2018, the Ugandan newspaper *The Daily Monitor* published two reports in juxtaposition. The first one, 'Police arrest 300 in operation', recounted that several hundred young men in Kampala had been incarcerated for at least a day as an attempt to curb street criminality. On the same page, a report entitled 'NRM party city youth to receive Shs 3.2b', described the donation of the equivalent of 800,000 USD to the government party youth in the capital who had complained about neglect and dire outlooks to find regular employment. The money, coming directly from President Museveni's coffer, should be used for creating car-washing bays as income generators and 'would help in enriching the skills' of urban party youth.[2] This strange simultaneity of repressive and fostering practices of the Ugandan government are not simply traditions of colonial rule. Yet, they show how power works in a setting that still bears colonial imprints.

[2] Kato, J. 2018: 'Police arrest 300 in operations' and Wandera, D. 2018: 'NRM party city youth to receive Shs3.2b' in *The Daily Monitor* (Kampala), November 8, 2018: 3.

The simultaneity mirrors the second feature listed above. Since colonial times, only a small proportion of the Ugandan economy is formalized, with a small minority of fully registered members of public social security schemes. The pension fund of the 'National Social Security Service', the most extended social security scheme, covers about 9.3 per cent of the total population (Munyambonera et al., 2018: 2). The provision of health and education is likewise bifurcated into a commercialized sector for those who can afford to buy such services, on the one hand, and, on the other hand, a much larger porous public system offering unreliable access to education and health services. While these services are formally free of charge in public institutions, Ugandans are used to paying informally at all levels. The only exception from that post-colonial continuity was seemingly the first decade of independence, the 1960s.[3]

While for a long time, the deficiencies of the Ugandan state as a 'service provider' – to use the parlance of the governance paradigm – has been attributed to the years of turmoil during the rule of Idi Amin (1971–1979) and an ensuing period of civil war, it has become apparent that core traits of this form of domination are part and parcel of colonial imprint in Uganda. Despite all universalist rhetoric and true ambitions of Ugandan politicians, international 'partners' in development, the four traits of – internationalization, bifurcation, power without knowledge and discharge – have been maintained. Their genesis and post-colonial afterlife can be narrated in three short chapters – early colonialism, the era of development in later colonialism and early independence and the current neoliberal regime of internationalized rule.

The historicity of social policies in the state formation of Uganda does, however, not consist in the survival of unchanged forms and institutions. It would also be inadequate to consider this to be an evolutionary process. Rather, it resembles what historians have called an eventful history,[4] as major periods of crisis interrupted, stopped or derailed processes that in other cases looked like regular and purposeful.

2.2 *Early Colonialism*

Uganda was a protectorate of the British crown between 1900 and 1962. De facto a colony, it was ruled along the idea that it should contribute to the empire by producing exportable goods and consuming

[3] Cf. Ssali (2018); Interviews K.S. in Kampala and Fort Portal, November, December 2018.
[4] Cf. Sewell (2005) and the introduction to this volume.

British products. A first wave of subjectivation aimed at an enforced participation of the 'natives' in the colonial cash economy. In order to acquire the money for the imposed hut tax, the adult males had either to enter the emerging wage-labour sector or to produce for the colonial market. This was on the basis of all colonial schemes that dissolved communal forms of economies and turned them into appendixes of first the imperial, then the world markets. Up until now, Uganda's exports consist mainly of agricultural products and labour (cf. Mkandawire, 2010).

Cotton, coffee and tea were the early main products that centralized marketing boards bought below world market prices so that the colonial administration could be funded from this margin. The creation and fostering of a sufficiently trained and healthy workforce became main requirements that spurred early efforts of health and education in the protectorate Uganda (cf. Vaughan, 1991). The urban bias, that characterizes both forms of 'social policy' till today, has their roots in these early colonial times.

The early colonial period was also the foundational period for the 'discharge' (Hibou, 1999) of conventional state functions to private institutions: throughout the colonial period, mission schools and hospitals offered by far more capacities, even if of low quality, than the colonial state itself. The health sector had a first extension with the recruitment of the imperial forces for World War I. In the early 1920s, the first hospitals were erected in Kampala and Entebbe.

Furthermore, already in these early colonial times, a bifurcation of welfare provision could be observed. While British 'expatriates' benefited early on from medical services close to the level of the metropole, the colonized had at first only access to the sparse installations of missions, scattered on the territory, and also not void of interest:

> Medical missionaries look for patients. It is true that missionary organisations need doctors to preserve the lives of missionaries. But they have also recognised in Western medicine an instrument for extending their influence among the people. To deliver their message they must find some method of attracting listeners. Where, as under direct rule, the people want education in order to get jobs, missionaries have provided schools. Where, as under indirect rule, education has less market value, they have provided hospitals. (Furnivall, 1948: 357–58)

2.3 *Late Colonialism and Early Independence*

As in the case of French colonialism in Africa, the last three decades of colonial rule (roughly 1930–1960) were a period of rapid expansion of state control and economic integration. In the case of Britain, the

'Colonial Development Act' of 1929 and the 'Colonial Development and Welfare Act' of 1940 marked a stronger interventionism and general planning that increasingly included welfare elements, but again clearly with a 'population' in Foucault's sense as target. But despite this stronger investment, service provision remained patchy and basic. Few hospitals but many dispensaries were built, and the introduction of secondary and tertiary education was not due to humanist ideals but curtailed to the necessary levels for the production of a colonial sub-elite needed to administer a growing economy.

There are at least three formations taking place here that became continuous features of Ugandan statehood after independence, up until present times. First among these was the birth of a representation that distinguishes between a society as an object and a government as a ruling agency, controlling and directing this population.[5] Second was the creation of a government staff, purposefully trained for that end. And the third element was a technology of government that became a general mode later: surveys and reports constitute the basis for the design of programmes and projects aiming at social and economic transformation under changing headings (see the chapter by Speich Chassé in this volume). This prepared the ground for the radicalized liberal government since the 1990s. The high-flying plans, however, rarely translated into social reality.

The field of education is emblematic in this regard. During colonial rule, several general reports were organized to assess the general situation. At the centre of the debate was always the question of how much education was at all desirable and affordable for a society that should consist of agriculturalists (cf. Ocheng, 2004: 90). In addition, since the 1950s at the latest, a planning logic with a ten-year rhythm was developed that should instigate a delegation of responsibility to local administration and single state agencies. The results, however, remained behind the governmental expectations, despite welcomed 'progress' in the subjectivication of Ugandans, as an exemplary quote from an annual report of a district commissioner shows:

> Unfortunately it cannot be said that the Batoro themselves are ready to take advantage of the great opportunities presented to them, and 1956 must go on record as a year of frustration and doubt when the sound and orderly progress of the District was marred by political difficulties. (Toro District Annual Report, 1956: 1)

[5] There had been, of course, pre-colonial forms of rule on the area that is now Ugandan territory. They had, however, not the governmentality of presiding a 'population' that needed to be transformed.

The period between 1930 and 1970 is thus the time in which an understanding of government emerged that later turned out to be directly compatible with neoliberal ideas. The plans stipulated development goals that should be reached through programmes and projects. Numeric benchmarks were in place already in the 1950s and 1960s. They concerned the standard number of administrative personnel per district, the achievements in infrastructure building, financial balancing of public accounts, school rates or medical service provision, while throughout the 1940s–1960s, the main worry was the size of cash-crop harvests and respective price levels.[6]

Yet despite considerable extension, welfare facilities remained chronically underfunded. The investment could not keep path with a rapidly growing population and the demand for formal education that was meanwhile generally seen as a precondition for acquiring the benefits of modernity.

District reports, like the one of Bunyoro District Annual Report for 1957 (1957: 19), reported the limiting number of teachers as the colonial administration could not even employ one teacher for each of the 334 classes. And while levels in primary schools would slowly increase, the late expansion of secondary schools had led to a shortage of buildings and teachers' houses so that again qualified teachers were lacking throughout the country.

When independence was gained in 1962, a considerable health care infrastructure had been established, consisting of urban hospitals, a number of rural health centres, nursing schools and two schools to train medical assistants, plus a network of health inspectors for the promotion of home hygiene (Okuonzi & Macrae, 1995: 125). This expansion continued during the first decade of Uganda's independence during which twenty-two new district hospitals were built. But this service provision remained concentrated in urban centres, among which Kampala stood out as only location with sophisticated health facilities.

Furthermore, secondary and tertiary education was expanded too, as the ideal of 'Africanization' especially of top echelons in the independent state ranked high on the political agenda. Yet in 1969, for example, Western expats were still the leading personnel in the Ministry of Finance. More than 242 foreign experts were in the country, together with an additional 197 volunteers. More than half of the experts stemmed from the USA, Canada and the UK, while only eight had Chinese and three Soviet passports (Mittelman, 1975: 158). The imperial

[6] Annual Reports of Madi and Tooro districts to the Governor of Uganda from the 1950s, Archive of the Mountains of the Moon University, Fort Portal, Uganda.

internationalization of Uganda's rule slowly changed into an international one (see the chapter by Lawson in this volume).

Colonialism left Uganda 'without a middle class to speak of' (Reid, 2017: 281). A thin merchant and entrepreneurial stratum of 'Asian' Ugandans was facing ethnic resentment, while a small technological and culturally elite socialized in colonial institutions overtook the independent state, following the routines and patterns of rule that they have acquired under 'the colonial masters'.[7] This stratum continued to rule Uganda, interrupted only by the period of turmoil under Idi Amin (1971–1979) and the years of civil war (1981–1986), during which most public institutions stopped working, in some areas for years. In Uganda's northern districts, massive political violence continued until 2005 with respective consequences for the provision of health and education.

2.4 *Neoliberal International Rule*

While the Ugandan government of the 1960s had displayed consistent scepticism towards foreign aid (Mittelman, 1975: 180), the new government in the late 1980s did not have any choice but to submit itself to the recipes of the International Financial Institutions (IFI). Yet, the independent government of the 1960s had continued to work with Five-Year Plans, and it had its – mostly international – commissions for the evaluation of 'development'. The colonial tradition of Five-Year Plans for 'development' had thus an afterlife in the 1990s when the World Bank introduced 'Poverty Reduction Plans' and the IMF started its 'Structural Adjustment Programs' (SAP). Aiming at reducing the role of the state, this led to a severe crisis of public service provision. Privatization was mandatory, and in Uganda like in other instances, it meant in fact the appropriation of the privatized agencies by the political class. The National Resistant Movement/Army (NRM/A) – still the current government – had started out in 1986 with an 'African socialism' rhetoric. Yet slowly, it adapted the IFI discourse as many of its members saw the new cumulative effects that the combination of political power and economic opportunity offered. Former predominantly publicly organized sectors like education and health became primary targets of private wealth accumulation by political entrepreneurs (cf. Médard, 1992), including ministers and secretaries of state (cf. Schlichte, 2008). The framing of 'national development' allows the settlement of this decisive power group with their international 'partners' (Rubongoya,

[7] This expression is still in use in contemporary Uganda, albeit with an ironic twist.

2018), not unlike the colonial arrangement of 'private indirect government' (Mbembe, 1991).

The aid industry that developed in this politically locked situation could easily connect with the colonial traditions of programmes, projects and reports. Ministries function as official partners, if it is not local NGOs, often led by politicians too, which act as contractors of projects. This political arrangement is, however, hidden behind a public and international debate about 'democratization' as if questions of political accountability of Uganda were still merely a national affair.

This internationalization of rule (cf. Schlichte, 2008; Morcillo-Laiz & Schlichte, 2016) does meanwhile include Chinese and since long also Indian companies and single entrepreneurs. It materializes in an international life-world of malls and hotels, SUVs, private colleges and private clinics. The opportunities of this internationalized class are worlds apart from the precarious, still porous and even for sub-Saharan African low standards of education and health facilities in the countryside and for the urban poor. The bifurcation between the legal status of the metropolitan citizen and the colonial subject that Mamdani and Fanon have scandalized for colonial times, has thus its current equivalent in the distinguished worlds of expat experts, entrepreneurs and high state officials that are connected to the poor majority by volatile connections of patronage, personal favour and charity.

3 The Welfare State in Colonial and Post-colonial Cameroon: Between Hybris and Renunciation

3.1 Initial Observations

In Cameroun, school is compulsory: children are expected to spend at least six years at school learning how to read, write and count; they learn the name of the countries' cities, its mountains, its rivers, its administrative regions and its national anthem (Cameroun: *Loi d'orientation de l'éducation* 1998, art. 17). Every year, however, some school children experience another aspect of Cameroonian statehood: they are not allowed to take the final exam because they lack any legal proof of their existence. Having no identity card or birth certificate, they eventually leave the school system without a diploma. In 2019, in the Far North Region alone, 38,163 pupils were in this situation of not being allowed to take the exam because they lacked a birth certificate (*L'oeil du Sahel*, 18 January 2019). Ironically, those children had a valuable knowledge about the state, but the state, in turn, did not even manage to learn and register their names.

Cameroon does not fit into the conventional narrative of state formation. In Foucault's theory of the state for instance, clinics, hospitals or schools function as 'tiny social observatories', in which the state can observe not only the pupils or the patients themselves, but also their parents, their families, their neighbours and eventually put the whole society under a regime of 'compulsory visibility' (Foucault, 1975: 213). There are, in Cameroon, some historical examples of biopolitical endeavours. However, these endeavours were mainly circumscribed in the realm of public declarations and symbol politics. State realizations in welfare provisions remained massively incoherent, poorly financed and often limited in their effects. There was a huge gap between grand promises of social engineering on the one side, and deceiving experiences on the other side. The tension between hybris and failure was not a side effect of colonial statehood: colonialism embraced failure, renunciation and powerlessness (Lachenal, 2010; Mbembe, 2013).

The state in Cameroon bears witness to this heritage. The Cameroonian constitution made grand promises about the social character of the state (*Constitution de la République du Cameroun*, 1996, Preamble). After his re-election as President of the Republic, Paul Biya reiterated this now usual commitment for better social protection, education of all, the construction of new hospitals and the provision of affordable housing (Speech by President Paul Biya, 6 November 2018). What about our unregistered pupils not allowed taking their final exam? Did the Cameroonian government promise to equip local police stations with the material to issue birth certificate?[8] Instead, Cameroon contracted a Dutch company with the production of a brand-new identity card and the general overhaul of its identification system. This foreign company promised to introduce a new identity card made out of polycarbonate with the 'biometric ten fingerprints' of its holder, as well as a microprocessor for electronic authentification (Gemalto, 2018). It was not merely about a modest goal of constructing a decent and functioning welfare system. It was about nurturing the utopia of biopolitical control with the help of a foreign enterprise. It was about invention of a new 'Cameroonian citizenship of the future' (Gemalto, 2018).

School children from the Far North Region, experience here the result of a long historical heritage. The internationalized structure of domination (Schlichte, 2017), the quasi-absence of basic state and administrative service in some corners of the country in a 'bifurcated' state

[8] Giving birth at home being one of the reasons for the absence of official registration. In the Far North, less than one out of five births is assisted by a health care professional and therefore likely to be registered (Linjuom Mbowou, 2013).

(Mamdani, 1996), the systematic incompletion of databanks allowed by the exercise of 'power without knowledge' (Breckenridge, 2008) and the 'discharge' of state responsibilities to private actors (Hibou, 1999; Mbembe, 1999).

3.2 *The Illusive 'Civilizing Mission' of the Early Colonial State (ca. 1884–1940)*

Cameroon was first a German protectorate (1884–1919), before becoming a mandate territory divided between British and French administration (1920–1944). The Kaiser's emissary obtained a protection treaty from local chiefs in 1884 and established a rudimentary administration and an armed force. Clearly, welfare services were not part of the plan.

Cameroon became a textbook case of 'extraversion' (Bayart, 2000). What mattered to colonial extraction was the control of the entry points to the territory (ports, urban centres, major axes) as well as productive enclaves (plantations and mines). Beyond these enclaves, the colonial territory was made up of large areas that were considered useless for the colonial economy – and therefore remained largely undocumented.

The few social services provided by the colonial administration were reserved for specific groups – German officers and administrators, white settlers, African employees of the state, soldiers, etc. The colonial administration focused on maintaining colonial order and securing European capital (Herbst, 2000). The 'civilizing mission' was left to the initiatives of missionaries, private companies and to welfare entrepreneurs who profiled themselves as benevolent colonialists.

Cameroon was relatively rich, resourceful and densely populated – it thus was an attractive field for missionary enterprises. The coastal region had witnessed several waves of Portuguese, Dutch, English, American and Jamaican missionaries since the sixteenth century. Since the end of the nineteenth century, missionary societies from different nations provided basic welfare services for the glory of their Nation and their God: the Baptist Missionary Society of London, the Swiss-German Basler Mission, the Baptist Mission of Berlin, the American Presbyterians, the French Catholics, the Société des Missions Evangéliques de Paris, etc. (Joseph, 1980). The logics of 'discharge' and 'extraversion' worked hand in hand: services in education or health provided by missionaries became arguments in the claims of competing European colonialism.

Welfare projects emerged through mix of personal initiatives, charitable financing and administrative support. Individual doctors, teachers or missionaries played the patriotic card and applied for support from the administration for their pet welfare projects. In the British territory, for instance, schooling remained the realm of the mission, through a system of 'Approved Voluntary Agency'. Another example was the hospital of French doctor Eugène Jamot, a centre to fight against sleeping sickness (trypanosomiasis); this received finances from the French colonial ministry as well as from private or semi-private actors (including the chemical and pharmaceutical firm Rhône-Poulenc). The field of colonial welfare provisions was structured by the competition between different churches, different private companies and different nations. The four features of state domination – internationalization, bifurcation, power without knowledge and discharge – were already entrenched before World War II.

3.3 *The Construction of a Cameroonian Welfare State (1940s–1986)*

Two factors lead to an increasing intervention of the state in welfare matters during and shortly after World War II. First, Africans massively protested against colonial domination. A series of social movements, workers' strikes and demonstrations took place in strategic cities like Dakar, Mombasa and Duala, forcing colonial powers to rethink colonial domination (Cooper, 1996). Second, international organizations now required information and minimum social provision standards for the colonized population (Article 73 of the UN Charter, June 1945; International Labour Organization Social Security (Minimum Standards) Convention, 1952).

This triggered a new ideology of 'development', 'welfare' and 'modernization'. The reformation of colonialism was meant to save empires. The British government pushed the 'Colonial Development and Welfare Acts' of 1940 and 1945, while the French government implemented a *Fonds d'investissement pour le développement économique*. In official discourses at least, the idea that 'traditional solidarities' ('family ties', 'tribal community', 'villages', etc.) would take care of the African workers' problems, was now complemented by a discourse on colonial welfare.

However, African syndicalists and politicians appropriated the notion of 'development' to criticize colonial rules and push for reform or even independence (Cooper, 1996; see also the chapter by Speich Chassé in this volume). It was a formative moment for the formation of an African discourse on welfare. After independence, the notion of 'development' remained a cornerstone of moral politics: the language of development and welfare enabled political and administrative elites to act as 'brokers' between international donors and local institution, that is, to articulate the language of modernization and the idioms of kinship, ethnicity and patronage.

In practice, however, social services largely followed a logic of 'enclaves' (Ferguson, 2005). In some territorially circumscribed areas, state servants, private companies and charitable organizations claimed for grand ambitions for social improvement. Military barracks, labour camps, sleeping sickness stations and leproseries were examples of biopolitical heterotopias. An example of such enclaves were the plantations of the 'Cameroons Development Corporation' a private enterprise that ran hospitals, dispensaries, schools, community institutions, water supply systems, roads, for its employees and their family. Another example was the 'medical government' of Haut-Nyong. The authority of the whole region was given exclusively to medical doctors by the French governor (Lachenal, 2010). Despite the investment and the (often brutal) medical administration, this episode was a fiasco for public health (diseases such as sleeping sickness and pneumonia actually spread) but it contributed nonetheless to the myth of the benevolent colonial state.

Cameroonian nationalists, especially the Union des Population du Cameroun (UPC) described colonialism not as a welfare state, but as a pathology (Mbembé, 1985). While French colonial elites marvelled about the 'good deeds' (*les bienfaits*) of French administration (*Marchés Coloniaux du Monde*, 1952), Ruben Um Nyobè accused France of not respecting its duty under international law to work for the political, economical, social and educational advancement of the population. France retaliated with one of the most brutal counter-insurgency wars in its history (1955–1971), with the systematic internment of the population, systematic tortures and concentration camps (Mbembe, 1996; Deltombe et al., 2011). Thus, the former colonial power ensured that formal independence (1960) and the unification of the two Cameroon (1961) could not mark a clear break with colonial legacy.

Under President Ahmadou Ahidjo (1961–1982), Cameroon became a single-party state led by the Cameroon National Union, and a stereotypical case of 'underdeveloped', 'neopatrimonial' and 'authoritarian' state (Eboko & Awondo, 2018). Cameroon benefited from sustained economic growth – at an annual rate of 5.4 per cent a year between 1960 and 1986 (Carbone, 2012). In spite of widespread corruption and low welfare expenditures, most macro-social indicators improved. Schooling rates were among the bests in Africa South of the Sahara – and they improved (from around 45 per cent in 1959 to 65 per cent in 1971 and 75 per cent in 1985) (Njiale, 2006: 55). Life expectancy at birth was of 41.7 years at independence, and already 54.2 years in 1985 (Carbone, 2012: 157–83). Some spoke of a 'Cameroonian miracle' (Aerts et al., 2000: 7).

3.4 *The Demise of the Embryonic Welfare State (1986–today)*

After the mid-1980s, the worsening terms of trade for major exports (cocoa, coffee, cotton) and the rapid decline in oil output led to one of the quickest impoverishment in Central Africa (Aerts et al., 2000: 8–10). Cameroon's economy contracted by 3.8 per cent a year between 1986 and 1994 (Carbone, 2012). This took place in a period of rapid demographic growth: there were 7.4 million inhabitants in 1975, there are ca. 24 million today. When President Ahidjo surprisingly resigned in 1982, his successor, Paul Biya (1982–today) invented a new, caricatural version of the neo-patrimonial state that Mbembe calls a 'government by negligence' (Mbembé 2017). As the saying in Cameroon goes: 'Corruption was corrupted.' The reproduction of a predatory political elite became the sole political ideology.

Eventually, SAPs came in as an antidote to debt and economic crisis. But the cure almost killed the patient. Cameroon signed for the first SAP with the IMF in 1988, swearing to implement massive cuts in state expenses. In spite of rapid demographic growth, the state employed less teachers, less physicians and less nurses in 1990 than it did fifteen years before (Kamdoum, 1994). State employee's salary were cut by 70 per cent, many taking jobs on the side or required tips and bribes for services that were supposed to be free (Dujardin et al., 2003). Schooling remained theoretically free of charge, but parents frequently now had to pay for their children to attend or for exams to be corrected. Access to basic health care was also theoretically free, but the real costs for accessing consultations and treatment rose.

The consequences of the SAPs on the population's health and education has been highly debated (Cornia et al., 1987; Pongou et al., 2006; Thomson et al., 2017). In Cameroon, governmental spending in welfare provisions dropped. Educational spending for every child aged six to fifteen years was divided by two between 1986 and 2000 (Njiale, 2006: 56). Health expenditure was reduced both in absolute terms and in share of national budget. Overall per capita health expenditure almost halved (Carbone, 2012). There was one teacher for 49 pupils on average in 1971, but only one teacher for 82 or 120 pupils in 2004 (Njiale, 2006: 62). Eventually, primary schooling rates dropped. The health system followed. The number of physicians per 1000 habitants had risen from 0.03 in 1960 to 0.8 in 1989, then dropped to 0.7 in 2008. In the 1990s, Cameroon was one of the few countries in which, in spite of an absence of war, life expectancy at birth was constantly dropping: one could expect to live 54.6 years in 1990, but only 50.5 in 2007 (Carbone, 2012).

Surprisingly, the claim for better welfare services rose at the moment when it was being attacked by the SAPs. Cameroon signed a series of international agreements promising profound ameliorations of the welfare states, from the Alma-Ata Declaration on Primary Health Care/ Health for All (1978) to the Jomtien World Declaration on Education for All (1990). However, state's investment in the welfare sector remained low. In 2019, the spending for welfare (18.6 per cent of state budget for health and education put together) was lower than the costs for the reimbursement of the debt (22 per cent of state budget) (République du Cameroun, Loi de Finances, 2019). The real spending probably looked even weaker, because 'only about two thirds of official allocations actually reached local facilities' (Carbone, 2012) because of corruption.

Thus, the delegation of social responsibilities and the dependence towards external donors are historical features of the Cameroonian state. The state's lack of interest for some categories of populations in certain regions, including school pupils in the Far North, is not an accident, but a legacy and part of a political strategy. For Francis Nyamnjoh, using Mahmood Mamdani's terminology, Ahmadou Ahidjo and Paul Biya borrowed and perfected the colonial legacy of 'decentralized despotism' (Nyamnjoh, 1999): Cameroon is a reliable and supporting state for some categories of citizens close to the government (as well as for international companies), and a contemptuous and distant despot for others. Thus, the politics of internationalized domination has a purpose: If a project is successful, the state can claim it and gain legitimacy. If a project fails, it justifies for a nihilistic ethos of 'non-interventionist intervention' led, once again, by external actors (Lachenal, 2015).

4 Conclusion

In this contribution, we have argued that the – albeit limited – competences of states are, like in 'developed' ones, neither new nor just of 'foreign origin'. Instead, they are the result of decades of transcontinental encounters and they show the historicity of both states. They also continue to operate in a highly internationalized manner, inserted into regional relations of power but also mirroring global claims and attempts of control and to care, but also of negligence and loopholes.

With our focus on the genesis and changes of social policies and their historicity, we find a further avenue promising to follow. What looks so strange and so different, is at the same reminiscent of processes and forms elsewhere. Accepting the historicity of political developments in Uganda and Cameroon actually allows us to see much clearer that similar processes, perhaps less visible and less pronounced might be at work elsewhere. Writing off entire segments of the society, establishing mere surveillance over 'ungoverned spaces' while celebrating 'charity' is not a foreign pattern to other parts of the world.

The criminalization of politics (Bayart et al., 1999) is not without echoes to what has happened in the former socialist parts of the world or in the West. There is, for example, a clear analogy between the historical bifurcation of the social question from the criminal question taking place at the end of the 19th century (Wacquant, 2010: 157) and 'poverty reduction' and policing in Uganda and Cameroon since the mid-1990s. The unequal distribution of the gains of privatization, the capture of state apparatuses by an entrepreneurial political class is by no means an African exception.

If we look at the genesis of the bifurcations, at the history of this internationalized production of a political situation, other aspects become visible. The interplay of mutual projections like the genealogy of racism in imperial times (cf. Arendt, 1951), the accepted paternalism of humanitarian aid (Barnett, 2011) are part of this and already established results of historical perspective on state formation and its international embeddedness.

References

Aerts, J.-J., Cogneau, D., Herrera, J., de Monchy, G. & Roubaud, F. (2000). *L'économie camerounaise: un espoir évanoui*, Paris: Karthala.

Badie, B. (1995). *La Fin des territoires*, Paris: Fayard.

Barnett, M. (2011). *Empire of Humanity. A History of Humanitarianism*, Ithaca: Cornell University Press.

Bayart, J.-F. & Ellis, S. (2000). Africa in the World: A History of Extraversion, *African Affairs*, 99(395), 217–67.

Bayart, J.-F., Ellis, S. & Hibou, B. (1999). *The Criminalization of the State in Africa*, Oxford: James Currey.

Breckenridge, K. (2008). Power without Knowledge: Three Nineteenth Century Colonialisms in South Africa, *Journal of Natal and Zulu History*, 26(1), 3–30.

Carbone, G. (2012). Do New Democracies Deliver Social Welfare? Political Regimes and Health Policy in Ghana and Cameroon, *Democratisation*, 19(2), 157–83.

Clapham, C. (1996). *Africa and the International System: The Politics of State Survival*, Cambridge: Cambridge University Press.

Cooper, F. (1996). *Decolonisation and African Society: The Labor Question in French and British Africa*, Cambridge: Cambridge University Press.

Cooper, F. (2002). *Africa Since 1940. The Past of the Present*, Cambridge: Cambridge University Press.

Cornia, G., Jolly, R., & Stewart, F. (eds.). (1987). *Adjustment with a Human Face: Protecting the Vulnerable and Promoting Growth*, New York: Oxford University Press.

Deltombe, T., Domergue, M. & Tatsitsa, J. (2011). *Kamerun!: une guerre cachée aux origines de la Françafrique (1948–1971)*, Paris: Editions La Découverte.

Dujardin, B., Dujardin, M. & Hermans, I. (2003). Ajustement structurel, ajustement culturel?, *Santé Publique*, 15(4), 503–13.

Eboko, F. & Awondo, P. (2018). L'État stationnaire, entre chaos et renaissance, *Politique africaine*, 2, 5–27.

Ferguson, J. (2005). Seeing Like an Oil Company: Space, Security, and Global Capital in Neoliberal Africa, *American Anthropologist*, 107(3), 377–82.

Foucault, M. (2004). La Naissance de la biopolitique. Cours au Collège de France (1978–1979), Gallimard/EHESS/Seuil.

Foucault, M. (1975). *Surveiller et Punir: Naissance de la prison*, Paris: Gallimard.

Furnivall, J. S. (1948). *Colonial Policy and Practice. A Comparative Study of Burma and Netherlands India*, Cambridge: Cambridge University Press.

Gemalto. (2018, January 28). Cameroon's new national identity card. Retrieved October 16, 2020, from www.thalesgroup.com/en/markets/digital-identity-and-security/government/customer-cases/new-national-identity-card-for-cameroon

Hennock, E. P. (2007). *The Origin of the Welfare State in England and Germany, 1850–1914: Social Policies Compared*, Cambridge: Cambridge University Press.

Herbst, J. (2000). *States and Power in Africa: Comparative Lessons in Authority and Control*, Princeton: Princeton University Press.

Hibou, B. (1999). La 'décharge', nouvel interventionnisme, *Politique Africaine*, 73, 6–15.

Joseph, R. A. (1980). Church, State, and Society in Colonial Cameroun, *International Journal of African Historical Studies*, 13(3), 5–32.

Kamdoum, A. (1994). Planification sanitaire et ajustement structurel au Cameroun (No. 29), Paris: CEPED.

Krasner, S. D. & Risse, T. (2014). External Actors, State-Building, and Service Provision in Areas of Limited Statehood: Introduction, *Governance*, 27(4), 545–67.

Kuhnle, S. & Sander, A. (2010). The Emergence of the Western Welfare State, in F. G. Castles, S. Leibfried, J. Lewis, H. Obinger & C. Pierson (eds.). *The Oxford Handbook of the Welfare State*, 73–92, Oxford: Oxford University Press.

Lachenal, G. (2010). Le médecin qui voulut être roi, *Annales. Histoire, Sciences Sociales*, 65(1), 121–56.

Lachenal, G. (2015). Lessons in Medical Nihilism: Virus Hunters, Neoliberalism, and the AIDS Crisis in Cameroon, in W. Geissler (ed.). *Para-States and Medical Science: Making African Global Health*, 103–41, Durham: Duke University Press.

Linjuom Mbowou, C. R. (2013). *Etre Sans Papier Chez Soi: Identification, Visibilité et Invisibilité dans les Marges Camerounaises du Bassin de Lac Tchad* (Memoire de Master Recherche de Science Politique), Paris: Université Paris 1 Pantheon Sorbonne.

Mamdani, M. (1996). *Citizen and Subject: Contemporary Africa and the Legacy of Late Colonialism*, Princeton: Princeton University Press.

Mbembe, A. (1991). Désordres, résistances et productivité, *Politique Africaine*, 42, 2–8.
Mbembe, A. (1996). *La naissance du maquis dans le Sud Cameroun, 1920–1960*, Paris: Karthala.
Mbembe, A. (1999). Du gouvernement privé indirect, *Politique Africaine*, 1, 103–21.
Mbembe, A. (2013). Sortir de la grande nuit: Essai sur l'Afrique décolonisée. La Découverte.
Mbembe, A. (2017). Au Cameroun, le crépuscule d'une dictature à huis clos, *Le Monde*, 9(10), 2017.
Médard, J.-F. (1992). Le 'Big Man' en Afrique: Esquisse d'analyse du politicien entrepreneuer, *L'Année Sociologique*, 42, 167–92.
Mittelman, J. N. (1975). *Ideology and Politics in Uganda: From Obote to Amin*, Ithaca: Cornell University Press.
Mkandawire, T. (2010). On Tax Efforts and Colonial Heritage in Africa, *Journal of Development Studies*, 46(10), 1647–69.
Morcillo Laiz, Á. & Schlichte, K. (2016). Rationality and International Domination: Revisiting Max Weber, *International Political Sociology*, 10(2), 168–84.
Munyambonera, E., Katunze, M., Munu, M. L. & Sserunjogi, B. (2018). *Expanding the Pension Sector in Uganda*, Research Series No. 143, Kampala: Makerere Economic Policy Research Centre.
Njiale, P. M. (2006). Crise de la société, crise de l'école. Le cas du Cameroun, *Revue internationale d'éducation de Sèvres*, 41, 53–63.
Noiriel, G. (1996). *The French Melting Pot: Immigration, Citizenship, and National Identity*, Minneapolis: University of Minnesota Press.
Nyamnjoh, F. B. (1999). Cameroon: A Country United by Ethnic Ambition and Difference, *African Affairs*, 98(390), 101–18.
Ocheng, M. T. K. (2004). Basic Education through Primary Education Cycle in Uganda. 1925 to 1999: Rationale and Analysis of Policy Changes (PhD dissertation), Kampala: Makerere University.
Okuonzi, S. A. & Macrae, J. (1995). Whose Policy Is It Anyway? International and National Influences on Health Policy Development in Uganda, *Health Policy and Planning*, 10(2), 122–32.
Pongou, R., Ezzati, M. & Salomon, J. A. (2006). Household and Community Socioeconomic and Environmental Determinants of Child Nutritional Status in Cameroon, *BMC Public Health*, 6(1).
Reid, R. J. (2017). *A History of Modern Uganda*, Cambridge: Cambridge University Press.
Rubongoya, J. B. (2018). 'Movement Legacy' and Neoliberalism as Political Settlement in Uganda's Political Economy. In J. Wiegratz, G. Martiniello & E. Greco (eds.). *Uganda: The Dynamics of Neoliberal Transformation*, London: Zed Books.
Schlichte, K. (2008). Uganda, Or: The Internationalisation of Rule, *Civil Wars*, 10(4), 369–83.
Schlichte, K. (2017). The International State. Comparing Statehood in Central Asia and Sub-Saharan Africa, in J. Heathershaw & E. Schatz (eds.). *Paradox of*

Power: The Logics of State Weakness in Eurasia, 105–19, Pittsburgh: University of Pittsburgh Press.

Thomson, M., Kentikelenis, A. & Stubbs, T. (2017). Structural Adjustment Programmes Adversely Affect Vulnerable Populations: A Systematic-Narrative Review of Their Effect on Child and Maternal Health, *Public Health Reviews* 38(1), 13.

Toro District Annual Report 1956, District Commissioner's Office, Fort Portal, Toro District, 20 March, 1957, Mountains of the Moon University Archive, Fort Portal, Box 414.

Vaughan, M. (1991). *Curing Their Ills: Colonial Power and African Illness*, Stanford: Stanford University Press.

Veit, A., Schlichte, K. & Karadag, R. (2017). The Social Question and State Formation in British Africa: Egypt, South Africa and Uganda in Comparison, *European Journal of Sociology*, 58(2), 237–64.

Wacquant, L. (2010). La fabrique de l'Etat neoliberal. 'Workfare', 'prison fare' et insécurité sociale, *Civilisations*, 59(1), 151–72.

Zartman, I. W. (1995). Introduction: Posing the Problem of State Collapse, in I. W. Zartman (ed.). *Collapsed States: The Disintegration and Restoration of Legitimate Authority*, 1–11, Boulder: L. Rienner Publishers.

5 Privateering, Colonialism and Empires
On the Forgotten Origins of International Order

Benjamin de Carvalho and Halvard Leira

1 Introduction

Studying IR historically has a number of implications, ranging from methods and methodologies to ontological questions and theoretical perspectives. Historical IR, then, broadly speaking, invites a rethinking of the fundamental assumptions so long taken for granted in IR. For as we have argued elsewhere, stories about the past are constitutive of how we see both the discipline and ourselves (Leira & de Carvalho, 2018). This is especially true in a discipline, which hitherto has remained largely ahistorical. Yet, approaches in IR – for example, constructivism and post-colonialism – which to some extent have emphasized the importance of the past to our current predicament have nevertheless tended towards an overly Manichean world-view which 'oversimplifies and politicizes the distinction between Orientalizers and Orientalized' (see the chapter by Schlichte and Stetter, in this volume). This, in turn, contributes to levelling differences between different colonial and post-colonial settings and overlooking differences between different *situations coloniales*.

Taking historicity and the associated notions of *longue durée* and eventful history seriously should logically imply questioning such *facile* dichotomies. While post-colonial scholarship has provided path-breaking and important analyses of how imperial and colonial apparatuses continue to structure our modern world, these imperial and colonial apparatuses themselves need to be the analytically unpacked and scrutinized. One way of doing that, as Schlichte and Stetter suggest, is to shift the analytical gaze from units like the modern state (or even empire) to processes, practices, and institutions and associated modes of historicity. This has the potential to uncover complex temporalities as well as heterogeneity in both causes and outcomes. Focusing on processes over the course of a *longue durée*, we believe, offers yet another type of engagement with the historicity of empires and states, as it promises to uncover different aspects of their engagements than if one were to focus on their apparatuses of government and their development alone. Not least does our engagement with privateering allow for a more legally nuanced historicity – one that showcases how the delimitation between legal (state) and illicit (non-state) activities is drawn up and eventually dichotomized. In fact, these dichotomies, which we today take for granted, are largely the product of specific historical contingencies rather than a unilinear drive towards the modern state. As Heyman and Smart have argued, zones of ambiguity or even illegality are deeply intertwined with state law:

> they do not stand apart from the state, nor the state from them. Having grown in necessary connection, state law and evasion of state law must be studied together. Often, governments tolerate ostensibly forbidden activities; even, [...] 'deviated pieces of the state' ally with, or 'condition' illegal networks. Certainly the state does not always conspire with crime, but it is intriguing to inquire after the conditions under which governments and illegal practices enjoy some variety of symbiosis and those which result in greater or lesser degrees of conflict. (Heyman & Smart, 1999, 1)

Our argument here, then, largely revolves around a largely forgotten history of state and empire formation, which seeks to go beyond rectifying the historical record in order to bear on current debates about 'failed states' and illicit practices of (Heyman, 1999).

In this chapter, we seek to go even further, shifting the focus away from units, anchoring our analysis instead in international institutions. We do so by focusing on the institution of privateering, and how it developed in and around processes of trade, imperial expansion, and state-formation over a period of more than 600 years.[1] For the purpose of this chapter, privateering can be broadly defined as maritime predation authorized by someone with recognized legitimate (sovereign) authority. Focusing on privateering allows us to highlight both the persistence of past institutions and the extent to which the present breaks with the past.

Historicizing international relations through the lens of privateering, immediately gives lie to both standard periodization and dichotomous post-colonial understandings of the world. From a *longue durée* or 'eventful history' perspective, privateering indicates that rather than periodizing through breaks between mediaeval, renaissance, early modern, and modern periods, one central 'event' was the growth of maritime trade from the twelfth century and onwards, enabling various forms of marine predation, and another such 'event' was the emergence of naval

[1] Our understanding of institutions here springs from the English School, cf. Colas (2016) on privateering as a 'derivative master institution'.

hegemony in the nineteenth century.[2] Privateering also belies neat static categorizations of 'public' and 'private', and the notion of a tidy development of state control over legitimate violence, as it continuously involved a plethora of different actors and was characterized by cooperation rather than gradual replacement. Likewise, privateering fits awkwardly within a standard post-colonial narrative. It emerged as petty squabbling between individuals of city-states, developed as a survival-strategy and a politico-religious tool for fledgling states in north-western Europe and quickly morphed into an empire-building strategy and a more regular institution of naval warfare. In this form, it was also adapted by hybrid actors in what would now be defined as the Global South, most prominently the so-called 'Barbary' regencies of North Africa, but also the American colonies fighting for independence from England and Spain. When it was formally 'outlawed' in 1856 by the Treaty of Paris, this was as a result of intra-European power dynamics, and not of relations between Europe and the wider world.

Privateering played an important role in the making and breaking of empires, and thus in the establishment of many of the macro-structures of the present (linking it thus to power, as suggested by mode 5). However, we will argue that privateering is perhaps most obviously present through its absence, and that the central mode of historicity, which connects the privateering past with our present is that of forgetting. In global politics, the Treaty of Paris of 1856 helped normalizing the idea of a modern state with a monopoly on legitimate violence and the oceans as a global common under the control of benign hegemons. Ambiguities between private and public violence at sea were forgotten, and the pirate remembered as the evil Other to the ordered ocean. Also forgotten was the extensive 'peripheral' agency, obvious in how privateering was used time and again to oppose the leading powers of the day. In academia, forgetting privateering has been essential to establishing and maintaining a state-centric and land-based understanding of the world and political developments in it. In the following pages, we hope to challenge this forgetting.

Thus, in terms of engaging with historicity, we do so along three of the modes outlined by Schlichte and Stetter in the introduction. While we do engage with their first two modes to some extent, by showing how a specific form of history, which largely omits privateering from its core contributes to structure our understanding of European overseas expansion (first mode) and how a phenomenon over time is given new meanings, tweaked and changed while retaining elements from different

[2] Thus, privateering matches well with other recent foci of naval history, such as marine insurance (Leonard, 2016).

temporalities (second mode), and obviously with the sixth mode through our emphasis on contingency and transformations along non-linear pathways, this chapter is perhaps more important in terms of dealing with historicity in that it probes the possibility of a seventh (or a subset of the first) mode, namely that of 'forgotten pasts'. This mode dovetails nicely with the chapters by George Lawson and Thomas Müller, which both deal with hidden histories, and how specific (key) aspects of past experience disappear from the core of how phenomena are historicized. This discussion is also relevant for the chapter by George Steinmetz. The question that becomes all the more pressing, then, is the role played by these forgotten or hidden histories. While giving a definitive answer is beyond the scope of the present chapter, we could nevertheless hypothesize that the extent to which certain aspects are successfully hidden or forgotten from our narratives about the past may be the condition of possibility of linear or progressive histories. Could it be, then, that only through forgetting can we project a specific progressive future, grounded in a 'progressive' past?

We will proceed as follows. First, we will provide a brief overview of the practice of privateering, its origins and changes. Second, we will show how privateering provided the impetus to colonize the American Atlantic coast and became a driver of imperial competition in the Americas, before it was used by colonies against their respective centres in their fight for independence. Finally, we will discuss how a focus on privateering forces us to question not only the state-centric ontology of IR, but also key post-colonial assumptions, through a discussion of the practice of privateering in the broader Mediterranean – the Barabary Corsairs. By way of conclusion, we draw attention to the historicity or *Geschichtlichkeit* of our focus on the *longue durée*, questioning not only periodizations and their aims, but also, through privateering, drawing attention to the extent to which the past still informs how we handle current problems and how the forgetting of privateering is central to how states and oceans are conceived of today.

2 Privateering: The Historical Trajectory of an International Institution

Despite being a common violent practice for around 600 years (from the thirteenth century to 1856), what we here refer to as 'privateering' is a woefully little understood phenomenon.[3] While 'piracy' has been

[3] The term is a partial anachronism, apparently emerging first in the middle of the seventeenth century (Rodger, 2014: 12), we use it hesitatingly for our entire investigation,

studied and celebrated in academe as well as in popular culture, privateering, which was a much more significant phenomenon, has been left largely alone, and even presumed to be simply a variety of the former, namely 'legalized piracy'. While the term 'privateer' and 'private-man-of-war' are terms, which emerge only in the late 1600s (Pennell, 2001: 70), the activity and legal foundation of the activity dates back to the thirteenth century and the custom of reprisal. Maritime predation was by no means a case of well-defined and clear-cut legal boundaries. In fact, as Cheyette (1970: 54) has argued, 'prisias, reprisilias, marchas – prizes, reprisals, and marques. To the men of the later Middle Ages, these terms all referred to the same thing'. As Rodger (2014: 6) points out, violence at sea was prevalent and largely ungoverned, and while there may have been pockets of authority governing some parts of the sea, there was yet no conception of right or wrong at sea, and 'robbery under arms was a normal aspect of seaborne trade'.

Rodger (2014: 6) doubles down on this point when he underlines that 'in the Middle Ages and the early-modern period, there were few non-combatants at sea'. The problem was thus how to govern maritime violence, how to allow for a limited form of reprisal in times of peace without disrupting the truces or peaces between princes. The solution became the application of the rules or reprisals, devised to deal with terrestrial violence, to violence at sea. The rules and laws governing seaborne violence became a way to regulate a certain amount of violence at sea also in times of peace, without disrupting truces negotiated on land.

As Neff (2005: 123) explains, the essence of reprisals was 'the seizing of property belonging to the fellow nationals of an original wrongdoer'. Reprisals were thus a way for a wronged party to 'obtain compensation for injuries or hostile acts, done by aliens who could not be brought to justice'. The authorization to undertake reprisals was granted through a letter of marque or reprisals.

Cheyette made the case that the distinction between privateering and piracy – between right or wrong at sea, so to speak, developed with the consolidation of monarchical power. In fact, he claims that they played a great part in helping about this consolidation. For monarchs increasingly saw their situation on land disrupted by violence at sea. Yet, as shown above, there was a need to allow for some degree of violence at sea as it allowed for the administration of a modicum of justice in a space in which monarchs were not yet attempting to monopolize force, in the way they were on land. The key became the monopolization of justice at

particularly since it could be argued that this specific term was coined to cover a new practice at the time.

sea. For where different lords and jurisdictions had claimed the right to address injustices and redresses in the past, during the fourteenth century monarchs sought to make it their sole prerogative to administer letters of reprisal and marque and adjudicate in matters of prizes (Cheyette, 1970). The fourteenth century thus saw the increasing codification of rules for violence at sea, rules which were to become central in the making of international law, and which where to govern maritime predation until 1856.

At any rate, the rules and practices of privateering remained relatively stable until the end of the sixteenth century, as the activity of French and English seafarers was still on the whole contained to the seas surrounding Europe. Thus, both the activity of privateering and the rules governing it survived the discovery of the New World, and even the first voyages beyond European waters by Iberian powers. What came to dramatically change this was thus not the fact that the European horizon had opened up, but the fact that powers who had been denied taking part in the spoils of colonial expansion by the Treaties of Tordesillas came to demand their share of it. In so doing, they were met with strong resistance from both Spanish and Portuguese ships. As French, English and Dutch seafarers ventured beyond European waters, the practices of privateering would change dramatically, even though the medieval rules governing it remained relatively unchanged.

3 New Worlds, New Religions and a Changing Medieval Institution

One of the reasons why privateering – after having been a relatively stable practice in European waters – came to change in character was that the practice no longer worked in favour of consolidating princes or 'states'. Until the 1550s, as Cheyette (1970) has emphasized, the increasing rule-making and regulation of 'privateering' worked in favour of monarchs. It not only gave monarchs authority over the seas, but it also worked to increase their projection of sovereignty on land. Now, this had changed. France, England and the Dutch – the three European powers with arguably the most experience in 'privateering' – had been excluded from the New World by the Treaty of Tordesillas. In order to make it into distant waters, relatively weak financially after prolonged religious conflicts, these states turned to privateering.

Privateering allowed them many advantages over building up their own navies. Firstly, it was relatively inexpensive, as the main burden lay in private hands. Secondly, it allowed these endeavours to venture into forbidden seas – how else were they to capture Iberian prizes? Thirdly, it allowed these states plausible deniability, as the state was not directly involved. Finally, and perhaps most importantly, in spite of all this, it was controlled by the state – albeit at a distance.

This was an age that was characterized by emerging seaborne empires, a globalizing balance of power and still 'intermediate relationships between war and peace, and between public and private initiative' (Grewe, 2000: 312; de Carvalho, 2015). We would go further and argue that privateering demonstrates how our contemporary understanding of public and private is itself a product of processes, which were not concluded until the nineteenth century. In their colonial endeavours, most states did not have the resources to project their military and political ambitions at sea. They therefore routinely relied on merchant shipping for advancing these: 'Private merchant ships were recruited to participate temporarily in naval operations, just as warships were sometimes temporarily assigned to serve the privateers' (Grewe, 2000). This reliance on private enterprise continued long into the nineteenth century – in spite of state navies having grown considerably stronger.

Privateering became the principal means of challenging the Catholic construction of the sea as a different kind of space, where control was granted by the Pope. Where the treaties of Tordesillas established Iberian empire through religious papal authority, a more secular conception of empire based on the emerging law of nations (*ex iure gentium*) provided challengers such as the French, Dutch and English with legal backing for their ambitions to trade freely where legal claims grounded in papal authority were not backed by effective occupation. Privateering was the weapon of choice of the challengers and came to reinforce both their ambitions for overseas influence, their penetration of the colonial trade, and their own colonial ambitions.

Huguenot privateering was temporally the first, but it lasted for a shorter time, and was different by virtue of being part of a civil war as well as the broader struggle (de Carvalho & Paras, 2015). However, the Huguenots were crucial both in providing harbour for Dutch and English privateers, and, perhaps even more importantly, teaching them the trade about sailing and plundering on the high seas and in the Americas.

4 Privateering in the Americas: Imperialism, Colonialism and Independence

Whereas the early English privateers soon looked to the Atlantic and the Caribbean, the early Dutch privateers were engaged in the immediate struggle for survival in and around the Dutch provinces, and later in the European theatre of war. The lack of overseas engagement was due to the domination of the Dutch in European maritime trade. Apart from an interlude in 1585–88, when Spain was preparing the Armada, Dutch intra-European trade on the Iberian continued largely unabated between 1568 and 1598. The main turn towards offensive privateering came when Phillip III issued a trade ban against Dutch commerce in 1598, leading the States-General to systematically start issuing privateering commissions ('t Hart, 2014: 136). Early privateering thus came under different guises, and different actors seem to have sought out different ways to ply this medieval institution.

English privateering, having emerged as an ad hoc tool to help co-religionaries in their continental challenges to Catholic Spain, had by 1600 become the main tool of maritime engagement of England. In the process, England had also turned from a polity focused mainly on securing the domestic strengthening of its reformation to a power that challenged Catholic supremacy wherever its ships would carry it (de Carvalho, 2014; 2016). This had happened without any serious ideological engagement. Granted, a number of writers and pamphleteers had engaged themselves in favour of a more sustained and ideological challenge to Spain. However, there had been little response from a queen and her council aware of the limitations of their military power. The importance of the practice of privateering cannot be overstated in the case of England. While promoters of overseas ventures lacked the means to launch large colonial ventures in the 1580s, two decades of privateering war against Catholic shipping had provided these means at the turn of the century. While English seamen lacked experience of the Atlantic in 1580s, that knowledge, including local knowledge of the West Indies, was common two decades later. While the English merchant fleet was modest before the war, it had experienced a boom over two decades (cf. Davis, 1962).

While the English saw to the Americas, the Dutch went east, with the most important colonial privateering ground being in Asia (cf. Borschberg, 2003; Phillips & Sharman, 2015). This was where most booty could be found, and where Dutch organization was strongest, with the East India Company (VOC) being funded in 1602. In its heyday, the VOC was the worlds' biggest company, but, as noted by Emmer (2003: 7), 'the commercial success of the VOC has obliterated the fact that, between its foundation in 1602 and the truce with Spain in 1609, the Company was much more an instrument of war than one of commerce'. The gains made from privateering then came to be essential for setting up the economic and military infrastructure, which allowed for further expansion in the ensuing periods (Borschberg, 2013: 52).

Privateering, which had only a century before been a largely atomistic practice, with little relevance for overall warfare and characterized by a number of related more or less institutionalized practices, was by the early seventeenth century not only a much more coherent institution with developing rules and regulations, it had proved to be a vital weapon in wars of survival and global reconfiguration. In the ensuing period, the institution would become further established, and spread to even more states, but it would not have the same transformative effects.

One obvious consequence of the intensification of privateering was that it became associated primarily with war. 'Private' use of force at sea would increasingly be seen as piracy. And, indeed, ends of wars would typically lead to privateers turning pirates. The first major example of this took place when the English made peace with Spain in 1604 and the Dutch and Spanish started negotiations about a truce in 1607. A number of former privateers (such as Peter Easton) then set up shop in Ireland and/or on Newfoundland and continued taking ships (Hanna, 2015: 64–67). Others took what must have seemed an even more radical route, taking their talents to 'Barbary', and setting in motion the Atlantic raiding of the Barbary corsairs (see below).

Even though some turned pirate or corsair, there was also plenty of room for regular privateering during much of the seventeenth century, with the Netherlands, France and England engaged in wars with others or with one another time and again through the century. Generalized privateering provided relatively cheap naval power, which could be mobilized and demobilized with much more ease than more regular naval forces. It should also be remembered that regular permanent 'battlefleets' were not established until the second half of the seventeenth century (Harding, 1999; Glete, 2000). And even when more regular navies were established, privateers continued to play an important role alongside them – during the first Anglo-Dutch war (1665–67), Dutch privateers captured roughly three times as many enemy ships as Dutch warships did, and during the second such war (1672–74) the capture rate was more than nine times higher (Harding, 1999: 104).

With such stunning success rates, it was possible to conclude that privateering was the most cost-efficient way of conducting naval warfare. This was at least what the French decided around 1700. During the reign as naval secretaries of Colbert (1669–83) and his son, the Marquis de Seignelay (1683–90), France tried, and partly succeeded, to establish the foundations of a navy to rival the English. However, there was no clear strategy for its use, and from 1695 onwards, Louis XIV decided to de-emphasize the navy. The opponents of the regular navy were not only the ones who would favour the army, but also those who favoured a *guerre de course* (a privateer war) rather than regular naval operations. Thus, during the remainder of the Nine Years' War as well as the war of the Spanish Succession (1701–13/14), France relied to a large extent on privateers for their naval presence. The sheer number of prizes taken (more than 5300 during the first of these wars, and more than 7200 during the second) suggests that the effort was successful, and during the 1690s there was indeed a heavy strain put on English trade (Harding, 1999: 157–58, 176–77). After 1700, however, the English were able to bear the loss. Even though their numbers were significantly lower, English prizes taken also offset some of the losses. These wars mark the apogee of French privateering, which then subsided during the wars of the mid-eighteenth century, only to reappear at a reduced level during the revolutionary wars.

Even if privateering was the strategy of choice, the French state was heavily involved. At the outbreak of war in 1688, the secretary of the navy, Seignelay, for example, commissioned four frigates for privateering, and persuaded the king and several members of the court and the naval administration to partake in the endeavour (Pilgrim, 1975: 258; Bromley, 1987: 187). Furthermore, as Bromley (1987: 187–212, 215–20) has discussed in detail, the French navy regularly lent ships, sometimes with crews, to privateers, at least in the Nine Years' War and the War of the Spanish Succession. Detailed regulations were also put in place, most famously the seminal *Ordonnance de la marine* of August 1681, better known as the *Ordonnance Colbert*, which among a host of other issues specifies both regulations for privateering and consular affairs, and continuously updated. Official regulations were coupled with prize courts, which in the colonies were often the first regular institutions, and consular networks. The French were pioneers in developing both regulations and networks, but the Dutch and English soon followed suit (Leira & de Carvalho, 2010).

During the eighteenth century, privateering took on a somewhat more subordinate role in the naval wars, even though they remained an important supplement to the regular navies. However, the growth of the British navy, and the increased emphasis on the navy as a standing force, implied both a reduced scope for British privateers, and increased risks for the privateers of other states. Whereas privateering had been highly profitable for many French outfitters and captains in the wars around 1700 and on aggregate an activity where the rewards outweighed the risks, in the wars of the second half of the eighteenth century, it is not clear that French privateering created an overall surplus. During the Revolutionary and Napoleonic Wars, however, French privateering again seems to have been a surplus activity. On the British side, privateering remained highly profitable in the wars of the middle eighteenth century, but decreasingly so thereafter.

On the other hand, when part of the British Empire revolted in 1775–76, privateering proved to be a key tool for the American colonists. A regular navy was way beyond the scope of the rebels, but privateering proved to be both efficient and effective. The same pattern was repeated in 1812, when US privateering also benefited from the already present French privateers, which had been a regular feature of the Napoleonic wars. Privateers were also engaged in the Latin American wars of independence, and again during the American Civil War. The use of privateering during the anti-colonial struggles warrants specific mention. Throughout the Americas, rebel authorities were issuing privateering-commissions to harm the trade of the imperial centre and bring in much-needed goods. The outfitters, captains and crews were sometimes locals, but particularly during the Latin-American revolts, foreigners were taking active part. Much like for the protestant polities of the sixteenth century, privateering was a weapon of the weak, and a remarkably effective one, at that (Starkey & McCarthy, 2014: 135).

However, the many parallel developments of state power, international law, steam propulsion, specialized warships and so forth made privateering less attractive both for states and for investors and captains. There was little protest when the treaty of Paris in 1856 simply declared that privateering was to be considered outlawed. The many practices, which had sustained the institution from the thirteenth century and provided it with the flexibility to change and adapt with the times, were no longer relevant.

5 The 'Barbary' Corsairs: Challenging Post-colonial Narratives

The final instalments of privateering in the Americas illustrate how peripheral aspiring states could turn the institution against the central powers of the international system. A more long-term example of the same, which further muddles the post-colonial dichotomy between centre and periphery, can be found in North Africa.

The history of Muslim/Christian hostility in the Mediterranean goes back to the ninth century, and for centuries 'the Saracens' were feared across southern Europe (Heers, 2003: 46), even establishing control over the alpine passes for half a century (Wenner, 1980). Around 1500, the term 'Barbary' was taken up in Italy, gradually coming to signify North Africa (Heers, 2003: 21). In the years around 1500, the Spanish and Ottoman polities were also both expanding their power in the Mediterranean, leading to the establishment of different groups of 'corsairs',[4] Maltese corsairs fighting for Christendom and Barbary corsairs fighting for Islam. Unlike most other maritime predators in history, for both parties the booty desired was primary humans to be sold or used as slaves. Apart from the occasional raid, piracy in North Africa had largely been littoral and a part-time income for a handful of men. With the Ottoman arrival, privateering/piracy became a polity-sanctioned major business (Heers, 2003: 31). In the sixteenth century, these men, under the Babarossas and their successors, doubled as (part of) the official Ottoman navy, and their leaders were Ottoman governors and admirals (Heers, 2003: 63). Gradually, through the seventeenth century, the cities (Algiers, Tripoli and Tunis chief among them, Sallee in Morocco was never under Ottoman control), became more and more independent, from the middle of the seventeenth century, Algiers was, for example, under Ottoman rule de jure, but the de facto power rested locally, with the leaders of the Janissaries and the corsair captains.

The corsairs have often been seen to occupy an ambiguous position in naval warfare, being something between pirates and a regular navy. Such an analysis, though, suffers from blatant orientalism. On the one hand, the corsairs were clearly the naval arm of the North-African regencies, often partaking in regular naval activities with the rest of the Ottoman fleet. On the other hand, within the political structures of the regencies, the captains had their own power-base, and acted more or less as they wished. This is a situation, which bears a strong resemblance to how the English organized their naval presence in the latter half of the sixteenth century, and it would seem as if it has been their exoticness rather than their practice which has branded them as pirates. This is not to say that the Barbary (or for that matter, Maltese) corsairs were just as other privateers. The legal system was quite different, with no element of reprisal, and no goal of weakening an opponent through crippling their trade. The main interest was capture of slaves, to be sold or ransomed.

Until the early seventeenth century, the corsairs relied largely on galleys, but with an influx of European privateers and pirates, some who turned renegado, others who remained Christian, larger sailing ships were incorporated into the corsair fleets. The corsairs then promptly cast their nets wider, raiding for slaves as far away as in Ireland and on Iceland in the 1620s and 1630s. As the navies of the large European

[4] In English, the term 'corsair' is more or less synonymous with 'pirate'; but in French, it signifies a privateer.

powers grew in strength, these states were able to make treaties with the Barbary regencies, ensuring the relative security of their own trade and population. The weaker states, unable to enforce treaties if need be, had to pay regular tribute to ensure the same freedoms, and, as the regencies depended on a steady influx of slaves and booty, it would be their policy to break treaties or declare tribute insufficient at irregular intervals, so as to always be at war with at least some European state, and thus rightfully be able to attack their shipping (Earle, 2003: 82–85). Interspersed with occasional smaller wars and bombardments, the situation remained stable until France invaded Algeria in 1830, gradually colonizing the countryside, and leading the other regencies to renounce their corsairing activities.

And how did the European states react against the corsairs? The sixteenth century witnessed repeated Spanish attempts at invasion and conquest, with little lasting result. During the next centuries, we see very little of the attempts at domination, discipline and eradication which became so commonplace elsewhere. Almost from the outset, diplomatic interaction was seen as a possibility, with the Franco-Ottoman alliance established in the 1530s as the first, shocking, example. This alliance led to joint naval expeditions, and a Barbary fleet wintering in Toulouse in 1544–45 (Heers, 2003: 83–87). The good relations between France and the Ottoman empire, including the regencies, lasted for several centuries, and French ships generally could trade unmolested with the North African cities from the second half of the sixteenth century (Heers, 2003: 115). The French were not alone; the English were entering into diplomatic negotiations with Sallee as early as in the 1620s (Ekin, 2006: 53), and from roughly the same time, the European states started appointing consuls to the Barbary ports. Being formally vassals of the Ottoman empire, the regencies could not receive diplomats in the name, but these consuls were generally considered to be more like diplomats than consuls, the French even being titled as *chargé d'affaires* in addition to the consular title (Windler, 2001a: 80). Once in a while, both the larger and the smaller European polities saw the need to redress the balance with the regencies, by bombarding the cities or even landing troops. By and large, however, the larger powers relied on treaties and diplomacy, and the smaller on the yearly bribes.

Even though some consuls suffered repeated indignities, the interaction between consuls and local authorities gradually became regularized. The interactions followed a pattern of repeated accommodation, with new and creative judicial spaces being created, allowing both parties to see the results as in line with their legal system (Pennell, 1994; Windler, 2001a; 2001b). Creative interaction and fluid judicial practices were possible until the end of the eighteenth century, since 'the diversity of the legal situations that characterized relations between Europeans and Maghrebis, but also between Europeans residing in Tunis corresponded to the plurality of status and jurisdictions in Europe' (Windler, 2001a: 93). Furthermore, since the development of 'international' law during the eighteenth century happened through the gradual expansion of positive law, through treaties, rather than through application of 'the universalist principles of a natural law of nations', a distinct set of norms for interaction could emerge in the Mediterranean (Windler, 2001b: 274). Towards the end of the eighteenth century, with the gradual rise of nations, the turn to Enlightenment rationalism and rapidly increasing European power, plurality was no longer accepted in the same way.

Increasing European power, combined with the political shifts that took place and the changes in the episteme that brought the modern political vocabulary to the fore and established the possibility of a general history marked by steady progress, spelled doom for 'backwards' and 'uncivilized' areas across the globe. A sign of things to come can be found in North American discourse. As Sutton (2009) demonstrates, as late as in the 1760s, newspaper descriptions were neutral, discussing corsairs and implying both equality and the possibility of friendship. From the mid-1780s, the protagonists were increasingly called pirates: 'The shift in terminology reflected a transformation in the American's view of the Barbary pirates, from men that had to be treated honourably to men that could be violently terminated' (Sutton, 2009: 61). Increasingly, the Barbary pirates were also compared with the Native Americans, as threatening progress and prosperity: 'in the American mind, the corsairs no longer belonged to states that could be diplomatically reasoned with, but to a menace to be exterminated through warfare in the name of American freedoms' (Sutton, 2009: 61). Thus, the eradication of privateering based in North Africa following the French conquest of Algiers in 1830, can easily be read as part of the establishment of a dichotomous world of Self and Other, of civilization vs. barbarism.[5]

Overall however, the privateering originating in North Africa provides a three-century counterpoint to any tidy dichotomous telling of the story of Western ascendancy.[6] The Ottoman Empire might, particularly around the outset of corsairing, have been considered Europe's 'demonic Other', but this Other was still a recognizable polity, which did

[5] Cf. Keene's (2007) analysis of anti-slavery treaties in the same period.

[6] Here we agree with Colas (2016), although we put somewhat less emphasis on economics and more on law and politics.

not represent a rejection of social order and discipline. Furthermore, as the centuries passed, the Otherness of the Ottoman Empire receded as regularized interaction replaced continuous war. The interaction with the regencies also demonstrates well the capacity for multiple forms of interaction in the classical age. Even though they were formally vassals of the Ottoman Empire, and polities of a radically different sort than many European ones, they could be treated as more or less equal in a 'tabulated order of states'. Likewise, even if the treaties and diplomatic interactions with the regencies were different than the ones found between European states, they were still regularized and institutionalized. As Colas (2016: 855–56) argues, privateering in the Mediterranean helped create a local international society, and the practices associated with the 'barbarians' were crucial in defining what later became known as the 'standard of civilization'. Barbary privateering should for centuries be seen as a partial producer of international society. However, when the epistemic shift around 1800 lead to a re-conceptualization of an international society consisting of formally equal sovereign states bound by natural international law and engaged in linear progress and development, the Barbary regencies were in trouble.

6 Conclusion

The social institution we have referred to as privateering obviously changed dramatically during the six centuries covered in this chapter, particularly in content. Nevertheless, there was an obvious continuity in many of the forms of the institution. Although the legitimate right to approve privateers could be contested, at an overall level privateering remained a legitimate international institution. And in many ways, it became interwoven in an ever-tighter web of legal regulations, starting with letters of marque and reprisal, but expanding to practises of ransom and parole, regularized prize courts, detailed privateering regulations, expanding consular networks to handle prizes taken to foreign ports and regularized prisoner exchange.

Furthermore, change tended to be incremental, based on gradual development of new practices, which sometimes changed the existing practise (such as with letters of marque and reprisal), sometimes added a new layer to the overall institution. We do find one major period of change in privateering practice, in the decades around 1600. Two changes in particular, which were to have lasting effect on privateering, stand out. The first was the change from individual privateering commissions to a generalized sanction of privateering. This change increased the states' direct interest in privateering and made it more exclusively an institution of war. The second change was from privateering as a relatively local phenomenon, to a truly global one. Both of these changes were directly related to how the aspiring powers of North-Western Europe sought to break the Iberian imperial duopoly; privateering proved to be the key both to weakening the Spanish and Portuguese grip on the Indies, but it also provided the financial muscle which would make further imperial expansion by particularly the Dutch and English possible.

As we have suggested in the preceding pages, the legacy of privateering, how our present is historicized by this institution, has less to do with any appropriation of terms, than with the macro-structures and historicity of international society. Privateering is one of the key institutions through which the modern world and modern international society found its form, and its history demonstrates well the malleability of institutions over the *longue durée*, the importance of key events for institutional change, the heterogeneity of both causes and effects associated with one institution and the necessity of unpacking the institutions associated with empire and colonialism.

Still, as mentioned in the introduction, privateering is primarily present today through its absence, and the key mode of historicity, which connects privateering to our present, is that of forgetting. At a basic level, this forgetting concerns 600 years of the history of maritime violence and how it continues to influence our current world. More importantly, the forgetting of privateering, which was enabled by the Treaty of Paris has enabled the perpetuation of two central myths of current international relations. The first is the statist myth, which considers states with a monopoly on legitimate violence to be the key actors in international politics, and the controllers of the world's oceans. Forgetting privateering has enabled the construction of a dichotomy between legitimate state-controlled naval force and illegitimate piracy, with no grey-zones. Thus, all private use of maritime violence is considered piracy. The Somali example is instructive. In 2010, it was asked whether Somalia was becoming 'a new Barbary' (Murphy, 2011). In an ironic twist, a current misinterpretation of the situation in Somalia was historicized through reference to a 'Barbary' that owes more to triumphalist civilizational myths than the three centuries of Barbary privateering (cf. Leira, 2017). Closely connected to the statist myth, is the landed myth. This holds that political authority is built and maintained on land and that the world ocean, outside of periods of outright war, can be considered a peaceful common. Forgotten in this narrative is how the end of privateering was intertwined with the rise of the naval hegemony, which has regulated the sea for almost two centuries.

Tying together the threads, we can conclude with a double, and in some sense mirroring, irony of forgetfulness. On the one hand, forgetting privateering comes with the obvious cost of negating 'peripheral' agency. Taking privateering seriously makes facile post-colonial arguments much harder. On the other hand, forgetting privateering serves to obscure the origins of naval hegemony, and to naturalize what is historically an extremely uncommon phenomenon, namely the freedom to travel the high sea without fear of predation. Taking privateering seriously thus also makes facile arguments about the freedom of the seas much harder. Privateering has shaped our world, and that it is present primarily through absence makes for inadequate analysis of the past and insufficient creativity in imagining the future.

References

Borschberg, P. (2003). Portuguese, Spanish and Dutch Plans to Construct a Fort in the Straits of Singapore, ca. 1584–1625, *Archipel*, 65, 55–88.

Borschberg, P. (2013). From Self-Defense to an Instrument of War: Dutch Privateering Around the Malay Peninsula in the Early Seventeenth Century, *Journal of Early Modern History*, 17, 32–52.

Bromley, J. S. (1987). *Corsairs and Navies. 1660–1760*, London: The Hambledon Press.

de Carvalho, B. (2014). The Confessional State in International Politics: Tudor England, Religion, and the Eclipse of Dynasticism, *Diplomacy & Statecraft*, 25(3), 407–31

de Carvalho, B. (2015). Private Force and the Making of States, c. 1100–1500, in R. Abrahamsen & A. Leander (eds.). *The Routledge Handbook of Private Security Studies*, 11–19, London: Routledge.

de Carvalho, B. (2016). The Making of the Political Subject: Subjects and Territory in the Formation of the State, *Theory and Society*, 45(1), 57–88.

de Carvalho, B. & Paras, A. (2015). Sovereignty and Solidarity: Moral Obligation, Confessional England, and the Huguenots, *The International History Review*, 37(1), 1–21

Cheyette, F. L. (1970). The Pirates and the Sovereign, *Speculum* 45(1), 40–68.

Colás, A. (2016). Barbary Coast in the Expansion of International Society: Piracy, Privateering, and Corsairing as Primary Institutions, *Review of International Studies*, 42(5), 840–57.

Davis, R. (1962). *The Rise of the English Shipping Industry*, London: Liverpool University Press.

Earle, P. (2003). *The Pirate Wars*, London: Methuen.

Ekin, D. (2006). *The Stolen Village: Baltimore and the Barbary Pirates*, Dublin: O'Brien Press.

Emmer, P. C. (2003). The First Global War: The Dutch versus Iberia in Asia, Africa and the New World, 1590–1609, *e-Journal of Portuguese History*, 1(1).

Glete, J. (2000). *Warfare at Seat, 1500–1650: Maritime Conflicts and the Transformation of Europe*, Milton Park: Routledge.
Grewe, W. G. (2000). *The Epochs of International Law,* New York: Walter de Gruyter.
Hanna, M. G. (2015). *Pirate Nests and the Rise of the British Empire, 1570–1740*, Chapel Hill: University of North Carolina Press.
't Hart, M. (2014). *The Dutch Wars of Independence: Warfare and Commerce in the Netherlands 1570–1680*, London: Routledge.
Heers, J. (2003). *The Barbary Corsairs*, London: Greenhill.
Heyman, J. M. (ed.). *States and Illegal Practices*, Oxford: Berg.
Heyman, J. M. and Smart, A. (1999). States and Illegal Practices: An Overview, in J. M. Heyman (ed.). *States and Illegal Practices*, 1–24, Oxford: Berg.
Keene, E. (2007). A Case Study of the Construction of International Hierarchy: British Treaty-Making against the Slave Trade in the Early Nineteenth Century, *International Organization,* 61(2), 311–39.
Leira, H. (2017). Political Change and Historical Analogies, *Global Affairs,* 3(1), 81–88.
Leira, H. & de Carvalho, B. (2010). Privateers of the North Sea: At Worlds End – French Privateers in Norwegian Waters, in A. Colas & B. Mabee (eds.). *Mercenaries, Pirates, Bandits and Empires*, 55–82, London: Hurst Publishers.
Leira, H. & de Carvalho, B. (2018). The Function of Myths in International Relations: Discipline and Identity, in A. Gofas, I. Hamati-Ataya & N. Onuf (eds.). *The Sage Handbook of the History, Philosophy and Sociology of International Relations*, 222–35, London: SAGE Publications.
Leonard, A. B. (ed.). (2016). *Marine Insurance: Origins and Institutions, 1300–1850*, Houndsmill: Palgrave Macmillan.
Murphy, M. (2011). *Somalia: The New Barbary? Piracy and Islam in the Horn of Africa*, London: Hurst Publishers.
Neff, S. C. (2005). *War and the Law of Nations: A General History*, Cambridge: Cambridge University Press.
Ordonnance de la marine, du mois d'aoust 1681 [Reprod.] (1714), Paris: C. Osmont.
Pennell, C. R. (1994). Accommodation between European and Islamic Law in the Western Mediterranean in the Early Nineteenth Century, *British Journal of Middle Eastern Studies,* 21 (2), 159–89.
Pennell, C. R. (2001). *Bandits at Sea: A Pirates Reader*, New York: New York University Press
Phillips, A., & Sharman, J. (2015). *International Order in Diversity: War, Trade and Rule in the Indian Ocean*, Cambridge: Cambridge University Press
Pilgrim, D. (1975). The Colbert-Seignelay Naval Reforms and the Beginnings of the War of the League of Augsburg, *French Historical Studies,* 9(2), 235–62.
Rodger, N. A. M. (2014). The Law and Language of Private Naval Warfare, *The Mariner's Mirror,* 100(1), 5–16.
Starkey, D. J. & McCarthy, M. (2014). A Persistent Phenomenon: Private Prize-Taking in the British Atlantic, c. 1540–1856, in S. E. Amirell & L.

Müller (eds.). *Persistent Piracy: Maritime Violence and State-Formation in Global Historical Perspective*, 131–51, London: Palgrave Macmillan.

Sutton, A. (2009). Atlantic Orientalism: How Language in Jefferson's America Defeated the Barbary Pirates, *darkmatter Journal*, 5, 53–67.

Wenner, M. W. (1980). The Arab/Muslim Presence in Medieval Central Europe, *International Journal of Middle East Studies*, 12(1), 59–79.

Windler, C. (2001a). Diplomatic History as a Field for Cultural Analysis: Muslim-Christian Relations in Tunis, 1700–1840, *The Historical Journal*, 44(1), 79–106.

Windler, C. (2001b). Representing a State in a Segmentary Society: French Consuls in Tunis from the Ancien Régime to the Restoration, *The Journal of Modern History*, 73(2), 233–74.

6 Where Did the Mongol Empire Go?
The Presences of a Eurasian Steppe-Nomadic Past

Einar Wigen and Iver B. Neumann

1 Introduction

In today's Russia, President Vladimir Putin is genuinely popular. Up until the 2022 invasion of Ukraine, he would probably win any free and fair election outright. There is little by way of a well-organized opposition with a broad popular backing. And yet, the regime makes a point of striking down what little there is of scattered dissent with much more publicized and physical force than what it would take to get the job done. In today's Turkey, President Recep Tayyip Erdoğan has a firm grip on the country, and yet he is willing to risk his popularity in order to overturn municipal elections that do not go his way. European influences have been heavily present in both states for centuries, and yet Russian and Turkish politics both look markedly different from the politics of the European Union. Furthermore, there are clear and oft-commented parallels between political life in the two states. What may explain this?

Our answer to this puzzle is that Russian and Turkish politics, and in an even greater degree Central Asian politics, display the present not only of European pasts, but also of steppe pasts. Political life is marked by complex temporalities, one we may call a steppe tradition. Organizationally, the last great instantiation of the fully fledged steppe tradition was the Mongol Empire. In the second half of the thirteenth century, this empire comprised the entire 'known world' from the Chinese coasts in the east to the forests of Eastern Europe in the west and from the Arctic Oceans in the north to Iran and Egypt in the south. Where it conquered, the empire also ruled, shaping a wide range of social and political phenomena and leaving an imprint upon the societies it conquered. The past of steppe-nomadic conquest may seem remote, yet it is nonetheless a lingering, but usually unacknowledged, presence. While George Lawson and Thomas Müller each brilliantly show in this volume how certain historical continuities of present institutions are hidden or conveniently underemphasised, the steppe legacy, largely constitutive of the Russian and Turkish presents, is forgotten.

There is something paradoxical about present-day attempts to rewrite recent world history as a long series of struggles against European imperialism, for such a framing does exactly what it is purportedly trying to avoid. By making struggle against Europe, the sine qua non of the past two hundred years of overall human experience, it privileges Europe, and so is by definition Eurocentric. In the introduction to this book, Klaus Schlichte and Stephan Stetter pointed to an alternative to this way of thinking about imperial and other determinants of present-day agency, namely to apply a historical sociology that would 'look for conflicting or overlapping temporalities, for mutual constitution, emerging interdependencies, variation and stabilization, translations and adaptations in processes'. Surely this is the way to go about understanding those areas where different imperial traditions, both Western and non-Western, are merging to inform present-day politics.[1] The Eurasian Steppe and its hybridized fringe states, with Turkey and Russia being prominent amongst them, would be one such area (and highlight the central importance of interpreting contexts deeply, as suggested by mode 4).[2] The mode of presence of the past in this area, we will argue, is top-dog clientelism. It is characterized by two factors. First, political life, from the everyday to that of the state administration, is upheld by chains of patron–client relations that end at the head of state. Secondly, whereas there will always be more than one line in play, there is little will to reach a modus vivendi with opponents or a collective mode of rule. The pattern is rather that the top dog refuses to acknowledge any equals, be that at home or abroad. The first of these factors is arguably the default of politics. The second has a number of parallels, but stands in direct opposition to the formal principles of democracy (with its concept of loyal opposition) and sovereignty (with its concept of reciprocity between sovereigns). Furthermore, and as also noted by Schlichte and Stetter, the point of this book is not to lay down covering laws, but to deliver what Sewell calls eventful histories; also where there are plenty of world-historical parallels, it has merit to demonstrate the specific processes – modes of historicity linked to complex temporalities – that produce a certain result, for these will necessarily be unique.

2 A Nomadic Imperial Tradition

Although the pre-history of the tradition imperial steppe tradition in Eurasia stretches back at least to the eighth century BC and includes some predominantly Iranic-speaking polities, the first documented Eurasian

[1] For more on imperial legacies, see George Steinmetz, this volume.
[2] On the modes of historicity see Section 4 of the introduction to this volume by Schlichte and Stetter.

steppe empire, that of the Xiongnu, hails from 209 BC (Di Cosmo, 2002). The best-documented and best-known empire in the Eurasian steppe tradition is the Mongol empire. Discussions of immediate precursors are usually referred to as Turko-Mongol in the literature. So are successors, although there is a bifurcation at the very end of the living tradition. At the time of their respective demise in the late eighteenth century, the Dzunghar empire was a Mongol affair, while the Crimean Khanate was a Turkic one.

Steppe empires emerged as a result of a fixed pattern that we may call polysynthetic. Some particularly ambitious young man would establish himself as head of a group of households. In the literature, such groups are usually referred to as tribes, and defined in terms of perceived common ancestry. As pointed out by James Scott, however, we have in this term, as well as in the categorizing scheme of which it is part, an example of how knowledge and power are so intertwined as to make the term misleading if not downright useful:

> States and empires have been founded by peoples conventionally understood as tribes – Jinggis Khan, Charlemagne, Osman, the Manchu. And yet, it would be far more correct to say that states make tribes, than to say tribes make states. Tribes are what have been called a 'secondary form,' created in two ways and only in the context of a state or empire. The antonym or binary to 'tribe' is 'peasantry.' The difference, of course, is that the peasant is a cultivator already incorporated fully as a subject of the state. Tribes or tribals, on the other hand, are those peripheral subjects not (yet?) brought fully under state rule and/or those who have chosen to avoid the state. (Scott, 2009: 257)

If a leader and his 'tribes' proved particularly good at raiding caravans and sedentaries, he would attract ever more of the familiar 'tribes', until the momentum was there to conquer more 'tribes' with other traditional allegiances. When taken to its logical extreme, as did Chinggis Khan and his lineage, the so-called Golden Kin, the resulting empire could envelop the entire steppe and begin to conquer sedentaries on a more permanent basis. When the founder of the empire died, there was, invariably, a succession struggle. Empires rarely survived for more than a couple of generations.

Following the Xiongnu and the Huns, particularly successful steppe empires organized along similar lines include the Uigur and the Khitan Empires. The Uigurs, whose powers peaked in the late eighth century, was a nomadic turned sedentary people that had considerable experience in ruling sedentary populations and cities. The Khitans were a semi-nomadic Turko-Mongol people that had established the Liao dynasty, been displaced, and returned as a key steppe force of the twelfth century (Sverdrup-Thygeson, 2012). The Mongols, which emerged as a close to irresistible military force in the first decades of the thirteenth century under the leadership of the man who was to become Chinggis Khan, were firmly ensconced in this tradition. The polity borrowed their alphabet (and used it until about a century ago), their way of setting up a chancery and the concept of scribes from the Uigurs. The Khitans, who were brought into the Mongol fold in 1218, had administered a loose and non-confessional steppe empire based on tribute extracted by decimally organized cavalry (Morgan, 1986: 49). For this, they had used intermediaries, and these are the direct predecessors of the *darugha* used by the Mongols.

Chinggis's key tool was his imperial guard, which had at its core his classificatory brothers (*anda*) and people who had chosen to leave their tribe to follow him personally (*nöker*). The guard, which included representatives of all the Mongolian tribes ('a useful form of hostage-taking'; Morgan, 1986: 90), and which was in effect Chinggis's household, numbered around 10,000 at the outset of his conquests.

Although the Mongols made eminent use of heavy wooden saddles and composite bows, their key advantage in warfare was their strategy. The Mongols emphasized protracted training, advance planning, multi-strand coordination and tight discipline. Alone at the time, they concentrated their thinking not on the single combatant or on a small group of soldiers, but on the *tümen* (Russian: t'ma), a unit ideally composed of 10,000 men. It was officially recognized that actual *tümen* would be undermanned (Allsen, 1987: 193). The land needed to man a *tümen* was also used by the Mongols as the basic administrative unit. At the height of its power, in the mid-thirteenth century, the Mongol empire, in the shape of four different polities, covered most of the known world, from the Pacific coast to Russian lands and from the high north to the waters outside Japan. India did not become a Mongol possession during the height of their rule, but was later conquered by the founder of the Mughal Empire, Babur, who claimed descent from Chinggis Khan.[3]

The Mongols lay claim to universal sovereignty. They conceived the world as a Mongol empire to be, under Chinggis Khan's successors, known as the Golden Kin. A *kuriltay* – a gathering of the successor lines – had to consecrate the choice of leader. All peoples were potential members of the universal Mongol empire. Allsen writes about these political

[3] The Mughal Empire (1526–1764/1857) was literally 'the Mongol Empire', Mughal being a variant of Mongol. Babur, however, spoke Turkic and wrote Chaghatay, a written language composed of Turkic grammar and suffused with Persian loanwords. Be that as it may, for all political purposes, the Mughal Empire originated as a post-Mongol empire, with Babur tracing his lineage back to both Chinggis and Tamerlane, and claiming *translatio imperii* from these two most famous Mongol empires.

ideas that they can be traced back to the Türk Kaghanate, and were in all likelihood relayed to the Mongols by the Uighur Turks. In the Mongol adaptation of this ideological system, it was held that Eternal Heaven (*Möngke Tenggeri*), the sky god and the chief deity of the [Shamanistic] steppe nomads, bestowed upon Chinggis Khan a mandate to bring the entire world under his sway. This grant of universal sovereignty gave the Mongols the right, or perhaps more accurately, placed upon them the obligation, to subjugate and chastize any nation or people refusing to join the Empire of the Great Mongols on a voluntary basis (Allsen, 1987: 42).[4]

The key principle of organization was kinship, both biological kinship and classificatory kinship. The language of the fights over succession was the one of the *jasagh*, the rules of the ancestors, which were supposed to be upheld and to which respect should be paid, not least when these were used creatively. There were multiple succession principles in play, including one whereby the youngest son follows his father, when it came to being the emperor – *khagan* – there was no automatic succession involved.[5] The candidates built alliances that felt one another out until one candidate emerged as the stronger one and called a *kuriltai* where the leading Chinggisid successors were to consecrate him (Allsen, 1987: 34). After Chinggis Khan died in 1227, his youngest son Tolui took over as regent, but in 1229 it was Ögödei who made *khagan*. When he died in 1241, a protracted fight between the Toluids and the Ögödeians ended when Tolui's oldest son Möngke made khagan in 1251. This protracted fight was of key importance to European history, and we will return to it below.

3 Mongol Imperialism

The analytical purchase of the terms imperialism and colonialism is tenuous for the Mongol empire. Whether we term the Mongol polity an empire or not does depend to a limited extent on our definition of the term empire. In extant literature, we may see this in the fact that the empires under discussion here, when being noted at all, usually come with an epithet: nomadic empires, riding empires, marching empires. If an empire is a polity that legitimizes its ruler through universalist conceptualizations, recognizes no other rulers as equals, and

[4] The idea of a heavenly mandate was, of course, also a Chinese idea (cf. Rachewiltz, 1971: 104).

[5] The existence of multiple principles meant, of course, that *de facto* power could be legitimized in different ways, leaving succession open for competition.

has world-encompassing conquest as its ultimate goal, then the Mongol empire was as imperial as polities come.[6]

The Mongol empire itself was formally centralized, initially around the power of Chinggis Khan and then around the senior among his successors. While new areas and populations were allocated to someone within the centralized ruling hierarchy to be treated as the polity treated grazing land to be allocated according to one's position in the unified hierarchy, in actual practice, as it conquered sedentary populations and grew out of its original proportions, the Mongols also engaged in ruling via a hub-and-spoke system in the sense described by Nexon and Wright (2007). When a ruler died, all of his subordinates of a certain rank needed to go to his successor to have his patent renewed. Given the means of transportation, the need to decide things locally and the limited number of people to man the central hierarchy, one could not but delegate power. To deny the imperial character of the Mongol empire would be a mistake, despite its formally centralized system of rule. The imperial character of the Mongol empire is much clearer when it comes to its universal ideology of rule. Chinggis Khan literally means 'Oceanic Ruler', where ocean implies that which encompasses the world. Hence, all lands were legitimate targets of conquest and no other ruler recognized as legitimate. There could only be one legitimate ruler, one top dog.

As a polity that was structured around an army whose twin objectives were conquest and the distribution of loot, but whose non-military population was relatively small, the Mongol empire would never have had the capacity for settler colonialism. Besides, as a peripatetic polity made up of nomads, settling was itself never a goal. Tribes and camping groups migrated, and their migration patterns extended to new areas as their armies conquered new lands, but it is doubtful how much insight one might get out of a discussion of whether to call this move colonial. What is clear is that if it was colonialism, it had more in common with how the Spanish king engaging in conquest of 'the New World' and what became the Philippines following the completion of the Reconquista. The political economy that drove the enterprise was not one of merchants, but through plunder, loot and the expansion of domains.

4 The Presence of Nomads and Their Descendants

Human remnants of the Mongol empire's four major offshoots are in evidence into the post-Mongol international order that followed it (Kotkin 2007). The Yuan dynasty in China lasted until 1348. The Ilkhans

[6] Cf. Jordheim and Neumann (2011) for a history of concepts of empire.

in Persia lasted approximately as long. In the northwest, however, where the Golden Kin stuck it out in the felt tent capital of Saray whence they could maintain a steppe-based lifestyle. Muscovy seems to have stopped paying tribute to the Kipchak Khanate sometime around 1470, and made an alliance with the Western part of what was left of it in 1502. Muscovy effectively swallowed its partner, and in 1507, Sigismund of Poland-Lithuania was 'granted' the western part from its last Khan. The Kipchak Khanate was no more.

In the steppe itself, unsurprisingly, the living tradition lasted longer. The Yuan dynasty had an afterlife north of the Chinese border. In the mid-fifteenth century, the Oirat Empire was a major steppe force (Purdue, 2005: 59). It was followed by one last Mongol imperial steppe polity, the Dzunghar Empire, which sported a new glue, Tibetan Buddhism. The first Mongol contact with Tibetan Buddhism since the thirteenth century occurred in 1566, when the Ordos Mongol Khutukhai Secen Hongtiji (1540–86) traveled to Tibet. In 1578, his successor Altan Khan gave Sodnam Gyamtsho 'the title of 'Dalai Lama' (Oceanic Teacher in Mongolian[7]), and the Dalai Lama declared Altan to be the reincarnation of Khubilai Khan' (Purdue, 2005: 66). The living imperial steppe tradition was liquidated by the expansion of two sedentary empires, Chinese and Russian, into the steppe.

Mention should also be made of one Mongolian offshoot, the Kalmyk, that moved west and arrived north of the Caucasus from Inner Asia in the 1620s, causing a characteristic ripple effect on the steppe by pushing the graze lands of the Nogays further west, which in turn became a factor in increasing the raids of the Nogays and the Crimean Tatars against Russian sedentaries (Khodarkovsky, 2004: 132–33).[8] By the seventeenth century, the Kalmyks were a major power in the western steppe. Having dominated Russia's seventeenth century steppe relations, in 1771 they refused to dismantle their political organization in order to accommodate Catherine the Great's imperial demands, and three quarters of them set off for Dzungaria in China, where they quickly became part of the Qing military.

The Crimean Khanate was the main successor to the Kipchak Khanate, and although they remained fairly stationary around the Crimean Peninsula and their capital Bakhchisaray, old steppe habits

[7] Note the similarity with the title Genghis Khan (his name was Temüjin), which means oceanic/universal khan/ruler.

[8] Subsequent ripple effects in the South were even greater: 'The arrival of desperate and destitute Kazakhs [in 1723] spelled disaster for the Central Asian khanates. The inhabitants of Samarkand and Khiva deserted the cities, Bukhara was besieged, and farmland and gardens were trampled by the Kazakhs' herds' (Khadorkovsky, 2004: 150).

died hard. Their political organization was certainly straight out of the steppe tradition:

> The leader of each clan, the bey, was chosen by the clan elders and was then confirmed by the Khan, in much the same manner that the Khan himself was confirmed by the Ottoman Sultan. At the time of confirmation the Khan would grant the new bey a iarlik or patent of authority over the lands of his clan. (Fisher, 1970: 10)

Furthermore, the Crimeans continued lucrative steppe pursuits like raiding, tribute-taking and slave trading. In 1571, Crimean Tatars attacked Moscow, and the attacks continued on a lesser scale. As Fisher (1970: 20) puts it, '[d]uring the seventeenth century Crimean raids on the Russians increased in intensity and frequency. The Khans often seemed dissatisfied with the money tribute and supplemented it with Russian captives, [perhaps numbering up to 200,000], who always brought a good price from Ottoman buyers'. After the Russian annexation in 1784, some 50–75 per cent of the Crimean Tatar population decamped for the Ottoman Empire (McNeill, 1964: 199). According to Kasaba (2009: 9; cf. Fisher, 1999: 181), as many as 900,000 Muslims left Crimea and the Caucasus in the eight years following the Crimean War (1853–56). In this case, the answer to where the Mongol-Turkic population went is Turkey. That is, in fact, the answer that usually applies. Of the Tatars who stayed on in Crimea, some 190,000 were deported by Stalin to Central Asia in 1944. Russia's continued persecution of the Tatars of Crimea constitutes a particularly glaring example of the presence of the past.

The Cossacks were another story, and present themselves as a key example of the hybridizing fallout of empire. They congealed not from pastoral households, but from runaways from all kinds of different polities towards frontier settlements. Boeck (2009: 14–15) puts it as follows:

> Up river from Azov, Cossack settlements began to arise in the late fifteenth century. At first drawn to Azov as a source for plunder, these Cossacks (a Turkic word for freebooters or independent operators) took up residence in the lower Don region. Like a parasitic organism that attaches itself to an unwilling host, the Don Cossacks drew their initial lifeblood from the Ottoman presence in the lower Don region. While at first they simply plundered the steppe and river caravans heading to Azov, Cossacks would accompany and protect travelers from depredations by Tatars and other Cossacks during river and steppe journeys from the mouth of the Don River to Muscovy. They also began to trade information on the Black Sea world to the Muscovites for weapons and supplies. Though geographically conjoined to Azov, the Cossacks of the Don became clients of a distant Russian tsar.

If we go by Scott's definition of tribes as by-products of state-making, then the Cossacks are an example of tribal formation on the frontier between the Russian and Ottoman Empires. The Cossacks also specialized in ransoming, a lucrative business in what was, in the days before American slave trade took off, the world's most active slave market (Boeck, 2009: 50–53). The ranks of the Cossacks were swelled by runaway serfs until the Peter the Great's crackdown in 1707 and the agriculturalization of the eighteenth century brought so many that the Turkic elements were marginalized and the Cossacks came across as increasingly Russian. Their way of life also shifted, with the raiding and trading typical of a steppe polity giving way to frontier duty for the tsar. This was also the direction of change for a number of traditional steppe polities. Furthermore, the Cossacks were like most, if not all, steppe polities in being dependent on town-dwellers for markets (Barfield, 1989; Khazanov, 1994).

The steppe polities and the Cossacks both perpetuated Mongol practices, but they did so in different ways. McNeill (1964: 115–16, 18) sums it up neatly when he writes that

> Cities and other seats of civilisation, e.g., a Polish nobleman's house, offered by far the best target for a raid, whereas fellow-feeling with enserfed villagers and the poverty of the peasants discouraged Cossack depredation in the countryside. The contrast may therefore be expressed as follows: In the time of Turkish-Tatar ascendancy [in the frontier region], city folk preyed upon villagers, whereas in time of Cossack apogee, villagers / attacked cities and city folk (…) This [the first decades of the seventeenth century, when sedentary polities were particularly weak] was the Cossacks' apogee. Like the Varangians of old, from a headquarters on the Dniepr interrelated bands operated all the way from the Baltic coast to the walls of Constantinople and from the Volga to the Carpathians; and everywhere booty-raiding and trading went hand in hand.

By the time of the Napoleonic Wars, physical remnants of the steppe tradition were reduced to territorially bounded units along the Russian-Chinese border. Contemporary examples include the state of Mongolia, Inner Mongolia in China, Buryatia and Tuvy in Russia. As marginalised groups within the Russian Federation, the latter two have been actively recruited for the invasion of Ukraine, where they have sustained many casualties fighting for Russia. The question we turn to now is the one of social remnants. What kinds of remnants of the Eurasian steppe tradition are in evidence? The hitch regarding wide-ranging historical discussions like the following is always the same; the number of variables in play is so large that it is very hard to establish that any one phenomenon is a causal effect of any one set of historical patterns. The argument must remain a tentative and somewhat underspecified one, at least until more work has been done.

5 Social Fact Remnants and the Imperial Eurasian Steppe Tradition

Having traced the steppe polities up to their demise in the late eighteenth century, we now turn to a discussion of remnants understood as social facts (as opposed to personnel). We begin with the most obvious case, which is Central Asia, and then proceed with the increasingly less clear-cut cases of Turkey and Russia. Before we proceed, however, we want to make note of a fourth case that is in need of further work, but that we leave out here for reason of space and lack of expertise. That is the Sub-Continent.

In terms of political tradition, both Pakistan and India were heavily influenced by the Mughal Empire (cf. Pardesi, 2018). The Mughal Empire is literally the Mongol Empire, with Mughal being a different transcription of the same word. It was a vast empire centred on Delhi from 1526 until the British expanded upon them, abolishing it in 1857 and claiming the title for Queen Elizabeth in 1876. The elites of the Mughal Empire were to a large extent Persians and Turks drawn from Transoxiana, but they were, like everyone else, heavily influenced by Mongol politics. The problem in determining Mongol influence is that much of the areas ruled by Mongols were ruled by Turks both before and after Mongol domination. And since Turkic and Mongol political tradition is so heavily intertwined and thus similar, it is almost impossible to tell what is a Mongol influence and what is a Turkic influence when it comes to political institutions and traditions.

Afghanistan is probably *the* key geography where sedentary-nomadic relations of the kind that emerged with the demise of the Mongols is still the order of the day. People wait to be told whom to vote for (Barfield, 2010: 331). This is reminiscent of the way the kuriltay was an institution for confirming the most powerful khan as *kaghan*, rather than an instrument for selecting the leader. If we believe Barfield, the Afghans take the elections to be a way to express their loyalty to the supreme force (the Americans) by voting for the man that this supreme force wants to rule. When the Americans did not explicitly say whom to vote for, the Afghans were at a loss. Similarly, elections in former Soviet republics in Central Asia, such as Kyrgyzstan, systematically elect the candidate supported by Moscow. This is not to say that there is no election fraud, but that the expectation on the part of the population is not that elections are instruments for selecting leaders, but merely to confirm the most powerful man as supreme leader.

It is also no coincidence that when the Central Asian republics (as well as Azerbaijan in the Caucasus) suddenly needed a political past upon which to base their identities as sovereign states after the fall of the Soviet Union, they reached to political lineages going back to the Mongols and to the same imperial title that the Mughals, the Muscovites and Ottomans claimed *translatio imperii*. This can hardly be called a historical accident, as many descendants of Chinggis Khan explicitly identify as such.[9] The memory of the Mongol Empire is still something to be used for political purposes, even though in Afghanistan the Mongol invasion is still remembered for its devastating consequences for sedentary civilization. Among the Hazaras, an outlying group of Mongolian-looking people in Pakistan and Afghanistan, many men can recite their genealogies going back about thirty-four generations to Chinggis Khan.[10]

In what can be termed a 'wider Central Asia', the political traditions we explore here were the main mode of conducting politics until the 1920s (Barfield, 2002). In some areas, most notably in Afghanistan but also in Iran, focusing on steppe and sedentary imbrication is arguably still the most relevant way of shedding light on state-society relations (Barfield, 2010). In Iran, the last explicit vestiges of the power of the nomads was shattered only in the 1930s, when Shah Reza Pahlavi blocked nomadic migrations by placing army units at strategic points (Barfield, 2002: 84).[11] Yet, in terms of the state itself, there can be little doubt that a symbiosis between Azeri Turkic elements and Persians is the *modus operandi*. Turkey may seem the odd one out, with almost ninety years of uninterrupted and outright adoption of Western practices. And yet, one way to see Mustafa Kemal is as a charismatic state founder, whose charisma is used by a clan (the Kemalists) to rule with the semi-divine authority of the founder.[12] This analogy to early Turkic states (and in particular the Ottoman) is useful as a heuristic device. Ruling (or at least trying to rule) in the name of the state founder (literally; Mustafa Kemal – Kemalists) is a typical trait of Turkic state building. As Peter Golden argues for the period immediately following the Mongol conquests of the thirteenth century,

> a new politically based system focusing on descent from troops that had served a particular historical figure or dynasty was emerging. This new system derives, I believe, from the institution of the (Mong.) *nökür* (pl. *nöküd*). (...) These were individuals who, for various reasons, had broken with or left their family-clan-tribal units and taken service with a lord. (Golden, 1992: 305)

[9] Chinggis Khan has a prodigious number of descendants, cf. Zerjal et al. (2003).
[10] www.freerepublic.com/focus/news/838099/posts.
[11] For how the Ottoman Empire dealt with nomads, cf. Kasaba (2009).
[12] While they do not use the concept of clan, the point is very similarly made by Parla and Davison (2004).

Golden does not go as far as tracing this institution into the present, but we argue that what happened during the break-up of the Ottoman Empire and the Russian Empire and again with the breakup of the Soviet Union, was that what Golden (1992: 305) terms 'politiconyms' took the place of ethnonyms, with an identity as Stalinist, Kemalist, Putinist taking the place of ethnic identity as the main social marker. Moreover, we would contend that the ethnogenesis of the category Turk, as it was formulated by the modern Turkish Republic, was in fact a question of loyalty to the state, and a possibility (for Muslims) of opting in or out of the political project led by Mustafa Kemal. As the Turkish slogan goes '*atam, iznindeyiz*' – 'my forefather [great leader], we are following in your path'. This is a direct influence not only of the steppe tradition, but an innovation that came about with the demise of the Mongol Empire. The first such politiconyms were derived directly from the names of descendants of Chinggis. It is still a way to denote political loyalty in Eurasia today.

While much of this explicit connection with the steppe past is not necessarily directly linked to previous political ways of doing things – nationalism is typically about making a specific past present in a very selective way – it can be selectively used by foreign policymakers when trying to build regional entities that they can then dominate (Wigen, 2019). Steppe-nomadic conquerors such as Tamerlane (a.k.a. Timur Lenk, 1336–1405) are celebrated by several present-day states as their political origin. Hence, the national narratives that legitimize these states are also to some extent shared across 'nation-states' and form the basis both for competition and mutual recognition in the present. More important is perhaps the propensity to celebrate an imperial past that was founded by a hybrid post-Mongol dynasty. This is in line with our claim elsewhere, that within the steppe tradition, there is a need to legitimize oneself as 'top dog', and hence the way to be historically and nationally distinct means remembering the time when the predecessor polity ruled the roost.

We see this imperial past present not only in 'national' narratives and practices, but also how parts of the regional international order are to an unusually obvious degree premised on a non-anarchical logic. The hierarchical order that manifests itself in much of Eurasia, where polities either seek to contest the position of the main power dominating all the others or simply find itself a patron and protector is a legacy of the steppe-nomadic past. It is also one where the European colonial projects, including the Russian, fitted nicely with the cultural preconditions of the steppe-hybridized polities they encountered. The latter did not simply give up without a fight, but many sought the aid of an outside power to protect themselves against the whims of the suzerain of the regional hierarchy.

Various elements of the steppe tradition were already part of European repertoires of rule, albeit in different form, at the time of European colonial empires started expanding. We would argue that this kind of cultural meeting typically re-actualizes such elements, although this is difficult to prove, and probably not always the case. Picking the lowest-hanging fruit first, we would point to Afghanistan, where Thomas Barfield has argued extensively that the position of 'president' (of a supposedly sovereign state) is typically attained by someone who claims to be able to mediate between an unruly set of tribes and an outside power that is willing to 'buy peace' (Barfield, 2010). Barfield traces this back to the relationship between the steppe nomads on China's northern frontier and the various Chinese empires through out history, which he himself has written on one of the few accounts of (Barfield, 1989). Using a the threat of a militarily-inferior 'unruly' set of polities against a clearly superior outsider to position oneself as ruler selected ultimately by that external superior power, is a move that is typical for steppe-tradition middlemen. Barfield points to Karzai, but Afghan history is full of them. As is the history of polities in what Russia calls it 'near abroad'. Most of those are selected not through popular vote or domestic support, but through their ability to attract the support of the 'khagan' in the area. Currently, this is Putin, but George Bush Jr. also tried to play this role. To the extent that Russia was a European colonial empire, the origins of this conquest and incorporation into the Russian Empire is a very clear example of how such a cultural meeting reactualized common parts of a repertoire where only some aspects are shared (Khodarkovsky, 2004).

6 Conclusion

It would be wrong to assume that only European imperial pasts are present in the contemporary international system, having left their marks on historical polities that are kept up by today's polities. The steppe tradition is still alive in parts of Central Asia. It has left a solid legacy in Turkey, as well as remnants in Russia. The differences between these polities and European ones are often observed. The debt they owe to the Eurasian imperial steppe tradition takes us one step closer to accounting for these differences.

The polities emerging from the steppe have always been hybridized, as their very way of life has agriculture as a precondition for emergence. Steppe polities were, furthermore, dependent upon sedentaries in order to sustain themselves. This hybridization became more pronounced in the tenth and eleventh centuries, as Turkic dynasties broke through Transoxiana and became rulers over sedentary populations and, as such, dependent on sedentary bureaucrats and advisors for running the administration. Furthermore, the influence of the steppe tradition was renewed every now and then up until at least the fifteenth century, as newly formed steppe confederations launched attacks and overran these earlier dynasties. Another exercise that kept established rulers of hybridized polities in touch with the steppe tradition was the need to frame their claims vis-à-vis steppe rulers in terms that were recognized by the nomadic soldiery. These would include tropes like the promising of more loot and the invocation of *qut*, the all-legitimizing fortune or divine will.

Given widespread hybridization, many polities who bear the marks of the steppe tradition have nonetheless put their steppe-nomadic past under erasure. This is, among other things, due to hybridization itself, for over the last two hundred years, the European tradition has fastened on how a proper polity, a state, is by definition sedentary. Other variants were treated as previous incarnations of an evolutionary sequence (on evolution and IR see Albert et al., 2023). It followed that an affinity to the steppe came to denote backwardness. Denial notwithstanding, contemporary Eurasian states have been influenced by the steppe tradition in ways that are still tangible. While the Eurasian empires may have perished, remnants of their statecraft linger. How else can one understand the political similarities that are to a large extent geographically coextensive with the Mongol Empire? While the aforementioned hybridity has created a wide range of differences in the local particularities, and there are different ways of relating to this past in how it is written into official historiography, the political traditions of polities ranging from the Mamluks in Egypt, via the Khazars and the Kipchak Khanate (a.k.a. the Golden Horde) in Russia, as well as the Mughals in India to the Mongols and the Yuan in China, make for a similarity in political traditions that can help to illuminate many similarities in the present. While a Mongolophonie would not have a wide membership, aspects of the imperial tradition disseminated and enforced by the Mongol Empire are still present across much of Eurasia, albeit in varying forms and arenas.

References

Albert, M., Brunkhorst, H., Neumann, I.B. & Stetter, S. (2023). *The Social Evolution of World Politics*, Bielefeld: transcript.

Allsen, T. T. (1987). *Mongol Imperialism: The Politics of the Great Qan Möngke in China, Russia, and the Islamic Lands, 1251–1259*, Berkeley: University of California Press.

Barfield, T. J. (1989). *The Perilous Frontier: Nomadic Empires and China*, Cambridge: Blackwell.

Barfield, T. J. (2010). *Afghanistan: A Cultural and Political History*, Princeton: Princeton University Press.

Boeck, B. J. (2009). *Imperial Boundaries: Cossack Communities and Empire-Building in the Age of Peter the Great*, Cambridge: Cambridge University Press.

Di Cosmo, N. (2002). *Ancient China and Its Enemies: The Rise of Nomadic Power in East Asian History*, Cambridge: Cambridge University Press.

Fisher, A. (1999). *A Precarious Balance: Conflict, Trade and Diplomacy on the Russian-Ottoman Frontier*, Istanbul: İsis Press.

Fisher, A. W. (1970). *The Russian Annexation of the Crimea 1772–1783*, Cambridge: Cambridge University Press.

Golden, P. B. (1992). *An Introduction to the History of the Turkic Peoples*, Wiesbaden: Otto Harassowitz.

Jordheim, H. & Neumann, I. B. (2011). Empire, Imperialism and Conceptual History, *Journal of International Relations and Development*, 14(2), 153–85.

Kasaba, R. (2009). *A Moveable Empire: Ottoman Nomads, Migrants & Refugees*, Seattle: University of Washington Press.

Khodarkovsky, M. (2004). *Russia's Steppe Frontier: The Making of a Colonial Empire, 1500–1800*, Bloomington: Indiana University Press.

Khazanov, A. (1994). *Nomads and the Outside World.* Madison, WI: University of Wisconsin Press.

Kotkin, S. (2007). "Mongol Commonwealth? Exchange and Governance across the Post-Mongol Space". *Kritika: Explorations in Russian and Eurasian History.* 8(3), 487–531.

McNeill, W. (1964). *Europe's Steppe Frontier 1500–1800,* Chicago: Chicago University Press.

Morgan, D. (1986). *The Mongols,* Oxford: Basil Blackwell.

Nexon, D. H. & Wright, T. (2007). What's at Stake in the American Empire Debate, *The American Political Science Review,* 101(2), 253–71.

Pardesi, M. S. (2018). Mughal Hegemony and the Emergence of South Asia as a 'Region' for Regional Order-Building, *European Journal of International Relations,* 25(1), 276–301.

Scott, J. C. (2009). *The Art of Not Being Governed,* New Haven: Yale University Press.

Sewell, W. H. (1996). "Historical Events as Transformations of Structures: Inventing Revolution at the Bastille". *Theory and Society,* 25(6), 841–881.

Sverdrup-Thygeson, B. (2012). "A Neighbourless Empire? The Forgotten Diplomatic Tradition of Imperial China", *The Hague Journal of Diplomacy,* 7(3) 245–267.

Wigen, E. (2019). O Brother, Where Art Thou? Kinship in Turkish Region-Building, in K. M. Haugevik & I. B. Neumann (eds.). *Kinship in International Relations,* 121–37, London: Routledge.

Zerjal, T. et al. (2003). The Genetic Legacy of the Mongols, *American Journal of Human Genetics,* 72(3), 717–21.

7 Where Would We Be without the Fog Lifting in Austerlitz?

Ruminations on the Uses of History and Sociology in IR

Mathias Albert

1 Introduction: 'Le Soleil d'Austerlitz'

On 2 December 1805, the battle of Austerlitz saw French troops under Napoleon fight Austrian troops under Emperor Francis II and Russian troops under Czar Alexander I. In an important side-event, Bavarian troops bound up a large contingent of Austrian troops near Iglau, thus keeping them effectively from intervening in the events at Austerlitz. Among many things, the battle, that within a day left more than 15,000 soldiers dead, also became legendary for 'le soleil d'Austerlitz' – 'the sun of Austerlitz'. 2 December had started with thick ground fog, turning early troop movements and skirmishes into erratic endeavours. Under these conditions, a battle that might have led to a clear result with a winner was barely conceivable (this is of course the counterfactual part of the legend). It is in this situation that Napoleon and his marshalls at around 8 a.m. in the morning saw the sun faintly appearing as a red globe behind the fog, indicating its imminent dissipation. The lifting of the fog through the sun of Austerlitz, instigated by Napoleon's own accounts afterwards, thus became a legendary part of the historical-mythical account of the battle.

As is always the case with major 'epic' events in history, the results of, and the evolutionary trajectories leading from, the battle of Austerlitz are manifold, and could be recounted and reconstructed in almost endless ways (for evolution and IR cf. Albert et al., 2023). For the sake of the argument to be developed here, that in a sense seeks to trace the aftershocks of Austerlitz in the present, two of these trajectories will be highlighted in the following; both are closely linked, yet obviously work on quite different timescales.[1]

[1] The original draft of this chapter included a third trajectory: in acknowledgement of the support of Bavarian troops, Napoleon granted Bavaria the status of an independent kingdom. This trajectory arguably is of different relevance to contemporary world

Firstly, Napoleon's victory in Austerlitz meant a short-term shift in the European balance of powers, a significant success in his attempt to establish dominance over Europe.

Secondly, the Treaty of Pressburg signed between Austria and France on 26 December 1805 not only led to substantial territorial gains by France and its allies at the expense of Austria, it also led to Francis II renouncing, on 6 August the following year, the title of the Holy Roman Emperor, thus formally ending the latter's existence after almost a millennium.

The first of these trajectories was the one with the most impact at its time. It signalled the real possibility of Napoleon advancing to dominate the continent. As is well known, history turned out differently, and in a story that ended in Waterloo saw Napoleon defeated. The structural implication of this became apparent during the Congress of Vienna in which the great powers first and foremost sought to establish an order that would prevent any single power from becoming dominant in Europe. The results were the European (not: 'global'!) 'Concert', as well as the balance-of-power, as the normative basis of the European system of world politics.

The second of these trajectories signalled a development of equally long-term structural importance. Although in reality a 'lame duck' in all but name for quite a while already, it was only with the formal end of the Holy Roman Empire that the main systemic alternative ordering principle to exclusive territorial rule disappeared (or at least was de-legitimized). 1805/6 in this sense was a kind of benchmark date that brought a development to its conclusion whose initial stylized benchmark date was 1648 (as the alleged first formal acknowledgement of exclusive territorial rule within the Empire as legitimate; what has become widely known as the 'Westphalian moment' or the 'Westphalian myth'). However, as this chapter will argue the long-term impact of the demise of the Holy Roman Empire was in shaping imaginaries and trajectories of how European imperial powers shaped global politics thereafter – here closely mirroring the first mode of historicity highlighted by Schlichte and Stetter. The decentralized way of how authority in the Holy Roman Empire was organized shaped – in complex evolutionary ways – trajectories of global empire(s) since the

politics compared to the other two trajectories, but without it, the author would have been born in a place that would have quite probably not have been part of Bavaria but of the Rhineland-Palatinate/Kurmainz or Hesse. The editors of this book thought this existential issue to be too parochial in order to be included in the main line of argument – however, when observing cultural patterns in the Mainz/Frankfurt/West Lower Franconian region it is easy to see the presence of a past that does not always map onto contemporary political borders.

early nineteenth century. It is in that sense that the present contribution defines modes of transformation, not as wilful practices of actors or even unintended consequences, but rather as evolutionary dynamics that pave the way for historical trajectories in which new social forms – such as European global empires or even the notion of global empire – borrow from previous forms, such as in this case the way of organizing political authority in the Holy Roman Empire. In doing so, the two modes of historicity most pertinent in this context are, on the one hand, the presence of several temporal layers in social and political phenomena (i.e. 'complex temporalities'), and, on the other hand, an evolutionary account of non-linear change.

The present chapter explores the contemporary system of world politics through the lenses provided by the trajectories mentioned. The emphasis here is on the 'lenses': looking through these will in some respects overstate the importance of some developments, while often underestimating or even ignoring other ones. While providing a specific comprehensive reading of some major structural shifts leading to contemporary world politics, this is something different from a comprehensive understanding. It is in this sense that the present argument is not only about the presence of a (Napoleonic, or better: anti-Napoleonic) past in the contemporary structures of the system of world politics, namely its decidedly anti-universalist, quasi-imperial, great power-based, yet still loosely integrated outfit. The aim in this sense is also to provide a methodological input into contemporary debates about global historical sociology. It seeks to demonstrate how stories and historical trajectories that unfold from a singular event leave their traces, and how they do this on various yet interlocking scales. The question of scales is important here, as it demonstrates that, on the one hand, any account of global historical sociology needs to reflect on the basic 'inclusiveness' of 'levels', yet also demonstrates that, on the other hand, there are limits as to what singular events and stories can contribute in this respect.

While this may at first seem like a rather theoretical exercise somewhat removed from the subject of the colonial (although decidedly sharing an understanding of the colonial in terms of its complex temporalities with the chapters by George Lawson and Thomas Müller), the perspective here is one that deliberately explores the structures of the colonial 'within' what is a Europe-centred system of world politics in the early nineteenth century. Firstly, it explores a period of turmoil that was re-stabilized in the Congress of Vienna that established a system that arguably paved the way for another century or so of the incorporation of large parts of the non-European world into the spheres of authority of European colonial empires and powers. The world would have looked very different had the Congress not established a system that defined world politics as a European system only. Secondly, the formal demise of the Holy Roman Empire can, among many other things, also be seen as the final establishment of the 'Westphalian' principle of exclusive territorial sovereignty as the norm for organizing political authority in the system of world politics. However, given that this system was conceived as a European one, its specific form of organizing political authority always was only partially characteristic of the organization of colonial rule. Admittedly stretching the analogy quite a bit, while the Holy Roman Empire ceased to exist in Europe, some of its typical elements with respect to organizing political authority continued in and through colonial rule globally. This not only led to the long delay in the establishment of exclusive territorial sovereignty as a global norm, but probably also left traces in the variety of forms of organizing political authority visible in the system of world politics until today.

The purpose of this argument is decidedly not to engage systematically with the tremendous amount of literature on either the role, or the rise and decline of, empires in world politics, on the one hand, or the role and the demise of the Holy Roman Empire, on the other hand. The purpose is to offer a highly specific cut through these themes in the interest of shedding light on contemporary world politics through following some specific, yet certainly non-conscious, evolutionary trajectories, in order to demonstrate one important way in which the past remains present in important ways.[2] Underlying this argument is what could be called a purely systemic understanding of empire: irrespective of its various instantiations and detailed forms of organization, empire is understood as but one important form of organizing political authority in the system of world politics.[3] It is a form that combines stratification and segmentation, usually expressed in strong centre-periphery differences. As a form of organizing political authority, it is not dependent on formality, however. Many forms of organizing political authority have always coexisted, and continue to coexist, in the system of world politics,

[2] It would have been possible to raise the question here of whether the Napoleonic wars resulted in what could be described as 'colonial experiences' within Europe as well. The interesting general question to be developed from this would then have been to ask whether forms of coloniality were always part of the concrete collective experiences and the resulting memories within the European cores of colonial empires. Klaus Schlichte thankfully remarked that this issue would merit a chapter of its own at least, and that the answer would probably depend on highly parochial, inner-German regional points of view on the differences between a Napoleonic 'colonization' and an 'occupation'.

[3] In this sense, it is about empires as a form of organizing political authority in modernity, that is since world politics assumes its characteristic as a subsystem distinguishable in the political system of world society – it is not about a grand theory of empires across history.

to varying degrees (cf. Albert, 2016). In this understanding – and thus possibly different to some of the other contributions to this volume (but notably quite in agreement with George Steinmetz' chapter), empire as a form of organizing political authority continues as a presence, although all formal empires currently might be things of the past, while, on the other hand, nation-states are not only a thing of the present, but very much were built in the past with and within empires (cf. Berger & Miller, 2015).

As mentioned above, the purpose here is 'methodological' in a sense that I hope to demonstrate some of the difficulties, yet also the promises of historical-sociological inquiry in the immensely complex context of world society. Historical-sociological analysis itself is difficult, but then in a sense also rather easy if it concentrates on social systems or contexts with more or less clearly defined boundaries (such as the 'system of states'). The difficulty arguably arises if such analysis on the one hand cuts across many of such contexts and systems, yet on the other hand retains an analytic perspective informed by abstractions that are typical for the social sciences ('levels', 'systems', etc.), but are mostly missing from the equally inclusive, yet relatively theory-remote accounts in the currently prominent tradition of 'global history'.

The remainder of this chapter will proceed in three main steps. The following section will briefly argue that while itself it is actually not the subject of the present inquiry in the narrower sense, the (fog at) Austerlitz is a good starting point not only for its concrete significance, but also for the theoretical questions it allows to raise. These questions pertain primarily to the levels, scales, time frames, and entanglements that play a role in historical sociological analysis, if that analysis is basically understood as pertaining to processes of social evolution. The following two sections will then pursue the two trajectories mentioned above in that spirit. In a sense, each of these sections tells a story that could be told by itself. The point here is, however, that all of them also can, and should be, told as related to one another, showing, as mentioned, both the difficulties and the promises of historical-sociological analysis in a world society context. The chapter concludes with some remarks on the vistas that such an analysis holds for the study of empire and coloniality in particular, as well as for the study of world society in general.

2 Levels, Scales, Time Frames and Entanglements

Levels, scales, time frames and entanglements arguably are key concepts in historical sociological analysis, which however are not always made explicit, let alone reflected upon in their relation to one another.

To students of international relations, 'levels' will be most familiar from Kenneth Waltz's three 'images' of how to view international relations (i.e. 'man', the 'state' and 'war', meaning the individual, collective and system level, respectively), and from Singer's (1961) classical treatment of the subject. Generally, it still seems to hold true that most of IR, historical and sociological analysis proceed on primarily one of these levels, treating other levels as boundary conditions. Underlying this practice is usually a claim, if only implicitly, that a level of analysis is in fact more than that, namely that it designates a relevant type of structure-formation, and that for the purpose at hand, it is more appropriate to concentrate on that particular kind of structure formation rather than on another, if related and interdependent one. This observation already hints at the suspicion that there might be something deeply problematic with a level-based analysis: even if acknowledging relations with other levels, and even if emphasizing an analytical character, level-based views tend to privilege an exclusive view of levels. What happens in one type of structure formation happens in that type only, even though it might be influenced, and in turn might influence, other types of structure formation.

The alternative is an inclusive view of levels. In such a view, the main issues here are not ontologically distinct types of structure formation, but different kinds of inclusion of different kinds of structure formation into social systems. The main question in this case changes from one that asks 'where' (i.e. at which 'level') something takes place, to one that asks 'how' something gets addressed by different social systems, allowing to draw a rather more sophisticated, if rather less parsimonious, picture of the evolution of social processes.

This observation regarding the issue of levels is intimately tied to questions of scale. Both are related, yet both often tend to be treated as meaning basically the same. Such a mix-up is somehow suggested by the levels-distinction between individuals, collective entities, and an overarching system – a distinction that would intuitively seem to neatly fit a distinction between, most notably, the local, the regional, and the global. However, quite obviously both distinctions are not the same, and although they might often overlap, there is no necessity that they actually do: an interaction between important diplomats is something that takes place on the individual level, yet on a global scale, while an intergovernmental treaty establishing a cross-border bicycle path takes place on the collective (state) level, yet on a local scale. The situation is further complicated by the fact that neither the levels- nor the scale-distinctions are the same as the distinction between micro-, meso-, and macro-levels, although here as well concepts tend to be used interchangeably.

Both the simplicity of levels- and scales-distinctions, as well as their usually more pronounced exclusive understanding, seem to primarily result from a somewhat mechanistic view of the social world, with a clear separation of ontological entities, forces, and causalities at work. It is not necessary to go into the myriad and the varieties of criticisms of underlying worldviews here, nor to provide an elaborate theoretical discussion of the many possible alternatives. Suffice it to say at this point that when looking at the social world, and notably including the modern system of world politics, as a mélange of social systems, in which levels are inclusive, then the latter cannot be defined primarily in terms of the kind of actorness they underpin (that is individual vs. collective), but need to be seen in terms of social emergence. Every higher level is characterized by emergent properties that cannot be reduced to the sum of properties of the respective lower level. It is in this sense that structure formation and modes of observation that underpin the evolution of the modern system of world politics are not simply the result of any number of battles and state actions. Thus, most notably, the emergence of 'balance of power' as the program through which the system of world politics observes itself is something else than the balancing behaviour of any number of states, although the latter is addressed in the former (inclusivity) (cf. Albert, 2016).

Similarly, as hinted at above already, it is important to recognize that although there frequently is a correlation between geographic and social systemic scale, they are not necessarily the same. Local events might have macro-effects, and global processes only micro ones (as well as any combination of intermediary steps). This seemingly simple observation points to an extremely complex issue when introducing time scales and evolutionary trajectories into the picture (witness the famous 'butterfly effect'). It also points to the fact that a social system (or indeed a plurality of social systems), whose history is composed of the endless evolutionary three steps of variation, selection and restabilization, is not only difficult to project regarding its future evolution. It is also very difficult to reconstruct, as strictly speaking its history is always not only the history of selections made, but also the history of those not made. The picture gets even more complicated if the evolution within and across social systems is not neatly synchronized. Still: reconstructing evolutionary trajectories arguably goes quite some way beyond the quite historical reconstruction of 'entanglements' (cf. Werner & Zimmermann, 2002). While that concept has gained quite some prominence in global history and beyond, it remains quite bereft of theoretical stringency of any kind. The argument of the present contribution is that evolutionary reconstructions, despite their inherent shortcomings, that proceed on the basis of not putting everything together in an entangled space, but on the basis of firstly identifying different systems, only to then recount their evolution and demonstrate mutual inclusivity, offer a more systematic and stringent form of a global historical sociology of the present. The present contribution is an explorative first cut in this direction, nothing more and nothing less.

3 The End of the Napoleonic Wars and the New Order

One could, of course, start somewhere else: in Jena, Auerstedt, Moscow, Waterloo, etc. Still, Austerlitz seems like an appropriate point. As hinted at in the introduction already, there is a certain symbolic value to the narrative or myth that surrounds it. In terms of a social evolution account, the fog could not have disappeared, the battle could have turned out differently, evolution could (with the value 'Napolenic victory' not selected) have continued otherwise. Beyond that hypothetical-theoretical remark, it is however important to acknowledge what Austerlitz stands for. After a range of advances that culminated in Napoleon's defeat of the Austrians in Ulm and most notably his taking of Vienna in November 1805, Austerlitz stands for the combined effort of Austria and Russia to halt Napoleon's drive for European domination, as well as, of course, for the fear that little to nothing would stand in his way after his victory (with the Prussians also arranging themselves with Napoleon). Although it is of course a highly stylized account, and although with much historical detail one might be able to make a similar argument for a later point in time (most notably Napoleon's advance towards and in Russia), it would seem legitimate to argue that Austerlitz was the point when all powers realized that the stakes were not realignments of the balance between the great powers, but the distinct prospect of full-scale Napoleonic hegemonic, if not imperial domination over all of Europe (this, it seems, was also mirrored in a particularly strong public reaction towards the news of the defeat at Austerlitz in Russia). The very fundaments of order were the issue, and this is what makes Austerlitz such an important event in the other storyline, that of the fate of the Holy Roman Empire (see Section 4 below) – and it is in this sense that for both European, as well as for later global history, Nipperdey's famous dictum on German history seems to hold as well: 'Am Anfang war Napoleon' ['In the beginning, there was Napoleon'] (Nipperdey, 1983: 11).

The immediate consequences of Napoleon's victory were laid down in the Peace of Pressburg that not only involved territorial gains by France and its allies, as well as the acknowledgement of the sovereignty of the Bavarian and Württemberg kingdoms, but propelled the demise of what was left in terms of formal structures of the Holy Roman Empire: 'Pressburg was universally received as a hammer blow, crushing whatever optimism remained' (Wilson, 2016: 653) – and that pertains to both optimism regarding the possibilities to prevent Napoleonic domination, as well as the possibilities to save the Holy Roman Empire. One could go one step further in this respect and argue that Austerlitz and Pressburg probably were a main traumatic episode in the overall Napoleonic trauma for the great powers of Europe that once and for all (up until the twentieth century, at least) instilled the paramount idea that even the maximization of individual gain must stand aside for the common good of preventing universal dominance of a single power – the Congress of Vienna's and the Concert's main motive, so to speak.

4 The Holy Roman Empire: Formal End but Not the End of Form?

From the perspective of the previous section's account, it would appear possible (and it has been done to that effect many times over) to put Austerlitz at the beginning of the ultimate chain of events that led to the formal dissolution of the Holy Roman Empire on 6 August 1806. Such an account of events and politics would recount the months between the end of 1805 and the summer of 1806 as a story of the (failed) attempts to rescue it.

The perspective adopted here is a different one: Austerlitz and Pressburg nudged the Holy Roman Empire into a specific evolutionary trajectory that, one could argue counter-factually, not only had an impact on the order of Europe, but to the system of world politics globally. In order to put that perspective into context, it is necessary to point out that the end of the Holy Roman Empire was never a singular event before which something existed, and after which it didn't exist. The end of the Holy Roman Empire in August 1806 was its formal abolition, yet also nothing more and nothing less than a cross-over point in a long story of the competition of two interwoven yet distinct trajectories in the evolution of political order.

Stylizing to a large degree, these trajectories are those of the imperial order on the one hand, and the territorial sovereign, later nationalist order on the other hand. While the long story of the displacement of the former by the latter is well-known and has been told in numerous versions, it is important to note that both were never self-enclosed forms of order with the according ideas that were pegged against each other. In addition, they were certainly not 'equal' competitors most of the time. Most notably, the Peace of Westphalia – still the most commonly used symbol for the success of the order of territorial sovereignty – in 1648 did not upset the imperial order. The laws and structure of the Holy Roman Empire remained intact and the limitation that territorial sovereignty induced was not a limitation on the Emperor, but 'the principal change was to explicitly deny military authority to mediate nobles, towns, and territorial assemblies' (Wilson, 2016: 174). This is to say that both trajectories were (and remain – see below) always densely interwoven, and not reflected upon as representing the struggle of competing orders until well into the eighteenth and particularly the nineteenth century; and indeed an argument could be made that the better part of that reflection actually was the result of an idealization of territorial-cum-national sovereignty against a particular representation of the Holy Roman Empire after its formal demise by nineteenth-century historiography: this included, particularly in Germany, the invention of a negative view of a 'rotten' Empire in comparison to an idealized medieval, 'old' Empire (a term still common in contemporary historiography). The romanticization of the past was part and parcel of the attempt to find a historical grounding for a German identity and the second Empire (cf. Wilson, 2016: 668–72). This romanticized and idealized account of the existence of a more or less 'pure' Old Empire existing until around 1250, as well as the according break with the new one that in a sense simply could go nowhere else but downhill clearing the path for territorial and national sovereignty, is still a very powerful narrative. As Wilson points out:

> These now traditional views survived Germany's total defeat in 1945 because they were shared by the victorious Allied powers. British, American, and French scholarship drew on the same detailed studies by nineteenth-century German historians for their interpretative framework, not least because this had been transplanted by the numerous intellectuals fleeing Germany in the 1930s that now held influential teaching posts in US universities. (Wilson, 2016: 678)

This deeply entrenched historical narrative is, I would argue, at the bottom of a major analytical short circuit in most depictions of the emergence of a 'modern' European and global system of world politics: it leads to mistaking the formal end of the Holy Roman Empire (even if allowing for attempts towards formal re-establishment after 1806) as the discontinuation of a specific evolutionary trajectory of one form of organizing political authority. However, both the form and the associated order persisted and continued to evolve: only marginally within a Europe increasingly characterized by nation- (and nationalist) states, but far more in what emerged as an important structure in the global system of world politics that emerged in the 'long' nineteenth century. Cutting short the argument to be further unfolded in a moment, one might say that what Napoleon achieved through Austerlitz was the end of the Holy Roman Empire in Europe, but not the end of its imperial form as a model for organizing political authority that it was, however pushed outwards towards the globe as a system increasingly characterized by colonial rule.

There is a rich literature that points to the fact that empires for a long time have been a constant form of organizing political authority available in various parts of the globe and connected to various civilizations (cf. Münkler, 2007). In terms of social evolution, empires might in fact be seen as something like an 'evolutionary universal' (e.g. the eye in the natural evolution of animals), fulfilling a specific 'governance function' (cf. Münkler, 2019). However, and despite a high degree of variation between different historical instantiations of empire, an integral part of imperiality has always been its geographical limitation – if not in aspiration, then in practice. There never existed a 'world empire' of truly global reach. The only empire that came – and that even remotely only – close to this in terms of planetary geographic coverage was the British Empire in the late eighteenth/early twentieth century. Other empires were 'global' in their self-perception of extending to the world they saw as relevant, either in terms of 'civilization', or in terms of the relevant space of power configuration,[4] the latter being the issue in the Napoleonic quests for European rule. The issue at hand here is somewhat different: namely that a specific form of Empire, namely the 'Holy Roman' one, in the course of its substantive demise, morphed into a different form, namely a global form of imperiality that, propelled through the co-evolution of the modern system of world politics in Europe and arrangements of colonial rule, established imperiality as a form of organizing political authority on a global social level, next to, and closely interwoven, with the global proliferation of territorial and later nation-statehood as 'legitimate' and quasi-natural forms of organizing political authority.

This is, first of all, a highly formalized argument about the evolution (which includes the appearance, disappearance, and transformation) of different forms of organizing political authority in the system of world politics. It is not an alternative story about the substantive demise and the continuation of the Holy Roman Empire, nor of other specific empires. The point regarding the Holy Roman Empire here is not on whether it 'really' ended in 1806, in 1795 (*Sonderfrieden zu Basel*), or any time before that, or on whether it 'continues' in the form of the European Union. The point is that its end marked the seeming formal

[4] Cf. Reinhart, 2015: 15 for a list of historical candidates in this respect.

discontinuation of a form of organizing political authority marked by multiple and overlapping lines of loyalty and authority next to the principle of sovereign equality, raising the point of whether and to which degree this form was afterwards actualized in 'informal' or indirect ways.

5 The Global Expansion Story Retold

What Napoleon achieved through Austerlitz was the end of the Holy Roman Empire, but not the end of the imperial form of organizing political authority (which is a truism in the sense that Napoleon's quest in itself was imperial). While ending in substance and name, however, it was the specificity of the Holy Roman Empire as a long-evolving, specific combination territorial and supra-territorial rule that was pushed towards another, systemic level, inextricably intertwined with the worldwide integration of spaces through colonial rule.

While at first sight, this argument might seem to bear some resemblance to a highly conventional account on the 'expansion of international society', there are fundamental differences to it, although a range of overlaps exist. There is, starting with Hedley Bull's notion of a 'new medievalism', a strong tradition of referring to the Holy Roman Empire as a form of organizing political authority that is markedly different from the alleged clear-cut way of carving up the political system of world society into territorial states, in which the principle of sovereign equality ensures that there is one, and only one, sovereign attached to a specific territory. Figures like 'new medievalism', 'complex sovereignty' and the like are then invoked in order to designate either residual or newly emerging forms in this respect, the latter most notably in relation to the European Union. This is an account usually strongly focused on Europe however. The argument pursued here is a different one: while Austerlitz and Pressburg led to the formal end of the Holy Roman Empire, it continued to function as a form of organizing political authority that was pushed outward globally, and subdued on an inner-European scale. This development was quite informal at times, yet contained elements of quasi-formality as well. It saw its most important bifurcation towards the end of World War II, when a de-legitimization of the global remnant of Empire led to a further intensification of informal empire.

The picture that will be drawn in the following is basically one that turns a picture of one or many disjunctures into a picture of staggered bifurcations. Many of these disjunctures have been criticized as providing either strongly distorted – or at least too simple – accounts of the evolution of the system of world politics in the 'long' nineteenth century. The most prominent motives in this respect are: the replacement of an imperial order by an order of sovereign equality between territorial states; the replacement of a dynastic order of powers by the sovereign nation-state, together with an internal homogenization of states; a global outward-expansion of a European society of states; a proliferation of empires with global reach and a form of colonialism that knew only specific one-way relations of domination and exploitation between imperial cores and peripheries; and, to various degrees interwoven with all of those, a narrative of industrial-economic, but also cultural and political modernization with at first a European, later a Western-Atlantic centre.

Very grossly over-painting the issue for the sake of argument one could say that none of these accounts ever were or are 'wrong', if the criterion for judging that would be faulty, sloppy or 'fake' historiography.[5] However, all can be criticized – and most criticisms arguably are variations of that – for neglecting contexts or failing to put themselves into context, ultimately not reflecting the orders of power and knowledge orders in which they are embedded.

One of the main problems in this context seems to be that most of the relevant storylines here are somewhat stylized. It has been mentioned already that the 'standard' English School account of some kind of one-directional, outward expansion of an essentially European international society (Bull & Watson, 1984) of states has long been challenged. It has been replaced by various accounts of 'globalization' of international society that takes into account both more (regionally) specific stories of the different forms of amalgamation of the orders of Western international society and varying traditions of organizing political authority, as well as the many effects that colonial practices had on European states (cf. Dunne & Reus-Smit, 2017). What this more nuanced account usually does not challenge is that at least for most of the first part of the nineteenth century, most notably between the Congress of Vienna and the Crimean War, there remained a rather pronounced difference between a European and an emerging global system of world politics. The system of world politics, if that is meant to be a social system that operates according to its own routines and (self-)observational schemes – in this case the 'balance of power' – is clearly first and foremost a European system. This system certainly does not form out of nothing, but rather builds on previous scripts, semantics and routinized forms of interaction. However, in terms of systemic evolution, including its formalization, it receives a tremendous boost by the traumatic experiences of possible Napoleonic dominance over Europe, without which the Congress of

[5] I at least leave it to historians to recount the degree to which that also existed.

Vienna would not have taken place. It would be plainly wrong to claim that diverging interests in other parts of the world in terms of influence and colonial possession would have played no role in that context; however, the observational scheme of balance of power remained focused on Europe, the system of world politics being a European one, which does not preclude the existence of a high density and variety of world political interaction beyond Europe.

The story starts to get really interesting, however, if read against the background of the spread and coexistence of different systemic or proto-systemic logics that underpin the ordering principles of (world) politics in this respect. This leads away from the sometimes difficult spatio-temporal connotations of 'expansion' or even 'globalization' accounts, and rather towards these very logics – and it is here that arguably the event, and timing of, Austerlitz and its aftermath was so important: the semantic and symbolic repertoires as well as the forms and intensities of interaction that allowed for the establishment of a specific modern system of world politics in Europe – in which states observed themselves and themselves against others through the observational scheme of balance of power, while otherwise treating themselves as formally equal (the status group of great powers) – where scarcely available to be actualized by imperial powers. That required the 'push' of Napoleon:

> It was the Napoleonic wars, and thus not the American, French, or the Haitian Revolution, that were responsible for the reshaping of the world of empires and nations in the Western Hemisphere and in the extended Europe. (Aydin, 2016: 81)

As Andreas Osiander observes in his critique of the 'standard' IR reading of the origins of a 'Westphalian system', 'the post-1648 Holy Roman Empire, on the one hand, and the seventeenth and eighteenth-century European system surrounding it, on the other hand, do not represent mutually exclusive paradigms. Instead, they are part of a spectrum' (Osiander, 2001: 277). The same holds true for the nineteenth century onwards, yet with a different constellation: the European system of states, on the one hand, and the global empire that first exists in but rudimentary form, on the other hand, are part of a spectrum – although one that particularly at the beginning of the twentieth century tilts extremely towards one end.

To quote Osiander again: 'If the European system as a whole can be called a loose, informal regime with few institutions … the empire was essentially a more developed regime with more elaborate institutions, providing a system of governance for matters of common interest' (Osiander, 2001: 279). If we substitute the form of a globalized empire as a specific form of organizing political authority for the specific (Holy Roman)

Empire that formally came to an end in 1806, then the early nineteenth century, with the particular instance of the Vienna Congress, turned this relation on its head: it was now the great power system (concert) in Europe that emerged as a more developed regime, while the relations between the great powers regarding their overseas interests and possession were more informal. The global empire was, in that sense, in statu nascendi, yet from thereon underwent a remarkable development over the course of a century. In the context of the newly emerging system of world politics, the nineteenth century in this sense was not only the story of the expansion of individual empires with core European states, nor the expansion of an international society. It was also the story of global imperiality as a form of organizing political authority related, but not identical to the territorial state-based order. Probably best symbolized as a collective rather than individual effort in the 1884/85 Berlin Conference on the division of Africa, this form of organizing political authority also included the institutionalization of international regulation of the globe in the late-nineteenth century (e.g. in time zones and a wealth of other 'world'-projects; cf. Krajewski, 2006), as well as, seemingly paradoxically, the global institutional mimicry of the territorial and later nation-state described by sociological neo-institutionalism as the emergence of a 'world polity' (cf. Meyer et al., 1997). Although individual empires exist, the global empire constitutes a distinct form of organizing political authority that mirrors the Holy Roman Empire in the duality of an imperial structure and a variety of different polities, in which the great powers constitute the main principalities. Both the Holy Roman Empire and the global empire address a similar problem, namely that of a lack of a central source of authority and legitimacy beyond individual authorities and sovereigns: the Holy Roman Empire found the solution to the problem of how to govern without the Pope in an Emperor with varying, but generally limited central authority; the global empire found the solution in how to govern without a world state in the United Nations' Security Council with varying, but generally limited general authority. Both require an underlying semantics of unity, the reference to (Western) Christendom on the one hand, and the figure of the 'international community' on the other hand.

Of course, much of what is observed here could be nothing more, and nothing less, than analogies. However, the argument that started with Napoleon and Austerlitz implies that something more might be at stake here, namely isomorphisms between orders old and new. These isomorphisms might best be illustrated by pointing out the two models and narratives that they do not comply to: firstly, they do not comply to the 'standard' IR account that sees world order as an order historically characterized by a more or less neat succession of empires and nation-states (if, that is, the account does not ignore empires altogether; cf. Stetter, 2019). Secondly, it also does not fully comply to the 'modified' account, which also provides the gist for the present book that largely retains a view of an exclusive relation between empires and nation-states, but sees them as being historically entangled in many ways, and that acknowledges that many (if not most) empires of the past live an afterlife in the present (arguments here ranging from the structuring effects of the Roman Empire in contemporary world politics (cf. Neumann & Nexon, 2018), to the continuation of the French one in the form of 'La Françafrique' (cf. Schlichte, 1998). In contrast to these two accounts, the argument here is to see empire as a form of organizing political authority that allows for a high degree of inclusivity as well. While most empires to varying degrees were inclusive in the sense that they had to find different arrangements for accommodating other forms of (locally) organizing political authority, an extreme degree of inclusivity was probably the hallmark of the Holy Roman Empire. It is this high degree of inclusivity that was copied into an emerging modern system of world politics that ironically received an evolutionary boost through an anti-imperial (i.e. anti-Napoleonic) moment. The Congress of Vienna laid the foundations of an order that permitted the emergence of a system of world politics in which territorial (and later nation-) statehood always coexisted with imperial/colonial forms of organizing political authority, only to see the 'governance function' of specific empires gradually replaced by international organizations in the late nineteenth and during the twentieth centuries. It is in this bold sense that one could argue that it was the great powers and the anti-imperial, anti-Napoleonic coalition that rescued some of the organizational logic of the Holy Roman Empire seemingly ended by Napoleon, and implanted it deeply in the DNA of the modern system of world politics.[6]

The Holy Roman Empire disappears in Europe as a result of Napoleon's victory, yet its ordering logic is gradually transformed and transferred to the global realm that is organized as network of colonial relations. It is in this sense that territorial-cum-national statism has always been more successful in displacing global (and individual) imperiality in historical

[6] This global empire is similar to the form of the 'global state' that Martin Shaw describes in his *Theory of the Global State* (Shaw, 2000), yet the argument here is that it continues the organizational logics of the Empire, with elements of state-formation being only rudimentary ('world statehood without a state'; cf. Albert & Stichweh, 2007). It should be emphasized that all this is about empire as a form of organizing political authority within the system of world politics, not about 'empire' as a pervasive societal ordering principle in the sense of Hardt and Negri (2000).

narrative rather than structurally (cf. Wilson, 2016: 667–78). This global empire paired with de facto coloniality continues until the present day, but its highly specific form is little or not at all captured by the post-colonial literature: it is a global ordering logic within the system of world politics that continues an evolutionary trajectory in that system (and this is first of all nothing else but a description of the existence of a form of organizing political authority; its normative assessment would be the subject of another contribution).

6 Conclusion

This chapter started with Austerlitz and presented a specific evolutionary account. Although this shares some similarities with event history (cf. Sewell, 2005), it could probably better be seen as the reconstruction of a specific evolutionary trajectory that simply starts with but one major selection in its history, although the trajectory could always be prolonged to before the event (cf. Brunkhorst, 2014 on this understanding of social evolution). The contribution that this chapter attempted to make in the context of the present volume is both about 'what' account is given and about 'how' it is given. The 'what' clearly pertains to the task of giving a more differentiated account regarding empire and coloniality than has become usual in simple accounts that tend to think in terms of global dyads rather than in a multiplicity of forms, levels, and regions. What this contribution has sought to argue is that empire comes in a variety of guises and organizational forms, but that varying logics of empire manifest themselves in different evolutionary trajectories and are embedded in the very historicity of contemporary forms of organizing political authority. As far as the link between imperialism and colonialism is concerned, it serves as a reminder that not only is colonialism not a uniform historical practice, but also European colonialism consists of practices that quite often emerged against the background of colonial practice within Europe before their global 'export'. Regarding the 'how', I would claim that the particular way of presenting the argument chosen in this contribution is to argue that while appreciating the inevitable historicity (*Geschichtlichkeit*) of the social world, recounting evolutionary trajectories is about providing stories about the presence of the past. These stories can be debated and scrutinized as being more plausible or less, they are necessarily open-ended and can be retold in different guises. Yet they ultimately remind us that when taking account of the presence of the past, it might just be possible to have an appreciation of historicity without having to ascribe a meaning to history (in this sense, a *Geschichtlichkeit* and its 'modes' of historicity without *Geschichtsphilosophie*).

References

Albert, M. (2016). *A Theory of World Politics*, Cambridge: Cambridge University Press.

Albert, M. & Stichweh, R. (2007). *Weltstaat und Weltstaatlichkeit: Beobachtungen globaler politischer Strukturbildung*, Wiesbaden: VS Verlag.

Albert, M., Brunkhorst, H., Neumann, I.B. & Stetter, S. (2023). *The Social Evolution of World Politics*, Bielefeld: transcript.

Aydin, C. (2016). Regionen und Reiche in der politischen Geschichte des langen 19. Jahrhunderts (1750–1924), in S. Conrad & J. Osterhammel (eds.). *Geschichte der Welt: Wege zur modernen Welt 1750–1870*, 35–253, Munich: C.H. Beck.

Berger, S. & Miller, A. (2015). Building Nations in and with Empires: A Reassessment, in S. Berger & A. Miller (eds.). *Nationalizing Empires*, Budapest: CEU Press.

Brunkhorst, H. (2014). *Critical Theory of Legal Revolutions: Evolutionary Perspectives*, New York: Bloomsbury Academic.

Bull, H. & Watson, A. (eds.) (1984). *The Expansion of International Society*, Oxford: Clarendon Press.

Dunne, T. & Reus-Smit, C. (eds.) (2017). *The Globalization of International Society*, Oxford: Oxford University Press.

Hardt, M. & Negri, A. (2000). *Empire*, Cambridge: Harvard University Press.

Krajewski, M. (2006). *Restlosigkeit: Weltprojekte um 1900*, Frankfurt: Fischer Taschenbuch Verlag.

Meyer, J. W., Boli, J., Thomas, G. M. & Ramirez, F. O. (1997). World Society and the Nation-State, *American Journal of Sociology*, 103(1), 144–81.

Münkler, H. (2007). *Empires: The Logic of World Domination from Ancient Rome to the United States*, Cambridge: Polity Press.

Münkler, H. (2019). Imperiale Ordnung. Die Governance-Leistung von Imperien, in E. M. Hausteiner & S. Huhnholz (eds.). *Imperien verstehen. Theorien, Typen, Transformationen*, 71–99, Baden-Baden: Nomos.

Neumann, I. B. & Nexon, D. H. (2018). Hegemonic-Order Theory: A Field-Theoretic Account, *European Journal of International Relations*, 24(3), 662–86.

Nipperdey, T. (1983). *Deutsche Geschichte 1800–1866: Bürgerwelt und starker Staat*, Munich: C.H. Beck.

Osiander, A. (2001). Sovereignty, International Relations, and the Westphalian Myth, *International Organization*, 55(2), 251–87.

Reinhart, W. (2015). Introduction, in W. Reinhart (ed.). *Empires and Encounters: 1350–1750*, 30–52, Cambridge: Harvard University Press.

Schlichte, K. (1998). La Françafrique: Postkolonialer Habitus und Klientelismus in der französischen Afrikapolitik, *Zeitschrift für Internationale Beziehungen*, 5(2), 309–43.

Sewell, W. H. Jr. (2005). *Logics of History: Social Theory and Social Transformation*, Chicago: University of Chicago Press.

Shaw, M. (2000). *Theory of the Global State: Globality as Unfinished Revolution*, Cambridge: Cambridge University Press.

Singer, J. D. (1961). The Level-of-Analysis Problem in International Relations, *World Politics*, 14(1), 77–92.

Stetter, S. (2019). Das Imperium schlägt (immer wieder) zurück: Imperien, Kolonialismus und Postkolonialismus im politischen System der Weltgesellschaft, in E. M. Hausteiner & S. Huhnholz (eds.). *Imperien verstehen. Theorien, Typen, Transformationen*, 255–77, Baden-Baden: Nomos.

Werner, M. & Zimmermann, B. (2002). Vergleich, Transfer, Verflechtung. Der Ansatz der Histoire croisée und die Herausforderung des Transnationalen, *Geschichte und Gesellschaft*, 28(4), 607–36.

Wilson, P. H. (2016). *The Holy Roman Empire: A Thousand Years of Europe's History*, London: Allen Lane.

Part II

Historical Sociology and the Imperial Fundaments of International Politics

8 The Afterlives of Empires

Notes towards an Investigation

George Steinmetz

1 Introduction

Empires have been the dominant forms of political rule for most of the past two millennia. Each time empires have declined or disappeared, there have been aftershocks and lasting legacies. Historians, literary and cultural analysts, and social scientists have explored the afterlives in colonialism as expressed in artefacts, melancholia, and nostalgia (Auslander & Holt, 2003; Gilroy, 2005; Hall & Rose, 2006; Steinmetz & Hell, 2006). This makes an archaeological excavation of the traces of empire more challenging but also more rewarding. These after-effects have also been occluded, overshadowed, and repressed. Yet this should not dissuade us. As Freud argued, and as contemporary neuroscience demonstrates, unconscious emotions do exist, and they can be studied (Kringelbach & Berridge, 2010). The unconscious may interfere with, or counteract, rational, conscious thought. Uncovering or disclosing hidden or invisible social structures is the very essence of science, including social science.[1]

This chapter is an attempt to survey the various ways in which present social life is permeated with colonial and imperial ideas, tropes, images, practices, and ruins.[2] My main focus is Europe, the metropole of the world's greatest modern colonial empires. I will also touch on imperial afterlives in the former European colonies and the United States. The problem of imperial afterlives has to be posed somewhat differently in the American case, where empire cannot yet be spoken of entirely in the

[1] This is contrary to authors who cast epistemological and even political and ethical aspersions on what they call 'depth hermeneutics', or the scientific practice of uncovering causal factors in accounting for empirical processes. In philosophical terms, this is an empiricist argument that seems to take issue with reality itself for being complexly layered, rather than ontologically flat. A related critique works by mistranslating Mannheim's term *enthüllen* as 'unmasking' (*entmasken* in German) or as 'unveiling' (*entschleiern* in German), rather than as the more straightforward 'uncovering'. This allows Baehr (2019), for example, to characterize the *enthüllen* approach as 'conspiratorial' and 'paranoid', and to assimilate it to a surveillance operation.

[2] For an overview of the study of ruins, including imperial ruins, cf. Hell and Schönle (2010).

past tense. Yet European colonialism and American imperialism have been connected in ways that give a special salience to the problem of imperial afterlives and central modes of historicity – such as the role of history in shaping reality (mode 1) and non-linear pathways (mode 6) outlined by Schlichte and Stetter in the introduction, but also the central role of the observer (mode 3) and the linkage of history and power (mode 5). Anti-imperialist and anticolonial ideas have circulated back and forth across the Atlantic. European colonial developmentalism and American modernization theory emerged in the same post-war period and addressed the same global regions, but while the first approach was premised on a continuing European colonial rule, the second was premised on a new world of legally independent states under the less formal umbrella of US hegemony (Cooper, 2004).

2 Europe, the United States and the Global South as (Post)Imperial Spaces

Empire's legacies are everywhere. European imperial leaders have been motivated by the Roman example and fixated on scenarios of Roman decline (Hell, 2009; 2019). And Modern Europe, according to Fanon (1961: 58), 'is literally the creation of the Third World'. At the same time, according to historian Pirenne, without the expansion of the Islamic empires in the eighth century, 'the Frankish Empire would probably never have existed and Charlemagne, without Mahomet, would be inconceivable' (Pirenne, [1927] 2014: 17; 1937). According to Hall (1996: 246), colonialism 'was never simply external to the societies of the imperial metropolis' but was 'always deeply inscribed within them'. The United States is the creation of its former slaves, a settler colonial state squatting on Indian lands, and a fading global empire. Historian Williams (1944) argued that 'slavery and the European slave trade provided the capital that financed the Industrial Revolution in England' (Tomich, 2015: 172).

The remnants of empire are ubiquitous, if one cares to look. Practices of science, law, architecture, engineering, religion, trace back to the Roman Republic and Empire. European languages bear the marks of the *Lingua Imperii* and *Lingua Coloniae* (to paraphrase Victor Klemperer). Words like empire, colony, protectorate, indigeneity, modernization, development, slavery and race have partly or exclusively imperial origins, and conjure up echoes of colonialism. The last explicitly colonial exhibition took place in Bordeaux as recently as 1950 (Lanxade, 1947), and museums of ethnography and non-western art preserved the spirit of the colonial fairs. Imperialism lives on in monuments and in the names of sports teams and mascots (Fenelon, 2017), streets, military bases, and towns, such as the villages that originated as resettlement camps for uprooted peasants created by the French army during the Algerian War of Independence. Ruins and artefacts of empire are strewn across former imperial domains, from the Palmyra archaeological site in Syria to the Varus Battle site in Kalkriese, Germany, to the abandoned Soviet and US military sites scattered throughout the world.

The afterlives of empire are not always as immediately visible as in a statue or street name, however, but often have a more spectral existence. This is perhaps especially true in places where genuine imperial politics have been out of reach for a longer time, such as Germany, Belgium and the Netherlands, or in the former Spanish and Portuguese colonies in the Americas, its cities filled with decaying colonial architecture and 'cholera', in the famous description by Gabriel García Márquez. Empire does not appear in explicit government policies or public statements but in euphemized, hidden, surreptitious forms. Large swaths of colonial and imperial history have been completely forgotten or repressed by both specialists and laypeople (Eckert, 2018).

This repression of imperial memory has several different sources.[3] In the decades after WWII, a vast number of Europeans were employed in numerous functions and professions in the overseas colonies, as colonial administrations engaged in developmentalism and social and educational policies. Yet the activities of these colonial experts were subjected to wholesale forgetting, as colonialism became distasteful to educated Europeans virtually overnight – just as Nazism quickly became taboo for respectable Germans after 7 May 1945. Forms of research that had been pioneered in the colonies were quietly terminated or brought under the control of postcolonial governments, or they were transferred to the metropoles, where their colonial origins were swept under the rug. Histories of French and British sociology written after 1960, for example, ignored colonial social research altogether (Steinmetz, 2013; 2017; 2023a).

The need to look beneath the surface may be even more urgent in the case of US imperial politics. The United States remains a colonial power today vis-a-vis its own indigenous populations, and it is routinely described as such by Native Americans. Paternalistic and denigrating

[3] Stoler (2011) rejects the psychoanalytic terms *amnesia* and *repression* in this context in favour of 'aphasia', but this term is more problematic: it comes from the natural sciences, and it has a *linguistic* emphasis, whereas repressed material also takes non-linguistic, embodied, emotional, visual and material forms. The word aphasia also elides the key *moral* dimension in discussions of forgetting (Ricoeur, 2004: 412–56). On strategic collective amnesia, the sociological counterpart to repressed individual memory in psychoanalysis, cf. Dimbath (2011).

symbols of Native Americans are still found in the names of sports teams, university secret societies, mass culture and everyday expressions. That said, the American empire has also been a 'hidden' one (Immerwahr, 2019). The US maintained systematic linkages to European imperial outposts in Africa via the trans-Atlantic slave trade, but US foreign policy was focused on the western hemisphere, as codified in the 1823 Monroe Doctrine. The United States was absent in the Scramble for Africa, although American marines joined the campaign against the Chinese Boxer Rebellion. The US annexed a scattering of formal colonies in the Spanish-American War, but again, this colonial mini-empire was short-lived and not widely acknowledged – however important it was for the inhabitants of the Philippines and Puerto Rico (Go, 2008). After World War Two, the US ascended to the role of global hegemon (Wallerstein, 2003), and contributed financially and politically to propping up the European colonial empires, giving 'the old imperialism ... a new lease on life' (Worsley, 1960: 106; Louis, 1977). In 1955, the US stayed away from the Bandung Conference to avoid 'complicat[ing] relations with European allies' (Parker, 2006: 886), but the following year the US thwarted the effort by France, the UK and Israel to stop Nasser's nationalization of the Suez Canal, pushing European colonialism closer to the brink. As European power faded, the US quickly moved to assume a leadership position across the previously colonized world. Ernest Gellner described this transition in Morocco near the end of the French Protectorate, observing that while Morocco was still 'a colonial territory' with France as the 'occupying, "protecting" power', the US position vis-à-vis France was becoming 'a bit analogous to the position the French hold vis-à-vis the Moroccans (if not, why should there be American bases in the French Empire?)'[4] An analogous passage from French colonialism to American imperialism occurred in Vietnam, as the Americans shifted moved from providing military assistance to the French and the Republic of Vietnam to sending in its own ground troops.

American imperialism also served to screen European memories of their recent colonial empires, as is suggested again by the Vietnamese example. After the French loss of Indochina in 1956, 75 per cent of the French population still affirmed in polls that it was 'very important' or 'pretty important' (*assez important*) that the colonies remained tied to France (Ageron, 1986: 46). The outspoken opposition of intellectuals like Sartre, Aron, and Bourdieu against the Algerian war does

[4] Gellner, 'Quatorze Juillet in Rabat', undated (1954), p. 2. Gellner papers, LSE, Correspondence, box 26.

not gainsay the fact that anticolonialism remained politically 'marginal' among the French through the end of the colonial era (Liauzu, 2007: 196). Opposition to the American war in Vietnam by French students and the French Left was a different story. The 1968 revolt began with Nanterre students' agitation against American imperialism in Vietnam (Duteuil, 1988). During an Anticolonial Day in the Latin Quarter on 21 February 1968, 'thousands marched, chanted, sang, and hanged and burned a giant effigy of Lyndon B. Johnson' (Keenan, 2018: 253). American imperialism and European (post)colonialism have been connected in unexpected ways.

The traces of the colonial past are most pervasive in the global South. According to Tunisian sociologist Elbaki Hermassi (1978: 250), 'there is general agreement among theoreticians that the structural defects of peripheral economies and societies result from their positions and roles within the capitalist world system.' This is confirmed by Samir Amin, Immanuel Wallerstein, and many others. Consider just a few examples. French and British policies of divide and conquer exacerbated Arab rivalries in the Middle East and contributed to the ongoing war in Syria (Fildis, 2011; Neep, 2012). The apartheid-era Bantustans in South Africa were the result of British and Afrikaner policies of indirect rule, and while the Bantustans were dismantled after the end of colonialism in 1994 and were reincorporated into the unified South African state, they still play disruptive political roles. In Namibia, German and South African colonial interventions sharpened the distinctness and salience of identities such as Ovaherero and Berg Damara (Steinmetz, 2007). German interventions in Rwanda before 1914 and Belgian policies afterwards accentuated the ethnic division between Tutsi and Hutu (Bindseil, 1988). Even more immediately destructive colonial aftereffects can be found in Algeria, where unexploded bombs from the French war continue to injure and kill people decades later (Larba, 2005). One might anticipate that the afterlives of empire are easier to perceive in the global South. Yet here too, certain aspects of the colonial past are obscured.

In sum, Europe is a descendent of the Roman Empire, an indirect product of the Arab empires of the Middle Ages, and the creation of its overseas colonies, including the slave plantation economies of the New World. The United States is a settler colony, squatting on Indian lands, and a declining global empire, whose imperial activities continue to wreak havoc worldwide. As recently as 1945, 'more than one-third of the world's inhabitants, occupying more than one-third of the land space of the globe' (Du Bois, 2007: 261), lived in colonies, and another large percentage lived in the European colonizing nations and the settler colonies with internal indigenous subject populations. Today, more than half of the member states in the United Nations are direct descendants of European colonialism, in addition to the seventeen Non-Self-Governing Territories recognized by the UN.[5]

It is therefore clear that we need to cast a wide net in defining our object. This excavation of meaning needs to include not just immediately visible signs but unacknowledged, hidden, euphemized, repressed and forgotten aspects of empire as well. We need to examine the resonances of remote historical periods, reaching back to the Roman Empire and beyond, together with more recent periods. We need to examine present-day imperialism and colonialism, since memory traces are not permanent, but are constantly being reconfigured. The rest of this chapter will try to organize this investigation, while providing some examples of the economic, political, legal, social and cultural aftereffects of empire in these diverse geospaces.

3 Economic After-effects of Empire

Generations of scholars of underdevelopment have detailed the ways in which parts of the world that were conquered by European colonizers continue to suffer from the effects of foreign rule. An entire generation of Francophone social scientists who began working on late-colonial Africa turned to the study of development and underdevelopment following decolonization (Samir Amin, Charles Bettelheim, Claudine Chaulet, Jean Cuisenier, René Dumont, Yves Goussault, Louis-Joseph Lebret, Pierre Marthelot, François Perroux, etc.). Immanuel Wallerstein's world system theory, which grew partly out of engagement with these French scholars, is premised on the argument that the global periphery remains peripheral by virtue of its consignment to production of raw materials (cf. Kohli, 2004; Mahoney, 2010). Slavery predated modern colonialism but took its harshest forms where the subjugation of enslaved laborers was combined with colonial practices of conquest and exploitation (Patterson, 1982).[6] Colonial-era slavery continues to structure some of the most pervasive inequalities in the Americas and the Caribbean (Wilderson, 2020).

[5] We should also consider the former colonies of Japan in East Asia and Oceania as well as internal colonialism vis-a-vis indigenous people in Russia, Israel, various Latin American countries, postcolonial Indonesia and of course, the other former British settler colonies, from South Africa to New Zealand; Han (1995); Chae (2006).

[6] Patterson describes the brutality of slavery in colonial Jamaica in his novel *Die the Long Day* (Patterson, 1972) and a slew of other publications (Greenland & Steinmetz, 2019).

4 Political and Legal After-effects of Empire

The International Order was an Imperial Order concerned with Great Power prerogatives (Simpson, 2004; Hobson, 2012; Lawson & Tardelli, 2013). International law's classical problem was to explain how order is created among sovereign states through inter-imperial cooperation. Colonies were denied statehood and sovereignty, and were therefore excluded from IR theory (Anghie, 2004: 3; Müller, this volume). Third-world sovereignty is thus distinctive in terms of its historical origins and is uniquely vulnerable and dependent. Lawson also suggests (this volume), however, that the basic patterns today are different from the colonial period due to an attenuation of divided sovereignty and the assumption of human inequality based on racism and the standard of civilization. Yet Lawson acknowledges that some of the old relations are also still present, for example in some of the forms of interventionism by core countries and the UN.

Colonialism has also shaped European states directly and indirectly. The very existence of the French Fifth Republic is due to the division within the French political class and public opinion around the Algerian War and the question of Algerian independence. Another example is the so-called 'Hottentot election' on 1907 in Germany, resulting from the Emperor's dissolution of the *Reichstag* after the majority voted to refuse further funding for the genocidal war against the Nama in Southwest Africa. The SPD lost thirty-eight of its eighty-one seats in the Reichstag as a result. The distant colonial war contributed to the genesis of the First World War by breaking the Socialists' previous momentum towards an absolute majority. Of course, Du Bois (2007) argued that both of the world wars of the twentieth century were codetermined by inter-imperial rivalry.

The very existence of many African states and nationalisms is the direct result of colonialism. This includes the names, national languages and borders of states, which often divide pre-existing polities, communities and economic and environmental unities. The remote border between the Burundi section of German East Africa and the Belgian Congo (Louis, 1963), which is still an international border, was defined through international negotiations and marked in the landscape to show where one coloniser's sovereignty gave way to another's (Figure 8.1). Miles's (1994) comparison of the long-term effects of French and British colonialism on both sides of the Niger–Nigeria border demonstrates the lasting effects of two different systems of rule on a single culture. On the one hand, Hausa villagers on the Nigeria–Niger border 'do not place their ethnic identity as Hausas above their national one as citizens of Nigeria or Niger and express greater affinity for non-Hausa co-citizens than foreign Hausas' (Miles & Rochefort, 1991: 401). On the other

Figure 8.1 Border Marker Belgian Kongo – German West Africa

hand, Hausa on the French and British sides of the border differ sharply in terms of the status, prestige and influence of traditional Hausa chiefs, which is lower in postcolonial Niger; in the practices of education, where there is a greater schism between educated elite and illiterate commoners among the Hausa of Niger; in religion, which is more subordinated to the state in Niger; in the local governing style, which is more militaristic governing on the Niger side; and in terms of nationalism, which is more important on the Niger side, and ethnic identity, more pronounced on the Nigeria side (Miles, 1994: 53, 111, 143, 246, 248).

Modern colonialism was defined first and foremost as a structure of foreign political domination and administration based on the *rule of difference* (Chatterjee, 1993), which divided the colonizers from the colonized in legal, social, cultural and economic terms. Colonial rulers frequently employed the principle of *divide and rule,* dividing the colonized against one another. This pattern of systematic, structured, proliferating social division permeated colonial states and societies at all levels, even if division was punctually undercut by resistance, governmental ineptitude, pragmatic adjustments and the breaking of rules.

Administrative and governing structures were bequeathed to the independent nations, along with a 'derivative' political discourse of nationalism (Chatterjee, 1986; cf. Balandier, 1952; Busia, 1956). Postcolonial societies inherited European-derived *state-cultures* (Steinmetz, 1999), as Mathur (2016) demonstrates in a case study in northern India and Miles (1994) in the cases of Nigeria and Niger. Prior (2020) analyses the effects of British approaches to governance on the rise of the 'strong man' leader type in Africa. Public and administrative law were carried forward from the colonial era. Basic categories of legal belonging and citizenship are traceable in many instances to the codification of customary law under colonial rule and the politics of Indirect Rule. Berda (2014) shows that administrative structures and institutional practices inherited from British colonial rule shape the trajectories of democratic states in Cyprus, India/Pakistan and Palestine/Israel. She focuses specifically on the ways legal and administrative tools used to control populations during conflicts and emergencies diffused throughout the British Empire, and how these imperial practices of security and surveillance shaped government practice in the independent successor states.

Additional connections between colonial and postcolonial politics can be found in the realm of parliamentary and electoral systems, political parties, and social movements. As many observers pointed out in the 1950s and 1960s, 'nationalism in the colonies starts by being anti-European; it is nevertheless itself European' (Busia, 1956: 4). Balandier demonstrated that African nationalism emerged within new messianic churches across Africa, and that it involved protest 'not just against religious depossession but [was also] a total reaction of Bantu peoples against the situation created by white colonisers' (Balandier, 1952: 66). Balandier traced the reciprocal relations between messianic movements and new African political parties in Gabon and the French Congo (Balandier, 1950: 103–4; Balandier, 1985: 466). Many of these churches and political parties still exist. In postcolonial Hong Kong, residents have embraced laws and institutions imposed by their former British colonisers in mainland Chinese rule. In Samoa, some of the institutions introduced by the German colonizers, such as the Land and Titles Court, have been maintained in the postcolonial state and are appreciated by many Samoans. German colonial anthropologist Augustin Krämer's *The Samoa Islands* remains in print (in English) more than a century after its original publication (1902–1903) and is regarded by many Samoans as a crucial reference work on their old traditions (Steinmetz, 2007). In the New Zealand parliament, there are currently seven dedicated seats for Māori representatives, a system that originated with the Maori Representation Act of 1867, which created the first four seats, in an effort to stabilise the Maori (Armitage, 1995: 143; Hess, 2018).

Domestic politics in the imperial metropoles were sometimes reconfigured by empire and empire's loss. Many writers have detailed the ways empires influenced European monarchies, churches, armies and navies and domestic politics. Hobson, Hobhouse and other liberals discussed the corrosive effects of empire on British democracy; Césaire (2000: 36) discussed the 'colonial boomerang' in France; Johnson (2004) discussed imperial 'blowback' in the US. Once European countries lost their colonies, other reactions set in. In Weimar Germany, for example, the responses to the loss of colonies due to the Versailles Treaty ranged from colonial irredentism and propaganda to nostalgia and melancholy. Responses also encompassed new forms of anticolonialism in the

German pacificist movement and the Berlin-based international League against Cruelties and Oppression in the Colonies (*Liga gegen Kolonialgreuel und Unterdrückung, renamed Liga gegen Imperialismus*), whose first congress in 1927 brought together anti-imperialists from 57 different countries and colonies (Steinmetz 2023b). In Germany, most of the statues of colonial heroes were erected after the loss of the colonies in WWI (Zeller, 2000). The colonial lobby successfully pushed for the creation in 1934 of an Office of Colonial Policy (*Kolonialpolitisches Amt*), whose futile aim was the reacquisition and administration of the lost colonies. Others simply mourned the loss of empire. Stefan Zweig recalled that Austria after WWI seemed an 'uncertain, gray, and lifeless shadow of the former imperial monarchy' (Zweig, 1944: 322). German settlers who were left over in Southwest Africa after WWI maintained a melancholy theater of their colonial past by assiduously maintaining an archipelago of German ruins and monuments in the African landscape. These ritualistic practices seemed to refuse to acknowledge their loss of power (Steinmetz, 2010).

In much of Europe, foreign aid, investment and political and military support still move along tracks laid down during the colonial epoch. This is obvious in the case of France, where the doctrine of *Françafrique* is explicit, and where military interventions in former French colonies continue up to the present. Some of the 'irrationalities' of French elite policy vis-à-vis Francophone Africa can only be understood in terms of a political habitus inherited from the colonial era (Schlichte, 1998). Germany is more surprising example of this, since it lost its overseas colonies so long ago. The small and sparsely populated African country of Namibia receives the highest per capita foreign aid of all countries in Africa from the German government.[7] This is a direct result of the widespread belief within the German political class in recent decades that German colonialism in Namibia was particularly brutal, and that some form of reparation is in order.

Colonial-era economic and cultural patterns also persist in the realm of tourism (Zytnicki & Kazdaghli, 2009). A quantitative study of tourism in fifty-six states found that 'residents of Europe and America show a preference for travel to destinations with strong historical/political ties and an equally strong aversion to travel to jurisdictions where no such connection exists', and that 'destinations rely heavily on former colonizers as a key source of visitors'. This is especially true of Dutch and French tourists (McKercher & Decosta, 2007: 453). Some analysts argue that the emphasis on tourism in former colonies distorts their economic development (Hall & Tucker, 2004), while others offer blueprints for sustainable forms of tourism (Carrigan, 2011). Critics argue that western tourists engage in

[7] German Development Cooperation with Namibia. https://windhuk.diplo.de/na-en/themen/dt-entwicklungszusammenarbeit/1050588

practices reminiscent of colonial relations (Sèbe, 2020). Others try to reimagine tourism in 'engaged' and 'anticolonial' guises (Vanden Boer, 2016; Aikau & Gonzalez, 2019). The Plantation Leyritz hotel in Martinique offers its mainly French tourists the opportunity to stay in former slave quarters (Stallings & Sullivan, 2007: 541), although it is unclear whether the tourists realize they are signing up for this when they book their vacation.

5 Lasting Social Effects of Colonialism

Social structures were radically transformed by colonialism, and many of these changes have persisted. In colonial Africa, Asia, and Oceania, tribes were circumscribed, reified, and invented out of whole cloth. Family structures were redefined directly by policy and indirectly by the perpetual, seething crises induced by colonialism. Balandier's studies in Gabon and Congo found that age and family structures in villages had been dramatically altered by the migration of young men to sites of European employment, and that female migrants to Brazzaville had escaped from customary gender roles (Balandier, 1955; 1985). Nearly the entire Samoan population became literate in the first decades of the 19th century as a result of the London Missionary Society's emphasis on literacy as a condition for membership in the church (Wilkes, 1845: vol. 2, 79). Religion was completely transformed by colonialism. In some places, missionaries and government officials violently suppressed entire religions (Clendinnen, 1987). Elsewhere missionaries sanctioned practices seen as 'fetishistic', and colonial states outlawed practices judged abhorrent to European sensibilities, as in the so-called repugnancy test (Mann & Roberts, 1991: 3–58). The French banned polygamy in some sub-Saharan African colonies while organizing government madrasas in their North African colonies and leaving polygamy untouched in Tunisia (Aron, 1957). Syncretic religions emerged throughout the colonial world in response to western contact, missionary cajoling and colonial policing, and these religions were studied by social scientists, starting with Leenhardt (1902) at the turn of the previous century; Herskovits, Bastide and Balandier in the middle decades of the twentieth century (Steinmetz, 2023a), and Jean and John Comaroff in the 1990s (Comaroff & Comaroff, 1991–1997).

Colonialism laid down the basic paths of migration from the global South to the North. Networks of colonial migrants emerged before independence (Banton, 1955; Montagne, 1957; Sayad & Gillette, 1976). This led theorists to analyse metropolitan race relations using colonial categories in the 1950s (Rex, 1959: 124). Since decolonization, migrants from the global South have been channelled disproportionately towards their former metropoles, for legal and linguistic reasons, although this relationship has weakened over time.

6 Imperial Cultural Hangovers

Most former colonies do not have a museum of the colonial era. This is understandable, since much of this memory is traumatic. The Herero of Botswana, whose ancestors were driven out by the Germans during the 1904 war, exhibit signs of trauma in recounting their national past (Durham, 1993). Yet some intellectuals argue that the colonial era is so important that it should be dealt with in public museums (Tharoor, 2017).

Countries across the Global South have had to deliberate what to do with monuments and commemorative structures left over from the colonial era (Çelik, 2019). At one extreme is the Republic of Congo, where the remains of Pierre Savorgnan de Brazza, the French explorer who founded Brazzaville, are housed on the banks of the Congo River in a white marble mausoleum with a museum, sculpture garden, and statue (Gettleman, 2006). It is rare, however, that former colonies bestow such honour on their colonizers. In Namibia, a bronze equestrian statue was left in Windhoek by the Germans and loomed over the capital city until 2014 (Figure 8.2). The cavalryman, unveiled in 1912, represented a commoner rather than a nobleman, but many Namibians believed

Figure 8.2 Equestrian statute Windhoek

Figure 8.3 Statue of Sam Nujoma

that it represented General Lothar von Trotha, who personally ordered the genocide of the Namibian Herero in 1904. What is undisputed is that the monument represents a 'general attitude of triumph over the vanquished Africans' (Koessler, 2015: 152). The memorial was finally demolished in 2013 and the statue moved into the courtyard of the old German fortress (Koessler, 2015: 148). It was replaced by a statue of Namibia's first president, Sam Nujoma, holding a copy of the Constitution of the Republic of Namibia in his hand, in front of a new Independence Memorial Museum (Figure 8.3). In 2022, Nambians finally removed the statue of Curt von François from the main street in the capital, Windhoek. Von François was the former military commander and imperial commissary of the German colony, who had massacred Witbooi women and children in 1893 (Steinmetz, 2007: 151–52).[8]

[8] Estimates of the number of Witbooi killed at Hornkrans on April 12 range from 80 to 150. The low estimate is from Lieutenant von François's telegram of April 12 in BA-Berlin, RKA, vol. 1483, p. 9. The high estimate is from Lieutenant Kurd Schwabe (1899, p. 35; 1910, p. 39). Missionary Olpp received a report from a Witbooi that was "so trustworthy that I can give the names of the fallen, wounded, and imprisoned"; the number of dead was 85 women and children and 10 men (VEM, RMG 1.404, p. 61).

It is difficult even to descry many of the traces of empire in the metropoles. One of the most powerful explorations of the hidden nature of French colonialism is the 2005 film *Caché* (*Hidden*) by the Austrian filmmaker Michael Hanecke. *Caché* examines an upper-middle class Parisian couple whose lives are disrupted by the eruption of long-suppressed memories having to do with events during the Algerian War, including the murder by the French police of a large number of protestors of Arab origin in Paris on 17 October 1961.

Some colonial traces in the metropoles have been transformed or removed. In Germany, public monuments and artworks commemorating colonial and imperialist actors, and even a slave trader, still exist, but in many cases, they have been contextualized or stored out of sight. Streets have been renamed, starting with Von Trotha Strasse in Munich, which became Hererostrasse in 2006. In 2010, a riverfront in Berlin's Kreuzberg district named after Otto Friedrich von der Groeben, who in the late 17th century founded the Brandenburg-Prussian slave trading colony in Ghana, was renamed after a German African writer, May Ayim. In December 2020, the Berlin Senate voted to change its *Strassengesetz* to permit the renaming of streets named 'glorify or make light of colonial injustice', in pursuit of an earlier Senate vote to accelerate the decolonization of public space.[9]

The terracotta relief sculptures of colonized African soldiers in Hamburg (Figure 8.4) represent a singularly obscure set of colonial traces. These large sculptures were hidden behind the gates of the Lettow-Vorbeck military barracks in Hamburg from their creation in 1938 until the closing of the barracks in 1992. They were thus viewed by generations of German soldiers, but rarely by the public.[10] In 2002, the Askari monuments were re-erected in a small, gated 'Tanzania Park' in Hamburg, which was initially described as a tribute to international understanding between Germany and Tanzania. Protests against this whitewashing of colonial history led to the installation of explanatory plaques in German, English, and Swahili (Möhle, 2007). Yet the monument is still difficult to access, as it was when I spent an entire day trying to get into the gated park to see it (Steinmetz, 2009).

[9] Berlin Senatskanzlei, 'Umbenennung von Straßen mit Kolonial-Namen wird vereinfacht', Pressemitteilung vom 01.12.2020. www.berlin.de/rbmskzl/aktuelles/pressemitteilungen/2020/pressemitteilung.1024065.php. Berlin's residents can be forgiven for not focusing on renaming the streets 'Lans' and 'Iltis' in the Dahlem district, which commemorate Naval Captain Wilhelm Lans and the warship Iltis, which Lans commanded in the imperialist campaign against the Chinese Boxer Rebellion in 1900.

[10] Other imperial traces inside the barracks include a 'Trotha House', embellished with a bas-relief portrait of the notorious general who initiated the genocidal war against the Namibian Hereo in 1904, and a stele memorializing troops who fell in colonial wars.

Figure 8.4 Askari relief by von Ruckteschell

An even more colonial *lieu de mémoire* in Germany is entirely invisible: this is the site of Berlin Africa Conference of 1884–1885, which set down the ground rules for the division of Africa among the European powers. This crucial event took place in the *Reichskanzlei* (Imperial Chancellery), which was destroyed after 1945 except for the underground *Führerbunker* complex, which was itself largely eliminated after 1989 (Figures 8.5 and 8.6). When artist Yinka Shonibare recreated the Africa conference in a life-size installation in Berlin in 2010, it had to be installed in a nearby Prussian church, as the original venue was long gone (Figure 8.7).

Another example of an entirely invisible imperial legacy is the site of the 1896 Berlin Industrial or Trade Exposition (*Gewerbeausstellung*), which included an exhibit of the German colonial empire, complete with live subjects from most of the colonies (Steinmetz, 2017a). The 1896 fair also included a 'Cairo Exhibit', which contained replicas of famous Egyptian mosques, city and university gates, a quarter-size reproduction of the Cheops Pyramid, and a small Egyptian peasant village. There were public lectures on colonialism and displays of the imperial monarchy and its military, including mock naval battles between miniature ships. This exhibition was dismantled after it ended in October 1896, with a few bits ending up in short-lived Berlin Colonial Museum, which was created using funds from the fair (Osayimwese, 2008). In 1949, the largest Soviet monument outside Russia was erected on the site of the 1896 fair. The Soviets were doubtless unaware of the hidden resonance between their own imperial presence and the imperial messages of the 1896 exhibition.

Figure 8.5 Congo Conference

Figure 8.6 Demolition of the Reichskanzlei

European museums that memorialize the colonial period had already started to euphemize colonialism before independence, calling themselves ethnological or art museums. The objects in ethnographic museums stem in large part from colonial plunder or from superficially fair trade or gifting practices that were structurally biased in favour of the conquering nations. The Hamburg Ethnological Museum (Museum am Rothenbaum), for example, owns a number of Benin bronzes and

Figure 8.7 Yinka Shonibare installation

Chinese treasures, some of which 'may have been looted in the imperial city and in public institutions of Beijing' during the German-led campaign against the Boxer Rebellion in 1900/1901.[11] Many of these European museums continued to exist after decolonization with little change until the 1990s or later (Aldrich, 2009). Since then, some of them have rearranged and contextualized their displays, often with the participation of historians and representatives from the previously colonized communities.

Colonialism was exhibited most explicitly in the Netherlands, Belgium, and France, and these are the countries in which colonial-era displays have been criticized and, to differing degrees, reconceptualized. The main national site for colonial memory in the Netherlands is the Amsterdam *Tropenmuseum* (Tropical Museum), which was originally created as the Colonial Museum, part of the Colonial Institute. After WWII it was renamed Royal Tropical Institute (Koninklijk Instituut voor de Tropen), and finally, *Tropenmuseum*. Bas-reliefs on the building's outdoor facade and indoor walls that are part of the original 1913 design by architect J. J. van Nieukerken draw the viewer's attention to key aspects of colonization, such as labour (Figure 8.8) and militarized interactions between Europeans and 'natives' (Figure 8.9).

When I visited the Tropenmuseum in 2018, it was still displaying a number of objects from an earlier exhibit on 'Dutch Colonialism', including a section called 'Colonial Theatre' (Bouquet, 2015). These are life-size wax figures of actual historical colonial personnages.

[11] https://markk-hamburg.de/en/loot-from-the-boxer-war-searching-for-traces-in-the-east-asian-collection/. I am grateful to Dr Susanne Knödel, Head Curator, Curator of the South- and East Asian Department at the Museum, for answering my questions about the Chinese collection during our conversation in January 2020.

Figure 8.8 Bas-relief I

Figure 8.9 Bas-relief II

Figure 8.10 Amsterdam Tropenmuseum I

Figure 8.11 Amsterdam Tropenmuseum II

They are placed inside cylindrical glass containers (Figure 8.10). As Tunno (2017) points out, 'wax or plaster life-size figures have a long history in museums and World Fairs, deriving from a more ancient tradition of wax works'; 'starting from the second half of the 19th century these displays developed in numerous ethnographic museums across Europe'. This approach therefore seems to place the culture of the dominating culture under the same scrutinizing surveillance that was earlier directed at the colonized. The fact that a few of the mannequins that are *not* enclosed in cylinders suggests that they have some autonomy from the core colonial enterprise: one is a Belgian colonial missionary-ethnographer working in the Dutch colony (Figure 8.11, left); another is a colonial artist and son of a sugar planter on Java (Figure 8.11, middle).

In Belgium, the enormous *Royal Museum for Central Africa* in Tervuren betrays its colonial origins immediately with the massive gilded figures standing beside the entrance doors, bearing titles such as 'La Belgique apportant la civilization au Congo' (Figure 8.12). This museum has also been reconceptualized with the help of African historians and citizens living in the community (Gryseels et al., 2005). In France, the key site for colonial memory is the *Palais de la Porte Dorée,* an exhibition hall that was originally the *Musée des Colonies* at the 1931 Colonial Exposition in Paris (Morton, 1998). It was subsequently renamed *Musée de la France d'Outre-Mer,* adopting the widespread euphemism 'outre-mer' (overseas) which replaced 'colonial' in official French discourse in the 1940s. In 1960, the hall was reconfigured again as a museum for African and Oceanic art, underscoring the widespread French pattern of transubstantiating colonialism in an aesthetic direction. In 2007, the hall became the home of the *Cité nationale de l'histoire de l'immigration* (Kiwan 2017). The bas-reliefs that adorn the palace's façade and the frescos on the ballroom walls

Figure 8.12 Musée royal de l'Afrique central

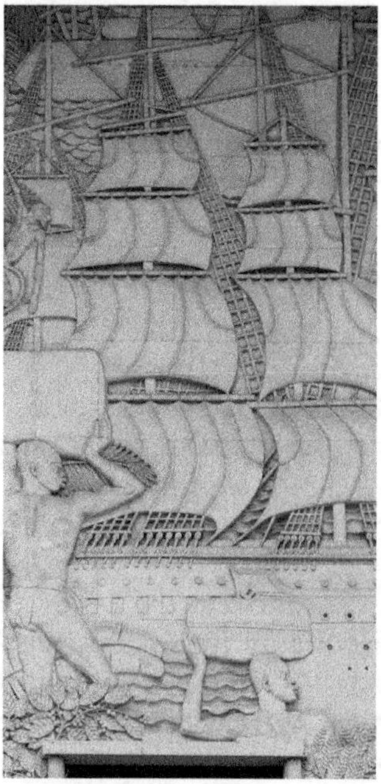

Figure 8.13 Palais de la Porte Dorée I

Figure 8.14 Palais de la Porte Dorée II

inside continue to remind visitors of its colonial origins (Figures 8.12-8.14), which contrasts with the tendency to deny the importance of the colonial past in discussions of race and poverty in France.

Compared to these reconfigured museums, the new Ethnological Museum at the Humboldt Forum in Berlin seems like a project from the era of high imperialism. Alexander von Humboldt was an imperial traveller whose accounts assimilated Amerindians to nature and described them in terms of their 'instrumental capacities' and availability for exploitation (Pratt, 2008). The Humboldt Forum is located within a building that represents the violent, anti-democratic monarchy of the Hohenzollerns, who attacked and annexed parts of France, Austria, and Denmark, giving rise to the Prussia-dominated *Kaiserreich* (the 'Emperor's Empire', literally), the state that accumulated an overseas colonial empire between 1883 and WWI. As for the museum's contents, the collection includes numerous objects obtained under coercive and unjust conditions in German colonies. These include the throne of King Njoya from the Bamum kingdom of Cameroon, which the German colonizers obtained as a putative 'gift' to Kaiser Wilhelm through a ruse, after Njoya refused to sell it (Geary, 1988: 92–93). The objects also include an outrigger boat from Luf island, which was also obtained in the context of German military aggression (Aly, 2021).[12] Discussions of

[12] There are several reasons for the difference between the Berlin museum and its counterparts in Paris, Tervuren, Amsterdam and Bristol, England (the British Empire and Commonwealth Museum). One is the greater presence in the latter three countries of immigrants from the former colonies of the country in question. Another is the destruction by Nazism of Germany's critical intelligentsia and the interruption of the 'natural' development of critical political and theoretical traditions. Finally, there is an effort to make Germany a normal European nation state with the trappings of royalty, thereby sweeping the country's anomalous twentieth century history under the rug.

Figure 8.15 IFAN Building Dakar

Figure 8.16 New IFAN Building

the 'provenance' of objects bracket the most important contextual factor, which was the fact that the collectors were usually the same people – or were protected by the people – who were invading, annexing, conquering, policing, and governing the societies producing these objects. It is astonishing that the Berlin museum does not attempt to create more distance between empire and its ethnographic collection but actually brings them closer together.

Science and education were deeply affected by colonialism in the metropoles and the global south. Many of the oldest and most prestigious universities and research institutes in the global south were created during the colonial era. Many maintained close connections to academic and scientific institutions in their former metropoles after independence. The Fundamental Institute for Black Africa (IFAN) in Dakar, for example, is the direct descendent of the French Institute for Black Africa (Figures 8.15 and 8.16). Hamburg University grew out of the German Colonial Institute before WWI, and continued to specialize in international studies through the Nazi era. Even after 1945, it was one of the only German universities where African history was offered at an advanced level.

Colonialism also had powerful effects on European science, including social science (Petitjean & Jami 1992; Tilley 2011). All of the human sciences, including economics, geography, history, law, psychology, psychoanalysis, and sociology, had important colonial offshoots (Steinmetz 2009; Singaravélou 2011). Anthropology was almost entirely focused on the global South and indigenous cultures inside the richer countries. There is one discipline, however, which suffered particularly from effects of disciplinary amnesia discussed above; sociology. Initial investigations, starting with Tenbruck (1992), pointed out that sociology before 1914 was largely organized around social evolutionary and cross-cultural comparative approaches grounded in an imperial episteme (cf. Connell, 1997). More recent research has ascertained that around half of the entire sociology discipline in Britain, France and Belgium carried out colonial research between 1945 and decolonization, and that most of the important sociological subfields were split between colonial and metropolitan foci (Steinmetz 2009, 2013a, 2013b, 2017b, 2023a). The key concepts and theories of the most influential present-day sociological theorist, Pierre Bourdieu, were forged in late colonial Algeria (Pérez, 2015; Steinmetz, 2020).

I want to conclude this section with two imperial themes circulating in the United States. As in Europe, these examples underscore the continuing power of imperial afterlives, along with growing efforts of decolonization and de-imperialization. The first example returns us to the theme of America's internal colonialism. In 2020, in the wake of the Black Lives Matter protests, an official portrait of Trump's first Secretary of the Interior, Ryan Zinke, was unveiled at the US Interior Department headquarters (Figure 8.17). On his first day in office, Zinke rode to work on a horse named after the fictional Native American character Tonto.[13] In the background of Zinke's portrait is Bears Ears National Monument. Zinke's only connection to Bear's Ears, which is 700 miles from his home state of Montana, is that he 'worked vigorously' while in office to drastically reduce the size of the National Monument, to 'the dismay of five American Indian tribes who maintain the butte is sacred ceremonial land to their tribal citizens' (Native News Online, 11 December 2020). The Department of the Interior, which is responsible for Indian reservations and other policies affecting Native Americans, has usually shown complete disregard for the fact that relations with

[13] Tonto is the name of the Native American companion of the Lone Ranger in the radio show from the 1930s (later turned into a television show). Tonto rescued the Lone Ranger, a Texas Ranger who had been ambushed and wounded.

Figure 8.17 Ryan Zinke portrait

Figure 8.18 Deb Haaland portrait

Native American tribes are a form of international relations within the borders of the United States. In 2021, however, US President-Elect Joe Biden nominated a Native American, Deb Haaland of the Pueblo people (Figure 8.18), to head the Department of Interior.

The second theme is imperial decline. The unmaking of American global hegemony is lasting longer than the winding down of the previous British hegemon, and it is occurring in an even more chaotic, unplanned, and often violent manner. Both US political parties are internally divided by intense disagreements around foreign policy, including their stance towards the conventional US global hegemonic posture. A further set of divisions among the hegemonists concerns the proper use of the US military. Significantly, the military is always the last component of hegemonic powers to be dismantled in every hegemonic cycle. Trump promised repeatedly to 'extract the United States from costly foreign conflicts, bring U.S. troops home, and shrug off burdensome overseas commitments', but ultimately he had not 'meaningfully altered the U.S. global military footprint he inherited' by the time he left office (MacDonald and Parent 2019). Biden has largely continued to pursue the same foreign policies as Trump, underscoring the distinctiveness of this arena compared to all other policy areas.

Commentators on Trumpist movement have focused mainly on the domestic American scene or on comparisons with other domestic political scenes in places like Britain and Hungary. The language of 'making America great' is implicitly assumed to have a domestic focus. But it is also possible to read this movement as a symptom of a further stage of the unwinding of the post-war imperial order (Hell & Steinmetz 2017). Geopolitically, Trump aligned himself with countries that were America's foes in the Cold War hegemonic configuration, and alienated post-war US allies. His ultimately hostile stance towards China reflected the inexorable pressures coming from the leading challenger to US hegemony; his friendly stance towards Russia reflected the fact that Russia is not a serious contender for global hegemony. Trump's ostensible aversion to military intervention was at odds with mainstream expert foreign policy views in both parties. Trump was therefore a symptom of the ongoing collapse of the assumptions that made up the post-war approach to US hegemony, and a contributor to that collapse.

Many observers recognize that the assault on the Cold War order has caused social and political disorganization, without a replacement paradigm coming clearly into view. But one frame that continuously resurfaces in political discourse is the decline of the Roman empire. The Trumpist invaders of statehouses across the US reminded many observers of violent zombies, but when they invaded the neoclassical US Capitol on 6 January 2020, US journalists and politicians quickly converged in describing them as a 'mob' – a term with imperial resonances – and some referred to them more significantly as 'barbarians' or 'Visigoths'.

7 Conclusion

Although it is inadequate to leave memorials to imperialists and colonial atrocities unmarked and uncontextualized, it is equally problematic simply to remove and repress these markers of collective memory. Imperial material can only be ignored only at the risk of its resurfacing in unexpected and potentially more damaging ways. These symbols should be excavated and reconstructed – but that is not enough. The imperial past should be worked through, in a joint effort involving careful research by scholars in dialogue with students and activists. The latter should include descendants of the colonized (or members of the currently colonized), and should also include descendants of the European or Euro-American colonizers. Some of the most subtle analyses of late colonialism, it turns out, were produced by social scientists employed by colonial research organizations, underlining here the importance to consider the third mode of historicity identified by Schlichte & Stetter in the introduction (i.e. the temporality of the observer). And as it also turns out, almost all of these social scientists, at least in the post-war period, opposed colonialism in one way or another. They also insisted that colonizer and colonized had to be analysed and interpreted relationally within a unified framework (Mannoni 1950; Balandier 1951; Memmi 1957). Colonialism and empire are constitutive aspects of European and American history, part of a joint history and the respective modes of historicity at play here, for better or for worse (such as the role of history in shaping reality and the importance of non-linear pathways). The sophisticated discussions and public practices directed at the memory of the Holocaust have shown that it is a mistake to simply erase the relevant traces, monuments, murals, buildings, and street names. This approach is naive about the workings of collective and individual memory and the political unconscious. Events during the past year in the United States, Britain, and Europe have suggested that protestors are often content simply to destroy these markers. Ultimately, such simple erasure of the past may have the same long-term effect as simply ignoring it.

References

Agblemagnon, F. N'Sougan. (1965). La différence de psychologie et de sensibilité provoque-t-elle une différence de comportement entre occidentaux d'une part, africaines de l'autre, quant aux méthodes de la recherche et quant à l'interprétation des résultats?, in *Association des universités partiellement ou entièrement de langue française, État et perspectives des études africaines et orientales*, 128–44, Montreal: Therien freres.

Ageron, C.-R. (1986). L'opinion publique face aux problemes de l'Union Française, in C.-R. Ageron (ed.). *Les Chemins de la décolonisation de l'empire colonial français: colloque*, 33–48, Paris: CNRS.
Aikau, H. K. & Gonzalez, V. A. (2019). *Detours: A Decolonial Guide to Hawaiʻi*, Durham: Duke University Press.
Aldrich, R. (2009). Colonial Museums in a Postcolonial Europe, *African and Black Diaspora: An International Journal*, 2(2), 137–56.
Aly, G. (2021). *Das Prachtboot. Wie Deutsche die Kunstschätze der Südsee raubten*, Frankfurt: S. Fischer Verlag.
Anghie, A. (2004). *Imperialism, Sovereignty and the Making of International Law*, Cambridge: Cambridge University Press.
Armitage, A. (1995). *Comparing the Policy of Aboriginal Assimilation Australia, Canada, and New Zealand*, Vancouver: UBC Press.
Aron, R. (1957). Nations et empires, in *Encyclopédie française*, 11.04-1–11.06.8, vol. 11, Paris: Société nouvelle de l'Encyclopédie française.
Auslander, L. & Holt, T. (2003). Sambo in Paris: Race and Racism in the Iconography of the Everyday Life, in S. Peabody & T. Stovall (eds.). *The Colour of Liberty: Histories of Race in France*, Durham, NC: Duke University Press.
Balandier, G. (1952). Contribution à une sociologie de la dépendence, *Cahiers internationaux de sociologie*, 12, 47–69.
Balandier, G. (1955). *Sociologie actuelle de l'Afrique noire: Dynamique des changements sociaux en Afrique centrale*, Paris: Presses Universitaires de France.
Balandier, G. (1985) [1955]. *Sociologie des Brazzavilles noires*. 2. Ed. Paris: Pr. de la Fondation Nat. des Sciences Po.
Balandier, G. (1950). Aspects de l'Évolution sociale chez les Fang du Gabon (Afrique Équatoriale française), *Cahiers internationaux de sociologie*, 9, 76–106.
Balandier, G. (1951). La situation coloniale: approche théorique, *Cahiers internationaux de sociologie*, 11, 44–79.
Banton, M. (1955). *The Coloured Quarter; Negro Immigrants in an English City*, London: Cape.
Banton, Michael. (1955). *The Coloured Quarter; Negro Immigrants in an English City*, London: Cape.
Berda, Y. (2014). Colonial legacy and administrative memory: The legal construction of citizenship in India, Israel and Cyprus. PhD dissertation, Sociology, Princeton.
Bindseil, R. (1988). *Ruanda und Deutschland seit den Tagen Richard Kandts*, Berlin: Dietrich Reimer Verlag.
Bindseil, Reinhart. (2008). *Ruanda im Lebensbild des Afrikaforschers, Literaten und kaiserlichen Residenten Richard Kandt (1867–1918)*, Trier: Ruanda-Komitee Trier.
Bouquet, M. (2015). Reactivating the Colonial Collection: Exhibition-Making as Creative Process at the Tropenmuseum, Amsterdam, in S. Macdonald & H. R. Leahy (eds.). *The International Handbooks of Museum Studies*, 135–55, vol. 4, Chichester: John Wiley & Sons.
Carrigan, A. (2011). *Postcolonial Tourism: Literature, Culture, and Environment*, New York: Routledge.
Çelik, Zeynep. (2019). Colonial statues and their afterlives, *The Journal of North African Studies*, 25(18), 1–16.

Césaire, A. (2000) [1950]. *Discourse on Colonialism*, New York: Monthly Review Press.

Chae, O.-B. (2006). Non-Western Colonial Rule and Its Aftermath: Postcolonial State Formation in South Korea. PhD dissertation, sociologySociology, University of Michigan.

Chatterjee, P. (1993). *The Nation and Its Fragments*, Princeton, NJ: Princeton University Press.

Chatterjee, P. (1986). *Nationalist Thought and the Colonial World: A Derivative Discourse*, London: Zed Books.

Chatterjee, Partha. (1993). *The Nation and Its Fragments*, Princeton, NJ: Princeton University Press.

Comaroff, J & Comaroff, J. (1991–1997). *Of Revelation and Revolution: Christianity, Colonialism, and Consciousness in South Africa*, Chicago: University Chicago Press.

Connell, R. (2007). *Southern Theory: The Global Dynamics of Knowledge in Social Science*, Cambridge: Polity.

Connell, R. W. (1997). Why Is Classical Theory Classical?, *American Journal of Sociology*, 102(6), 1511–57.

Cooper, F. (2004). Development, Modernization, and the Social Sciences in the Era of Decolonization: The Examples of British and French Africa. *Revue d'histoire des sciences humaines* 1(10), 9–38.

Dimbath, O. (2011). Wissenschaftlicher Oblivionismus. Vom unbewussten zum stratgeischen Vergessen, in O. Dimbath (ed.). *Soziologie des Vergessens: theoretische Zugänge und empirische Forschungsfelder*, 297–316, Konstanz: UVK Verlagsgesellschaft.

Durham, Deborah. (1993). *Images of Culture: Being Herero in a Liberal Democracy (Botswana)*. 2 vols. PhD Thesis, University of Chicago.

Duteuil, Jean-Pierre. (1988). *Nanterre 68: vers le mouvement du 22 mars*, Maul'eon: Acratie.

Eckert, A. (2018). Jenseits von Europa. Elias, Bourdieu, Balandier: Im Zeitalter der Dekolonisierung was die 'koloniale' Soziologie Avantgarde ihres Faches. *Frankfurter Allgemeine Zeitung*, December 19, p. 3.

Fanon, F. [1961] (2004). *The Wretched of the Earth*, New York: Grove.

Fenelon, J. V. (2017). *Redskins? : Sports Mascots, Indian Nations and White Racism*. New York, NY: Routledge, Taylor & Francis Group.

Fildis, A. T. (2011). The Troubles in Syria: Spawned by French Divide and Rule, *Middle East Policy*, 18(4), 129–39.

Geary, C. M. (1988). *Images from Bamum. German Colonial Photography at the Court of King Njoya. Cameroon, West Africa, 1902–1915*, Washington, DC: Smithsonian Institution.

Gettleman, J. (2006). An African Rarity in Congo: Honors for Brazza, Its Colonial Governor, *International Herald Tribune*, November 29.

Gilroy, P. (2005). *Postcolonial Melancholia*, New York: Columbia University Press.

Go, J. (2008). *American Empire and the Politics of Meaning: Elite Political Cultures in the Philippines and Puerto Rico during U.S. Colonialism*, Durham: Duke University Press.

Gryseels, G., Landry, G. & Claessens, K. (2005). Integrating the Past: Transformation and Renovation of the Royal Museum for Central Africa, Tervuren, Belgium, *European Review*, 13(4), 637–47.

Hall, C. M. & Tucker, H. (eds.). (2004). *Tourism and Postcolonialism: Contested Discourses, Identities and Representations*, London: Routledge.
Hall, Stuart. (1996). When Was 'The Post-Colonial'? Thinking at the Limit, in Iain Chambers & Lidia Curti (eds.). *The Post-Colonial Question: Common Skies, Divided Horizons*, 242–60, New York: Routledge.
Hall, C. & Rose, S. O. (eds.). (2006). *At Home with the Empire : Metropolitan Culture and the Imperial World.* Cambridge: Cambridge University Press.
Hell, J. (2009). Imperial Ruin Gazers, or Why Did Scipio Weep? *The Germanic Review*, 84(4), 283–326.
Hell, J. (2019). *The Conquest of Ruins: The Third Reich and the Fall of Rome*, Chicago: University of Chicago Press.
Hell, J. & Schönle, A. (eds.). (2010). *Ruins of Modernity*, Durham: Duke University Press.
Hell, J. & Steinmetz, G. (2017). 'A Period of Wild and Fierce Fanaticism': Populism, Theo-Political Militarism, and the Crisis of US Hegemony, *American Journal of Cultural Sociology*, 5(3), 373–91.
Hermassi, E. (1978). Changing Patterns in Research on the Third World, *Annual Review of Sociology* 4, 239–57.
Hess, Kimberly. (2018). Paradigms and Power in the Policymaking Process: The Institutionalization of Māori Political Inclusion in Nineteenth Century Aotearoa/New Zealand. Unpublished paper, University of Michigan, Sociology Department.
Hobson, J. M. (2012). *The Eurocentric Conception of World Politics: Western International Theory, 1760–2010*, Cambridge: Cambridge University Press.
Immerwahr, D. (2019). *How to Hide an Empire: A History of the Greater United States*, London: Penguin.
Johnson, C. (2004). *Blowback: The Costs and Consequences of American Empire*, New York: Henry Holt and Co.
Keenan, B. S. (2018). 'The US Embassy Has Been Particularly Sensitive about This': Diplomacy, Antiwar Protests, and the French Ministry of Foreign Affairs during 1968, *French Historical Studies*, 41(2), 253–73.
Kiwan, N. (2017). Remembering on the City's Margins: The *Musée de l'histoire de l'immigration* in Paris, *Journal of Contemporary European Studies*, 25(4), 426–40.
Krämer, A. (1902–1903). *Die Samoa-Inseln*, Stuttgart: E. Schweizerbartsche Verlagsbuchhandlung.
Kringelbach, M. L. & Berridge, K. C. (eds.). (2010). *Pleasures of the Brain*, Oxford: Oxford University Press.
Koessler, R. (2015). *Namibia and Germany: Negotiating the Past.* Münster: Westfälisches Dampfboot.
Lanxade, J. (1947). Le Stand de l'Institut National de la Statistique et des Études Économiques à la Foire Coloniale et Internationale de Bordeaux, *Bulletin de l'INSEE*, Novembre (No. 9), 47–64.
Larba, S. A. (2005). Legs du colonialisme, *La Dépêche de Kabylie*, December 4. www.depechedekabylie.com/kabylie/13075-legs-du-colonialisme/.
Lawson, G. & Tardelli, L. (2013). The Past, Present, and Future of Intervention, *Review of International Studies*, 39(5), 1233–53.
Leenhardt, M. [1902] (1976). *Le mouvement éthiopien au sud de l'Afrique de 1896 à 1899*, Paris: Académie des sciences d'outre-mer.

Liauzu, C. (2007). *L'histoire de l'anticolonialisme en France du XVIe siècle à nos jours*, Paris: Armand Colin.

Louis, W. R. (1963). *Ruanda-Urundi, 1884–1919*, Oxford: Clarendon Press.

Louis, W. R. (1977). *Imperialism at Bay: The United States and the Decolonization of the British Empire 1941–1945*, Oxford: Clarendon Press.

MacDonald, P. K. & Parent, J. M. (2019). Trump Didn't Shrink U.S. Military Commitments Abroad – He Expanded Them. The President's False Promise of Retrenchment. Foreign Affairs, 3 December. www.foreignaffairs.com/articles/2019-12-03/trump-didnt-shrink-us-military-commitments-abroad-he-expanded-them.

Mahoney, J. (2010). *Colonialism and Postcolonial Development: Spanish America in Comparative Perspective*, Cambridge: Cambridge University Press.

Mann, K. & Roberts, R. (eds.). (1991). *Law in Colonial Africa*, Portsmouth, NH: Heinemann.

Mannoni, O. (1950). *Psychologie de la colonisation*, Paris: Éditions du Seuil.

Mathur, N. (2016). *Paper Tiger: Law, Bureaucracy and the Developmental State in Himalayan India*, Delhi: Cambridge University Press.

McKercher, B. & Decosta P. L. (2007). Research Report: The Lingering Effect of Colonialism on Tourist Movements, *Tourism Economics*, 13(3), 453–74.

Memmi, A. (1957). *Portrait du colonisé, précédé du Portrait du colonisateur*, Paris: Buchet/Chastel.

Miles, W. & Rochefort, D. (1991). Nationalism Versus Ethnic Identity in Sub-Saharan Africa, *American Political Science Review*, 85(2), 393–403.

Miles, W. (1994). *Hausaland Divided: Colonialism and Independence in Nigeria and Niger*, Ithaca: Cornell University Press.

Möhle, H. (2007). Kolonialismus und Erinnerungspolitik. Die Debatte um die Hamburger 'Askari-Reliefs', in S. Hobuß & U. Lölke (eds.), *Erinnern verhandeln. Kolonialismus im kollektiven Gedächtnis Afrikas und Europas*, 196–209, Münster: Westfälisches Dampfboot.

Montagne, R. (1957). *Étude sociologique de la migration des travailleurs musulmans d'Algérie en métropole.* Paris: Ministère de l'intérieur, Direction des affaires d'Algerie, Bureau des affaires sociales musulmanes.

Morton, P. A. (1998). National and Colonial: The Musée Des Colonies at the Colonial Exposition, Paris, 1931, *The Art Bulletin*, 80(2), 357–77.

Müller, T. (forthcoming). Collective Hegemony after Decolonisation: Persistence Despite Delegitimation. This volume.

Neep, D. (2012). *Occupying Syria under the French mandate: Insurgency, Space and State Formation*, Cambridge: Cambridge University Press.

Osayimwese, I. I. 2008. Colonialism at the Center: German Colonial Architecture and the Design Reform Movement, 1828–1914. PhD, University of Michigan.

Parker, J. (2006). Cold War II: The Eisenhower Administration, the Bandung Conference, and the Reperiodization of the Postwar Era, *Diplomatic History*, 30(5), 867–92.

Pérez, A. (2015). *Rendre le social plus politique: Guerre coloniale, immigration et pratiques sociologiques d'Abdelmalek Sayad et de Pierre Bourdieu.* Doctoral thesis, EHESS.

Petitjean, P. and Jami, C. (eds.). (1992). *Science and Empires. Historical Studies about Scientific Development and European Expansion*, Dordrecht: Kluwer Academic Publishers.

Pirenne, H. (1937). *Mahomet et Charlemagne,* Paris: Presses Universitaires de France.

Pirenne, H. [1927] (2014). *Medieval Cities: Their Origins and the Revival of Trade,* Princeton: Princeton University Press.

Pratt, M. L. (2008). *Imperial Eyes: Travel Writing and Transculturation,* London: Routledge.

Prior, C. (2020). Reverberations of Decolonisation: British Approaches to Governance in Post-colonial Africa and the Rise of the 'Strong Men', in B. Sèbe & M. G. Stanard (eds.). *Decolonising Europe? Popular Responses to the End of Empire,* 57–72, New York: Routledge.

Ricoeur, Paul. (2004). *Memory, History, Forgetting,* Chicago: University of Chicago Press.

Rex, John. (1959). The Plural Society in Sociological Theory, *British Journal of Sociology* 10(2), 114–24.

Sayad, A. & Gillette, A. (1976). *L'immigration algérienne en France,* Paris: Éditions Entente.

Sèbe, B. (2020). Oases of Imperial Nostalgia: British and French Desert Memories after Empire, in B. Sèbe & M. G. Stanard (eds.). *Decolonising Europe? Popular Responses to the End of Empire,* New York: Routledge.

Simpson, G. (2004). *Great Powers and Outlaw States: Unequal Sovereigns in the International Legal Order,* Cambridge: Cambridge University Press.

Singaravélou, P. (2011). *Professer l'Empire : Les sciences coloniales en Cœur sous la IIIe République,* Paris: Publications de la Sorbonne.

Stallings, D. & Sullivan, M. (2007). *Fodors Caribbean,* New York: Fodors.

Steinmetz, G. (1999). Introduction: Culture and the State, in G. Steinmetz (ed.). *State/Culture,* 1–49. Ithaca: Cornel University Press.

Steinmetz, G. & Hell J. (2006). The Visual Archive of Colonialism: Germany and Namibia, *Public Culture,* 18(1), 141–82.

Steinmetz, G. (2003). The Devil's Handwriting: Precolonial Discourse, Ethnographic Acuity and Cross-Identification in German Colonialism, *Comparative Studies in Society and History,* 45(1), 41–95.

Steinmetz, G. (2005a). Return to Empire: The New U.S. Imperialism in Theoretical and Historical Perspective, *Sociological Theory,* 23(4), 339–67.

Steinmetz, G. (2005b). The Genealogy of a Positivist Haunting: Comparing Prewar and Postwar U.S. Sociology, *boundary 2,* 32(2), 107–33.

Steinmetz, G. (2007). *The Devil's Handwriting: Precolonial Ethnography and the German Colonial State in Qingdao, Samoa, and Southwest Africa,* Chicago: University Chicago Press.

Steinmetz, G. (2009). The Imperial Entanglements of Sociology in the United States, Britain, and France since the 19th Century, *Ab Imperio,* 4, 23–78.

Steinmetz, G. (2010). Colonial Melancholy and Fordist Nostalgia: The Ruinscapes of Namibia and Detroit, in Julia Hell & Andreas Schoenle (eds.). *Ruins of Modernity,* 294–320, Durham, NC: Duke University Press.

Steinmetz, G. (2013a). A Child of the Empire: British Sociology and Colonialism, 1940s–1960s, *Journal of the History of the Behavioral Sciences,* 49(4), 353–78.

Steinmetz, G. (2013b). Major Contributions to Sociological Theory and Research on Empire, 1830s–Present, in G. Steinmetz (ed.). *Sociology and Empire,* 1–50, Durham, NC: Duke University Press.

Steinmetz, G. (2017a). Empire in Three Keys: Forging the Imperial Imaginary at the 1896 Berlin Industrial Exhibition, *Thesis Eleven*, 139(1), 46–68.

Steinmetz, G. (2017b). Sociology and Colonialism in the British and French Empires, 1940s–1960s, *The Journal of Modern History*, 89(3), 601–48.

Steinmetz, G. (2020). Soziologie und Kolonialismus: Die Beziehung zwischen Wissen und Politik, *Mittelweg 36*, 3(June–July), 17–36.

Steinmetz, G. (2023a). *The Colonial Origins of French Social Thought*, Princeton: Princeton University Press.

Steinmetz, G. (2023b). Richard Wilhelm, China, und der deutsche Antikolonialismus. *Historische Urteilskraft*, 5 (magazine of the German Historical Museum, Berlin).

Stoler, Ann Laura. (2011). Colonial Aphasia: Race and Disabled Histories in France, *Public Culture*, 23(1), 121–56.

Tenbruck, F. H. (1992). Was war der Kulturvergleich, ehe es den Kulturvergleich gab? In Zwischen den Kulturen?, in Joachim Matthes (ed.). *Zwischen den Kulturen?: die Sozialwissenschaften vor dem Problem des Kulturvergleichs*, 13–36, Göttingen: O. Schwartz.

Tharoor, S. (2017). *The Need for a Museum on British Colonisation of India*. http://shashitharoor.in/writings_my_essays_details/145

Tilley, H. (2011). *Africa as a Living Laboratory: Empire, Development, and the Problem of Scientific Knowledge, 1870–1950*, Chicago: University of Chicago Press.

Tomich, D. W. (2015). Capitalism and Slavery Revisited: The 'Williams Thesis' in Atlantic Perspective, in C. A. Palmer (ed.). *The Legacy of Eric Williams: Caribbean Scholar and Statesman*, Mona, Kingston, Jamaica: University of the West Indies Press.

Tunno, G. G. (2017). *From Mannequins to Contemporary Art: Madonna (after Omomà and Céline), 2008 by Roy Villevoye at the Tropenmuseum*. www.traces.polimi.it/index.html@p=2266.html/.

Vanden Boer, D. (2016). Toward Decolonization in Tourism: Engaged Tourism and the Jerusalem Tourism Cluster Issue, *The Institute for Palestine Studies*, 65. https://oldwebsite.palestine-studies.org

Wallerstein, M. I. (2003). *The Decline of American Power: The U.S. in a Chaotic World*, New York: New Press.

Wilderson, F. B. (2020). *Afropessimism*, New York: Liveright Publishing Corporation.

Wilkes, C. (1845). *Narrative of the United States Exploring Expedition during the Years 1838, 1839, 1840, 1841, 1842*. 5 vols, Philadelphia: Lea and Blanchard.

Williams, E. (1944). *Capitalism and Slavery*, Chapel Hill: University of North Carolina Press.

Worsley, P. (1960). Imperial Retreat, in E. P. Thompson (ed.). *Out of Apathy*, 101–40, London: New Left Books.

Zeller, J. (2000). *Kolonialdenkmäler und Geschichtsbewusstsein*, Frankfurt: IKO.

Zweig, S. (1944). *Die Welt von Gestern, Erinnerungen eines Europäers*, Stockholm: Bermann-Fischer.

Zytnicki, C. & Kazdaghli, H. (2009). *Le tourisme dans l'empire français. Politiques, pratiques et imaginaires*, Paris: Publications de la Société française d'histoire d'outre-mer.

9 Divided World

Encountering Frantz Fanon in Kabul

Teresa Koloma Beck

> The colonised world is a world divided in two. The dividing line, the border, is represented by the barracks and the police stations. In the colonies, the official, legitimate agent, the spokesperson for the coloniser and the regime of oppression, is the police officer or the soldier.
>
> Frantz Fanon (1965), *The Wretched of the Earth*, 3.

1 Introduction

The quote above is taken from the opening passages of Fanon's seminal work *The Wretched of the Earth* (1965), in which the philosopher and social scientist develop a micro-sociology of colonial society. At the core of his reconstruction is the idea that life in the colonies is organized around a key distinction: the one between colonizers and the colonized. He elaborates how this distinction structures not only systems of thought and the logics of politics, but also the material realities of the lifeworld of colonialism. He reconstructs how it produces and is reproduced in particular socio-spatial arrangements, which create a world of the colonizers set apart from that of the colonized. And he shows how this lifeworldly structure shapes the particular and complementary subjectivities.

As a sociologist working in conflict and violence research, I had long been familiar with Fanon's work. He had proposed an original microsociology of violence and violent domination, merging critical Marxian thought with the body phenomenology of Maurice Merleau-Ponty.[1] He was the first to have most meticulously analysed how a system of violent domination comes to be inscribed into the bodies of people and how it uses these bodies as sites of its own reproduction. He had demonstrated that not only do people live in colonialism, but colonialism also lives in people.

[1] Marx himself had been strongly influenced by the phenomenological thought of Edmund Husserl, which resonates especially in his early works. For Merleau-Ponty, in turn, Marx had been an important inspiration, along with Husserl and Heidegger. For a systematic discussion of the interrelations between Marx and Merleau-Ponty cf. Miller (1976).

I had read Fanon as a sociologist of violence and domination whose analyses of the *colonial condition* had been inspired by the liberation struggles of his time especially on the African continent. Therefore, I was surprised to discover strong resonances with this work in a place which in lay debates is frequently – if incorrectly – praised for having withstood attempts at colonial conquest since Alexander the Great and, many centuries later, Genghis Khan: Afghanistan. In 2015, I had spent two months in Kabul and surrounding provinces for ethnographic research. The aim was to explore how a protracted armed conflict affects the organization of everyday life, with a particular analytical focus on socio-spatial arrangements. Motivating this research was a growing interest in the dimension of space in the interdisciplinary field of conflict and violence research. Sceptical towards an expanding body of literature, which reconstructed places in war as places in chaos and without social order,[2] I had set out to explore the social and material realities of war-affected lifeworlds.[3]

It was, hence, to my own surprise that in the ethnographic process, Fanon's considerations on colonial society became one of the most recurrent theoretical resonances. I found myself navigating a city divided into two worlds: one for the people who came from outside and were part of the humanitarian and military intervention; and another for the so-called local population. The continuous presence of foreigners working with international and foreign non-governmental organizations, of journalists and researchers from outside is, of course, common throughout the so-called developing world. Striking in Kabul were the efforts undertaken to keep the world of 'the locals' and the world of 'the internationals' apart. From the separated parking lots at the airport (cf. Andersson & Weigand, 2015) and the fortified compounds of peacebuilding and development

[2] In political science, these debates take place under headings such as 'ungoverned territories' (Rabasa et al., 2007) or 'areas of limited statehood' (Risse, 2011). In German historical violence research, 'spaces of violence' (ger. 'Gewalträume) has become an influential concept of reference (Baberowski, 2015). For an overview of all these debates, cf. Koloma Beck (2016).

[3] The research took place in the framework of an interdisciplinary French-German research group on 'Spaces of Violence', funded by the German Federal Ministry of Education and Research, at the Centre Marc Bloch at Humboldt University Berlin. During field research in and around Kabul, I was embedded with an Afghan civil society organization that specialized in grassroots peacebuilding initiatives throughout the country. Participant observation was the key method of data generation. Observations were documented in field notes of about 200 printed pages. Furthermore, I conducted: six in-depth biographical interviews with Afghan women and men who worked close to the intervention project; two real group discussions with young people; five drive-along-interviews, two of which into neighbouring provinces; and five expert interviews. Most of the interviews and conversations took place in English. Translators were present in the focus group discussions. In many day-to-day situations, for example in the office, Afghans with English skills volunteered as informal translators.

organizations, which were scattered throughout the city (cf. Duffield, 2010), to hotels, restaurants and gyms for internationals with airport-style security procedures, I felt reminded of Fanon's reconstruction of colonial society as a world cut in two; a world whose internal borders were marked by barracks, walls and checkpoints, which in turn were guarded by agents in arms.

In this contribution, I will take a closer look at this resemblance between Fanon's description of the world of late colonialism and my ethnographic observations in the world of humanitarian intervention in Kabul. The objective, however, is not polemicize about the neo-colonial character of humanitarian politics. Instead, the analysis aims to understand sociologically how a socio-spatial constellation, which has been described as the product of a particular form of domination and a particular world political order, comes to be re-enacted in a very different space and time, and a very different world political context.

The Afghan case seems to be of particular analytical value when considering the historicity of contemporary forms of internationalized domination and governance (mode 5), because its political history differs significantly from the patterns of settler colonialism and decolonization, which typically inform – explicitly or not – writings on the presence of the colonial past in the so-called developing world. While in these discursively emblematic contexts structural resemblances like the one described above might appear as a simple continuity, the same observation calls for greater sociological scrutiny in the Afghan context. How to explain that history seems to shape present realities in a place that is geographically and culturally distant and detached from the original events? In this sense, the following analysis attempts to contribute to understandings of the *longue durée* of colonialism in world society – but also to irritate them.

Looking at the case of Kabul, I will explore in the following how the socio-spatial order of everyday life described by Fanon comes to reappear in the lifeworld of an intervention society. I will argue that the systematic attempts to isolate the lifeworld of the foreigners from those of the local populations respond in both contexts to the same perceived problem: security for those from outside in a context of foreign rule. In this sense, humanitarian interventions are part of the 'afterlife' of empires (see Steinmetz in this volume). Yet, while the similarity of the problem explains the strong structural resemblances, I will also show that the overall conditions have changed dramatically: while enforced segregation was consistent with the discourses that justified colonialism, it is at odds with contemporary humanitarian thought which is supposed to frame contemporary intervention politics.

Methodologically, the chapter aims to illustrate the productivity of microsociological approaches in the study of the historicity of world politics and world society (which links it to mode 3 which highlights the centrality of the observer). Thus, while thinking about the relation between humanitarianism and colonialism in general generates insights regarding continuities and discontinuities, focus on micro- and meso-level social dynamics sheds light on how the latter are reproduced and challenged in mundane practices and everyday (inter-)actions.

Section 1 situates the Afghan case within the history of imperialism and colonialism. Section 2 summarizes Fanon's reconstruction of the 'divided world', so as to explore, in Section 3, how seemingly similar socio-spatial arrangements come to be reproduced in the context of Kabul's intervention society. Finally, I will discuss what such an analysis can contribute to the understanding of the historicity of contemporary world society.

2 Imperial and Colonial Past

The history of Afghanistan is marked by its location at the crossroads of regions and empires. For most parts of its known history, it belonged to larger empires, frequently constituting a frontier zone in which conflicts with neighbouring powers were staged or had to be absorbed (Barfield, 2004: 267). Somewhat polemically, the anthropologist Thomas Barfield describes the region as 'a territory that was historically overrun by every major power in pre-modern times' (Barfield, 2004: 263). To this day, the history of the country is marked by foreign rule or respective attempts in varying guises. From the early nineteenth century onwards, the region moved into the focus of what came to be known as the 'Great Game', in which the British and the Russian Empires rivalled for dominance in Central Asia. Against the background of imperial competition, Afghan diplomats succeeded to negotiate independence from Britain. In 1919, Afghanistan became the first sovereign state with a Muslim majority population to enter the international arena.

The modern Afghan polity was, hence, formed in confrontation with external forces. Living with imperial powers, in relations of collaboration as well as resistance, is deeply inscribed into the modern history of the country and constitutive to the modern Afghan state. Politics came to be defined not by the institutionalized logic of 'colonial domination' (Trotha, 1994), but by dynamics of 'fuzzy sovereignty' (Monsutti, 2012), in which power is appropriated and enacted in shifting constellations of distinct and competing networks of actors. In the light of these historical experiences, the Soviet intervention in 1979[4] as well as the international military and humanitarian intervention that had started in late 2001[5] appeared as repetitions of a pattern rather than as distinct political enterprises. Internationalized structures of domination and governance were not an exception, but a rule (see also Glasman & Schlichte in this volume).

Although in its recent history, the Afghan region never became part of a successful colonial project, as a zone of influence of crucial importance to the British Empire, it became subject of an imperializing culture. The imperial imaginary dwelled on the ostensible 'otherness' of the region's inhabitants, especially regarding the particularities of religious life. It nourished civilizing phantasies and served to enact and affirm the civilized and enlightened status of the colonizing society. The anthropologist David Edwards provides a telling example in his account of uprisings around the Afghan-Indian border in 1897, shortly after the establishment of the Durand-line. He describes how these borderlands became a target for a British *mission civiliatrice*, which posited enlightened Englishmen against 'mad mullahs' (Edwards, 1989). The rhetorics employed in this conflict at the end of the nineteenth century seem to echo much of the discourse on Afghanistan today. Even in the absence of a colonizing project in the narrower sense, Afghanistan, hence, came to occupy a particular place in the colonial imaginary that divided the world according to the progress of civilization.

Different, however, from other world regions dominated by the empires of the nineteenth and early twentieth century, in Afghanistan the imperial disdain for certain aspects of cultural and religious life did not prevent them from flourishing. Its status as a zone of influence rather than a ruled territory as well as its comparatively early independence facilitated Afghanistan's rise, in the early twentieth century, as the heartland of Muslim modernism (Green, 2011). From its independence onwards, it became a battleground for modernization as national elites as well as foreign policymakers and activists were electrified by the experiment of stimulating economic and societal development in a predominantly rural, ethnically diverse, Muslim society. Reform politics

[4] The Soviet Union had been the first state that granted independent Afghanistan international recognition. The attempt to create a modern Muslim society inspired the imagination of Soviet politicians and intellectuals early on (cf. Nunan, 2016). In late 1979, Soviet troops entered the country to support the government of the People's Democratic Party of Afghanistan (PDPA), which in a coup in 1978 had declared a People's Republic and was struggling to stay in power. The operation developed into an internationalized civil war that came to an end only in 1989 with the Cold War itself.

[5] This intervention was launched in response to the attacks of 11 September 2001, whose instigators were suspected to reside in the country.

as well as intensified intellectual exchanges led to the emergence of an intellectual elite, which identified as Muslim, but opposed the fundamentalist positions of clerical leaders (cf. Dorronsoro, 2000). In the anti-colonial struggles of the 1960s and 1970s, Afghanistan, therefore, became a major source of inspiration in Asian countries with significant Muslim populations.

Despite the absence of experiences of modern colonial rule, Afghanistan came to be implicated in the global dynamics of colonialism and decolonization. Its regular encounters with imperial politics granted the region a place in imperial and colonial imaginaries – not only as an object of possible conquest, but also as an epistemic object, whose presumed Otherness made it a side for modernistic self-assertions – pointing to the relevance of several modes of historicity for the Afghanistan case, such as temporality of observers (mode 3) and the role of power (mode 5). This symbolic importance was heightened by the fact that in the absence of continuous colonial engagement, actual knowledge on the country remained limited. As historian Nivi Manchanda points out, until today policy making in and for Afghanistan takes place on the basis of an 'emergency episteme', produced during politically motivated spikes of interest and in response to very tangible problems (cf. Manchanda, 2017). As a consequence, foreign and international politics engaging Afghanistan were frequently more telling about the concerns on the part of the interveners, than about problems in the country itself; contemporary intervention research is no exception in this regard.[6]

Even without a history of prolonged colonial rule, Afghanistan participates in the global experiences of colonialism and decolonization in very particular ways. Are the structural resemblances between the socio-spatial organization of everyday life in Kabul today, and Fanon's reconstruction of the lifeworld of colonial society a simple continuity after all? To pursue this question, let us first take a closer look at Fanon's original analysis.

3 Divided World: Fanon's Sociology of Colonialism

In the opening chapter of *The Wretched of the Earth* Fanon sets out to analyse the social dynamics of colonial society. Titled 'On violence', this text has become controversially famous for insisting on the necessity of physical force to realize decolonization. This chapter, however, is more

[6] A case in point are women empowerment policies; while their effects in the country are ambivalent, they reliably serve to reenact and reassure Western femininity and Western womanhood (cf. Koloma Beck, 2018).

than a manifesto of anti-colonial struggle. It provides a fine-grained analysis of social life in the colonies.[7] Inspired by phenomenological studies of the lifeworld, he reconstructs colonialism in terms of experience. The analysis, therefore, operates at the intersection of subjective and social, bodily and material dynamics. The separation of colonizers and colonized in physical space is the starting point of this inquiry. From there he explores the modes of its (re-)production as well as its effects on the social and the individual level.

Fanon's text has been criticized not only for its political position but also for an alleged short-sightedness of his analysis. His argument about the Manichean division of colonial society was considered deficient, as it obscured the diversity of the populations in the colonies and the complex interplay between them (cf. Bayart, 2016: 140–42). Such arguments seem to be based on a misunderstanding of Fanon's methodological and theoretical approach. They read the reconstruction of a lifeworld in the perspective of a particular subjectivity as an argument about societal structures in general. Fanon himself contributes to this misunderstanding, by failing to address methodological questions explicitly. Knowing, however, his major intellectual sources (Marx, Freud, Sartre, Merleau-Ponty), it is plausible to read his text as a deliberately and necessarily situated attempt at a sociology of experience. It is this methodological and theoretical perspective which makes his work interesting to this day.

Fanon describes colonial society as a specific topological order, a world divided, or compartmentalized, into two confronting zones: there is the city of the colonizers built in stone, stable and clean, 'its belly is permanently full of good things' (Fanon, 1965: 4); and there is the city of the colonized, a famished shantytown, a 'world with no space, people are piled one on top of the other, the shacks squeezed tightly together' (Fanon, 1965: 4–5). Both zones coexist next to each other, and are, yet, detached and disconnected.[8]

Sociologically interesting is Fanon's reconstruction of the social and individual dynamics by which this physical separation is (re-)produced. On a practical level, it is enforced by agents in arms – by police officers, gendarmes or soldiers – who control the borders and guard against unwanted intrusions into the world of the colonizers. To the colonized, these actors are the living interface of domination, 'the spokesperson for the colonizer' (Fanon, 1965: 3). By them they are 'put in place'. They regulate the spaces in which the colonized can move and exist, they

[7] For an insightful re-reading of Fanon as a sociologist cf. Go (2016).
[8] On binary classifications of people as an important part of (the legacy of) imperial rule see also the contributions of Go as well as of Glasman and Schlichte in this volume.

define their space of life. Lucidly, however, Fanon describes that policemen and soldiers with their guns alone cannot stably (re-)produce the segregated colonial lifeworld. The separation also has to be normatively justified. Indigenous populations are described not simply as inferior but as inherently immoral (Fanon, 1965: 6–8). With colonial brain research 'proving' natural limitations regarding moral behaviour as well as biological dispositions towards aggressiveness (Fanon, 1965: 219–34). 'The native' is described as a risk, which turns the measures undertaken to restrict and control her space of life into acts of self-defence. In the language of contemporary IR research, colonial society is a securitized space, organized around the construction of the colonial Other as a threat.

Fanon elaborates that these practices of segregation imply more than restricted access to certain places in the world. The socio-spatial arrangement just described organizes everyday life. Being restricted in mobility, having to life in tight and crowded places, being regularly exposed to control procedures are experiences which condition subjectivities and body structures of the colonized. Fanon compellingly describes the bodily tensions which erupt occasionally in rituals, practices or in intra-group violence (Fanon, 1965: 1920).

It needs to be highlighted, however, that separation in this context does not mean isolation: the zones of colonizers and colonized are clearly separated, but not hermetically closed. Colonizers enter the zones of the colonized in their efforts to control and govern these spaces. And the colonized come to work in the households and offices of the colonizers, trimming their gardens, cooking their food, washing their cloths and making their beds. In colonial societies, crossing from one zone to the other is a delicate and highly regulated but absolutely indispensable social practice.

It is important to understand that the constellation described by Fanon is not just about a separation of worlds – which, in fact, could be observed in any major city, where social heterogeneity is typically organized in 'neighbourhoods' and 'quarters' – but about an asymmetric division, which is unilaterally imposed and enforced by the protagonists of a large-scale political project of domination; a division which is even more pronounced as those who impose it come from the outside. It resonates with Georges Balandier's description of the 'colonial situation' as characterized by the imposition of domination by a foreign, racially and culturally different minority, claiming racial and/or cultural superiority, on a local majority population with dramatically less material resources (Balandier, 1951; see also Speich Chassé in this volume).

Most interestingly, however, this asymmetric division does not only create dynamics of separation, but also dynamics of attraction and desire: the lifeworld of the colonized gains a specific orientation. Similar to the landscape of war, described by the social psychologist Kurt Lewin (cf. Lewin, 2009), this world is not 'round', not open to all sides, but has a direction. As the colonized observe and serve the life and world of the colonizers without being able to share it, their own world comes to be oriented or directed towards that which cannot be reached. The relation of the colonized to the world of the colonizers is, hence, marked by tension: 'The colonist's world is a hostile world, a world which excludes yet at the same time incites envy' (Fanon, 1965: 16). It becomes a place of desire – right within reach and, yet, unattainable. Echoing Hegel's dialectic of master and slave, Fanon, hence, highlights that the very same practices and dynamics, which separate colonizers and colonized also create an intimate connection between them. It is a relation of dependence, which is more forcefully felt by the colonized, whose lifeworld and actions are restricted by the colonizers. Similar to Balandier, Fanon describes colonialism as a specific type of society produced from antagonistic relations and conflict (Balandier, 1951).

Fanon's phenomenological analysis of colonial society is theoretically and methodologically interesting, as it reconstructs how colonialism as a system of domination with global reach produces and is reproduced in a topological order, that is, in a specific spatio-social arrangement, and a related order of practices. He elaborates how this global order implodes into situations of interaction. And he shows how not only politics, but bodies and selfs are shaped in this process. Long before social sciences started to discuss the necessity of a 'spatial turn' (cf.Soja, 1989, 1996; Massey, 2005), he elaborated a most insightful reconstruction of the interrelations between space, power and subjectivity.

4 'Safe Places': Segregation in the Intervention Society

In most former colonies, the strictly divided lifeworld described by Fanon has become something belonging to the past. Surely, the post-colony, too, is marked by striking socio-economic inequalities. But the latter is no longer organized around a racially coded distinction between 'foreign rulers' and 'natives'. Yet, the socio-spatial arrangements described by Fanon seem to systematically re-emerge in a different type of context: in places of humanitarian military interventions. In the highly internationalized contemporary crisis zones from Afghanistan and Iraq to Mali or Darfur, we find again social spaces, which are organized around the need of powerful outside actors to separate and distance themselves from indigenous populations. The humanitarian projects of peacebuilding, aid and democratization are run out of fortified compounds which sustainably transform the localities in question (Smirl, 2008, 2015; Duffield,

2010, 2012; Andersson & Weigand, 2015). What to make of these seeming continuities? What do they tell us about the historicity of global politics? In the following I am going to show, that there might be more to neocolonial patterns of internationalized governance than a mere reproduction or re-enactment of imperial imaginaries and knowledges.

Ethnographic exploration of Kabul's 'divided world' revealed that this socio-spatial arrangement was produced primarily not by ideologies or ideas, but by very practical concerns. As in Fanon's colonial society, division was driven by a security rationale: the context in question was marked not only by humanitarian aid, but also by military and political efforts to end an ongoing internal conflict and to reshape state and society. As these international efforts are welcomed by some and contested by others, interveners consider local populations not only as people in need whose hearts must be won, but also as a potential threat. Intervention societies are, therefore, characterized by the juxtaposition of internal conflicts, on the one hand, and resistance towards or open struggle against the intervention on the other. Protecting against the latter – which means protecting against dangerous parts of the indigenous population – becomes a major concern in the practical organization of interventionism.

What did field research in Kabul reveal about the practical solutions found to this problem? The most obvious insight was that, as in Fanon's reconstruction of colonial society, the interveners' quest for security created and articulated itself within a particular topological order. Security was conceived in terms of 'safe places'. And the latter were defined, essentially, by keeping potentially dangerous Afghan nationals outside. This security rationale was, of course, well founded. Almost one and a half decades into the intervention project, the insurgency was all but contained. Yet, similar to the insurgents who had generalized their resistance against the intervention to such a degree that everyone and everything related to it had become a potential target, the intervention itself had generalized its threat perception to include everyone and everything appearing Afghan or 'local'. As in similar intervention theatres, 'making safe places', hence, first and foremost meant putting distance between local/Afghan lifeworlds and the world of internationals (cf. Andersson & Weigand, 2015).

On the level of practices, this logic was epitomized by what Mark Duffield, scholar in critical peace and conflict studies, has named the 'fortified aid compound' (Duffield, 2010): permanent, quasi-military architectural structures designed to protect international humanitarian interveners against a potentially contentious population. Behind high concrete walls, topped with barbed wire fences, the protagonists of the intervention worked and lived detached from the practical problems and normative requirements of the actual local context. Huge logistical efforts were undertaken to uphold within these bunkerized spaces, living standards and working conditions which met 'Western' expectations. On their inside the fortified compounds of humanitarian interveners in Kabul, hence, looked similar to those in Mali or South Sudan (Andersson & Weigand, 2015; Duffield, 2012).

In a sociological perspective it was, however, interesting to observe, that these physical structures on their own cannot account for security. Massive as they are, they can never be closed, because at least occasionally people have to get in and out. Like the bunker, the fortified compounds of the humanitarian missions have doors and gates – vulnerable openings, traffic through which had to be controlled. So, the physical structures erected to create 'safe places' need complementary social processes to reliably fulfil their task. Systems of rules were defining who, under which conditions and at what hours was allowed to pass, were conceived to regulate entrances and exits. Procedures and personnel were put into place to enforce them. The physical structures which most visibly divided the world of the 'internationals' from the world of the 'locals' were hence embedded in a multitude of social practices, which regulated access and modulated experiences within and around them.

The practical arrangement I had found to facilitate my research, put me in a unique position, to observe some of these processes more closely. I had embedded myself with an Afghan civil society organization, which since the early 2000s had been engaged in grassroots peacebuilding initiatives. It was chiefly funded by Western and international donors, but enjoyed particular legitimacy in the Pashtun-dominated provinces of the South, where resistance against the intervention was most longstanding and most pronounced. I was, hence, embedded in a milieu of liberal but culturally self-confident Afghans who worked in the surroundings of the intervention project, but right at the frontier between their lifeworld and that of the interveners on whose funding and support their organization depended. Crossing between these two worlds – alone or accompanied by Afghan colleagues/informants – was a practical necessity. And it also became an important heuristic engine.

For many of my Afghan research informants, the logic of fortification, which organized central parts of the city, created frequent experiences of rejection, exclusion and humiliation. Working in the surroundings of the intervention project, they had frequent contact with the world of the interveners. These encounters, however, were usually organized in ways, which made their status as merely tolerated visitors unmistakably clear. Control procedures performed at the entrances of fortified compounds, for example, were by rule more extensive for Afghans than for 'internationals'. Frequently, Afghans who did not work inside the compound would find it difficult to gain access at all – even if they had a legitimate reason for their visit. During my stay, the Afghan organization I was working for, once sent me to a meeting, which was only remotely related to the projects I was working on. When asking my superior why not the actual expert on the topic was attending instead, she explained that the meeting took place in a highly securitized compound, to which the competent Afghan colleague would be denied access. Even within the compounds, contacts between local and international staff was regulated and restricted. There were, for example, different canteens. One informant, who used to work for a US-government contractor, told me that for meetings outside the compound, he and his American supervisor always had to ride in two different cars. Besides these formal organizational procedures, informal rules played an important role, too. Given that the 'international staff' of the intervention reflected the phenotypical diversity of the global population, belonging to this group was not evident, but had to be performed. Crucial in this regard were practices of distinction, which displayed – in speech, clothing or other lifestyle choices - attributes of Western Modernity. Many women working for international organizations paraded attributes of Western femininity, even if they had to interact with Afghan collaborators. Complaints about the indigestibility of Afghan food were common, especially among those 'internationals' whose lives were mainly confined to the compounds. Collective alcohol consumption, which typically plays a role in expat communities, was in the Afghan context also symbolically charged. These and similar practices of distinction produced distance towards Afghans even under the conditions of immediate proximity.

Most importantly, however, the security rationale of the intervention and the related admission procedures operated not only at the gates and check posts of the fortified compounds of the humanitarian organizations. It was mimicked in all public places, which intended to attract 'internationals' as their clientele, among them not only shops, banks, restaurants and hotels, but also businesses and organizations that wished to cooperate with the protagonists of the intervention, such as the Afghan organization I was embedded with. The impact of fortification went, hence, far beyond the compounds themselves. It shaped the city space.

As a consequence, Afghans who worked or lived in the surroundings of the intervention project found themselves navigating a segregated urban space, which eerily resembled the constellation described by Fanon. It was a divided world with borders marked by checkpoints and sally ports manned by armed guards, who acted as the living interface of a global order of domination.

Humanitarian interventions are truly global political projects. Yet, they are based on a starkly asymmetric representation of world society: well-functioning, 'modern' or 'civilized' regions on the one hand and 'problem zones' on the other (Calhoun, 2004), which call for the re-establishment of 'normality'. In the social and symbolic centres of intervention societies, this asymmetrically binary world order is regularly produced in situations of interaction and in organizational arrangements, designed to keep people identified as 'local' at bay and to put them in their place.

Despite such regular experiences of rejection and exclusion, for many Afghans who worked within and around the intervention project, the world of the 'internationals' was also a place of desire. Although they remained critical of certain aspects of Western lifestyle, they longed – some of them desperately – for a life in an 'open society'. The world of the 'internationals' in Kabul, their compounds, hotels or restaurants, were places desired not so much for their prosperity, but for their affordance of personal liberties; there, it was possible to escape cultural, political and religious constraints. The desire for such liberties was, of course, not shared by Afghans in general. It was typical for the people with whom I mainly interacted during field research: they belonged to the cultural elite of the country, but not to its political or economic one. They were middle-aged or young, many had lived abroad, as exiles in neighbouring countries or as students, and some had been strongly influenced by emancipatory politics under Soviet rule. One way or another, they had become familiar with forms of interaction and self-expression, which general social norms in their country did not permit. Therefore, they longed for places (or situations) in which these rules were suspended. As in Fanon's description, such places were literally within reach, but refused to take them in.

5 Same but Different

What can we learn from this inquiry into the presence of the colonial past in contemporary world society? While the similarities of the lifeworlds created by late colonialism, on the one hand, and humanitarian interventionism, on the other, are striking, there are some pronounced differences. The most obvious one is the normative context. Whereas colonialism seized and exploited distant territories to further essentially national interests, humanitarian interventions are said to be put in place in the interests of humanity. Within the epistemic order of colonialism segregation of the 'natives' was consistent, as the latter were considered – at least initially – as not (yet) fully developed humans. This did not only justify the strict separation of lifeworlds, but also pre-emptively delegitimized any claim they could make. To humanitarian interventionism, by contrast, the socio-spatial exclusion of local populations appears as a security necessity that is normatively problematic. Humanitarian interventions are founded in and justified by universalized norms and values, most important of all the idea of universal human dignity. Whereas colonizers could justify their actions by their superior stand on the evolutionary ladder, humanitarianism operates under the assumption of an equal value of all human life. The declared goal of the intervention and the reasons for its existence is to transform the society intervened upon so as to further these values. Thus, while in the colonial situation the image of the 'dangerous native' had been consistent with the colonizers' narrative about the world and their own place in it, efforts to shield humanitarian interventions from the people they came to protect are at odds with the principles of humanitarianism and, hence, risk to jeopardize the legitimacy of intervention project and to create new security problems.

In my research, I, therefore, could also observe how the divided world of interventionism was contested not only by Afghans, but by people belonging to the intervention themselves. Some of these instances were rather mundane: I met 'internationals' who proudly told that they got their weekly meat supply in the city's 'butcher street'; it was their way to create moments of personal proximity to a context from which they felt constantly being pulled away. Another typical example is the many urban legends about intervention staff dodging security protocols to eat in 'local' restaurants or to socialize in less securitized private houses where 'internationals' as well as Afghans were welcome. Some of the stories, however, were more dramatic, as when former intervention staff turned humanitarian ideals into a personal responsibility, supporting long-term and out of their private resources Afghans whom they had met during their stay in the country. This privatization of humanitarianism escalated upon the complete pull-out in summer 2021, when countless people who had once worked and lived in Afghanistan as soldiers, police(wo)men, aid workers, journalists, researchers or business(wo)men tried to support and protect former Afghan collaborators.

The very diversity within the milieu of the interveners was another constant source of contestation and dissent. Whereas all large intervention organizations are structurally dominated by staff from the so-called Global North, many of the employees come from the developing world. The conflict between 'the West' and 'the rest', which conditions interactions between interventionists and Afghans, is, hence, mirrored within the milieu of the intervention itself. Especially among 'internationals' who worked for smaller international or national organizations and/or whose origins were not (only) in the Global North a kind of counter-culture could be observed. Proximity to the local context was its guiding ethos, put into practice by learning regional languages, dressing according to local customs, driving in worn, low-profile cars, buying bread, vegetables and other food in small stores or on stalls in the street, and by socializing with Afghans in appropriate ways. This solidarization with the local context was typically accompanied by a certain estrangement from the dominant intervention culture.

Against the background of these complexities, it would be sociologically short-sighted to relate the similarities observed between the colonial and the interventionist lifeworld to a simple continuity of colonial domination. The comparative analysis developed in this chapter has shown that in both cases the segregation of space is enacted first and foremost as a practical response to a perceived security problem. The epistemic and normative horizons conditioning this perception, however, differ significantly – and with that, as explained just above, the possibilities for contesting this order.

There is, however, one indisputable continuity between colonial and intervention societies. Both are sites, which play a crucial role in the constitution of world society. Colonial and intervention societies can be conceived as arenas in which the power and knowledge structures of world politics collapse into concrete places and condition existences within them. This way, an abstract and global epistemic, normative and political system is performed, stabilized and made negotiable in human interaction. The crucial point is that these interactions are conditioned as encounters not between 'Frenchmen' and 'Algerians', 'Americans' and 'Afghans', but between the 'Universal' and the 'Particular', the 'Global' and the 'Local'. Colonizers as well as humanitarian interveners position themselves as representatives of humanity, as agents of a planetary social whole; furthering the interest of the latter justifies their arrival in the first place. As these ideas, however, are put to work in concrete social spaces the distinction between the Global and the Local engenders social practices of exclusion. For the 'locals' it creates experiences of the Global without belonging to it, experiences of the world in the form of exclusion.

It is no coincidence, that these dynamics were first analytically reconstructed by a scholar who was himself a colonial subject. Fanon's work is a telling example of how the historicity of the observer informs analytical perspectives. In the power centres of world society, globalization was experienced and theorized as a process of circulation, expansion, and communication driven by technological innovations; in the colonies, by contrast, it appeared as a continuous struggle in everyday interactions. Reading Fanon not only as a sociologist of violence and colonialism, but as a sociologist of globalization reminds us that historicity is necessarily situated. Considering the historicity of world society and world politics, therefore, is not only an exercise in historical analysis. It is also an exercise in perspectivation.

References

Andersson, R. & Weigand, F. (2015). Intervention at Risk: The Vicious Cycle of Distance and Danger in Mali and Afghanistan, *Journal of Intervention and Statebuilding*, 9(4), 1–23.

Baberowski, J. (2015). *Räume der Gewalt*, Frankfurt: Fischer.

Balandier, G. (1951). La situation colonial: approche théorique, *Cahiers Internationaux de Sociologie*, 1(110), 44–79.

Barfield, T. J. (2004). Problems in Establishing Legitimacy in Afghanistan, *Iranian Studies*, 37(2), 263–93.

Bayart, J. F. (2016). Relire Fanon, *Politique Africaine*, 143(3), 137–43.

Calhoun, C. (2004). A World of Emergencies: Fear, Intervention, and the Limits of Cosmopolitan Order, *Canadian Review of Sociology/Revue Canadienne de Sociologie*, 41(4), 373–95.

Dorronsoro, G. (2000). *La Révolution Afghane des Communistes aux Tâlebân*, Paris: Karthala.

Duffield, M. (2010). Risk-management and the Fortified Aid Compound: Everyday Life in Post-interventionary Society, *Journal of Intervention and Statebuilding*, 4(4), 453–74.

Duffield, M. (2012). Challenging Environments: Danger, Resilience and the Aid Industry, *Security Dialogue*, 43(5), 475–92.

Edwards, D. B. (1989). Mad Mullahs and Englishmen: Discourse in the Colonial Encounter, *Comparative Studies in Society and History*, 31(4), 649–70.

Fanon, F. (1965). *The Wretched of the Earth*, London: Macgibbon & Kee.

Go, J. (2016). *Postcolonial Thought and Social Theory*, New York: Oxford University Press.

Green, N. (2011). The Trans-border Traffic of Afghan Modernism: Afghanistan and the Indian 'Urdusphere', *Comparative Studies in Society and History*, 53(3), 479–508.

Koloma Beck, T. (2016). Gewalt – Raum: Aktuelle Debatten und deren Beiträge zur raumsensiblen Erweiterung der Gewaltsoziologie, *Soziale Welt*, 67(4), 431–50.

Koloma Beck, T. (2018). Liberating the Women of Afghanistan, *Socio*, 11, 57–75.

Lewin, K. (2009). The Landscape of War, *Art in Translation*, 1(2), 199–209.

Manchanda, N. (2017). The Imperial Sociology of the 'Tribe' in Afghanistan, *Millennium*, 46(2), 165–89.

Massey, D. B. (2005). *For Space*, London: SAGE Publications.

Miller, J. (1976). Merleau-Ponty's Marxism: Between Phenomenology and the Hegelian Absolute, *History and Theory*, 15(2), 109–32.

Monsutti, A. (2012). Fuzzy Sovereignty: Rural Reconstruction in Afghanistan, Between Democracy Promotion and Power Games, *Comparative Studies in Society and History*, 54(3), 563–91.

Nunan, T. (2016). *Humanitarian Invasion: Global Development in Cold War Afghanistan*, New York: Cambridge University Press.

Rabasa, A., et al. (2007). *Ungoverned Territories: Understanding and Reducing Terrorism Risks*, Santa Monica: Rand Corporation.

Rendall, J. (1982). Scottish Orientalism: From Robertson to James Mill, *The Historical Journal*, 25(1), 43–69.

Risse, T. (ed.) (2011). *Governance without a State? Policies and Politics in Areas of Limited Statehood*, New York: Columbia University Press.

Smirl, L. (2008). Building the Other, Constructing Ourselves: Spatial Dimensions of International Humanitarian Response, *International Political Sociology*, 2(3), 236–53.

Smirl, L. (2015). *Spaces of Aid: How Cars, Compounds and Hotels Shape Humanitarianism*, London: Zed Books.

Soja, E. W. (1989). *Postmodern Geographies: The Reassertion of Space in Critical Social Theory*, London: Verso.

Soja, E. W. (1996). *Thirdspace: Journeys to Los Angeles and Other Real-and-Imagined Places*, Oxford: Blackwell.

Trotha, T. (1994). *Koloniale Herrschaft: Zur soziologischen Theorie der Staatsentstehung am Beispiel des 'Schutzgebietes Togo'*, Tübingen: Mohr.

10 The Colonial Origins of Policing
The 'Domestic Effect' in the UK and the US

Julian Go

1 Introduction

If we are to fully apprehend the historicity of the international order, as the present volume urges us to do, then we must also apprehend the bifurcation that undergirds it. The 'international order' does not just consist of relations between nation-states. The very idea of an *international* order relies upon a conceptual and practical bifurcation between the 'international' on the one hand, and the 'national' on the other: a binary distinction, in other words, between the inside/outside, the internal/external, or the domestic/foreign (Walker, 1993). This binary is both conceptual and practical. It is conceptual because it is an idea: the idea that the world can be divided into something called an 'international' order that is ontologically distinct from a 'domestic' order – the idea that there really is an inside and outside to states. The binary is practical, however, in the sense of *practices*. The binary idea has been solidified and perpetuated through various regimes or assemblages of state power: legal regimes that declare who is a citizen and hence 'inside' and who is not, a panoply of institutions that exercise 'sovereignty' over 'domestic' territory and which deal in 'international' law, and so on. It is through these very regimes that the 'state effect' is produced (Mitchell, 1991) and, along with it, the 'domestic effect' – the *appearance* of a domestic space and hence the *appearance* of two distinct spaces that we call the international and national, the foreign and domestic, in the inside and outside.

The present chapter explores the origins of one such regime of state power that institutes the bifurcation between the international and national: the states' *dual regime of coercion.* All states have this dual regime: they have, at minimum, the 'military' or army on the one hand and 'police' on the other (and often more besides). This regime precisely manifests the bifurcation between the international and national: the 'military' functions in foreign-international space while the 'police' functions in domestic-national space. The former deals with 'foreigners', the latter with 'citizens'. The former deals in territory over which the state does not claim sovereignty, the latter deals in the states' 'own' territory. In his classic comparative analysis of policing systems in Europe, Bayley (1975: 327–28) stresses this distinction in his very definition of what 'policing' is. 'An army', he avers, 'uses force to defend a community from threats outside itself; a police force protects threats from within.'

This distinction between the 'police' and the military is an historical accomplishment, just like the international order itself. The perpetuation of policing in the modern world is likewise a historical accomplishment. To understand this history, therefore, is also to illuminate one of the crucial bases of the international order. This chapter accordingly seeks to uncover the origins and reproduction of the states' dual regime of power whereby the police and the military stand as two distinct institutions. In so doing, it helps illuminate one of the many areas in which 'historicity', as discussed by Schlichte and Stetter in their introduction to this volume, has structured the international order, in particular the sedimented forms of power and domination shaped by historicity (mode 5), and of complex temporalities involved in the reconfiguration of such power constellations (mode 2).

In this chapter, I will discuss two crucial moments in the history of the states' dual regime of power. The first is the emergence of modern policing itself, which did not happen in the Western world until 1829 with the creation of the London Metropolitan Police. I discuss the origins of the London Metropolitan Police in the first part of the chapter. As I will show, the London Metropolitan Police was one of the first state institutions of coercion to deal exclusively with 'domestic' territory that was separate from the army: a 'third arm' of the nation-state that was neither society nor the military. In the second part of the chapter, I discuss the creation of new power capabilities in urban policing in the United States in the early twentieth century. This involved various new tactics and techniques like 'hot spot' policing that significantly enhanced the ability of police to control domestic populations while constructing criminality as a distinct spatial target of intervention. These tactics and techniques would later spread throughout the world and persist in police departments nearly everywhere.

The larger point of the discussion below is not to reveal the historical significance of these two developments. Historians already know their significance. The point rather is to show that both developments in policing were inextricably intertwined with colonialism. The very idea of a civilian police separate from the military, as well as many of policing's tactics, technologies and tools, came originally from the colonial world.

In revealing this relation, the present chapter has been influenced by and contributes to an emerging literature that has shown the various ways in which policing in the UK and the US has been entangled with and shaped by colonialism overseas.[1] But the relation discussed in this chapter is not about 'entanglements' or 'connections'; it is more precisely focused upon *origins.* As we will see, it is not enough to say that the founding of the London Metropolitan Police was 'entangled' or 'connected' with the colonial site. It is more precise to say that the London Metropolitan Police *originated* in the colonies – and even more precisely, in Ireland. Similarly, the policing capabilities in early twentieth-century America were not just 'entangled' with or 'connected' to the colonies; rather, *they were born there*, and specifically, in the Philippines. Therefore, as opposed to showing just relations or 'connected histories' this chapter operates in the genealogical mode, showing the *colonial* origins of policing. Schlichte and Stetter (this volume) remind us that the study of international orders needs to be focused on 'sedimented forms' of colonial domination and imperial power embedded in the international order but which are so 'deeply engrained' that we barely notice them. The chapters in this volume reveal some of these forms as they are sedimented and often hidden in, for instance, broader culture (chapter by Steinmetz in this volume) or international organizations (chapter by Lawson in this volume). The story told in this chapter thus contributes to this project of excavation by revealing the colonial underpinnings of the one of the crucial components of our current bifurcated order which makes 'the international' thinkable.

2 The Emergence of the 'Police' in London

Like so many other aspects of what we today think of the 'international order', domestic policing is a relatively recent thing. While the activity of 'policing' in the broadest sense of the word (as in to 'maintain civil order', 'to organize or regulate') could be said to have been operative since the early modern period, the system of policing that we are familiar with today is a relatively new invention. Up until the mid-1700s, the typical usage of the term 'police' had been a verb rather than a noun – as in 'to police' – and in the latter meaning it was just thought of as a state of civilization. In 1694, the definition of police in the *Dictionnaire de l'Académie française* defined police as 'order.' Diderot, Voltaire and Rousseau had used the term *policé* in opposition to *sauvage* to suggest that policed states are civilized states. It was not until the mid-1700s that 'police' began to refer to an organized force, institution, or administrative

[1] For a sample of this growing literature, cf. Bell (2013), Ellison et al. (2008), Sinclair (2006) and Sinclair and Williams (2007). The seminal piece for the English police is Brogden (1987). For recent US police history, cf. Schrader (2019).

agency that operates in sovereign territory. Even then, it was often synonymous with simply 'government.' Adam Smith equated 'police' with any form of state regulation (Hay & Snyder, 1989; Neocleous, 1998).

By the early 1800s, two sets of institutions came close to approximating modern policing as we know it today. On the one hand, in England, the closest institution approximating a modern police force was little else than an agglomeration of constables and night watchmen. Residents of a town simply reported people suspected of a crime to a constable who in turn brought the suspect before the justice of the peace. They were not obliged to investigate crimes or prosecute them. Nor was their role to patrol the town to secure order. Instead, volunteers served as watchmen who patrolled the streets – and only at night (Critchley, 1978: 29–30). There had also developed various private means of policing, afforded by the wealthy classes; and the Bow Street Runners, a small emerging group for chasing down criminals in one area of London. But there was no single department for all of this. As for major incidents of disorder, such as rioting, officials were forced to call in the army (Lyman, 1964).

On the other hand, moving away from England to across the continent, a somewhat different 'policing' tradition had emerged with France's national *gendarmerie*, created in 1791. This emerged from the ashes of France's previously existing system of royal armies and guards, and Napoleon spread it to other European countries in the early 1800s, leading to the creation of the Gendarmerie in Prussia, the Netherlands, Italy's present-day *Carabinieri* and various other European policing institutions (Emsley, 1999b). These policing institutions, however, were still not domestic police departments as we know them today because they were not separate from the military. Scholars like Emsley (1999a) refer to this model of policing as the 'state military' model exactly because they have been typically branches of the military. The emergence of a 'third arm' between society and the military had not yet emerged.

The change came with the London Metropolitan Police, established by an Act of Parliament in 1829. This was novel in several respects. First, it organized an array of diverse activities into a single department and rationalized crime management into a single system. The 'motley assortment of part-timers, entrepreneurial thieftakers and amateur volunteers' that had dealt with crime in London previously was finally transformed into a full-time force of professionals organized into a single bureaucratic hierarchy (Reiner, 2000: 51). This was a force of initially 3,000 men under the control of the Home Secretary. Crucially, they were professionals, not volunteers, wearing uniforms and carrying rattles and short truncheons. They patrolled the streets regularly, charged with maintaining order, preventing crime and pursuing criminals throughout most of London. Their mandate was 'to prevent crime and disorder' (Reith, 1956: 140). One of the men behind the act, Sir Robert Peel, was proud of the new police's discipline and appearance, making a stark contrast with the earlier rag-tag group of watchmen. He wrote to his wife in 1829, 'I have been again busy all the morning about my Police. I think it is going very well, the men look smart, and a strong contrast to the old watchmen' (quoted in Lyman, 1964: 153).

The London Metropolitan Police was also novel because it created a new coercive institution that was not part of the army: a third arm existing between society and the military. As noted already, prior to the London Metropolitan Police, officials had to call in the army to manage outbursts of mass violence, riots or public disorder. The Peterloo massacre in August 1819, when up to 80,000 demonstrators were charged by the British calvary, had been only the most recent example: for decades previously there had been repeated instances of mass unrest that summoned the need for military intervention. The Gordon Riots of 1780, for example, had required 12,000 soldiers. In 1821, in preparation for the gathering of potential 'mobs' during Queen Caroline's funeral in 1821, the government concentrated half of its 22,000 soldiers in Britain around London, leading to violent clashes between the public and the army (Palmer, 1977: 637). To many officials, this constant reliance upon the army was no longer feasible. Furthermore, the propertied classes had grown more and more fearful of labour unrest and threats to their property, not least as radical and revolutionary ideas among workers had been sprung since the 1790s (Philips, 1980: 182). The army could not always manage these situations, nor could the disorganized array of constables and watchmen.

These rising fears required innovation. Something new was necessary, and officials and parliamentarians had been groping for solutions. In 1821, amidst the riots in London over Queen Caroline, the Duke of Wellington suggested that 'Government out, without the loss of a moment's time' to create some kind of 'police in London or a military corps, which should be of a different description from the regular military force.' In 1823, he repeated that the idea that the state should create a new force, under civil rather than military control, to deal with 'domestic insurrection and disturbance' (Palmer, 1988: 289). Sir Robert Peel in 1826 wrote to his friend similarly of the need for 'some kind of local force' that would be separate from the army (Peel & Parker, 1899: I, 405).

The London Metropolitan Police, proposed mainly by Peel, was the solution. Initially, Peel had hoped police departments to be formed across all of England, not least in the manufacturing districts where worker discontent had erupted, but for political reasons he and his supporters narrowed it to London first (Gash, 1961: 490–97; Philips, 1980). In either case, the bill was proposed expressly as a substitute for military intervention; a means by which the state could use force in strictly domestic – as opposed to foreign – territory (Philips, 1980: 182). The 'state civilian' model of policing, as opposed to a national *gendarmerie* controlled by the military, was thus born (Emsley, 1999a). To deal with crime and domestic disorder on home territory, to manage the affairs of citizens, and to generally regulate the social order, the 'new police' in London (as it is sometimes called) was birthed to replace the army. When Parliament debated the bill that would create the London Metropolitan Police, Peel told his fellow legislators that with the new police, they will 'be able to dispense with the necessity of a military force in London'.[2] Accordingly, as the historian Stanley Palmer (1977: 644) notes, the 'Queen Caroline riots of 1821 were the last time that the people and the British Army clashed in the streets of London. After 1829 ... military intervention was not necessary, for the new police were always able to control demonstrations and contain mobs.' The Army could now direct its attention to 'foreigners' on 'foreign' territory, that is, to the 'international' sphere.

If the London Metropolitan Police was radically novel, it was also seminal. In the 1830s, officials in the cities of Boston and New York in the United States sought alternatives to their existing constable and watch system on the one hand and, on the other, to the army for dealing with domestic disorder. Inspired by the London Metropolitan Police, they created their own police departments: Boston in 1838 and New York in 1845. Various other cities followed in subsequent decades, creating the modern police departments that today dot America's map. Other countries were also influenced by London's new police. As he reorganized the Paris police in the mid-1850s, Napoleon emulated the London Metropolitan Police (Emsley, 1999b: 3). By now, every country has its own version of the civil domestic police, following London's lead. The ubiquity of it is what enables scholars like Bayley (1975) to say that the army is the force dealing with 'outside' the nation while the police deals with 'threats from within'. The ubiquity of it also perpetuates the idea that there actually is an 'inside' as opposed to an 'outside' in the first place.

The London Metropolitan Police was both novel and seminal, but the idea for it did not emerge from thin air. To the contrary, it had a precedent and an inspiration. As I will now show, the model for it was the Irish Constabulary, a colonial counter-insurgency force of the English colonial state in Ireland. In other words, the London Metropolitan Police, and hence the very notion of a civil police separate from the army operating in domestic territory, was largely a colonial invention.

[2] Peel in *Hansard's Parliamentary Debates* xxi, 15 April, 1829 p. 883

On one level, it is hardly surprising to claim that policing has colonial origins. After all, postcolonial countries today owe much of their modern-day police forces to the period of colonial rule. One of the key tasks of the American colonial state in the Philippines, after subduing the Philippine Revolution, was to replace the Spanish *guardia civil* with a modern police force. It did the same in all of its colonies. Similarly, British colonial rule arguably created the first policing institutions in nearly all of its former colonies, often developing policing capacities in response to counter-insurgencies that in turn laid the basis for postcolonial policing (Eck, 2018; on postcolonial policing cf. Hönke & Müller, 2016). By the same token, national police in African countries today have their roots in the colonial era (Beek et al., 2017). Whether British, French or Portuguese colonialism, policing today in African countries owes much 'to the long shadow of colonial African policing', as Schlichte (2017) summarizes.

Still, this leaves open the question of policing in the imperial metropoles. If the origins of policing in postcolonial states in Africa, Latin America or Asia lie in colonialism, what about metropolitan policing that was supposedly exported to the colonies in the first place? In other words, what about policing in the imperial metropoles rather than just in the colonies or ex-colonies? What about the London Metropolitan Police?

In fact, the London Metropolitan Police was merely a modified copy of three prior paramilitary policing institutions in colonial Ireland: the Dublin Police force established in 1808, the Peace Preservation Police established in 1814, and the Irish Constabulary of 1822 (which essentially replaced the Peace Preservation Police). Notably, the three men most strongly credited with creating the London Metropolitan Police in 1829 and securing the passage in parliament of the act creating it were three friends and members of the Conservative Party: Robert Peel, the Duke of Wellington as Prime Minister and Henry Goulborn. All three had been chief secretaries of Ireland; and each oversaw the creation of one of these Irish policing bodies. The Duke of Wellington (then Sir Arthur Wellesley serving as Irish Chief Secretary) created the Dublin Police in 1808, Peel oversaw the Preservation Police in 1814 and Goulborn the Irish Constabulary in 1822.

The primary function of these Irish military forces had been simple: rather than fighting 'crime' per se they were meant to quell disorder and violently squash rebellion. They were counter-insurgency forces. The Dublin Police Force was created as a response to the uprisings in Dublin in 1803. The Peace Preservation Police for the rural areas was a response by Peel to the perceived 'barbarism' of the rural Irish and the 'state of lawless society' in the districts that Peel wanted settled by the English (Peel & Parker, 1899: I, 121–22). And while he feared such criminal activity, he was more horrified by the thought of insurrection which, he believed, was always brewing. The problem was that the British Army, which during the Napoleonic Wars had a presence in Ireland of some 50,000 strong, had fallen by 1813 to only 11,000 regular troops (while the English in Dublin Castle estimated that 40,000 were needed to effectively patrol the country). A paramilitary police force was the solution. Peel accordingly wrote that the idea behind the Peace Preservation Force was 'an armed civil force under the order of chief magistrates' to cover the rural areas, and that its main purpose was to crush 'insurrectional and turbulent' elements (PP, V. XXII January–May 1816). The Irish Constabulary established later under Goulborn was merely an extension of this force. Peel explained that it would best take the function of the military, acting on its own without the army's help 'for the suppression of mobs of all kinds' (Peel & Parker, 1899: II, 123). It later became a model for paramilitary policing throughout the Empire. By the end of the nineteenth century, senior British military officer Sir Hugh Rose remarked 'no system of police has ever worked better for the suppression of political agitation, or agrarian disorder, than the Irish Constabulary' (quoted in Arnold, 1986: 26).[3]

The London Metropolitan Police was in this sense an invention of colonial coercion. Indeed, Peel modelled it directly after the colonial counter-insurgency forces in Ireland that he himself had helped create and oversaw during his time as Chief Secretary of Ireland. The hierarchical structure of the force resembled the military hierarchy of the colonial forces that Peel and others had instituted. The London force was under the command of the Home Secretary, just as the colonial police in Ireland was under the command of the Lord Lieutenant at Dublin Castle. It was divided into seventeen divisions of 165 men each, with an officer entitled the 'superintendent' in charge of each division. The superintendent position reproduced the position of 'superintending magistrate' of the Peace Preservation Police. The London force even borrowed military titles: working with the superintendent in each division were four inspectors and sixteen 'sergeants' (Critchley, 1978: 50). It follows that when Peel first contemplated who should head the London force, he wrote to his friend that the ideal would be 'a military man conversant in the details of the police system of Ireland' and thus he sought out Irish magistrates for the job (Peel & Parker, 1899: II, 114). It was appropriate that one of the two first commissioners of the new London Metropolitan

[3] In fact, the Irish Constabulary was also the model for colonial policing throughout the Empire, from India to Burma and British Columbia (Ellison & O'Reilly, 2008). It was also a model for the first state police system in the US, the Pennsylvania State Police.

Police was Charles Rowan, a Lieutenant-Colonel in the British army who had been in Ireland previously. The other, Richard Mayne, was a barrister who had also been in Ireland.

Not only the form but also the function of the London Metropolitan Police had a colonial complexion. Early histories suggested that the motive for Parliamentary supporters of the bill establishing the police force was fear of rising crime. Some statistics at the time indicated that crime may have been rising indeed, but those statistics were also disputed (Reiner, 2000: 38). Rather than 'crime' in general, it was insurgency in particular that fuelled the formation of the force. London had seen riots every single year since 1815, and the *Times* published stories of violence almost daily (Lyman, 1964: 151). The rise in violence and rioting coincided with the economic downturn that plagued London in the years following the close of the Napoleonic War. This and the related impact of the unpopular Corn Laws of 1815 exacerbated fears of insurgency. It did not help that the monarchy was unpopular at the time and that republican views were being expressed loud and clear. For the urban elite and landed gentry, the spectre of revolution was real (ibid).

As noted, the army had been the main recourse to thwart mob violence or mass demonstrations. But this option became less and less viable as the years progressed. The emergency use of the army to quell disorder was like a sledgehammer applied in response to bursts of violence, and it was not pretty, amounting sometimes to 'drastic procedures' bordering on war', as one historian puts it (quoted in Reiner, 2000: 26). The use of the militia was another option, but it was politically unreliable: deputies of the militia were often from the same working-class strata as the rioters themselves. And in either case, anything resembling military power to be used on English citizens was anathema. For example, in 1822, Peel chaired a committee that looked into a Napoleon-style continental force as a possible solution for England. It concluded that such a force would be 'odious and repulsive' to English citizens (Ellison & Smyth, 2000: 13). A permanent professional police force that acted *like* a colonial military force but was not in fact the army was deemed by Peel, the Duke of Wellington, and their friends in Parliament to be the best solution. The London Metropolitan Police was the result.

3 The US: From the Philippine-American War to America's Cities, 1905–1920s

In 1845, New York City created one of America's first modern police forces. Albany and Chicago followed in 1851 and the rest of the country in subsequent decades. By the 1880s, every major city in the US had a London-style police force, each therefore bearing the hidden imprint of the latter's military-colonial origins. Yet, in the early twentieth century, policing in the US would take on even more military-colonial features.

What happened in the early twentieth century? One was the creation of mobile police squads and pin-mapping or 'hot spot' policing. This is a dominant feature of policing in the US today. It involves, first, the identification of 'hotspots': urban neighbourhoods where the crime rates are highest. For this, data on crime is mapped onto areas and then used to predict where crime is most likely. Mobile police forces are then deployed to saturate those areas. This was a profound change from city policing in earlier periods of American history. As noted above, police departments were established in the middle to late part of the nineteenth century, modelled after the London Metropolitan Police. And like the London Metropolitan Police, the police forces were divided into distinct districts and 'beats'. The common practice was for policemen to patrol their respective beats – a few blocks or miles of territory. Policemen rarely if ever left their own confined areas. Hot spot policing, by contrast, involves concentrating force in particular areas with highly mobile police units or 'squads' with the capability for rapid deployment.

The change to more mobile units, concentrated force, and statistical mapping occurred in the early twentieth century along with multiple other changes in policing at the time. The early twentieth century, in fact, was known as the 'reform era' of policing in the US; a period when police forces were 'modernized' and 'professionalized' – transformed from their original establishment in the mid-nineteenth century. The changes were multiple, involving a variety of innovations such as the new data collection on neighbourhood crime and then using it for 'pin mapping': putting pins marking criminal activity onto maps of the city. The changes also involved developing new tactical approaches for controlling territory and regulating bodies, not least mounted patrolmen who replaced foot patrols with mounted patrols using horses, bicycles, wagons and later motorcycles, electric wagons and eventually automobiles.

Historians have already discussed these developments and their significance: after all, these were the operations and tactics that spread throughout the US later and then to other parts of the world. Through new groups like the International Association of Police Chiefs, temporary military occupations and state-building projects, and an array of police consultants, advisors and aid programs, the police innovations that had developed in America's cities in the early twentieth century were slowly spread to countless other countries, starting with Central American and Lati American countries and then extended to other regions (Kuzmarov, 2012; Schrader, 2019).

Yet, historians have yet to recognize that many of the new policing tactics and techniques originated in America's new overseas colony, the Philippines. Just before the reform movement, the US had seized the Philippines from Spain in 1898. It had then embarked upon a war of conquest to defeat the Philippine revolutionary government at Malolos, labelled by the US as an 'insurgent' force. The war cost 500,000 Filipino lives. It was America's largest overseas war to date; and its first guerilla war overseas campaign. The US Army was crucial for the counter-insurgency campaign. And to meet the exigencies of the war, the Army had to innovate. For example, the Army faced Filipino guerilla units moving swiftly through a complex terrain of rivers, jungles and mountain villages. In this context, large-scale cordon-and-sweep campaigns and close-order formations were useless. Instead, the US Army had to use 'open order' operations: it had to divide into small mobile units to move through foreign terrain, gather intelligence, and then rapidly deploy. This essentially amounted to what is known as the 'hike', combining what later became more commonly known as 'reconnaissance-in-force' and 'search-and-destroy' missions (during the later Vietnam War), which enabled the American forces 'to match the mobility of the *insurrectos* [insurgents]' (Linn, 1991: 98).

Such tactics required an unprecedented reliance upon calvary units and 'special detachments of mounted infantry and scouts' or 'elite' forces who 'bore the brunt of the counterguerrilla war, acting in reconnaissance, strike, and mobile reserve capacities, functions in which they quickly developed an expertise' (Birtle, 2009: 114). It also required new intelligence-gathering practices. To survey the ostensible hordes of nonwhite Filipinos – anyone of whom could be an insurgent, in the Army's mind – and to collect information on nationalist activists and would-be guerrillas, the Army ended up forming three new services amounting to an original counterintelligence unit known as the Division of Military Information – the very 'first field intelligence unit in its hundred-year history' (McCoy, 2015: 7). The Division created novel records-keeping and information-gathering techniques: it established a mapping section and utilized new telegraph lines constructed across rural and urban territories to survey territory and track insurgents. With this information, the elite mobile units would then hunt down insurgents and raid their camps.

The police reform movement drew directly from this imperial-military apparatus in the colonial Philippines.[4] We can see this more clearly by focusing upon August Vollmer, chief of the Berkeley Police Department starting in 1905. In nearly all histories of the police reform movement, Vollmer is a leading character. Textbooks and historical accounts refer to him as 'the father of modern policing' (Oliver, 2017). This is because Vollmer innovated most of the police reforms and changes associated with the police reform movement, from mounted to patrols to data collection and crime mapping mentioned above. So influential were his changes that by the 1910s police departments around the country, from Los Angeles to Chicago to Detroit, brought him in as a consultant or as Chief to modernize their departments.

There was nothing especially unique about Berkeley to account for why Vollmer was so innovative. However, what is important is that Vollmer had previously been a key member of America's rising imperial-military regime. He had served in the Spanish-American war and then stayed on to police the city of Manila. Then the Philippine-American war broke out, and Vollmer served in that counter-insurgency effort until late 1899, after which he returned to Berkeley. In 1905, he became Berkeley's Chief of Police. This experience was Vollmer's main inspiration for his policing innovations.

Consider Vollmer's mobile police forces. In fact, Vollmer was the first to mount his entire police force. But his idea for mounting patrolmen did not come from thin air: it came from the US Army's counter-insurgency operations in the Philippines.[5] Vollmer in fact had been among those handpicked to join the new elite mobile units of the army in the Philippines. These mobile units embodied the army's new counter-insurgency approach, tasked with penetrating the country's interior to hunt down insurgents in a range of missions. Using the intelligence gathered by the Army's new intelligence systems, Vollmer and his unit thus tracked down, surrounded, and attacked insurgent camps – either by taking small boats through jungle rivers or mounted on horses. They were also called upon to respond swiftly to insurgent strikes in and around the city of Manila and further into Luzon.

In mounting his police forces in Berkeley, and later in Los Angeles, Vollmer drew from this experience. Like the terrain surrounding the city

[4] I discuss these developments in greater detail in Go (2020).

[5] Mounting forces on horseback had been used by the British empire, not least in Canada to give rise to the mounties. Mounted forces were also used by the army in conquering Native-Americans in the Plains and for militarized patrols like the Texas Rangers. But for Vollmer, the more immediate inspiration came from the Philippines.

of Manila, both Berkeley and Los Angeles covered vast territory, while Vollmer only had a handful of men to cover hundreds of square miles. Furthermore, crimes were occurring all around the city. In Los Angeles, bank robberies had sprung up throughout different districts. To meet the problem, Vollmer put his Berkeley police force on bicycles and, later in Los Angeles, created a new elite mobile division of three hundred men. These were to be just like the mobile elite soldiers in the Philippines on horses or small boats navigating the rivers of Luzon. Vollmer's mobile units, wrote one reporter after interviewing Vollmer at the time, 'put into effect some of the methods he used in chasing river pirates on the Pasig [River] and bushwhackers in the steaming wild jungles' (*Honolulu Star*, 5 June 1923: 1).

The new mobile units were not only going to prevent crime, they were going to deploy rapidly in response to crimes, just as mobile units in the Philippines responded to insurgent strikes, following the principles of the military's open-order operations. Shaw, a journalist who interviewed Vollmer about his innovations, later explained: 'Vollmer ... believed that the military techniques of war could be applied to the police war against criminal enemies' (AVP C7a: Shaw, ch. 38). In his own writings he stressed how mobility was a key military operation applicable to policing (AVP, Carton 3, 'Organization'). As Vollmer explained to his force: 'We must be able to move men rapidly from one scene of action to another. Concentration of force *is supremely important in military science,* and it will be important to the task we have at hand.'

Vollmer also innovated in police intelligence. Rather than relying upon a single detective for crimes like theft or murder that had already happened, he created at Berkeley and later Los Angeles new police divisions devoted entirely to intelligence-gathering and analysis to help hunt down criminals. This too was inspired by his experience in the Philippines. Just as the US Army created a special Division of Military Information in the Philippines to identify, track and predict insurgent activity in the Philippines, Vollmer created an 'Intelligence Division' within his police force. As he explained to his officers: 'we are up against a tough fight against organized criminal enemies. To make the most of the forces at our command, we will have to operate according to the principles of military science.'

Furthermore, the origins of Vollmer's 'pin mapping' or 'crime mapping' lie in the colonial Philippines. Vollmer began doing this in the Berkeley police department soon after returning from the Philippine-American war and later encouraged other police departments to do the same (Schutt, 1922; AVP, B48a). This was a duplicate of the methods used by the Division of Military Information which had done similar mapping, using pins to track the locations of troops and insurgent attacks, while innovating upon the method (by, for example, attaching slips of information to each pin). So just as the military mapped out the location of insurgent strikes across the topography of Central Luzon, Vollmer taught the intelligence units of his force to map out criminal activity across the city (in one case, for example, mapping out bank robberies). Vollmer explained that this was one of the first principles of policing: 'to develop strategy, which simply means "making war on maps"'. He further explained in public and in private correspondence this 'principle of strategy' was not only homologous with military methods, but came from it (AVP, B40a, C7a).

The case of Vollmer and urban policing attests to the larger point of this chapter. In theory, policing is a nationally endogenous institution. While armies are meant for foreigners and colonial subjects, policing is meant for citizens. While armies are meant to operate on territory 'outside' the nation, policing is meant for the 'inside'. In this sense, policing is a crucial aspect of the dual regime of power by which the very distinctions between the inside and outside, the internal and the external, and the national and the foreign are maintained. The irony is that policing has not originated nor has it developed over time endogenously to the nation. This chapter has shown that modern policing as we know it today has colonial origins. Novel coercive forms were created in colonial Ireland and they were brought back to London. New counter-insurgency practices were developed in the colonial Philippines and they were imported back to the United States. These forms and practices did not so much 'diffuse' or 'connect' sites as they did move from one site – that is, the colonial, the foreign, the Other – to another site: the 'metropole', 'domestic' and 'national'.

Such movement continues to this day, even as it is sometimes challenged in ways that nonetheless reproduce the bifurcation. In 2014, for example, in Manchester, New Hampshire, word was spread that the city's police department was going to receive millions of dollars' worth of surplus military equipment from the government, including a mine-resistant armoured vehicle. The mainly white residents of the town protested vehemently, some holding up signs saying 'More Mayberry, Less Fallujah' (*WSJ*, 4 February 2014: A3). Of course, the reference here was to the fictional, peaceful and idyllic white small town of Mayberry, North Carolina, and its bumbling but benign, well-intentioned and friendly white police chief, Andy Taylor. They protested because they feared that militarized policing would turn their otherwise peaceful Mayberry-like town into the site of American imperial violence far off, over there, in Iraq. Theirs was thus a protest against the blurring of the lines between the 'domestic' (read: peaceful, white, Christian, America) and 'foreign' (read: violent, colonial, brown, Muslim, Iraq). In other words, the protestors wanted to make sure that the bifurcation between the domestic and the foreign, the metropole and colony, the inside and outside was firmly upheld.[6]

All evidence suggests the protestors were unsuccessful. Around the United States the so-called 'militarization' of the police – with its colonial and imperial origins – has continued unabated. But even if such protests were unsuccessful, by their very terms they contribute to the *domestic effect*, reproducing the idea of a separation between Mayberry and Fallujah, the inside and the outside, the domestic and the foreign; indeed the national from the international.

Archives and Abbreviations

AVP The Papers of August Vollmer, Bancroft Library, University of California, Berkeley

PP The Papers of Sir Robert Peel, British Library, Add MS 40202

References

Arnold, D. (1986). *Police Power and Colonial Rule: Madras, 1859–1947*, Delhi: Oxford University Press.

Bayley, D. H. (1975). The Police and Political Development in Europe, in C. Tilly (ed.). *The Formation of National States in Western Europe*, Princeton: Princeton University Press, 328–79.

Beek, J., Gopfert, M., Owen, O. & Steinberg, J. (eds.) (2017). *Police in Africa: The Street Level View*, Oxford: Oxford University Press.

Bell, E. (2013). Normalising the Exceptional: British Colonial Policing Cultures Come Home, *Mémoire(s), identité(s), marginalité(s) dans le monde occidental contemporain* 9. http://mimmoc.revues.org/1286

Birtle, A. (2009). *U.S. Army Counterinsurgency and Contingency Operations Doctrine, 1860–1941*, Washington: Center of Military History.

Brogden, M. (1987). The Emergence of the Police: The Colonial Dimension, *The British Journal of Criminology*, 27(1), 4–14.

Cosmas, G. (1998). *An Army for Empire: The United States Army in the Spanish-American War*, Shippensburg: White Mane Publishing Co, Inc.

Critchley, T. A. (1978). *A History of Police in England and Wales*, London: Constable.

Eck, K. (2018). The Origins of Policing Institutions: Legacies of Colonial Insurgency, *Journal of Peace Research*, 55(2), 147–60.

Ellison, G. & Smyth, J. (2000). *The Crowned Harp: Policing in Northern Ireland*, London: Pluto Press.

[6] The racial dynamics involved in the colonial origins of policing require more space to fully elaborate, but cf. Go (2020).

Ellison, G., Smyth, J. & O'Reilly, C. (2008). From Empire to Iraq and the 'War on Terror': The Transplantation and Commodification of the (Northern) Irish Policing Experience, *Police Quarterly,* 11(4).

Emsley, C. (1999a). A Typology of Nineteenth-Century Police, *Crime, Histoire & Sociétés / Crime, History & Societies,* 3(1), 29–44.

Emsley, C. (1999b). *Gendarmes and the State in Nineteenth-Century Europe,* Oxford: Oxford University Press.

Gash, N. (1961). *Mr. Secretary Peel,* Cambridge: Harvard University Press.

Go, J. (2020). The Imperial Origins of American Policing: Militarization and Imperial Feedback in the Early 20th Century, *American Journal of Sociology,* 125(5), 1193–254.

Hay, D. & Snyder, F. (1989). Using the Criminal Law, 1750–1850: Policing, Private Prosecution, and the State, in D. Hay & F. Snyder (eds.). *Policing and Prosecution in Britain 1750–1850,* Oxford: Clarendon Press, 3–54.

Hönke, J. & Müller, M.-M. (eds.) (2016). *The Global Making of Policing: Postcolonial Perspectives,* London: Routledge.

Kuzmarov, J. (2012). *Modernizing Repression: Police Training and Nation-Building in the American Century,* Amherst: University of Massachusetts Press.

Linn, B. (1991). Intelligence and Low-Intensify Conflict in the Philippine War, 1899–1902, *Intelligence and National Security,* 6(1), 90–114.

Lyman, J. L. (1964). The Metropolitan Police Act of 1829, *Journal of Criminal Law and Criminology,* 55(1), 141–54.

McCoy, A. W. (2015). Policing the Imperial Periphery: The Philippine-American War and the Origins of U.S. Global Surveillance, *Surveillance & Society,* 13(1), 4–26.

Mitchell, T. (1991). The Limits of the State: Beyond Statist Approaches and Their Critics, *American Political Science Review,* 85(1), 77–96.

Neocleous, M. (1998). Policing and Pin-Making: Adam Smith, Police and the State of Prosperity, *Policing and Society,* 8(4), 425–49.

Oliver, W. (2017). *August Vollmer: The Father of American Policing,* Durham: Carolina Academic Press.

Palmer, S. (1977). Before the Bobbies: the Caroline Riots, 1821, *History Today,* 27(10), 637–44.

Palmer, S. (1988). *Police and Protest in England and Ireland, 1780–1850,* Cambridge: Cambridge University Press.

Peel, R. & Parker, C. S. (1899). *Sir Robert Peel. From his private papers. Edited for his trustees by Charles Stuart Parker. With a chapter on his life and character by his grandson, the Hon. George Peel,* London: J. Murray.

Philips, D. (1980). *'A New Engine of Power and Authority': The Institutionalization of Law-Enforcement in England 1780–1830,* V. A. C. Gatrell, B. Lenman & G. Parker (eds), London: Europa Publications.

Reiner, R. (2000). *The Politics of the Police,* Oxford: Oxford University Press.

Reith, C. (1956). *A New Study of Police History,* London: Oliver and Boyd.

Schlichte, K. (2017). Policing Africa: Structures and Pathways, in J. Beek, M. Göpfert, O. Owen & J. Steinberg (eds.). *Police in Africa: The Street Level View,* Oxford: Oxford University Press, 19–26.

Schrader, S. (2019). *Badges without Borders,* Berkeley: University of California Press.

Schutt, H. (1922). Advanced Police Methods at Berkeley, *National Municipal Review*, 11(3).

Sinclair, G. (2006). *At the End of the Line: Colonial Policing and the Imperial Endgame 1945–80*, Manchester: Manchester University Press.

Sinclair, G. & Williams, C. A. (2007). 'Home and Away': The Cross-Fertilisation between 'Colonial' and 'British' Policing, 1921–85, *The Journal of Imperial and Commonwealth History*, 35(2), 221–38.

Walker, R. B. J. (1993). *Inside/Outside: International Relations as Political Theory*, Cambridge: Cambridge University Press.

Part III

Global History and the Imperial Fundaments of International Politics

11 Unearthing the Coloniality in the International through the Genealogy of IR in Japan and Beyond

Tomoko Akami

1 Introduction

This chapter argues that the notion of the 'International' contributed to making the knowledge of modern trans-border interactions 'a-colonial'. The notion so far had defined a conceptual framing for understanding political, economic, legal, social, intellectual, cultural and institutional interactions across political boundaries especially since the mid-late nineteenth century. Although the 'Global' is now becoming increasingly prominent, it remains to be the core concept of the inter-(nation) state system, on which the disciplines (or sub-disciplines) of IR, International Law and International History have been based. Accordingly, this chapter tackles the notion of the International as a case for the fifth mode of historicity, expounded in Introduction of this book: it had been historically constructed and had been accepted as 'apolitical', making certain power dynamics of international politics invisible. It argues, therefore, revealing colonial aspects of the notion explicitly would allow us to recognize and examine so far neglected diverse and complex power dynamics of trans-border actions.[1]

Below I shall do so in two ways. First, I suggest two different concepts, namely 'inter-imperial' and 'inter-colonial', for framing trans-border interactions, not as *the alternative* to that of 'inter-national', but rather, to capture other layers of interactions which meshed with inter-national interactions. I briefly summarize how imperial/colonial factors have not been discussed as *constitutive of* the International in the above three disciplines until recently, largely because of an almost exclusive focus on Euro-America where the inter-state system was assumed. Integrating

[1] I thank for the comments of the editors and the participants of the two workshops in 2018 and 2019, and also thank the ANU College of Asia and the Pacific and the Rockefeller Archive Center for research funds. This chapter is a part of my broader project 'Towards a globalized knowledge of history of international relations', funded by the Australian Research Council.

non-Euro-American experiences and sources into this knowledge, therefore, I suggest, necessitates facing the coloniality of the International. Further, I argue the concepts of inter-imperial and inter-colonial would allow us to identify and examine imperial polities and their interactions, which had been invisible in the discourse of the International, but which had been dominant in extra-Europe, and this would help us to globalize our knowledge of modern international relations.

Second, after showing the different framings, which could acknowledge neglected imperial polities and their lateral relations, the chapter examines another neglected 'coloniality' in the International, Colonial Policy Studies in the genealogy of the discipline of IR. I use the case study of Japan, as it is a non-Euro-American case, and not Anglo-American cases that so far have been defined as *the* genealogy of IR. This case study of Japan suggests, I argue, the ambiguous impacts of Colonial Policy Studies in IR in Japan in its formative period, and the presence of the past ensuing therefrom.

While the first, third and fourth modes of historicity discussed in the Introduction by Schlichte and Stetter are well ingrained in historical works, if not in many of IR works, examining the case of Japan in a global historical context suggests a different understanding of 'temporality' (the third mode of historicity). This is because 'Japan' became a formal empire almost at the same time when most of the other (maritime) empires formalized their empires, institutionalizing the colonial administrations and creating the departments and other state apparatus at the respective imperial metropolitan centres. Those from the Japanese empire, whom I focus on in this chapter, therefore, had *contemporary* interactions with their counterparts in the other empires (and the colonies, including Japan's own), although when and how these interactions manifested may have not been unanimous (the sixth mode of historicity). This chapter will examine these contemporary interactions, and, therefore, the mutual constitutivity of the ideas across the regions, by taking a relational approach, suggested by HSIR, especially 'Global Historical Sociology' (Go & Lawson, 2017), as well as 'Global Relational Studies' (Sakai, 2020), rather than an essentialist approach of Global IR (Buzan & Acharya, 2010).

2 Making the Coloniality Visible in the Notion of the International: Different Framings of Inter-Imperial and Inter-Colonial

Until recently, the colonial factors had not been problematized as constitutive of the concept of the International, which was closely tied to the notion of the inter-(nation) state system. Although great works, such as Mommsen and Osterhammel (1986), Hardt and Negri (2000), Burbank and Cooper (2010), have examined empire, imperialism and colonialism, little attempt has been made to conceptualize them as constitutive of the modern international system. Especially in and after the era of the League of Nations, which has been understood to have advocated the new norm of 'self-determination', most scholars in the three key disciplines, mentioned above, almost exclusively focused on national sovereign states, not imperial polities, as the basic units of the International.

As suggested in the Introduction of this book, the notion of International Society by the English School (Bull, 1977; Bull & Watson, 1984), the most history-oriented school in the discipline of IR, for example, is a-colonial: it is defined as the society of national sovereign states; it had originally been formed as the society of the Christian nations within Europe, and *then* expanded to the rest of the world. Bull and Watson's influential work of 1984 hardly referred to the fact that many of these 'national sovereign states' in Europe were already 'global' with their formal or informal colonies before this society 'expanded' to the rest of the world (Akami, 2013). Dunne and Reus-Smit's (2018) recent work addresses this fatal omission of colonialism, but does not internalize colonialism or reconstruct its basic framework.

In contrast, recent works of international law have problematized colonialism as constitutive of international law. Koskenniemi (2001) and Third World Approach to International Law scholars/practitioners have argued that empires shaped modern international law, legitimizing their formal and informal colonizations (Koskenniemi, 2001; Anghie, 2005; Orford, 2012). By revealing that modern international laws perpetuated the power hierarchy between (former) empires and their (former) colonies, they advocate reforms to redress the current structural injustice.

Meanwhile, a growing number of historians have begun to examine histories of international organizations as a part of the formation of the modern global governing norms and institutions (Iriye, 2002; Pedersen, 2007). Yet, many so far have focused predominantly on Euro-American cases, which tended to accept the standard inter-state system, and adopt the 'a-colonial' notion of International Society. Accordingly, the dominant analytical framework has been the national-international binary (Sluga & Clavin, 2017), leaving little space for imperial polities and their lateral relationships.

Although the Euro-American centricity has so far been largely discussed in terms of culture or civilization, the omission of the coloniality in the scholarships on the International could be understood as the assumed centrality of the inter-(nation) state system. National sovereign states indeed became a new reality in a large part of the Americas in the early nineteenth century, and *the* norm in Europe with the end of the continental empires after 1919. Yet many of these 'national' states of Europe and North America continued to function as 'imperial' governments, governing colonial administrations beyond their metropoles, and imperial polities with different degrees of sovereignty dominated beyond Euro-America. Because (with a few exceptions) most of these imperial polities were not regarded as legitimate 'independent' actors in the inter-state system, the three key disciplines on the International largely neglected or dismissed them in their analyses. The inter-war period was, therefore, understood as the period of the challenge of nationalism *and* imperialism against 'liberal internationalism'.

In the past few years, however, historians have started to pay a greater attention to imperial polities in extra-Euro-America, and tried to internalize them into their analyses (cf. Legg, 2014; Monteiro & Jerónimo, 2018). I have also focused on lateral relations across these imperial polities (conceptualized as inter-imperialism and inter-colonialism) in Asia and their significance in the League's global governing projects (Akami, 2016, 2017).

While these works have demonstrated the constitutivity of the Colonial in the International, they also suggest why unearthing the coloniality in the International (the fifth mode of historicity, discussed in Introduction) is important. The notions of inter-colonial and inter-imperial within the discourse of the International at the League and League-related organizations, for example, allow us to examine neglected actors (e.g. colonial administrators and experts based in extra-Euro-America) and complex power dynamics they created. Such analyses have not been possible by the existing frameworks of national versus international, imperial versus national, or imperial versus international. By recognizing the neglected diverse actors, which had been made invisible by the historically constructed notion, we can ask a new set of questions that address complex power relations[2]: whether projects of the League or the UN prioritized shared interests of (former) empires or those of (former) colonial peoples; whether 'local' experts advanced the interests of their newly independent states and/or their peoples through international projects of the UN; or whether they were co-opted into supporting former empires' shared priorities.

[2] Such complex relationships, which cannot be explained by the framework of colonizer versus colonized, as elaborated in Introduction, are well captured in the chapter by Teresa Koloma Beck.

3 Unearthing Colonial Policy Studies and Its Legacies in a Genealogy of IR in Japan and Beyond

3.1 *Colonial Policy Studies as the Past in the Present Discipline of IR*

The second way of making the coloniality explicit in the notion of the International is to trace 'Colonial Policy Studies' in the genealogy of the discipline of IR, and examine their legacy and/or 'disappearance' in the discipline. Vitalis (2015) and Schmidt (1998) have pointed out that Colonial Policy Studies had been significant in the formation of the discipline of IR in the US. Vitalis (2015) suggests that this aspect has disappeared in the discipline, which indicated a submersed, fundamentally racist nature of the discipline.

In contrast, the case of Japan shows a clear lineage of Colonial Policy Studies in the 'discipline' of IR,[3] with its ambiguous implications. This has been explicitly acknowledged. In 1969, Kawata Tadashi[4] (1925–2008), whose textbook on IR (first published in 1958) has been regarded as the best of this kind in Japan (Ōhata, 1996: 394), noted that one genealogy of the 'discipline' of IR could be traced back to 'Colonial Policy Studies' (Kawata, 1996: 357). The first course on colonial policy studies was given by Nitobe Inazō (1862–1933) at the Kyoto Imperial University in 1903, which he then taught at the Tokyo Imperial University in 1909–20 (Kawata, 1996: 374–75). Nitobe, a Quaker (and better known as a prominent inter-war 'liberal internationalist' who served as Under-Secretary of the League of Nations in 1920–26), was an expert of agricultural economy (PhD from Halle University),[5] and a colonial technocrat who contributed to modernizing the sugar industry in Japan's colony, Taiwan, in 1901–6. Based on this experience, he was asked to teach the first course on the subject in Japan, becoming the founder of Colonial Policy Studies. Yanaihara Tadao (1893–1961), a Christian (No-Church Sect) and an economist, took over the course in 1923. He taught it until late 1937, when he was forced to resign from the university because of his public anti-war stance, as the Sino-Japanese War broke out. The course continued to be taught during the war (Kawata, 1996: 380).[6]

[3] I use the term, 'discipline', with inverted commas for the case of IR in Japan, because of its explicit inter-disciplinary (or anti single-discipline) stance from its beginning in 1956. Baji's recent work also locates Colonial Policy Studies in a genealogy of IR in Japan, and its studies especially on the South Sea (the Pacific islands) contributed to making the racially hierarchical knowledge of IR and creating the idea of Global South (Baji, 2022).

[4] All Japanese names in the text have been written as in Japan: a surname first and a given name last.

[5] It is now Martin-Luther-Universität Halle-Wittenberg.

[6] During the wartime, Nagao Sakurō taught the course in 1937–38, and then Tōhata Seiichi (Faculty of Agriculture) taught it in 1939–44.

This colonial policy studies became a part of the 'discipline' of IR in the 1950s. When Yanaihara was called back to Tokyo University immediately after the war, he renamed the course as '*Kokusai keizai ron* [Theories on International Economy]', and taught it until he became the university chancellor in 1951 (Kawata, 1996: 380). Kawata, who had been his student since 1946, took it over in 1964 (Kawata, 1996: 383).[7] Both Yanaihara and Kawata understood this course as an integral part of the 'discipline' of IR, and they contributed to the foundation and development of the Japanese Association of IR (JAIR). Kawata became its president in 1982–84, while Yanaihara led the establishment of the Association of International Economy in 1950, and became its first president (Kawata, 1996: 382).

3.2 *Ambivalent Factors of Colonial Policy Studies in Japan, the 1900s–1910s*

Before 1910s, the most dominant field in forming the knowledge of the International in Japan was International Law. The term, international, is said to have first appeared in Japan in 1873 in a book title, 'International' Law (*Kokusai hō*) (Akashi, 2004: 4). For the government (both Shogunate and Meiji), International Law was the vital knowledge and skill for conducting competent foreign policy and achieving international prestige. It became a requisite knowledge for career diplomats, while its 'non-official' experts served as advisors to the state. The Japanese Society of International Law (JSIL) was established in 1897, and started its journal in 1902 (initially called *Kokusai hō zasshi* [the *Journal of International Law*], and then *Kokusaihō gaikō zasshi* [the *Journal of International Law and Diplomacy*] after 1912).

The JSIL linked itself to the Institut de Droit International (1873–) and the International Law Association (1873–) (Akami, 2018a),[8] and together promoted the inter-national framework of the 'science' of International Law. Yet these Japanese experts at the JSIL could not avoid the imperial/colonial issues. 'International' relations for Japan were defined by power hierarchy among imperial polities of diverse degrees of sovereignty in their region, not equal national sovereign units. This was evident in unequal clauses Japan concluded with Euro-American countries in 1858–67 (repealed fully only in 1911). Furthermore, while Japan became a parliamentary democracy and constitutional monarchy in 1889, the expertise of

7 Yanai Katsumi, a Marxist economist, taught the course in 1951–63.

8 The Japanese national branch of the ILA was, however, not established until 1920 (Akami, 2018a).

International Law was crucial for its conducting imperial wars 'legally' and after-war negotiation of formal (legal) colonization in the 1890s–1910s (Dudden, 2005; Akami, 2018a). The post-Chinese hegemonic order of Northeast Asia was, therefore, the modern inter-imperial order, not the inter-(nation) state system (the so-called Westphalia system).

While the 'science' of International Law focused on the inter- (nation) state system, the gap between this 'science' and geopolitical reality was to be filled by *Shokuminchi seisakugaku* [Colonial Policy Studies]. In this context, Nitobe's Colonial Policy course of the 1900s–1910s produced the knowledge in which the Colonial and the International were mutually constitutive, not exclusive. According to the currently available contents of the course, which were based on the lecture notes of 1916–17,[9] his course was a general introduction to colonization, colonies, and colonial policies, not specific to Japan's colonies or colonial policies. It was divided into nine parts: first four on general historical trends of colonization and colonies; next four on methods of colonization, categories of colonies and colonial policies; and the last on the principles of colonial policies (Nitobe, 1969). He discussed general colonial governance as a part of broader international relations, while reinforcing a hierarchical world order based on the notion of civilization, and implicit military, economic and moral power relations.

Nitobe course was, therefore, intended to constitute a part of a modern 'discipline' on the International. He aimed it to be a 'social science' combining emerging fields of demography, economics (used the notions of capital and production), agricultural economy, cultural and religious relations, politics, and domestic and international law with general world history (Nitobe, 1969: 165). Despite its delivery style as a general talk (Ōuchi, 1969: 646; Yanaihara, 1969: 8) and its lack of theoretical coherence or pedagogical projection, Kawata stresses Nitobe's course was 'science' (social science), distinguished from most other colonial policy works of the time on two points: first, his was a broader scholarly analysis on the subject, not ad hoc technical analyses; second, it was independent from political and business interests (Kawata, 1996: 375–76).

Like many of non-Marxist pioneering IR works in the following decades, Nitobe's 'science' was science of management, not science to challenge power structure of international relations. His course predated the publications (either in original or in Japanese translation) of

[9] The notes were taken by Yanaihara as a student, supplemented by two other, which Yanaihara edited in 1937–42, and published in 1942. The only major change from the original notes was the term for aboriginal people (Nitobe used 'the natives', *Dojin*) (Yanaihara, 1969, originally written in 1942: 7–9).

the works by Lenin, Hilferding, Kautsuky, Luxemburg or Bukharin. As Kawata suggests, Nitobe should still have been aware of critical works of imperialism, such as that by Kōtoku Shūsui (1901) or by J. A. Hobson (1902), but chose not to embrace their stances (Kawata, 1996: 376). Rather, quoting Salisbury (three-time Conservative Prime Minister of Britain in 1885–1902), Nitobe understood that colonization was inevitable for a vital nation (Nitobe, 23), and it was best and logical for the world to utilize the (under-utilized) resources, especially in the 'under-developed' areas (Nitobe, 48, 167).

Yet, within this imperial framework, Nitobe developed a critical perspective, based on his Christian humanitarianism.[10] This was evident in his attitude towards the 'natives' in the colonies. While colonization was inevitable and even good for the world, he argued, its mission should be not for exploitation, but for humanitarian goals and the betterment of the world as a whole. In his view, the ultimate objective of colonization should be the benefit to the 'natives' (Nitobe, 1969: 165). There were, therefore, two ambivalent factors in his Colonial Policy Studies: one to see empires as the managers of world affairs; and another, the paternalistic objective of their policies to improve the conditions of the 'natives'.

3.3 Scientification of the International and the Place of the Colonial in the Era of the League of Nations

In the 1920s, the International was even more solidly based on the dominant inter-national framing, and focused on relations among national sovereign units. The League of Nations (founded in 1920) played a significant part in this process. The League was the first inter-governmental organization for global governance. Counteracting the Communist International, it advocated 'self-determination' as a new norm, and promoted a non-socialist/communist internationalism. The League also put great efforts in its publicity (Akami, 2018b), while the associations to promote the League of Nations were established in various countries, including the US (non-League member), and disseminated its notion of the International. The Japanese Association of the League of Nations (JALN), founded in 1920, was one of them, and soon began to publish its journal, *Kokusai chishiki [International Knowledge]* (Akami, 2018a). As a result, the term, *Kokusai* (inter-national), entered into peoples' everyday discourse.

[10] He was christened by a methodist missionary in 1878, while he was at the Sapporo Agricultural College at the same time as his classmate, Uchimura Kanzō, who later developed Non-Church Sect, was. Nitobe became a Quaker when he was studying at John Hopkins University in 1884–87. He married a Quaker, Mary Elkinton, in Philadelphia in 1891.

Adding to the previously dominant experts of International Law and Diplomatic History, the League fostered new experts of the new 'scientific' field, 'International Politics' (*Kokusai seiji*), which gradually occupied a dominant position in the knowledge of the International. The League inspired the foundation of organizations of these new experts, and mobilized them for its 'technical' works (Giddens, 1987). These new organizations included the Royal Institute of International Affairs (London, and its dominion/colonial branches), the Council on Foreign Relations (CFR, New York) and the Institute of Pacific Relations (IPR, initially Honolulu). The League's International Committee for Intellectual Cooperation also began a project to establish a 'scientific study' of international relations for international peace, the International Studies Conference (ISC, 1928–54). The ISC is now regarded as an origin of the discipline of IR in the US and the British Empire (Long & Schmidt, 2005; Long, 2006; Rietzler, 2009; Riemens, 2011; Cotton, 2013; Pemberton, 2019). It held twelve conferences in 1928–39, continued executive meetings during the war. The fifteenth and last conference was held at Windsor in 1950 under the auspices of UNESCO before it ceased in 1954 (Long, 2006).[11]

Despite of strong involvements of the Americans (the Rockefeller Foundation, the Carnegie Endowment for International Peace, the CFR and the IPR), the 'International' of the ISC was largely European before 1945. Its executive office was in Paris, where most of its meetings were held[12]; its main members were from Europe; and its main concerns were European inter-national affairs. It had nonetheless made efforts to involve those from non-Euro-American 'national sovereign' states, especially Japan, from the beginning, and that effort continued during and after the Manchurian Crisis (1931–33).[13] Japan's representatives participated informally but actively in the 11th ISC conference in Prague in 1938, and formally at the 12th ISC conference in Bergen in 1939, which became the last one before 1945 (Akami, 2020). While ISC's executive meetings continued among members of the Allied countries during the war, there was no sign of Asian members' participation.

[11] On a related, important conference on IR theory in 1954, cf. Guilhot (2010).

[12] Director to Gentlemen, 19 March 1930; Picht to Babock, 11 December 1930 (on the executive meeting on 17 January 1931), Box 351/K.I.1.a, UNESCO Archives (UNESCOA), Paris.

[13] Japan sent a representative to a meeting in London on 11–12 March 1929, which discussed the first ISC conference in Berlin in 1928, and the ISC's discussion on Japan's participation in its conferences and the Japanese group's membership began in 1930 and continued until 1939 (Akami 2020).

In this Euro-centred ISC, the Colonial was not totally neglected at the ISC or League's 'technical' operations. At the same time, the ISC's Colonial was largely a part of European affairs. In late 1935, the ISC started to include 'colonial question' as one important topic on the main theme of the ISC 1937 conference, 'Peaceful Change'. Various European countries participated in this study group, and examined economic, social, and political aspects of colonial issues relevant to 'Peaceful Change' in 1936–38.[14] In contrast, League's technical operations in extra-Europe incorporated more perspectives of 'locals' in the colonies. The International Labour Organization set up the committee to improve labour conditions in the colonies (Monteiro & Jerónimo, 2018). The League of Nations Health Organization (LNHO) also incorporated inter-colonial expert networks in Asia in the 1920s, which influenced the revision of the International Sanitary Convention in the mid-1920s (Akami, 2016). Through these networks, the LNHO also tried to implement holistic approach to rural health problems of the peoples in colonial Asia in the 1930s (Akami, 2017).

Yet, combined with a zeitgeist for a quest for science of the time and an almost exclusive focus on Europe, an inter-national framework defined intellectual discourse and administrative/organizational frameworks at the ISC. As the Rockefeller Foundation envisaged, the ISC secretariat at the International Institute of Intellectual Cooperation at Paris was a coordinating body of studies on international relations across the designated 'national' institutions.[15] Its annual conferences were to synthesize these 'national' perspectives in the 'national' studies by the 'national' institutes. The ISC invited John Condliffe, Research Director of the International Secretariat of the IPR (ISIPR), to report on the IPR's conference methods, which combined data papers produced by 'national' branches and round table discussions, as a model the ISC could emulate.[16]

[14] Kittredge to Walker, 10 Dec 1935, RG1/100S/Box 105/Folder 953; Kittredge to Walker, 23 March 1936, RG1/100S/Box 105/Folder 954, Rockefeller Archive Center (RAC). 'Peaceful Change: Note by M. Bourquin', January 1936, R4007/5B/2381/2381/Jacket 3; 'Outline of a Questionnaire on Colonial Aspects of the Problem of Peaceful Change', by H. O. Christophersen, May 1936, R4011/5B/21696/2381/Jacket 2: ISC, 9th session, Madrid, 27–30 May 1936; ISC, 10th session, Agenda, Plenary Sessions and Round Table Meetings, Paris 1937, Colonial Problems by H. O. Christophersen, R4012/5B/25952/2381/Jacket 3, League of Nations Archives (LNA).

[15] Kittredge to Walker, 15 February 1935, RG 3/Series 910/Box 7/Folder 60, RAC.

[16] Condliffe to Luchaire, 23 March 1930, on his confirmation of his attendance to ISC executive meeting, Box 351/K.I.1-a, UNESCOA; '[J.B. Condliffe's paper for ISC executive meeting]' (C88.1930), Box NOOCR-000363/K.I.3.1929-47, UNESCOA. Condliffe also developed 'international research projects' which the ISIPR commissioned to individual researchers or its national councils (Akami, 2002: 133–36).

While this 'global' zeitgeist that inspired the League, the ISC and the IPR was embraced in Japan in the 1920s, the International and the Imperial/Colonial were not always sharply demarcated. New expertise of International Politics emerged in Japan in the 1920s, and so did a new bleed of experts in the field. A few started to teach courses, entitled *Kokusai seiji* [International Politics], in the mid-1920s and the early 1930s, which stressed multilateral processes and institutions with peace as its clear objective, and they were keen to establish it as a 'scientific' field (Kawata, 1996: 337–39, 341). These new experts clustered at the JALN (1920–) and the Japanese Council of the IPR (JCIPR, 1925), as well as at the JSIL. Among them, the division between International Politics, 'Colonial Policy Studies', and studies on certain countries or regions was not always clear. To be sure, some new experts of International Politics are devoted in studying the League, its conventions, its related organizations, or politics surrounding the League. Yet, for many experts in Japan, 'regional' affairs were also 'international' affairs, and overlapped partially also with 'colonial' affairs, and all were discussed together in the journals of the JALN and the JSIL.

In this context, Yanaihara took over Colonial Policy course at the Tokyo Imperial University in 1923–37. Kawata argues that Yanaihara attempted to establish Colonial Policy Studies as a 'coherent social science based on objective and scientific analysis', and this led him to voice a strongest criticism of Japan's colonial policies in his time (Kawata, 1996: 377). Scholars dispute this evaluation of Yanaihara's stance to colonialism (Imaizumi, 1996; Nakano, 2013). On one hand, Yanaihara acted on the absolute pacifist position, based on his belief in the 'No-Church' Sect of Christianity, and he was forced to resign from his job after his public condemnation of the policy of the Japanese government and general attitudes of the Japanese people towards China at the outbreak of the Sino-Japanese War. He held on the position throughout wartime (1937–45). This was contrasted with many experts of international (and regional) affairs at the JCIPR, who were mobilized to Japan's wartime operations (Akami, 2002).

On the other hand, Yanaihara did not challenge colonialism in general. The contents of Yanaihara's course are available in the fourth edition (1933) of his *Shokumin oyobi shokumin seisaku* [*Colonization and Colonial Policy*], which was originally published in 1926, and dedicated to Nitobe (Yanaihara, 1963a: 5–6). Yanaihara inherited traits of Nitobe's course, but expanded substantially on policies on land and aboriginal peoples, and added policies on labour, banking, industry and finance. He then published his analyses on Japan's colonial policies in Taiwan (1929), Manchuria (1934) and the mandate territories in the South Pacific (1935), and on British colonialism in India (1937). In these works, Yanaihara incorporated not only demography (on over-population), but also theories of Marx, Lenin, and Luxemburg, to explain the causes of colonialism by class and capitalism (and monopoly capitalism) (1963a: 68–74). He refuted non-economic motivations provided by Joseph Schumpeter and Leonard Woolf, such as pure desire to conquer or national prestige (Yanaihara, 1963a: 77–88).

Although using the notions of class and capitalism, he was not Marxist, and argued that 'colonialism' could also occur even in a socialist system. This was because 'civilised societies [whether capitalist or socialist] still had to contribute to the development of the production of the whole [global] society by transferring capital, labour and technology to the areas where no one lived or where a level of civilisation of the people was low, and production power was not developed' (Yanaihara, 1963a: 75). For Yanaihara, 'colonialization' was virtually migrations of social groups to a new land, which was a 'mother' country's territory, and as long as under-developed lands existed on the globe, such movements would occur (Yanaihara, 1963a: 465). He saw colonialization was inevitable, and sought for peaceful and non-exploitive ways, as Nitobe did.

Yanaihara, however, furthered Nitobe's teaching to a point that could potentially challenge international power hierarchy, and prompt an anti-imperial perspective. This point of possible departure was his greater incorporation of the perspective of colonial peoples, than metropolitan imperial perspectives. Yanaihara stressed that one most significant lesson he learned from Nitobe was the notion of colonial policy based on a respect of human integrity (Yanaihara, 1963a: 5). Nitobe had argued that the ultimate objective of colonial policies should be the 'welfare' of the 'natives'. This objective, Yanaihara argued, could not be achieved by subjugation or assimilation; it could be achieved only by cultivating autonomy among the colonial peoples, while connecting them to the whole [global] society (Yanaihara, 1963a: 468–70). Here, Yanaihara regarded the British Commonwealth as an ideal model, in which colonial peoples could achieve 'autonomy' [*Jishu*], although not 'independence' [*Dokuritsu*], within a protective imperial framework (Yanaihara, 1963a: 478–79).

According to Kawata (1996: 369), this perspective shaped Yanaihara's methodology in his works on Taiwan, Manchuria and the South Pacific islands. It was based on fieldwork, visiting the place of research subject, gathering data on the spot, and analysing these data 'scientifically', while understanding local issues from local perspectives. It is unclear whether Yanaihara learned Chinese and Pacific island languages to do these fieldworks. He maintained a hierarchical view on civilization, and he did not argue for independence of colonial peoples. But his 'Colonial Policy Studies' corresponded to a prototype of 'Area Studies', which the IPR was concurrently pioneering in this period; they were studies on contemporary affairs of an area, based on a field work, acquiring local language and knowledge, and using social scientific methods and theories. Yanaihara's work on Japan's mandate in the South Pacific was indeed written for, and published as an IPR's research series in 1940.[17]

Yanaihara's works of Colonial Policy Studies were pioneering works not only for 'Area Studies', but scholars regard them also as pioneering works of IR. Sakai and Nakano see this aspect in: first, his understanding of 'colonialization' as global-scale 'migration of social groups' (Yanaihara used the term, the 'emergence of the world'); and second, his recognition of the British Commonwealth as a model of the world federation (Sakai, 2004; Nakano, 2013). Moreover, Imaizumi draws our attention to Yanaihara's argument: the colonies were the global linking nods where all the problematics of international power imbalance manifested (Imaizumi 1996: 144). In 'History of colonialism as a part of the development of world economy' (1929), Yanaihara argued: world politics and world economy emerged as the reality after World War I, to which colonization contributed significantly; and 'colonies became political and economic contact points and link of diverse points on the globe'. 'Because of this', he continued, 'they became *the cores of various international problems*' (Yanaihara, 1963b: 141–42). Yanaihara, therefore, saw a colonial site not as an object of a specific empire's policy, but as the manifestation of core problems of international relations. Significantly, almost a decade later, Yanaihara's view was echoed in one report by the Netherlands' group for the ISC in 1937: 'The colonial question is not an isolated problem, but … linked with the entire complex international politics'.[18]

Yanaihara's Colonial Policy Studies could be understood as pioneering works for the new fields of 'Area Studies' and IR, which were left with its ambivalent imprints. Despites his accepting colonialism and a hierarchical view of the world, his ultimate objective of Colonial Policy Studies was peace of the world, which position he maintained at an expense of his job and income, and under severe pressures during wartime. His Colonial Policy Studies in Asia and the Pacific, may have had a potential to develop locally based knowledge and counter-metropolitan perspectives. At the same time, a majority of these works were conducted and

[17] The Japanese version was published in 1935.
[18] B. Schrieke, 'Memoire Netherlands No.4: Colonial Question', March 1937, p. 16, R4014/5B/25952/2381, LNA.

advanced as wartime strategic and economic studies for Japan's military expansion and occupation in Asia and the Pacific (Hara, 1984; Suehiro, 2006). Such developments were not unique to Japan, and had a parallel in the Allied countries. The ISIPR and IPR's international research and conferences were serving as the wartime think tanks on Asia and the Pacific for the Allied forces (Akami, 2002: 257–74). When these IPR's works were taken over by Area (in this case, Asian) Studies in the US after the war, their strategically driven nature was even enhanced during the Cold War period. Yet, there was also an aspect that these 'Area Studies' and their scholars inspired and were driven by anti-imperial and nationalist movements in Asia and beyond.

3.4 Legacies of the Colonial in the Making of the Discipline of IR (the Presence of the Past), the 1950s

In the era of the UN, the notion of the International, based on national sovereign units, could now be applied globally, as decolonization occurred across the regions. International conventions, the UN, its agencies, and other international and regional organizations reinforced this 'inter-national' framework. This was best represented by an image of the UN as the globe surrounded by the national flags.

In this context, there were attempts to establish IR as a coherent and distinct discipline in various countries in the 1950s. Here, nationalism in Asia became *the* most dominant issue for the experts in the field in Asia and the Pacific-rim countries. Submersed, neglected, or overshadowed in the mainstream thinking was the continued existence of diverse forms of imperial polities, and hierarchical relations in international affairs. They were anomalies in the knowledge of International Relations, International Law and International History. While Marxist, neo-Marxist, and critical theorists problematized power imbalance, using the notions of neo-colonialism, dependency, and world system, the orthodox IR theories focused on the management of the inter-state system, and dealt with colonial/post-colonial issues (such as poverty in Africa, food shortage in Asia) as external problems, which the powers and their international organizations had to fix and manage, rather than the fundamental problem inherent in international politics, as Yanaihara suggested. Their framework was the national-international, which also defined (and limited) their remedial methods: to assist them to become a 'proper' state, or take the problems out from an 'inter-national' space, and squeeze them into the relevant 'national' jurisdiction (e.g. refugees), rather than examining the root causes in the power dynamics which had caused these problems in the first place.

Japanese experts reflected, and were engaged with these *contemporary* developments. Towards the end of the US-led Allied occupation (1945–51), they started to re-join governmental and non-governmental international organizations. The JCIPR, for example, was re-established in 1946 (JCIPR, 1947: 2), and became one of the first to send its representatives to a non-governmental international conference in 1950 (Lucknow, India), when Japan was still under the Allied occupation. It quickly re-established its international connections (including those with India and the ROC in Taiwan) in the 1950s. Most members of IPR's national councils were to become founders of International Relations and/or 'Area Studies' in this formative period. Japan joined UNESCO in 1951, a few months after it concluded the San Francisco Peace Treaty, and five years earlier than its entry to the UN (1956). There is, however, so far no record of Japanese participation at the last ISC conference at Windsor in 1950, now under the auspices of UNESCO (Rose, 1952).

While the JCIPR, the JALN and the JSIL had been mobilized for war, their members emphasized a 'new and clear departure' from the past, when they re-organized their respective post-war organizations.

This was not the case for the Japanese Association of International Relations (JAIR), which was established in 1956 as a brand-new organization, and paradoxically, here we see a clear continuity from the pre-war Colonial Policy Studies. While the founders used the JAIR for its English title, the Japanese name for the association and its journal (since 1957) used *Kokusai seiji* (International Politics), not *Kokusai kankei* (International Relations). Yet, despite this narrower association with Political Science, the JAIR has been distinct in its multi-disciplinary nature, and included History and Area Studies in its scope. This has been the case since its foundation for a few reasons. First, its founding members, including leading figures, came from Diplomatic History, and as a result, History has constituted one of the core components of the JAIR (Ōhata, 1986: 178). Second, main figures in the JAIR argued that 'International Relations' needed to be a comprehensive social science, rather than a narrowly specialized discipline. Kawata Tadashi was most articulate. In 1962, he argued that IR should be a basic knowledge of a new generation, which should analyse complex international affairs, and be a coherent, comprehensive, and integrating study, combining relevant disciplines of Sociology, Political Science, Economics, History, Law, and Human Geography (Kawata, 1996: 321). In 1963, he further argued: 'IR should be more than Political Science', examining not only power relations, but also 'norms of international relations, and philosophical, legal, economic, and moral backgrounds of the global society that was to emerge soon' (Kawata, 1996: 329). This statement echoed that of Alfred Zimmern at the ISC in the 1930s, but was contrasted to the views of the founders of the 'discipline' of IR in the US in the mid-1950s, who regarded these earlier ISC efforts as non-scientific' and 'fragmented' (Long, 2006; Guilhot, 2010, 2017).[19]

Third, the JAIR inherited pre-war Colonial Policy Studies and other studies on the regions, many of which had developed significantly during wartime for Japan's military operations and occupation in Asia and the Pacific. Kawata took over the former Colonial Policy Studies course, which Yanaihara had renamed as '*Kokusai keizai ron* [Theories on International Economy]' in 1945. Furthermore, Tōhata Seiichi, who had taught Colonial Policy Studies during wartime, also led the foundation of Asian Studies in post-war Japan, which were not only for Japan's strategic and economic policy objectives, but also for comprehensive understanding of the region based on local knowledge and fieldworks (Suehiro, 1997: 53–55). Kawata especially regarded Area Studies as integral to IR: 'Area Studies without an international perspective would be narrow, irrelevant to broader concerns', while 'IR research that [lacked] concrete knowledge of histories and current conditions of a specific region would be an empty theory' (Kawata, 1996: 327–28). This was a stark contrast to what was going on in the US in the 1950s on which a Rockefeller officer commented: 'there is a sharp divorce between [IR and Area Studies]'.[20]

4 Conclusion

This chapter argued the need to unearth the coloniality which had become invisible in the current knowledge of the International, and showed two ways to do so. First, it demonstrated how the frameworks of inter-imperial and inter-colonial would allow us to acknowledge and examine the roles of neglected imperial polities and their complex relations in international politics. Second, it explored the meaning and legacy of 'Colonial Policy Studies' in a genealogy of the discipline of IR. In Japan, Yanaihara identified 'colonial sites' as the problematic manifestation of diverse power dynamics, and the core of international politics. His Colonial Policy Studies also became 'International Economy' after the war, while what he planted in his Colonial Policy Studies were also taken up by emerging

[19] Their positions to 'social sciences', however, were complex, as the 'realists' were against behavioural social sciences and also stressed the significance of norms in the mid-1950s (Guilhot 2010, 2017).

[20] 'A program for International Studies' [n.d, but after 1953], p. 36, RG 3/Series 910/Box 7/Folder 61, RAC.

'Area Studies', and both fields were included within the scope of the JAIR in the 1950s. In these 'succeeding' fields, ambiguous power dynamics, which were evident in Yanaihara's Colonial Policy Studies, permeated: it suggested the continued empire (big power)-centred, strategically driven knowledge; but it also contained the potential for counter-imperial, locally based perspectives, concerns and methodologies. For us to find out the exact impacts of its legacies in the present, we need detailed studies on current specific policies and projects. What this chapter showed, however, is how such neglected power dynamics in the disciplinary knowledge of what we now call IR could be unearthed.

The case of Japan is also significant on the issue of temporality. Because of the timing of Japan becoming a formal empire (1895) and that of decolonization in Asia, a moment to challenge collective hegemony by post-colonial states of Latin America at The Hague in 1907, as shown in the chapter by Müller, was also the moment to consolidate inter-imperial cooperation for Japan, which now asserted its equal status as a formal empire *and* a constitutional monarchy/parliamentary democracy. Japanese experts were closely engaged in contemporary debates across the empires, and digested, negotiated, and reshaped their ideas not only for Japan's colonial policies, but also for inter-imperial governing order and institutions as indicated in Lawson's chapter in this book.

The case of Japan may appear unique, but its presence of the past in the current disciplinary knowledge of IR may only be more explicit than in Anglo-American contexts, and there may be similar cases in other 'national' contexts. Moreover, it suggests a constructive way of unearthing and integrating the separated 'disciplines' within a nation and across the nations. The fact Yanaihara found a right scholarly framework in International Economy for his Colonial Policy Studies after 1945 suggests that that field itself may have had a similar colonial genealogy in other countries, and this may also be the case for 'Development Studies'.[21] The making of a 'scientific' discipline of IR in the US, and to some extent in the British Commonwealth, has so far been a process of making it 'a-colonial' and 'ahistorical', asserting its 'autonomy' by demarcating it from the 'rest' of the knowledge fields, including 'Area Studies'. Unearthing the colonial past in the presence for the discipline of IR is finding new ways of constructive collaboration with the 'others', which trend I believe this book promotes, and I also detect in Japan (Sakai, 2020).

[21] Here, there may also be the legacy of colonial statistics in making the 'Third World' in the UN era, discussed in the chapter by Daniel Speich Chassé.

References

Akami, T. (2002). *Internationalizing the Pacific: The USA, Japan and the Institute of Pacific Relations in War and Peace, 1919–1945*, London: Routledge.

Akami, T. (2013). The Nation-State/Empire as a Unit of an Analysis of the History of International Relations: A Case Study in Northeast Asia, 1868–1933, in I. Lohr & R. Wenzlhuemer (eds.). *The Nation State and Beyond: Governing Globalization Processes in the Nineteenth and Early Twentieth Centuries*, 177–208, New York: Springer.

Akami, T. (2016). A Quest to be Global: The League of Nations Health Organization and Inter-colonial Regional Governing Agendas of the Far Eastern Association of Tropical Medicine, 1910–25, *The International History Review*, 37(1), 1–23.

Akami, T. (2017). Imperial Polities and Inter-colonialism in Shaping Global Governing Norms: Public Health Expert Networks in Asia and the League of Nations Health Organization, 1908–1937, *The Journal of Global History*, 12(1), 4–25.

Akami, T. (2018a). Experts and the Japanese Association of the League of Nations in the international context, 1919–1925, in P. O'Brien & J. Damousi (eds.). *League of Nations: Histories, Legacies and Impact*, 158–78, Melbourne: Melbourne University Press.

Akami, T. (2018b). The Limits of Peace Propaganda: The Information Section of the League of Nations and its Tokyo Office, in J. Brendebach, M. Herzer & H. Tworek (eds.). *Exorbitant Expectations: Communicating International Organizations in the 19th and 20th Centuries*, 70–90, London: Routledge.

Akami, T. (2020). Japanese Participants at the International Studies Conference and the Institute of Pacific Relations in the Twenty Years' Crisis, *Rockefeller Archive Center Research Reports* (19 November), 1–31.

Akashi, K. (2004). Japan's 'Acceptance' of the European Law of Nation: A Brief History of International Law in Japan, c. 1853–1900, in M. Stolleis & M. Yanagihara (eds.). *East Asian and European Perspectives on International Law*, 1–22, Baden-Baden: Nomos.

Anghie, A. (2005). *Imperialism, Sovereignty and the Making of International Law*, Cambridge: Cambridge University Press.

Baji, T. (2022). Colonial Policy Studies in Japan: Racial Visions of Nan'yo, or the Early Creation of a Global South, *International Affairs*, 98(1), 165–82.

Bull, H. (1977). *The Anarchical Society: A Study of Order in World Politics*, New York: Palgrave.

Bull, H. & Watson, A. (eds.). (1984). *The Expansion of International Society*, Oxford: Oxford University Press.

Burbank, J. & Cooper, F. (2010). *Empire in World History: Power and the Politics of Difference*, Princeton, NJ: Princeton University Press.

Buzan, B. & Acharya, A. (eds.). (2010). *Non-Western International Relations Theory: Perspectives on and beyond Asia*, London: Routledge.

Cotton, J. (2013). *The Australian School of International Relations*, New York: Palgrave Macmillan.

Dudden, A. (2005). *Japan's Colonization of Korea: Discourse and Power*, Honolulu: University of Hawai'i Press.

Dunne, T. & Reus-Smit, C. (eds.). (2018). *The Globalization of International Society*, Oxford: Oxford University Press.
Giddens, A. (1987). *The Nation-State and Violence*, Berkeley: University of California Press.
Go, J. & Lawson, G. (eds.). (2017). *Global Historical Sociology*, Cambridge: Cambridge University Press.
Guilhot, N. (ed.). (2010). *The Invention of International Relations Theory: Realism, the Rockefeller Foundation, and the 1954 Conference on Theory*, New York: Columbia University Press.
Guilhot, N. (2017). *After the Enlightenment*, Cambridge: Cambridge University Press.
Hara, K. (1984). *Gendai Ajia kenkyū seritsushiron*, Tokyo: Keisō shobō.
Hardt, M. & Negri, A. (2000). *Empire*, Cambridge, MA: Harvard University Press.
Imaizumi, Y. (1996). Yanaihara Tadao no kokusai kankei kenyū to shokuminchi seisaku kenkyū, *Kokusai kankeigaku kenyū*, 23, 137–48.
Iriye, A. (2002). *Global Community: The Role of International Organizations in the Making of the Contemporary World*, Berkeley: University of California Press.
JCIPR (Nihon taiheiyō mondai chōsakai). (1947). *Yōran*, Tokyo: Kyōeidō.
Kawata, T. (1996). *Kokusaigaku I: Kokusai kankei kenkyū*, Tokyo: Tokyo Shoseki.
Koskenniemi, M. (2001). *The Gentle Civiliser of Nations: The Rise and Fall of International Law 1870–1960*, Cambridge: Cambridge University Press.
Legg, S. (2014). An International Anomaly? Sovereignty, the League of Nations and India's Princely Geographies, *Journal of Historical Geography*, 43, 96–110.
Long, D. (2006). Who Killed the International Studies Conference?, *Review of International Studies*, 32(4), 603–22.
Long, D. & Schmidt, B. C. (eds.). (2005). *Imperialism and Internationalism in the Discipline of International Relations*, Albany: State University of New York Press.
Monteiro, J. P. & Jerónimo, M. B. (2018). Internationalism and Empire: The Question of 'Native Labour' in the Portuguese Empire, 1919–1961, in S. Jackson & A. O'Malley (eds.). *The Institution of International Order: From the League of Nations to the United Nations*, 206–33, London: Routledge.
Mommsen, W. J. & Osterhammel, J. (1986). *Imperialism and After: Continuities and Discontinuities*, London: Allen & Unwin.
Nakano, R. (2013). *Beyond the Western Liberal Order: Yanaihara Tadao and Empire as Society*, New York: Palgrave Macmillan.
Nitobe, I. (1969). *Shin Nitobe Inazō zenshū, vol. 4*, Tokyo: Kyōbunkan.
Ōhata, H. (1996). Kaisetsu, in T. Kawata (ed.). *Kokusaigaku I: Kokusai kankei kenkyū*, 387–94, Tokyo: Tokyo Shoseki.
Ōhata, T. (1986). 'Nihon kokusai seijigakkai 30 nen no ayumi', *Kokusai seiji* (October), 168–93.
Orford, A. (2012). The Past as Law or history? The Relevance of Imperialism for Modern International Law, *IILJ Working Paper 2012/2*, 1–17, New York: New York University School of Law.
Ōuchi, H. (1969). Kaisetsu, in I. Nitobe (ed.). *Shin Nitobe Inazō zenshū, vol. 4*, 645–49, Tokyo: Kyōbunkan.

Pedersen, S. (2007). Back to the League of Nations: Review Essay, *The American Historical Review*, 112(4), 1091–117.

Pemberton, J.-A. (2019). *The Story of International Relations, Part One: Cold-Blooded Idealists*, Cham: Palgrave Macmillan.

Riemens, M. (2011). International Academic Cooperation on International Relations in the Interwar Period: The International Studies Conference, *Review of International Studies*, 37(2), 911–28.

Rietzler, K. (2009). American Foundations and the 'Scientific Study' of International Relations in Europe, 1910–1940. PhD thesis. University College London.

Rose, S. (1952). The University Teaching of International Relations: International Studies Conference, 16–20 March 1950 by G.L. Goodwin, *International Affairs*, 28(2), 274.

Sakai, K. (2020). Gurōbaru kankeigaku ha naze hitsuyō nanoka, in K. Sakai (ed.). *Gurōbaru kankeigaku I: Gurōbaru kankeigaku towa nanika*, Tokyo: Iwanami Shoten.

Sakai, T. (2004). 'Shokumin seisakugaku' kara 'kokusai kankei ron' e, in T. Asano & T. Matsuda (eds.). *Shokuminchi teikoku Nihon no hōteki tenkai*, Tokyo: Shinzansha.

Schmidt, B. C. (1998). *The Political Discourse of Anarchy: A Disciplinary History of International Relations*, Albany: State University of New York Press.

Sluga, G. & Clavin, P. (eds.). (2017). *Internationalisms: A Twentieth Century History*, Cambridge: Cambridge University Press.

Suehiro, A. (1997). Sengo Nihon no Ajia kenkyū, *Shakai kagaku kenkyū*, 48(4), 37–71.

Suehiro, A. (2006). Ajia chōsa no keifu, in A. Suehiro et al. (eds.). *'Teikoku' Nihon no gakuchi, vol. 6*, Tokyo: Iwanami Shoten.

Vitalis, R. (2015). *White World Order, Black Power Politics: The Birth of International Relations*, Ithaca: Cornell University Press.

Yanaihara, T. (1963a). Shokumin oyobi shokumin seisaku, in T. Yanaihara (ed.). *Yanaihara Tadao zenshū, vol. 1*, Tokyo: Iwanami Shoten.

Yanaihara, T. (1963b). Sekai keizai hatten katei toshiteno shokuminshi, in T. Yanaihara (ed.). *Yanaihara Tadao zenshū, vol. 4*, Tokyo: Iwanami Shoten.

Yanaihara, T. (1969). Henja jo (originally written in 1942), in I. Nitobe. *Shin Nitobe Inazō zenshū, vol. 4*, Tokyo: Kyōbunkan.

12 Was the Rise of the 'Third World' a Theory Effect?

International Relations and the Historicity of Economic Expertise

Daniel Speich Chassé

1 Introduction

International Relations in the second half of the twentieth century were structured by a series of cleavages of which the North-South-Divide was a major one. This chapter asks how the opposition of rich and poor nations became a clear-cut topic in world political communication. The focal point is the notion of a 'Third World'. The initial observation is that this specific discursive formation emerged only post-1945, then grew to considerable importance, and again vanished as of the 1980s from the diplomatic debates. The interest here is in its rise. Was this a discursive phenomenon only and if so, how did it relate to material change? To what extent were colonial and imperial formations functional for the emergence of the said notion? And in what ways can a presence of the colonial and imperial past be discerned in current political communication along this line of inquiry?

I take the 'Third World' to be an effect of theory. That is not to play down the material weight of inequality between rich and poor parts of humanity. The point is rather to highlight the importance of discourse in historical change and in shaping reality (as insinuated by the first mode of historiticity developed by Schlichte and Stetter in the Introduction). After having had several 'cultural turns' in social theory, it seems quite clear that both, modes of perception and material facts, need to be considered. In the digital knowledge-society, in which we live today, the productive drive of concepts is obvious.[1] With the supply of numerical communications rising, that is, 'Big Data', for example, on GDP per

[1] The concept of theory effect here is taken from Bourdieu through Diaz-Bone, 2007. In the social studies of science and technology, it has become familiar to understand knowledge and expertise not as mere representational devices but as productive systems in their own right (cf. MacKenzie, 2006).

capita on all sovereign nations as produced through the Penn World Table,[2] the demand for critical data studies also increases. The question in this chapter is how material differences in standards of living across the planet have been conceptually framed over the twentieth century through numerical communication. Colonial experiences and imperial moves were crucial in establishing a global epistemic order, the historical trajectory of which shall be roughly sketched. In view of the sources underlying this contribution, it seems quite clear that both, colonialism and imperialism played a crucial role in the history of the international order not only materially but also epistemically and thus bear witness to a presence of the past. The core argument is that (firstly) decolonization and the End of Empire in the 1950s and the 1960s lead to conceptual confusion and that (secondly) economic knowledge production through macroeconomic statistics helped solve this impasse. Quite clearly, history not only shaped global material difference itself but also the cognitive ways in which agents tried to make sense out of their social realities. In my example, it is economic expertise that acquired a certain power in shaping the present out of the past. Its historicity is – at least – twofold: On the one hand, post-1945, the economics discipline gained substantially in importance as a chief source for the legitimizing of political rule. Statistically grounded measures of collective economic wealth play out centrally in global politics. On the other hand, the conditions of the possibility of this rise of economics can historically be accounted for. They are to a certain degree contingent and point to complex temporalities (mode 2). We could at least imagine the possibility that not economics, but social anthropology had become the chief source of expertise on global cleavages at the epoch of imperial decline. But anthropology gave way to economics in the hierarchy of the social sciences to this task. Historicity lies in the eye of the beholder – and requires a need for interpretation as suggested by mode 4 – and always cries for interpretation in view of a critique of power relations. Thus, knowledge production as a (contingent) historical practice must be set on the very same level as power games or material struggles over natural resources.

The chapter is structured in four steps. The first part aims at concretising the discursive formation of the 'Third World' as a singular phenomenon which was epistemologically rooted in quantitative economic expertise. Second, I take up some notions originally coined by the French sociologist Georges Balandier in order to better understand major shifts in global political communication and to propose an analytical framework that might inform future studies. The third section focusses on the

[2] www.rug.nl/ggdc/productivity/pwt/ (seen on 24 February 2019).

history of quantitative (i.e. statistical) economic knowledge. It recalls the relative (un)importance of quantitative economic knowledge in imperial practice before roughly the 1950s. The fourth section then looks at the way in which economists post-1945 gained an almost 'imperial' position in stabilizing global expertise on socio-economic inequality and difference in the emerging world society. Most certainly, the 'Third World' never only was an effect of theory but rather a political concept uniting relatively poor nation states across the world in their struggle against material post-colonial dominance. But still, when looking at global historical legacies, the importance of shared concepts and theory effects cannot be neglected.

2 The Phenomenon

The notion 'Third World' shows a peculiar historical pattern in global political communication. It rose to prominence in international discourse around 1960 and declined as of the 1980s. In opposition to the two Cold War blocks it designated a third group of relatively poor nations with a past of having been dominated by Europe. The background to its history is decolonization in Asia and Africa after World War Two[3]. The notion 'Third World' needs to be situated in a larger history of the perception of global difference. It connects both to changes in the order of knowledge and, more specifically, to the history of economic statistics.

Initially, the notion 'Third World' was coined in France by Alfred Sauvy in 1951, who drew parallels to the discourse of empowering a 'Tiers Etat' during the French Revolution. Sauvy's term gained strength through the writings of Georges Balandier. And Peter Worsley introduced it in Anglo-Saxon discourse soon after.[4] The term took up considerable power with the UNCTAD Conferences as of 1964 and is still sometimes used in framing emancipatory perspectives from the back side of industrial capitalist dynamics (Murphy, 1984; Prashad, 2007). Two aspects are important. First is a fundamental disorientation in global communication that went along with the end of formal European hegemony post-1945. European and North-American scholars in the epoch of Imperial decline were unsure as to how to prolong definitional authority over the state of the planet. And second, macroeconomic abstractions such as the GDP proved helpful in this task.

[3] How Latin America came into this global knowledge regime is another story not subject to this chapter.

[4] Balandier (1956). There is a rich literature on the topic (cf. Tomlinson, 2003; Berger, 2004; Dirlik, 2004; Solarz, 2012; Dinkel, 2014; Speich Chassé, 2015).

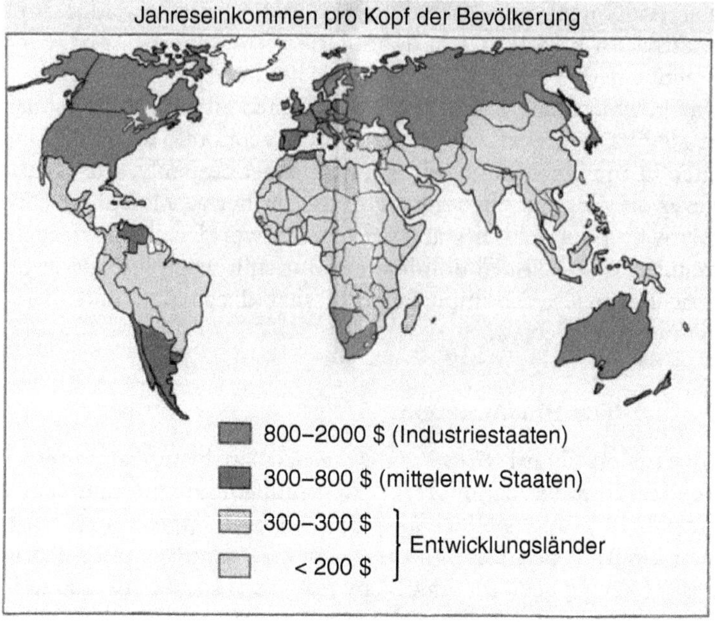

Figure 12.1 Map of the family of nations

My interest in the phenomenon was triggered initially by coming across a world map in a West-German publication of 1962 (Figure 12.1). It showed all nations grouped according to their gross domestic product (GDP) and drew a stark line between dark grey (rich) and light grey (poor) nations on this epistemic ground. What French scholars framed as the 'Third World' in the 1950s obviously seemed to be very helpful in making sense of global constellations at that time also in the Bonn Republic. Thanks to macroeconomic statistics, a complicated world could be simplified on a map. Researching on economic knowledge about the globe, I have not come across such a map earlier than 1962. I wonder, why? Economic difference was key to imperial and colonial discourse. But only in the framework of a global family of assumedly sovereign nations, according to a Westphalian System, that came up with decolonization worldwide post-1945, economic theory became the foundation for a new global imaginary.

The statistical evidence underlying Figure 12.2 shows a sharp incline in the usage of the term 'Third World' as of the 1960s. A search on Google N-Gram brings into evidence that at some points in history some discourses lost importance while others gained. Figure 12.2 also shows clear evidence for a loss in importance of the usage of the term 'Third World' as of the 1990s. Again, the question is, why? Maybe material

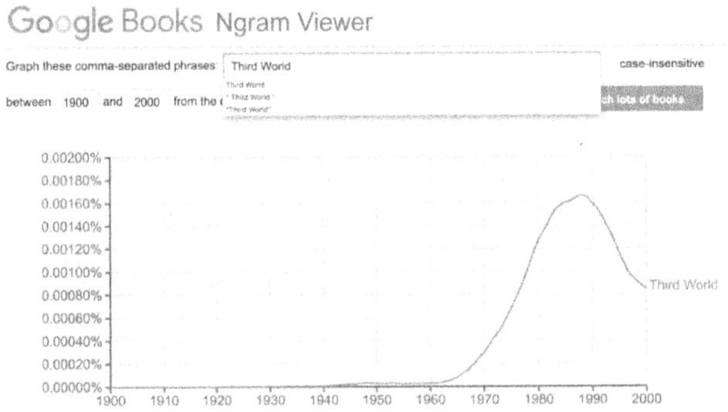

Figure 12.2 Google N-Gram query

differences at that period evaporated, so that there was no more need for a collective term for poor nations after ca. 1990 as opposed to more wealthy collectives? I would rather assume that other discursive formations gained ground with the rise of neoliberal political economy at that specific time (Cooper, 2005; Ferguson, 2006; Slobodian, 2018), in order to keep persistent material difference in living standards across the globe an object of political communication in world society.

The map in Figure 12.1 and the graph in Figure 12.2 bear evidence of a specific global communication form concerning world inequality during the second half of the twentieth century. Focus on the rise of the term: How and why did this specific order of knowledge grow out of European colonial practice during – roughly – the hundred years from the middle of the nineteenth to the middle of the twentieth century? A further question is, as to what extent this specific epistemic regime bears witness to its imperial past up until today. Knowing the world in abstract terms such as those of macroeconomic statistics became important during the very last years of European colonial rule, that is, ca. 1945–1960. Accommodating difference in global political communication in the terms of quantitative macroeconomic indicators then rose to a chief form of world politics that seems without alternative nowadays.

Abstract speak on wealth and poverty in the terms of GDP became globally prominent precisely at the moment of imperial decline, that is, the 1960s. This observation leads to the question as to what extent colonial and imperial legacies were written into a post-colonial knowledge regime. As of 1945, when the United Nations were founded in San Francisco, a new international political order gained ground with new agents such as the FAO, WHO, UNESCO, UNDP and others. All these bodies strongly based their activities on seemingly objective statistical data. Hard facts in the terms of numbers could represent the view of the administrators of these bodies clear-cut differences in the global condition concerning educational prospects, the availability of food and job opportunities and the provision of health care. Obviously, to this statistical view, some new states lacked important achievements in these perspectives (African and Asian nation states and Latin American as well as some Oceanian), while others fully complied (the USA, Canada and OEEC members generally).[5]

Recall the dark grey versus light grey distinction in Figure 12.1. In the immediate post-colonial years, statistical abstractions helped keeping a well-established cognitive order in place: assumedly, in imperial times, supreme senders of wealth and civilizational values were set against poor and demanding 'primitive' communities located 'over-seas', that is, at the periphery of imperial space. With the decay of the colonial order during the 1960s the macroeconomic measurement of GDP per capita reset knowledge on global inequality in a framework that seemed objective to European and North-American eyes. But it further transported old Europe- and US-centred norms, thus evidencing a present of the colonial past.

Depicting the world in macroeconomic terms in two groups of rich (dark grey) and poor (light grey) countries is factually undercomplex. Such an epistemic logic held up high the notion of a 'Third World' and obviously was plausible in global political communication only during the three decades between the 1960s and the late 1980s. Data in Figure 12.2 show that global discourse quickly departed from this categorization as of 1989. But during the first three decades in the existence of the UN System, such a North-South-antagonism was crucial and went largely unquestioned by chief agents.

One interest (which cannot be addressed in this chapter) is why the logic of holding up the notion of a 'Third World' collapsed in the 1980s. Another question is why it came up in the first place. I argue that in explaining the emergence of this specific discursive constellation one needs to go back in history to the early comparative work by one sociologist of Empire and colonialism which to-day is largely subject to oblivion. More specifically, I propose including the historical upcoming of social scientific expertise, such as quantitative macroeconomic statistics, into a narrative of political communication within the analytical framework of a 'société globale' according to Georges Balandier (Balandier, 1951; Steinmetz, 2014).[6]

The end of imperial rule was closely connected to the rise of statistical thinking which enhanced the capacity of modern (i.e. 'Western')

[5] On abstract speak in OECD cf. Hongler (2019).
[6] A critical discussion and a collection of sources can be found on www.livingbookabouthistory.ch/en/book/la-situation-coloniale (viewed on 03 March 2019).

societies to know their present condition in a seemingly objective way (Porter, 1986). More precisely, quantification propelled understandings of society and 'the economy' as mechanical devices that would deliver certain results in 'development' if run correctly (Mitchell, 1998). In the global twentieth century, the connection between statistical knowledge and development plans for poor nations became even more complicated as it encompassed an increasing number of instances of social difference. The power of statistics was helpful in reducing complexity and in creating a global framework for political communication.

3 A Balandierian Approach to 'Third World' Discourse

Rulers all over the world today need to take numerical facts and statistical figures into account when trying to gain legitimacy, irrespective of the veracity of data (Speich Chassé, 2016). We are confronted with a major power-function of such expertise, which is important in order to understand recent global history. The mechanism has been described by James Ferguson and others under the heading of a 'depoliticization' which in itself is a political move (Ferguson, 1990). Economists in development economy relate to however fictitious long time-series of seemingly factual data without connecting their interest to the historical condition of their very possibility.

Economic modelling should allocate more resources to the criticism of sources according to historians' methodology (Jerven, 2013). At the same time, the field of international development historiography booms (Hodge, 2016). Both these trajectories might be questioned on the basis of Georges Balandier's analysis of the colonial situation. This seminal text first appeared in 1951 and was one major source of inspiration for Frederick Cooper and Ann Laura Stoler to talk of 'Tensions of Empire' (Cooper & Stoler, 1997; Bayart, 2010). It called those grand narratives of the human condition in question that made the European experience a global template for modernization and that set all other experiences far from it in a series of fundamental dichotomies such as: 'Black' versus 'white' complexion or 'rich' versus 'poor' national economies in the statistically grounded epistemology of a 'first' and a 'second' world versus a 'third'; in the opposition of an assumed 'West' against the 'Rest' or in the current wording of a 'Global South' as opposed to a 'Global North'.[7] There are so many inconsistencies in the history of categorizing global difference that some demand for theory emerges.

[7] Note the geodetic absurdity of fusing compass directions with the adjective 'global' and keep in mind the discursive position as opposed to the geographical position of states like Nepal and Bhutan (discursive South but geographical North) or Australia and New Zealand (discursive North but geographical South).

In an interview on the occasion of the 50th anniversary of the independence of many African states that was conducted by Alexandre Bonche in 2010 (Bonche, 2010), the late Georges Balandier talked of his fascination as a child with the exotic overseas world that was on display at the 'Exposition Coloniale' in Paris in 1931. We can understand the rest of his intellectual life as an anthropologist as having partly been dedicated to a fundamental critique of this fantasy.

After World War Two Balandier ventured to Senegal. In his 1957 book, 'Afrique ambiguë' he wrote:

> Lorsque j'arrivai à Dakar en 1946, j'étais surtout animé par une volonté de fuite et dépaysement. L'expérience ethnologique que je souhaitais avait la valeur d'une retraite au sens original du mot: je désirais disposer d'un recul suffisant pour mieux me reprendre en mains après une époque ne m'ayant guère laissé le temps de la réflexion; j'éprouvais le besoin d'accéder à une forme d'existence radicalement nouvelle. J'abordais l'Afrique moins pour elle qu'en fonction de moi-même. (Balandier, 1957: 275)

Upon arrival in Dakar, the young anthropologist quickly lost sight of the object on which he had intended to produce new knowledge. Contrary to his expectation of being confronted with a completely exotic world, what he found in the capital of French West Africa was an ambiguous complex of different historical trajectories and socio-political identities of which he himself as a social scientist turned out to be an integral part. He started to check his romantic childhood imagination against his own present situation in the colonial context. In this, the analytical instruments that he had gathered during his studies in Paris were of little help.

When Balandier arrived in Dakar, anthropology was a discipline held in high esteem by colonial administrators because this art of describing distant cultural formations promised a way of making sense out of the everyday routines of the many subjects under their rule (Tilley, 2011). French ethnographers like Marcel Griaule, for example, were captivated by the rich material culture of the Dogon while the famous Dakar-Djibouti-Mission, of which Michel Leiris was a part, gathered thousands of strange seeming items for display in Paris (Leiris, 1934; Griaule, 1938; de L'Estoile, 2007). But the young scholar quickly and surprisingly clearly understood that ventures like those by Griaule or Leiris produced no helpful scientific vision of West African social collectives but rather one that changed the life of the Dogon (and other people) dramatically. In the 2010 interview, at old age, Georges Balandier expressed his wonder that when one visited the Dogon decades after the early French ethnographers, the local guide would cite from Griaule's work in order to explain 'true' Africa.

Social scientists always have been part of the social totality they pretended to observe from a however distanced position. Accordingly, to

Balandier, single groups like the French, Wolof, Libanese, or Peul all formed core ingredients to Senegalese sociability, despite their respective identity constructions. In the 1951 text, Balandier thus suggested a sociology of the colonial situation as a totality rather than an ethnography of distant others. He wrote:

> ... que la ‚colonie' (société globale) se compose en général d'un nombre de groupes plus ou moins conscients de leur existence, souvent opposés les uns aux autres par la couleur, et qui s'efforcent de mener des vies différentes dans les limites d'un cadre politique unique. (Balandier, 1951: 61)

The term 'société globale' that Balandier used is telling. It served to describe the social situation of a place like Dakar, Senegal, that through French imperial expansion had as a social sphere become even more hybrid as it had already for a long time been due to its geographical locality (on the fringe of Islamic rule and exposed to European maritime expansion by, first, the Portuguese). The adjective 'globale' refers to the fact that he overserved in Dakar very different forms of sociability among single discernible groups which at the same time engaged in manifold interaction among each other. In Dakar, in the late 1940s, Balandier found a global society very locally, the chief structures of which, to-day, apply to the world as a whole.

My argument is that this experience still informs globality and that in its analysis the history of knowledge is not less as important as the reconstruction of seemingly objective economic needs. Just as ethnographers like Marcel Griaule became part of the game, so are international experts in economic development and statistics nowadays.

In the 'societé globale' of the colonies, different social entities converged that referred to colonial power in different ways but still summed up to one single social collective. According to Balandier, it is important to focus on the functional aspects of diversity in analysing the process of communicative convergence that makes up the totality of a 'colonial situation', hence a 'global society'. The – however critical – assumption that one single group of agents (i.e. the 'West' or a 'First World') successfully pressed their views through all social channels upon the 'Rest' (or a 'Third World') misses the interactive complexity at stake. Balandier observed for the French colonial presence:

> Chacune de ces fractions participe de manière différente à la société globale; le contact de races et de civilisations qu'impose, encore, la colonisation n'a ni la même signification ni les mêmes conséquences pour chacune d'elles – il doit être étudié en fonction de cette diversité. (Balandier, 1951: 70)

To this view, the fundamental separation between Western and non-Western ways of organizing collective life never was a sound basis for analysing global reality, but rather one of the characteristic traits of the 'colonial situation' itself that needed to be subject to social scientific study.

Generalizing a Balandierian approach for the purposes of this chapter means that the interesting question is the function of key notions in global discourse for different local polities. Balandier thought that the current language too strongly separated 'le "primitiv" et le civilisé, le païen et le chrétien, les civilisations techniques et les civilisations arriérées' (Balandier, 1951: 70). He criticized the notion of a clash of cultures that dominated social theory. Rather, he emphasized 'que le contact se fait par le moyen de groupements sociaux – et non entre cultures existant sous la forme de réalités indépendantes' (Balandier, 1951: 71). On whatever epistemic ground singularized cultural entities stood against each other, social scientific scholars were invited to analyse such situations as a totality, say a global presence. In a self-reflective move, Balandier not only questioned age-old categorical difference between own (European, Christian) social collectives and others (Black, African, Muslim), but also specifically questioned the role of knowledge production (as in his own discipline of Ethnography) which he saw as a part and parcel of the ongoing global power games.

Since the middle of the twentieth century, when one French social scientist ventured into Western Africa, social scientific modes of knowing the world have become politically highly relevant and need to be carefully subject to analysis. This is especially true for economic statistics. Rather than framing the world, they must be considered a part of the game.

4 Imperial economics

The epistemic basis of Figure 12.1 lies in geodetic surveys and population censuses and in a comparative system of national accounts that was invented by the economist Richard Stone (and others, such as Simon Kuznets) on behalf of OEEC and the UN around 1950 (Stone 1951; United Nations, 1953). But how – and why? – economic knowledge production became so prominent in global politics post-1945? (Speich Chassé, 2011; Macekura, 2017). I have shown that the notion 'Third World' is largely an effect of social scientific theory and statistics. And I have also argued that social scientific knowledge production needs to be assessed as one part of the game. Along with a Balandierian analysis of the colonial situation, macroeconomic expertise has a social function and cannot serve as whatever 'objective' basis for analysing world society. So, a closer look at history seems helpful. I assume that understanding the history of statistical economic knowledge practices can explain the peculiar career of the notion 'Third World' in the post-imperial and in the post-colonial global politics of difference.

Comparative macroeconomic statistics have a history that needs to be measured against the present past of imperial and the colonial rule.

Quite surprisingly, macroeconomic statistics played a minor role in the long and violent history of European imperial expansion way up until the middle decades of the twentieth century. The focus here is on Africa post-1945.[8] Current research tends to emphasize the modernity of the imperial project. Some authors have suggested understanding European activities overseas during the age of high imperialism as 'laboratories of modernisation' (van Laak, 2004). The Indian post-colonial scholar Arjun Appadurai analysed the cultural conditions of expanding European notions of modernity on a global scale (Appadurai, 1996: 115). Recent work on India has followed his proposal and inquired into the statistical tools that gained importance in the British Raj already during the second half of the nineteenth century. But what about Africa? For East Africa, Christophe Bonneuil argued that planning was a chief continuity across the rupture of decolonization. Joseph Hodge and Véronique Dimier produced ample evidence for the fact that many European professionals found little problems in prolonging their careers from the British and the French colonial service into the administrations of the newly emerging nations or international organizations (Bonneuil, 2000; Hodge, 2007; Dimier, 2014. Cf. Gupta, 2012; Kalpagam, 2014). But despite these continuities, it is striking to see how much less use European authorities made of social scientific expertise in distant ruling than in governing the metropolitan polities during the same epoch.

Let us take a closer look at the British example. The beginning of a systematic knowledge production by British colonial administrators on their African possessions was a project called the 'African Survey' that took place in the 1930s (Hailey, 1938). The epistemic basis of this statistical work was the qualitative inquiry of anthropologists like Bronislaw Malinowski who was en vogue at the time. The volume included descriptions of different African languages, popular cultures, religions and regions but only very few quantitative data. None of the statistical techniques that were being hotly debated during the 1930s among social scientists in view of the British, the US, French, Italian and German domestic social situation were reflected in the Hailey-Project.[9] The work of the German-British ethnographers Richard and Hilde Thurnwald is a case in point who shared a decided interest in economic questions but consciously refrained from statistical analysis in their work on East Africa (Thurnwald, 1935; Steinmetz, 2010). As Helen Tilley has shown, the main idea in the African Survey by Lord Hailey was to record assumedly

[8] A look at other world regions, especially Asia, might foster a different picture.

[9] This holds especially true for quantitative economic statistics. On the state of the art in the 1930s cf. Stamp (1934).

ancient forms of collective life that were thought to vanish in the course of the European civilizing mission, but not to compute a full statistical assessment that included abstract values of economic productivity as measured by area and population number (Tilley, 2011).

It is difficult to understand the statistical ignorance of imperial authorities such as the British in Africa historically. In a Balandierian analysis, one can assume that it was simply not functional to their aims. These authorities did not invest adequate manpower nor material means in the gathering of information probably because it did not seem necessary from a metropolitan perspective to do so in order to economically profit from the overseas possessions before 1945. The specific whereabouts of the subaltern were largely irrelevant to imperial governmentality. Racist prejudice made European overlords refrain from counting what to their view simply did not count. To sum up, during Interwar Imperial rule, in Africa at least, the social sciences, and numerical statistics, mainly helped to protocol social formations that were held to be totally different from the colonizing ones. In this specific connection, the social sciences were being used to stabilize worlds apart rather than focussing on the interplay between them let alone gaining an adequate understanding of the 'other'.

During the middle decades of the twentieth century, the epistemic order changed and economic statistics gained a new importance as a mode of knowledge about global difference. I suggest assigning this process to a change from the imperial to the colonial as a new form of much more close and deeper governance of distant territories (Steinmetz, 2014: 79). The history of the epistemic techniques behind the notion of a 'Third World' shows disconcerting continuities from imperial to colonial times that directly lead to the knowledge order of the subsequent age of constrained national sovereignty in the Global South as opposed to full sovereignty in the Global North.

5 Economic 'Imperialism'?

There are historical reasons as to why economics became so important a resource of political deliberation in global politics post-1945.

The Second World War changed colonial needs especially for France and Great Britain. Due to a significant Dollar shortage capital investment in the colonies was intensified what went along with a deepening of governance. As the Asian possessions were lost to Europe with the independence of India in 1947 and with the concomitant French and Dutch violent frictions in Indochina and Indonesia, Africa became a new focus under European imperial eyes (Cooper, 2011).

This went along with a change in form from sheer brutality to more subtle forms of domination. During the War, in the British experience, economic statistics had been helpful in more rationally allocating scarce resources within one seemingly closed economic system, that is, the national economy. Experts like the economist E. A. G. Robinson who had been on the scientific board of the Hailey Survey, demanded more sound knowledge on the colonies' economic state and potential in order to widen such an approach to all of the British Empire (Deane, 1948). But the early attempts at statistically creating sound social accounts for all economies at the periphery of British Rule all completely failed. They produced very modest results in terms of facts but debated at length the methodological problems of computing a sum-total of national income (GDP) for non-Western economic life (Deane, 1953; Prest, 1953; Peacock & Dosser, 1958).

Such discursive uncertainty also prolonged into the organizational innovations at the epoch of imperial decline. Namely, a fundamental insecurity reigned during the founding years of the United Nations Organization (1942–48) as to how categorically organize a family of nations. At the pledging conference for the Technical Assistance Program, that later gave rise to the United Nations Development Program (UNDP), in 1950 one observer noted:

> It is difficult to give a precise definition of an underdeveloped country. No country can be considered as fully developed in all respects. However, the intention underlying the programme is to help those countries which do not possess within their own borders the elements necessary for their development, i.e., neither technical knowledge nor adequate financial means for securing such knowledge from abroad. 2. From a practical standpoint, an under developed country would be any one that considered itself as such. (UN Archive Geneva, UNOG GX 26/01, 30.01.1950)

In this quote, there are many insecurities as to what targets the emerging development machine (J. Ferguson) should concentrate on. Many other sources bear witness of a specific irritation at that epoch concerning the categorial order in world politics. One diplomat from Ceylon (Sri Lanka) is purported to have stated at a conference of the *General Agreement on Tariffs and Trade* (GATT): 'An underdeveloped country is like the giraffe – an animal difficult to define, but easy to recognise'. Paul G. Hoffman, the first director of UNDP, repeatedly stated that it was impossible to define a Third-World-country on sound terms, but every Western expert would intuitively know when he or she was in such a place (Renschler, 1966: 12). In view of the definitional complexity, one US-American scholar in a review on work by M. F. Milikan, E. Shils, J. Lacouture, J. Baumier and others in 1963 simply invented a hypothetical country (that he baptized 'Nudexia') in order to help focus the booming literature on international development and to create a unity out of the manifold different situations at the periphery (Boyd, 1963).

Simplifying the legacy of European colonialism in a new world map that confronted poor nations (light grey) to rich nations (dark grey) according to GDP-statistics was a way out of the cognitive impasse of decolonization for European and North American agents (Figure 12.1). This epistemic setting provided the basis for a new notion – the 'Third World' – to emerge globally as an effect of statistically grounded development economical theory.

Already the mandate system of the League of Nations had furthered inter-imperial cooperation in technical respects (Pedersen, 2015). New norms of good governance increasingly assigned importance to the gathering of statistical information. The founders of the UN in San Francisco created an Economic and Social Council (ECOSOC) that aimed at preventing future wars through planning economic development on a global scale. The first UN-Secretary General Trygve Lie conceived of the organization as a 'clearinghouse for skills and 'knowhow'' (Lie, 1954: 146f). He wanted the organization to become a forum for the exchange of technical expertise.

African leaders strongly reacted to these promises of state-run technical internationalism.[10] In 1958, a regional economic commission for Africa was established in the UN-System. Earlier on, other such regional UN-Commissions had been founded. Most renowned in development history is CEPAL, the Latin American UN regional commission for economic development, that was located in Santiago de Chile under Raul Prebisch and that is remembered as the cradle of Dependency Theory (Dosman, 2008). In Africa, the Ethiopian Emperor Haile Selassie strongly engaged in the regionalizing of the UN. He offered a plot of land in his capital of Addis Ababa where an 'Africa Hall' was to be constructed as a new conference venue. The official founding ceremony of the institution (but not of the building that was finished later) was seen as a symbol of African renewal stating that the ECA was 'Africa's own commission' (Misteli, 2016). The new organization had little formal power and would later engage in a detrimental competition with OAU. But during its first years of existence, it played an important role as the envisioned clearing house of

[10] Strong evidence for this can be found in the biography and the writings of Nkwame Nkrumah, who envisioned a new African internationalism that based on technocracy, with Accra as a centre (Nkrumah, 1963).

knowledge. Several international professional bodies started to hold meetings at the new Addis Ababa venue. And ECA officers engaged in many statistical endeavours across Sub-Saharan Africa. Listening into them speak (1965):

> Economic planning is now a commonly acclaimed ideal in the underdeveloped countries, particularly in Africa. ... With the disintegration of the colonial system, planning in the former African colonies and protectorates underwent a complete metamorphosis. (Ben-Amor & Clairmonte, 1965: 473)

A great quest for statistical inquiries arose, which challenged the administrators of late British imperial rule. After World War Two, they practically overnight were forced to confess that their mode of governance was technologically outdated. For example, in 1961, officials from the East African colonial administrative body explained to an international audience at a conference of the 'International Association for Research in Income and Wealth' (IARIW) that was hosted by the UN Economic Commission for Africa in Addis Ababa, that the Colony of Kenya did not possess very sophisticated statistics (Kennedy et al., 1963).[11] They confessed that, measured against the norms of a new international discourse of statistical transparency, British colonial administration had little to say:

> It is, therefore, not possible to construct a useful series of *per capita* real incomes. Nor, because of the absence of useful price indicators is it possible to produce a satisfactory series showing changes in aggregate real domestic product. (...) Except in the obvious and elementary sense of providing an outline-map of the economy, the National Accounting material is not sufficient to be of great help or assistance in development planning; certainly, it has not been used in East Africa. (Kennedy et al., 1963: 391–410)

Comparative economic statistics on a global scale were a mere fantasy according to this source. But local authorities had to comply. Consequently, the East African Statistical Department compiled a substantial documentation in 1959 not on facts, but on the methodological problems of African economic fact gathering (Colony and Protectorate of Kenya, 1959). This local move that was repeated all over the world during the 1960s, created a basis for global economic income statistics to become such a plausible communicative device in the emerging world society.

[11] The authors indicated 'that the basic statistical information is quite inadequate in many cases with respect to certain important sectors of the economy' because of the 'small amount of resources which have been devoted to statistical collection in East Africa' (Kennedy et al., 1963: 389).

6 Conclusion

What colonial or imperial trajectories can be detected in 'Third World'-discourse until today? To what extent is it theory-bound? How to explain the sudden rise of a new epistemological order on global difference as is evident in the figures shown above?

As of the 1950s, the analysis of one planetary social formation has become the focus of a new sub-discipline in sociology, political science and historiography. The headings of a 'global community' (Iriye, 2002), a 'World polity' (Meyer, 2009), a 'Weltgesellschaft' (Luhmann, 1971) or a 'World System' (Wallerstein, 2004) address current phenomena of globalization. They could more strongly reconsider colonialism and – generally – overcome their amnesia concerning Balandier.

The aim here is to make the historical impact of the social sciences in the colonial encounter visible as one agent of change among others from the imperial to the colonial and further into the post-colonial situation that came to be structured according to the Westphalian system of a planetary family of nations. The current name for this move is 'decolonization'. In this, the rise of the discipline of economics was most prominent.

While imperial rule largely neglected quantitative modes of knowledge, late colonialism and the post-colonial development-industry embraced them with whatever ambiguous success. Only with the process of decolonization the notion of a 'Third World' became globally important as an effect of theory. My findings suggest that this move was initially connected to a shift in distant rule from an imperial regime that was largely disinterested in statistics to a late colonial regime that took such governmental techniques up however incompletely. With decolonization imperial expert-commissions and administrative units simply gave over to new agents like the United Nations' ECOSOC and UNEPTA, and national development agencies, while the order of knowledge did not change. We find here a strong instance of a presence of the past.

My argument in this chapter is that macroeconomic statistics should not be taken as a somewhat innocent rendering of global economic differences through the twentieth century, but rather as a cognitive mode of reducing the complexity of global society in the age of imperial decline. Agents behind this specific approach must be considered one social community among others that needs to be studied – according to Balandier – in its social function towards the diversity of a global whole. For sure, looking at the rendering of global difference in quantitative terms today shows specific legacies of colonialism and imperialism.

The material presented bears evidence of a very close connection between power and knowledge. Legacies of colonial times abound. More research is needed on the logic and on the form of governance in the conflictive transformation process from Empires to the family of nations. To be sure, in this global transformation, the composition of a comparative framework of national GDPs was an engine, rather than a camera (MacKenzie, 2006). It was based on a radical methodological nationalism and gave rise to economics as a seemingly all-encompassing way to describe social life across the planet. I still wonder as to what extent old colonial notions of difference prevail.

References

Appadurai, A. (1996). *Modernity at Large: Cultural Dimensions of Globalization*, Minneapolis: University of Minnesota Press.

Balandier, G. (ed.). (1956). *Le 'Tiers Monde'. Sous-développement et développement, Travaux et Documents, Cahier no 27*, Paris: Presses Universitaires de France.

Balandier, G. (1951). La situation coloniale. Approche théorique, *Cahiers Internationaux de Sociologie,* 11, 44–79.

Balandier, G. (1957). *Afrique ambigüe*, Plon: Paris.

Bayart, J. F. (2010). *Les études postcoloniales. Un carnaval académique*, Paris: Karthala.

Ben-Amor, A. & Clairmonte, F. (1965). Planning in Africa, *Journal of Modern African Studies*, 3(4), 473–97

Berger, M. T. (2004). After the Third World? History, Destiny and the Fate of Third Worldism, *Third World Quarterly*, 25, 9–39.

Bonche, A. (2013). *Entretien avec Georges Balandier: 50 ans d' independences ambigües? Paris.* www.livingbooksabouthistory.ch/en/book/la-situation-coloniale#chapter-1-3

Bonneuil, C. (2000). Development as Experiment. Science and State Building in Late Colonial and Postcolonial Africa 1930–1970, *Osiris*, 15, 258–81.

Boyd, A. (1963). Review: The Third World, *International Affairs*, 39, 564–69.

Colony and Protectorate of Kenya. (1959). *The Domestic Income and Product in Kenya – A Description of Sources and Methods with Revised Calculations for 1954–1958*, Nairobi: Government Press.

Cooper, F. (2005). *Colonialism in Question*, Berkeley: University of Berkeley Press.

Cooper, F. (2011). Reconstructing Empire in British and French Africa, in M. Mazower et al. (eds.). *Post-War Reconstruction in Europe: International Perspectives 1945–1949*, Oxford: Oxford University Press.

Cooper, F. & Stoler, A. L. (1997). Between Metropole and Colony: Rethinking a Research Agenda, in A. L. Stoler & F. Cooper (eds.). *Tensions of Empire: Colonial Cultures in a Bourgeois World*, Berkeley: California University Press.

de L'Estoile, Benôit. (2007). *Le goût des autres: De l'éxposition colonial aux arts premiers*, Paris: Flammarion.

Deane, P. (1948). The Measurement of Colonial National Incomes: An Experiment, *The Economic Journal*, 59(236), 593–95

Deane, P. (1953). *Colonial Social Accounting*, Cambridge: Cambridge University Press.

Diaz-Bone, R. (2007). Habitusformierung und Theorieeffekt: Zur sozialen Konstruktion von Märkten, in J. Beckert et al. (eds.). *Märkte als soziale Strukturen*, Frankfurt: Suhrkamp.

Dimier, V. (2014). *The Invention of a European Development Aid Bureaucracy: Recycling Empire*, Basingstoke: Palgrave Macmillan.

Dinkel, J. (2014). 'Dritte Welt': Geschichte und Semantiken, Version 1.0, Docupedia-Zeitgeschichte, 06 October 2014, http://docupedia.de/zg/Dritte_Welt?oli-did=97388.

Dirlik, A. (2004). Spectres of the Third World: Global Modernity and the End of the Three Worlds, *Third World Quarterly*, 25(1), 131–48.

Dosman, E. J. (2008). *The Life and Times of Raul Prebisch*, Montreal: McGill-Queen's University Press.

Ferguson, J. (1990). *The Anti-politics Machine: Development, Depoliticization, and Bureaucratic Power in Lesotho*, Cambridge: Cambridge University Press.

Ferguson, J. (2006). *Global Shadows: Africa in the Neoliberal World Order*, Durham: Duke University Press.

Griaule, M. (1938). *Masques Dogons*, Paris: Institut d'ethnologie.

Gupta, A. (2012). *Red Tape: Bureaucracy, Structural Violence, and Poverty in India*, Durham: Duke University Press.

Hailey, W. H. (1938). *An African Survey: A Study of Problems Arising in Africa South of the Sahara*, London: Macmillan.

Heintz, Bettina (ed.) (2005). *Weltgesellschaft: Theoretische Zugänge und empirische Problemlagen*, Stuttgart: Lucius & Lucius.

Hodge, J. (2007). *Triumph of the Expert: Agrarian Doctrines of Development and the Legacies of British Colonialism*, Athens: Ohio University Press.

Hodge, J. (2016). Writing the History of Development (Part 2: Longer, Deeper, Wider), *Humanity: An International Journal of Human Rights, Humanitarianism, and Development*, 7(1), 125–74.

Hongler, P. (2019). *Den Süden Erzählen: Berichte aus dem kolonialen Archiv der OECD (1948–1975)*, Zürich: Chronos.

Iriye, A. (2002). *Global Community: The Role of International Organizations in the Making of the Contemporary World*, Berkeley: University of California Press.

Jerven, M. (2013). *Poor Numbers: How We Are Misled by African Development Statistics and What to Do about It*, Ithaca: Cornell University Press.

Kalpagam, U. (2014). *Rule by Numbers: Governmentality in Colonial India*, Lanham: Lexington Books.

Kennedy, T. A., Ord, H. W. & Walker, D. (1963). On the Calculation and Interpretation of National Accounting Material in East Africa, in L. H. Samuels (ed.). *African Studies in Income and Wealth*, Chicago: Quadrangle Books.

Leiris, M. (1934). *L'Afrique fântome*, Paris: Gallimard.

Lie, T. (1954). *In the Cause of Peace: Seven Years with the United Nations*, New York: Macmillan.

Luhmann, N. (1971). Die Weltgesellschaft, *Archiv für Rechts- und Sozialphilosophie*, 57, 1–35.

Macekura, S. (2017). Development and Economic Growth: An intellectual history, in I. Borowy & M. Schmelzer (eds.). *History of the Future of Economic Growth*, London: Routledge.

MacKenzie, D. (2006). *An Engine, Not a Camera: How Financial Models Shape Markets*, Cambridge: MIT Press.

Meyer, J. W. (2009). *World Society: The Writings of John W. Meyer*, Oxford: Oxford University Press.

Misteli, S. (2016). Prendre en compte la décolonisation. Les débuts de la Commission économique pour l'Afrique des Nations unies (1958–1965), *Revue d'histoire diplomatique*, 130(2), 162–76.

Mitchell, T. (1998). Fixing the Economy, *Cultural Studies*, 12(1), 82–101.

Murphy, C. N. (1984). *The Emergence, of the NIEO Ideology*, Boulder, CO: Westview Press.

Nkrumah, K. (1963). *Africa Must Unite*, London: Heinemann.

Peacock, A. T. & Dosser, D. (1958). *The National Income of Tanganyika 1952–54*, London: H. M. Stationery Off.

Pedersen, S. (2015). *The Guardians: The League of Nations and the Crisis of Empire*, Oxford: Oxford University Press.

Porter, T. M. (1986). *The Rise of Statistical Thinking 1820–1900*, Princeton: Princeton University Press.

Prashad, V. (2007). *The Darker Nations: A People's History of the Third World*, New York: The New Press.

Prest, A. R. & Stewart, I. G. (1953). *National Income of Nigeria*, London: Cambridge University Press.

Renschler, W. (1966). *Die Konzeption der technischen Zusammenarbeit zwischen der Schweiz und den Entwicklungsländern*, Zürich: Europa Verlag.

Schmitt, M. (1962). *Die befreite Welt: Vom Kolonialsystem zur Partnerschaft*, Baden-Baden: August Lutzeyer.

Slobodian, Q. (2018). *Globalists: The End of Empire and the Birth of Neoliberalism*, Cambridge: Harvard University Press.

Solarz, M. W. (2012). 'Third World'. The 60th Anniversary of a Concept that Changed History, *Third World Quarterly*, 33(9), 1561–73.

Speich Chassé, D. (2011). The Use of Global Abstractions. National Income Accounting in the Period of Imperial Decline, *Journal of Global History*, 6(1), 7–28.

Speich Chassé, D. (2015). Die 'Dritte Welt' als Theorieffekt: Ökonomisches Wissen und globale Differenz, *Geschichte und Gesellschaft*, 41(4), 580–612.

Speich Chassé, D. (2016). The Roots of the Millennium Development Goals. A framework for Studying the History of Global Statistics, *Historical Social Research*, 41(2), 218–37.

Stamp, J. (1934). Methods Used in Different Countries for Estimating National Income, *Journal of the Royal Statistical Society*, 97(3), 423–55.

Steinmetz, G. (2010). La sociologie et l'empire: Richard Thurnwald et la question de l'autonomie scientifique, *Actes de la recherche en sciences sociales*, 185(12), 12–29.

Steinmetz, G. (2014). The Sociology of Empires, Colonies, and Postcolonialism, *Annual Review of Sociology*, 40(77), 77–103.

Stone, R. (1951). *The Role of Measurement in Economics: The Newmarch Lectures given at University College London 1948–1949*, Cambridge: Cambridge University Press.

Thurnwald, R. & Thurnwald, H. (1935). *Black and White in East Africa: The Fabric of a New Civilization. A Study in Social Contact and Adaptation of Life in East Africa*, London: Routledge.

Tilley, H. (2011). *Africa as a Living Laboratory: Empire, Development, and the Problem of Scientific Knowledge 1870–1950*, Chicago: Chicago University Press.

Tomlinson, T. (2003). What Was the Third World?, *Journal of Contemporary History*, 38(2), 307–21.

United Nations (1953). *A System of National Accounts and Supporting Tables*, Studies in Methods, Series F, Vol. 2, New York: United Nations Press.

van Laak, D. (2004). Kolonien als 'Laboratorien der Moderne?', in S. Conrad & J. Osterhammel (eds.). *Das Kaiserreich transnational: Deutschland in der Welt 1871–1914*, Göttingen: Vandenhoeck & Ruprecht.

Wallerstein, I. (2004). *World-Systems Analysis: An Introduction*, Duke: Duke University Press.

13 The Past and Its Presence in Ottoman and Post-Ottoman Memory Cultures

The Battle of Kosovo and the Status of Jerusalem

Anna Vlachopoulou and Stephan Stetter

The past is never dead. It is not even past.

William Faulkner

1 Introduction

In this chapter, we discuss how the 'double' historical experience with imperial politics shapes memory cultures in Ottoman and post-Ottoman spaces (cf. Wigen, 2013; Anscombe, 2014; Busse, 2021). Thus, firstly, there is the historical experience in today's Turkey, and throughout the Balkans as well as Arab states, Israel and other countries, of having been situated in the Ottoman Empire – an imperial entity that ruled over these territories often for several centuries. Central here is, as we will highlight, the creeping transformation of the Ottoman Empire during the long nineteenth century: the Empire 'modernized', thereby acquiring a self-understanding as a modern imperial power and, with the rise of Turkish nationalism, also as a quasi-colonial power. The century-old millet-system endured, but was increasingly framed in terms of ethno-nationalist, and then also racial, and at times even genocidal terms. This went hand in hand with an increasing mobilization by political and social movements representing non-Turkish communities throughout the empire that were seeking political autonomy or national self-determination, often leading to new state formation (on state formation in Africa see the chapter by Glasmann and Schlichte in this volume). Thus, the Ottoman Empire faced, since the first half of the nineteenth century, various forms of locally determined and/or nationalist-oriented resistance from within, such as from Greeks, Serbs, Bulgarian, Kurds, Arabs, Jews and others. Memory cultures in such communities often emerged in relation to this experience with late-Ottoman imperialism. This historical (and to some extent contemporary, given Turkey's neo-Ottoman resurgence under President Erdoğan) experience with a form of non-Western imperialism 'from within' is, as we will argue, one facet of the Ottoman and post-Ottoman complex memory culture.

Secondly, then, due to the declining power of the Ottoman Empire during the nineteenth century, European powers increasingly shaped politics in Ottoman realms, usually in an attempt to foster their own great power interests, thereby exploiting the (relative) weakness of the Ottoman Empire vis-à-vis these other great powers. The Ottoman Empire became depicted as the 'sick man of Europe' and in the context of this imperialism 'from the outside' (on nineteenth century mainly Concert of Europe imperialism see the chapters by Müller and Albert), Great Britain, the German and Russian Empires, Austria-Hungary, France, Italy and over time the US as well entered the scene (compare the chapters by Müller and by Albert in this volume). This came with often quite obvious imperial and colonial ambitions, battling over who would fill the vacuum left by the decline and dissolution of the Ottoman Empire, either through quasi-colonial imposition as in the British and French mandates after World War I or through informal forms of imperial power projection. Take, for example, the successive Russo-Ottoman wars during the nineteenth century, the German alliance with the Ottomans up until the end of the First World War or the competition between the US and the Soviet Union, and then again Russia, over geopolitical influence in different parts of the erstwhile Ottoman Empire. Add to this the increasing relevance of transnational cultural, economic and political entanglements that arose in global modernity in the form of links between Ottoman and post-Ottoman societies, associations and people with counterparts in the rest of the world, including diaspora communities (e.g. on the role of Palestinian diaspora cf. Said, 1995). In the Arab provinces and the Middle East in general, imperial succession to the Ottomans came in form of formal occupation or informal prerogatives by Great Powers and the establishment of colonial regimes (aka mandate system) or 'client states', substantially delaying independence and self-government of the populations in the region or limiting their scope of sovereignty. The erstwhile South-eastern European provinces of the Ottoman Empire gradually achieved independence from the Ottomans since the early nineteenth century while at the same time balancing or fighting imperial ambitions by European powers (and the US) in the form of cultural outreach, political pressure and economic control, with some of these territories undergoing an interim phase from Ottoman to Habsburg imperial rule before gaining independence.

This double imperialist experience and how it is reflected in the way history is incorporated into the collective memory (Halbwachs, 1980; Erll, 2011), will be analysed in this chapter in relation to two cases that offer a snapshot on the different experiences of the (former) Ottoman provinces. Firstly, the myth that developed around the Battle of Kosovo in particular for Serb nationalism but also Albanian memory culture. And then, secondly, the status of Jerusalem and the city's religious-political symbolism. While it harkens back to a past event, (collective) memory and its cultivation is of course a phenomenon of the respective present. As laid out in the Introduction of this volume, the past – Kosovo and Jerusalem in our specific case – is 'constantly enacted and constructed in the present' through various forms of memory cultures. Following Erll (2011), we conceive of memory culture as a wide set of sociocultural narratives and practices of collectively remembering (and forgetting) specific aspects of the past (Erll, 2011: 96). This also relates to how cultural memory is invoked in various social contexts from politics to education and from media to popular culture. Focusing on the linkages between memory cultures and national identities our two cases of Kosovo and Jerusalem highlight that memory cultures revolve not so much about history, a concrete memory of it or the myth around it, but the ways in which it can (and is) turned, on transnational scales, into an instrument by leaders, political movements, interest groups or individuals with distinct political agendas. Thus, the analysis of memory culture concerning Kosovo and Jerusalem has to take into consideration different modes of historicity sketched out in the introduction: not only different temporalities but also different power structures, since different actors shaped, interpreted and used the collective memory of these events in different points of time in certain historical contexts (mode 4). We emphasize in particular how the memory cultures studied in this chapter gained political significance as a way of resisting to what is perceived as foreign rule either by imperial powers or another conflict party making claims on the same territory. Moreover, memory cultures transform and play a particular role in legitimizing authority over territory for non-great powers. Finally, memory cultures are not locally contained but 'migrate' to the international level. There are local-global entanglements of considerable relevance to memory cultures, for example, because they become part of imperial politics and complex relations between outside actors and parties on the ground. Imaginaries of Kosovo and Jerusalem, thus, not only affect politics in the territories under erstwhile imperial or colonial tutelage, but also imperial actors as we discuss inter alia with a view how imaginaries of the Balkans and the Holy Land shape US politics. Doing so, this chapter traces how memory cultures pertaining to Kosovo (Section 2) and Jerusalem (Section 3) changed over time, how they interplayed with imperialist ambitions in the respective regions and global power relations and looks at how memory cultures were used (and abused) by different actors.

2 Memory Cultures in Ottoman and Post-Ottoman Realms I: The Battle of Kosovo

On 28 June 1389 (15 June O.S.) the Ottoman army led by Sultan Murad I. and the Serbian army led by Prince Lazar Hrebeljanović met in battle on the so-called Field of Blackbirds (Kosovo Polje) in the vicinity of Priština. Both leaders lost their life on the battlefield. This is about as much as historians know with some degree of certainty. Early reports claimed Serbian victory, but the battle probably ended in a draw (Emmert, 1990). Although Serbia remained independent for another seventy years, the Battle of Kosovo became engrained in Serbian collective memory under Ottoman rule as the end of the Serbian medieval kingdom and the beginning of 'five centuries long Turkish yoke' (Djokić, 2009: 219–20).

Almost immediately after the battle, legendary accounts emerged in folk ballads and poems. The early versions of the Kosovo legend in the fourteenth/fifteenth century, accentuated religious motifs and centred around the figure of Prince Lazar, who was canonized shortly after he had died on the battlefield (Zirojević, 2000: 190). Prince Lazar – the legend goes – on the eve of the battle was offered the choice between a kingdom in heaven and a kingdom on earth. By choosing the heavenly kingdom as Prince Lazar did, he would lose his live and the battle to the Ottomans but secure heavenly redemption for the Serbian nation. Thus, the military defeat was turned into moral victory (Djokić, 2009: 220).

Over the centuries, the myth evolved. Written chronicles, popular epics and oral traditions influenced one another and cross-fertilized, adding more details and tropes. While there is no single, uniform version of the Kosovo myth, by the seventeenth century three basic features are discernible: the motif of sacrifice, personified by the aforementioned Prince Lazar who chose the heavenly over the earthly kingdom and died on the battlefield. The motif of treason, personified by Vuk Branković, son-in-law of Prince Lazar. He is said to have betrayed the Prince by withdrawing his forces from battle, thus causing the Serbian loss. The motif of selfless heroism and revenge against the Ottomans, personified by the figure of Miloš Obilić, a Serbian noble and another son-in-law of Lazar. He is said to have killed Sultan Murad I. being slain himself in the act.[1] This three-layered legend (religious sacrifice, betrayal, heroism and revenge) was over the centuries told and retold, sung, narrated,

[1] While Vuk Branković is a historic figure there is no trace of him leaving the battlefield or taking sides with the Ottoman forces in historical sources. The historicity of Miloš Obilić is disputed.

staged and finally written down, copied and widely disseminated, with the different motifs dominating the narrative at different times, taking firm roots in the collective memory of people in the region and beyond (Zirojević, 2000: 190–94). The legend of the battle was finally incorporated into the collection of epic ballads, compiled by the reformer of the Serbian language Vuk Karadžić. The stories of Lazar, Branković and Obilić were thus canonized and made accessible to literate Serbians 'arming them with the core ingredients of a new nationalist faith' (Cohen, 2014: 11–12).

Serbian nationalism – like most nationalisms – looked to the foretime, to the 'golden age' of the nation, thus creating a 'usable past' (Smith, 1997) and the Kosovo myth, which bore several usable features, lend itself to this end very conveniently. The myth itself referred to a golden age, to the medieval Serbian kingdom featuring Serbia's biggest territorial expansion. While the myth recounted the loss of this kingdom it also turned the loss into a moral victory and promised the resurrection of the state: like Jesus who sacrificed so that his people would live, Prince Lazar had sacrificed so that Serbia would resurrect. The reference to betrayal on the battlefield by the Judas-like Vuk Branković explained the loss of the kingdom in a way that allowed for externalization of blame and at the same time called for (national) unity. The reference to bravery and the revenge taken by Miloš Obilić provided for a heroic identification figure, inspired action and promised success in the liberation of the nation. All three figures with the respective motifs they represent, 'survive as an integral part of Serbian collective discourse', that centres around an encounter with the Ottoman Empire (Djokić, 2009: 221).

The Kosovo myth could therefore be handily and frequently be invoked during the struggle for independence from the Ottoman Empire in the modern era. Djordje Petrović, better known as Karadjordje, leader of the first Serbian uprising (1804–1813) called on the people to 'throw off, in the name of God, the yoke which the Serbs carry from Kosovo to this day' (Nenadović, 1893: 260–61). In the years after the 1848 revolutions, Serbian nationalist-revolutionary youth organizations kept referring to the medieval Serbian kingdom, to Kosovo and to the need to resurrect past glories. The declaration of war against the Ottoman Empire in 1876 referred to Kosovo, and the heritage of the medieval kingdom and its end in Kosovo was appropriated both by the Karadjordjević and the Obrenović dynasties in their rivalry over Serbian rule – underlining the central role of the myth in the late-Ottoman Empire (cf. Djordjević, 1991).

While the motif of sacrifice (Prince Lazar) dominated the early centuries, the nineteenth century was dominated by the motif of heroism and revenge (Miloš Obilić). Especially in Montenegro, where many people believed that they were descendants of survivors of the Battle of Kosovo who had fled to the mountains, the Kosovo myth was deeply engrained in the collective memory. Prince-Bishop Petar Petrović Njegoš (r. 1830–1851) further popularized the myth in his long poem 'Mountain Wrath', which depicts a fictional execution of Slavs/Montenegrins who had converted – as many Bosnians did a few centuries ago – to Islam, making extensive references to the Battle of Kosovo and especially to Miloš Obilić (Zirojević, 2000: 196–98; Djokić, 2009: 224–25).

After Serbia had won her formal independence in 1878 following the Congress of Berlin, the Kosovo-myth-turned-national-narrative took on additional functions, now connected to nation-building and state-building processes in a modern international order with the old motifs serving new objectives: the myth served to reinforce and legitimize both domestically and internationally the notion of a Serbian nation by providing for identification figures and calling on the (shared) collective memory of the Serbian nationals. It legitimized the new state by constructing a historic continuity between the medieval Serbian kingdom and 'modern' Serbia and between the medieval heroes and 'modern' Serbs, thus alleging a perennial nation/statehood. It however clashed with other emergent collective memories aiming to justify independence from the Ottomans, and the European powers of the day. Thus, as far as Serbia is concerned, the reformulated myth promised territorial expansion of the new state by postulating a claim on Kosovo and the region West of Kosovo (Metohija), the scenes of the myth, since the European powers had not included these areas into the newly minted Serbian Principality. The 500th anniversary of the Battle of Kosovo (1889) was therefore of utmost importance for the new kingdom and saw the elevation of St. Vitus' Day (15/28 June, the day the battle was fought) to a national holiday (Ekmečić, 1991), further stressing the territorial claims that Serbia deduced from the myth. When during the First Balkan War (1812) Serbian troops finally marched into Kosovo, the intensity of the physical space seemed overwhelming: 'When we arrived on Kosovo [...] our commander spoke: 'Brothers, my children, my sons!' His voice breaks. 'This place on which we stand is the graveyard of our glory. We bow to the shadows of fallen ancestors and pray God for the salvation of their souls.' His voice gives out and tears flow in streams down his cheeks and grey beard and fall to the ground. He actually shakes from some kind of inner pain and excitement.' one soldier recalls (Emmert, 1990: 133–34).

With the founding of the Yugoslav state (1918), the need for a more inclusive narrative arouse and efforts were made to mould the Kosovo myth from a Serbian national narrative into a Pan-Slavic one, that reconstructed resistance to the Ottomans as a broader Slavic affair, handily epitomized by the Slavic-dominated political set-up of Yugoslavia. The celebrations of the anniversary in 1939 thus tried to embrace Croats and Slovenes (but not Kosovars, Bosniaks although being Slavs and others) – with only limited success. After the establishment of communist rule in Yugoslavia (1945) the Kosovo myth for some time lost significance and was overshadowed by the new foundational myths, mainly about the wartime heroism of communist partisans (Emmert, 1990: 126–41; Bieber, 2002: 99).

After the death of Tito in 1980, the Kosovo myth quickly acquired renewed significance and a new scope. In the wake of student's protests demands for the status of full republic for the autonomous province of Kosovo arose amongst Albanian Kosovars, posing the first nationalist challenge of the post-Tito status quo (Bieber, 2002: 99). After the suppression of the protests but with tensions still simmering, a new Kosovo-related theme emerged in Serbia's nationalist discourse: The Great Migration of the Serbs. This narrative recalled the year 1689 when forces of the anti-Ottoman Holy League had captured Belgrade, Niš, Kosovo and advanced as far as Skopje only to lose it again to the Ottomans in the following year. Fearing Ottoman reprisals, thousands of refugees from the region, including Arsenije III, the patriarch of Peć, crossed the Danube and found shelter on the Habsburg side of the new border (Malcolm, 1998: 139–40). This seeded a sense of betrayal vis-à-vis the West in Serbian memory culture. Adding this feature to a modern nationalist discourse – in an international order dominated by the West – thus worked quite easily and served a variety of purposes. In a way, it replayed the motifs of the Battle of Kosovo Polje by depicting the Serbs suffering a martyr's faith by resisting Ottoman (Muslim/Albanian) barbarians. It reinforced the idea of Serbia as a coherent ethno-nationality since the fourteenth century and her heroic nature fighting for freedom against all odds. It hinted to a tradition of persecution of the Serbs by others, and betrayal by the West, throughout history which was now enriched by a rhetoric of ethnic cleansing and even genocidal tendencies by Kosovo Albanians against the Serbs living in the autonomous province. And it 'reconcile[d] romantic national history with awkward modern reality', explaining the Albanian demographic majority in Kosovo by depicting them as historical late-comers and beneficiaries of the Serbian expulsion, settling in Kosovo after the fact (Bieber, 2002; Anscombe, 2006: 767).

By exploiting political tensions and socio-economic grievances in Kosovo, the Serbian leadership under Slobodan Milošević mobilized nationalist sentiments and utilized the thus created 'usable past' for their political agenda within Yugoslavia. In March 1989, when changes to the Serbian constitution were made, Kosovo was stripped of her (Malcolm, 1998: 343–44). Only three months later, the Kosovo myth reached its highest visibility – including in international media – during the 600th anniversary of the Battle of Kosovo in which the place of the battle, the Field of Blackbirds, played a leading role as now fully globalized memory space. According to some estimates up to one million spectators gathered in Gazimestan (the memorial site on Kosovo Polje) outside Priština to commemorate the battle of 1389. Milošević used his speech to further the Kosovo-related motifs in the nationalist discourse, thereby stoking the support of public opinion for his goals (Bieber, 2002: 100–3).

The next high point of the Kosovo myth in Serbian nationalist discourse came with renewed tension in Kosovo, leading to war in 1998/1999. The Serbian leadership drew on the Kosovo myth to stress Serbia's claims to the region and object to Western influence. The military intervention of NATO and the bombardment of Serbia then sparked rhetoric of Serbian martyrdom and activated the collective memory of Serbian victimization by a foreign imperialist enemy, comparing NATO 'imperialism' to Ottoman impositions, but also invoking deeply seated suspicions of Western betrayal, existing since the Holy League days. Support for Milošević declined after the war and the 'Kosovo question' was pushed aside by more pressing problems in post-war live, such as social and economic difficulties, political change and considerations of Serbia's relation to the EU (Bieber, 2002). Yet, the declaration of independence by Kosovo in 2008, recognized by a majority, but not all EU member states, as well as the broad presence of international organizations and NGOs on the ground are still often framed in the context of the Kosovo myth as it pertains to occupation of 'Serbian territory' and to Serbia being a victim of betrayal and foreign occupation.

On the Albanian side of the conflict, the battle of Kosovo Polje played no major role but has to be discussed here because myths of Albanian statehood relate to similar temporal schemes that invoke a memory culture that contradicts the Serbian theme. Thus, the late nineteenth-century Albanian nation-building myth reached even further back than Medieval times claiming ancient presence of Albanians in the region. According to the 'Illyrian theory', Albanians were descendants of ancient Illyrians and settlers in the region before everybody else – especially the Slavs – arrived. Thus, Serbs were the late-comers and their claim to Kosovo was considered null and void. Kosovo Albanians rejected Serbian claims by rejecting the Serb/Yugoslav official name of the region: 'Kosovo and Metohija' (Kosovo: the field of blackbirds; Metohija: the land of (Orthodox) monasteries') or short 'Kosmet'. When Albanian communists took control over the province under its semi-autonomy within the Yugoslav state (1968), they changed the official name into 'Kosovo' in which form it remained until 1989 when Kosovo was stripped of her autonomy (Pavković, 2001: 3–5; Schwandner-Sievers & Fischer, 2002), until becoming independent by 2008.

The potent symbolism of the Kosovo myth was not lost on European and international powers who used the myth according to their own objectives. The nineteenth century saw a rise of tourists, scientists, diplomats, eccentrics and spies travelling to the Ottoman or former Ottoman regions of south-eastern Europe and a plethora of respective travelogues and reports were published. The descriptions of the regions, people, their lives, customs and histories were heavily loaded with Orientalist terms and not only served broader imperialist objectives of control and domination but at times also very concrete political goals (Said, 1979; Hammond, 2004; Todorova, 2009). They usually conveyed an impression of south-eastern Europe being inhabited by violent barbarians, incapable of self-government and in desperate need of European (or British or French or American) civilization and guidance. During the First World War, Serbia became an ally to the West and the Kosovo myth was used to create pro-Serbian (and thus anti-Central Powers) sentiments. For the Habsburg Empire and the Central Powers Kosovo was a powerful anti-Serbian symbol – Gavrilo Princeps, who had assassinated the Austrian Archduke and his wife in Sarajevo on the symbolic St. Vitus day 1914, knew Njegoš' poem by heart and heavily identified with Miloš Obilić (Djokić, 2009: 224, 229–30).

The end of the Cold War saw South-eastern Europe re-emerge in European perception together with the imperialist derogatory rhetoric albeit not as overtly as in the previous century. Now not the primitive lifestyle and barbarism was blamed for the violence that was depicted as inherent in the region, but an alleged ethnic diversity and a supposed tendency of South-eastern Europeans to become too easily emotionalized by identity issues. The Kosovo myth was used this time as one argument for the existence of ethnic and religious fanaticism that led to Muslims, Orthodox and Catholics in the Balkans hating and slaughtering each other since time immemorial until today – all achievements of European enlightenment being lost on these people (Mazower, 2000: 4 ff.). This rhetoric was absorbed by political decision-makers as well. The reluctance of US President Bill Clinton and NATO to intervene in the wars of Yugoslavia's disintegration was held to be influenced by the belief that intervention would be futile, after all the Balkan people had always been killing each other. This belief was apparently if not triggered at least reinforced by Robert Kaplan's *Balkan Ghosts*, which had circulated in Washington: handed to Bill Clinton by Colin Powell, read by the President and Ms. Clinton – as Kaplan himself mentions in the preface of the 2005 edition of his book (Halberstam, 2001: 228; Kaplan, 2005).

Thus, the Kosovo myth indirectly had made its way from Serbian collective memory to international political discourse.

3 Memory Cultures in Ottoman and Post-Ottoman Realms II: The Status of Jerusalem

As outlined in the previous section, the myth of the battle of Kosovo in a sense found its way from the 'inside' to the 'outside', that is, from the particularities of Serb and to a lesser degree Albanian identity to a global recognition epitomized by the global attention to the 600th anniversary of the battle – being strongly politicized by the Yugoslav government of the time, and gaining global attention in media and international political circles. In contrast, then, memory cultures revolving around the 'idea and reality' (Mayer & Mourad, 2008) of the status of Jerusalem evolved from a somewhat opposite direction (for a general overview cf. Montefiore, 2011). To be sure, the city was central for Jewish identity already during antiquity, when memory cultures revolving around the temple played a prominent role for example during the Jewish Babylonian exile during the sixth century BCE. However, the immense religious significance of this city to three major and transnational religions – (post-expulsion) Judaism, Christianity and Islam – highlights in particular the global dimension of memory cultures linked to Jerusalem – including claims that there is a distinct field of research that is called 'Jerusalem Studies' on this contested city (Fendius, 2016). Moreover, during the nineteenth centuries outside powers 're-discovered' Jerusalem as part of their respective imperial ambitions, arguably starting with Napoleon's campaign in Egypt and Syria from 1798 to 1801 (Montefiore, 2011: 333) – while the political appropriation of Jerusalem as a pinnacle of Arab/Palestinian and Israeli/Jewish nationalist discourse, that is, a particularization, set in at later stages. This is not to say, that the religious and the political are neatly separated. Thus, nationalist memory cultures on Jerusalem strongly draw from a perception of historical 'rights' based on a particular reading of the city's religious significance as well as debates on who was there first and who has a demographic majority. However, arguably more than in the case of the battle of Kosovo, such particularistic readings stand in a tension with the 'universal' image of Jerusalem as a 'heavenly city' and as a place belonging to all three religions and two people.

For more than a millennium, Jerusalem has been the capital of various autonomous Jewish kingdoms and suzerain states – from the times of King David, considered the founder of the city under this name, around 1000 BCE to the expulsion of the majority of Jews from the then Roman province of Judea after the failed Jewish uprisings around 135 CE – in the wake of which the Romans renamed the province into *Syria Palaestina*. Jerusalem is central to the Jewish holy texts, namely the Torah, and the city became a central point of reference – more as a spiritual metaphor than as a concrete place – in the rabbinical traditions that evolved in exile (Levine, 2008). This changed since the emergence of Zionism, which increased the status of Jerusalem as a concrete city central to Jewish and Zionist/Israeli identity. Today, the Kotel (Western Wall), a remnant of the erstwhile second Temple, that was located on the Temple Mount, is one of the central prayer sites of global Judaism. In Christianity, Jerusalem's holy status derives from the city's significance as the place of the suffering, burial and – according to Christian belief – the resurrection of Jesus Christ. Jesus of Nazareth wept in the Garden Gethsemane at the foot of the Mount of Olives, endured his passion when carrying his cross on Via Doloroso in today's Old city and was buried and resurrected at Golgotha, the place where under Roman Emperor Constantine and Empress Helena, the Church of the Holy Sepulcher was built. For the crusaders, as later on for European (and nominally Christian) powers during the nineteenth century, this religious meaning of Jerusalem was then mixed with political objectives of exercising control over the city and its population. Islam, finally, heralds Jerusalem – or Al-Quds – as one of its holiest cities, next to Mecca and Medina, the direction of prayer in early Islam having been oriented to Jerusalem and not Mecca (El-Khatib, 2001). Al-Quds is the place, where according to the Quran and the Hadith, the prophet Muhammad arrived during a night-ride on the horse-like creature Al-Buraq. From there Muhammad ascended into heaven and conversed with prophets from Adam to Moses and Jesus as well as with God, before returning to Earth. It then was after the Muslim conquest during the seventh century CE, that the Al-Aqsa mosque as well as the Qubbat al-Sakhra (Dome of the Rock) were built on the Holy Plateau or, according to its Muslim name, the Haram Al-Sharif. With the exception of the crusader's Kingdom of Jerusalem (1099–1187) and prior to the British Mandate (1922–1947), from the seventh century until the end of World War I, Jerusalem was governed by Muslim overlords: from the Ummayads, to the Mamluks and then in particular the Ottomans who ruled over the city from 1516 until 1917. It also was an Ottoman ruler, Suleiman the Magnificent, who built the 'signature' city walls of Jerusalem. Yet, the slow demise of the Ottoman Empire during the nineteenth and early twentieth century meant that European powers made increasing inroads, claiming not only a special responsibility for the Ottoman Empire's Christian communities and a guardianship for Christian holy places, but also leaving visible marks on the cityscape that reflected their political ambitions: the Russian compound, the German

Colony or the French Hill are Jerusalem neighbourhoods that testify to this imperial outreach and the way the city became incorporated into imperial memory cultures that ascribed specific meaning to the city as an element of imperial identities.

To be sure, already prior to the emergence of modern imperialism and nationalism, Jerusalem provided fertile ground for political and often religiously grounded (exclusive) memory cultures – and conflicts revolving around opposite memory cultures. Thus, in pre-modern eras, the city witnessed manifold instances of political strive that underline the city's political significance. Take the already mentioned tensions between Jews and Romans, when the Romans actually renamed the city as *Aelia Capitolina* after the expulsion of Jews; or the conflicts between (West European) Crusaders, on the one hand, and Muslim-Arabs as well as Orthodox Christians, on the other. And, finally, strive between the Ottoman overlords and increasingly assertive European powers, the latter often trying to link up with local communities striving for self-determination.

Note here that from the perspective of metropolitan elites in Istanbul, Jerusalem was until the mid-nineteenth century more of a peripheral province. The concrete city was not central to Ottoman memory culture and politics – as it has not been for Christians after the end of the crusader's kingdom until Napoleon's ventures in the region or for Jews prior to the emergence of Zionism. This peripheral status is well expressed by the observation that Jerusalem was part of the larger Vilayet of Syria and only became a distinct province (sandjak or mutassarifat of Jerusalem) in the late-Ottoman Empire, in 1872. This underlies the growing political significance the city acquired during the nineteenth century not only in the eyes of the Ottomans, but of local populations and European imperial powers as well. While religious memory cultures pertaining to Jerusalem were strong amongst Jews, Christians and Muslims, political invocations of memory cultures related to the city's status remained low until the rise of modern European imperialism and the global spread of nationalism. Thus, after centuries of largely uncontested Ottoman rule – when people belonging to all three major religions co-existed in the city – the nineteenth century witnessed growing struggles over Jerusalem's political status, firmly placing particularistic memory cultures pertaining to the status of Jerusalem on domestic and international political agendas.

Challenges to Ottoman rule came, firstly, 'from above' – that is, the international level and in particular from European imperial powers – as well as, secondly, from 'below', that is, from local communities that increasingly defined themselves in nationalist terms, based on memory cultures that were meant to both oppose imperial outreach and legitimize the respective emergent nationalist discourse. As far as the challenges from above are concerned, over the course of the nineteenth century a (non-violent) 'war' of the European consuls (Wasserstein, 2008) set in, with European imperial powers and their diplomatic representatives in the city advancing opposing claims about Jerusalem, often by invoking memory cultures linked to specific religious traditions and serving particularistic imperial agendas. Distinguishing themselves from what Europeans framed in Orientalist terms as a 'backward' and faltering Ottoman Empire (and local populations) inferior to the self-proclaimed European-Christian civilizational model, the Middle East and the city of Jerusalem became firm part of European imperial geopolitics and imaginaries. In that context, Jerusalem's religious significance increasingly fused with political ambitions. The Russian Empire not only had concrete territorial ambitions over Ottoman lands (albeit not in Jerusalem), it also framed itself as the protector of the Ottoman Empire's huge Christian orthodox population – Czarist Russia, under the leadership of the Orthodox Church, organized annual pilgrimages from Russia to Jerusalem, with pilgrims in increasingly huge numbers visiting Jerusalem during the Easter festivities (cf. Montefiore, 2011). Other imperial powers followed suit. From Great Britain that set up schools and Anglican missions in Jerusalem, to France (and also Austria-Hungary and Italy) who claimed to protect both the local Catholic Christians as well as other Christian churches following the Latin rite.

The protestant-dominated German Empire – a country that had a huge Catholic minority – became under Emperor Wilhelm II a close ally to Sultan Abdülhamit II. Protestants of the Temple Society, coming from the Wurttemberg region, built the German Colony neighbourhood in Jerusalem in the 1880s. The German Emperor visited Jerusalem in 1898, receiving a lot of media attention both in the Ottoman Empire, Germany, and elsewhere. Invoking memory cultures of Jerusalem as a multi-religious city, and trying to garner international support for Germany's geopolitical ambitions, in particular support by the High Porte, Wilhelm made political gestures addressing various religious communities in the Ottoman Empire and beyond. First and foremost this was directed to his German-Protestant constituency at home, pleased by the building of a huge Protestant religious complex in the Old City, with the Lutheran Church of the Redeemer and associated educational institutions at its centre. Aiming to balance French support for Catholics and British support for Jews, Wilhelm also sponsored the establishment of a huge Catholic religious site on Mount Zion, while meeting Zionist leader Theodor Herzl at Jaffa Gate. Wilhelm made sure not to forget addressing the Muslim community as well, albeit mainly in Damascus where he visited the grave of Salah Ad-Din and invoked memories of an alleged cooperation between Muslim rulers and the Frank kings in the eighth century CE obviously as a matrix for his relationship with Abdülhamit. What matters here is that all these imperial imaginaries of Jerusalem drew from a distinct invocation of memory cultures. These various policies by the German Empire and other external powers pronounced some aspects of the city, for example, protecting a specific religious rite or the multi-religious character of the city. Other elements of memory cultures were forgotten though, for example, by not recognizing or by downplaying the religious significance of the city for others or by neglecting a linkage between such religiously grounded memory cultures and political objectives. Such imperial imaginaries ultimately served a double purpose: on the one hand, they were part of a wider competition between European imperial powers over global influence. On the other hand, they fettered concrete projects on the ground: such as the Ottoman-German military alliance, with the German and Ottoman Armies jointly defending Ottoman Jerusalem at the end of World War I and German orientalist and diplomats playing a noteworthy role in the Ottoman Sultan's call for jihad against the Entente powers in 1915 (Jung, 2014). Concrete territorial imperial claims then were central to the British-French Sykes-Picot agreement of 1916, which foresaw a joint administration of Jerusalem by both imperial powers, only to be superseded by the unilateral British conquest of the city in 1917 under General Allenby and the League of Nation formalizing the British Mandate for Palestine in 1922.

Since the second half of the nineteenth century, these imperial ambitions were increasingly mirrored by a growing political awareness of local populations, a challenge to imperial Ottoman and later on British rule 'from below' (for Jerusalem in the late-Ottoman and British era cf. Jacobson, 2011). While Jerusalem over time acquired a pivotal and antagonistic place in mainstream Palestinian/Arab vis-à-vis Israeli/Jewish memory cultures, a coalescing between religious significance and political objectives only gradually developed. Until the ultimate demise of the Ottoman Empire, memory cultures in parts of both communities continued to draw from a multi-religious imaginary inspired by a belief in a modernizing and potentially reform-oriented Ottoman Empire. Thus, many Arab/Palestinians (both Christians and Muslims) as well as Jews (both local Jews and Zionists of European origin) sought some form of self-determination within a changing Ottoman Empire, but not necessarily independence, as for example the later Israeli prime minister David Ben-Gurion after his immigration into Ottoman Palestine (who then of course changed his position later on). Arab-Muslim and Arab-Christian allegiances shifted strongly in the course of World War I and an increasing disillusionment with the Ottoman Empire that culminated in the Arab revolt of 1916 – also nurturing exclusive Arab territorial claims on Jerusalem that emphasized in particular Muslim memory cultures. Central here was the war-time Hussein-MacMahon correspondence in which the British promised the Sharif of Mecca – whose sons later on ascended, under British tutelage, to the thrones of Transjordan, Syria and Iraq – political control over specific Arab-populated territories, to which most Arabs and certainly the Sharif naturally counted Al-Quds/Jerusalem (on local and expat Christians in Jerusalem during the British Mandate cf. Alnaimatt, 2017). On the other hand, though, in the Balfour Declaration of 1917, the British also promised to the Zionist movement a national home for the Jewish people in Palestine. To this, the Zionist movement naturally counted Jerusalem, although at this time Jewish population centres that emerged in the context of successive rounds of immigration by Jews from Europe since the 1880s, which mainly came as a response to lacking integration or experiences with outright anti-Semitism in various European nation-states and empires, were mainly located in other parts of Palestine.

In the first decades of the twentieth century, particularistic memory cultures pertaining to Jerusalem became central for local populations when opposing territorial claims from both external actors as well as by what over time became the opposing party in the emergent Israeli-Palestinian conflict – albeit assumptions between both sides about the Ottoman period and the Mandate years and 'what constitutes history' are surprisingly similar between both parties (Doumani, 1992). Notwithstanding episodes of Arab/Palestinian-Jewish/Israeli attempts to share memory cultures on Jerusalem – from the Faisal–Weizmann Agreement of 1919 to the Israeli-Palestinian 'Geneva Initiative' of 2003 and other proposal aiming to render Jerusalem a 'shared city' for all religious and national groups (Nasrallah, 2016) – mainstream memory cultures on Jerusalem became increasingly exclusive and mutually incompatible. This was, first of all, directed against 'external' claims by Ottomans/Turks and the British – notwithstanding some post-Ottoman nostalgia amongst some Palestinians that endured during the 1920s (Doumani, 1992).

With a view to what became contrasting Palestinian and Israeli memory cultures related to the status of Jerusalem, it is important to note that this was not so much about denying the religious significance of Jerusalem for the respective opponent. Rather, it revolved around rejecting territorial and political claims that could be made on such a basis. As far as the status of Jerusalem in Arab/Palestinian and Jewish/Israeli memory cultures is concerned, there is thus an underlying ambivalence. Thus, while for the Zionist movement prior to the war of 1967, during which Israel conquered the Eastern parts of the city, including the Old City,

Jerusalem was at times in and at other times out of focus (Mayer, 2008), Palestinian memory cultures oscillated between highlighting the huge religious significance of Jerusalem and an equally pervasive emphasis in modern Palestinian identity on various Palestinian cities that together make up the national fabric (Khalidi, 1997). However, and notwithstanding such nuances, the general trend for both national movements was an emphasis on exclusionary notions of Jerusalem, focusing on 'own' claims and historical rights (as in the Israeli national anthem that elaborates on the meaning of Jerusalem for the Jewish people or the location of Yad Vashem, the World Holocaust Memorial Centre, in Jerusalem) as well as highlighting the own sacrifices for the city, while downplaying the political relevance of the city for the other side. Memory culture is clearly visible here. Thus, ever since the Zionist movement defended the road from Tel Aviv to Jerusalem in the war of 1948, rusty tanks and artillery of the Zionist forces until today flank the Israeli Highway No. 1 connecting these two major cities. At the same time, in Israeli memory culture, this defence of West Jerusalem is linked to a narrative that remembers the division of the city between its Israeli parts and the Jordanian administered Eastern parts as an era of pain during which the city was physically divided and Jews were prevented from praying at the Kotel. The Palestinian national movement and people, in contrast, suffered a painful defeat in 1948 and then again in 1967 (Said, 1995), the former remembered in Palestinian memory culture in particular for the forceful expulsion of Palestinians in Israeli-controlled areas and the beginning of the Palestinian refugee issue, the *al-nakba* (catastrophe) – the latter, being associated with the Israeli occupation, as *al-naksa* (setback). Yet, while being defeated politically, the most central places of the city were – from 1948 until 1967 – at least controlled by Arab overlords, the Hashemite kingdom.

These two opposing narratives and memory cultures hardened after the war of 1967. The physical separation of Jerusalem was ended but not the separation of memory cultures. In Israeli politics and popular culture, the perceived liberation of Jerusalem became a central topic, figuring in iconic images of soldiers praying at the Western wall and the notion of united Jerusalem became central to popular culture as well (such as the famous song 'Jerusalem of Gold'). It also had concrete political consequences, first and foremost the formal annexation of Jerusalem in 1980, until today not recognized under international law but a firm legal and political fundament in Israeli politics. For Palestinians opposing what they perceived as a conquest of the city, objections to the ensuing Israeli occupation had, on the one hand, a grassroot dimension of memory culture with most of the 300,000 Palestinians living in Jerusalem rejecting Israeli citizenship and boycotting municipal election, a trend only recently slightly changing. On the other hand, Jerusalem acquired a renewed relevance for the Palestinian national movement with the establishment of the Orient House in the Jerusalem neighbourhood of Sheikh Jarrah in the 1980s as an informal and after the Oslo-Agreements of the 1990s semi-formal representation for the Palestine Liberation Organization and affiliated institutions.

The Ottoman past does not play a very visible role in either Israeli or Palestinian memory culture, although touristic branding by both sides heavily plays with the architectural beauty of the Ottoman city walls. Also, the first steps of modernizing the city, including the building of roads and of modern commercial centres, date back to the late-Ottoman era. Somewhat ignoring this, memory cultures on both sides often construct instead a linear continuity between today's political claims and perceived historic rights that usually ignore both the Ottoman era and the physical presence of the other side of the conflict. The perceived continuity from the times of King David to modern Israel – and the exclusion of Arabs and Palestinians from this narrative – was notably in the 'Jerusalem 3000' celebrations of the Israeli-controlled Jerusalem municipality during the late 1990s. On the other hand, the iconic image of the (golden) Dome of the Rock is a central element for flags, posters and gatherings, including cabinet meetings, of the different Palestinian parties and plays a prominent role in Palestinian popular culture and resistance culture, for example, in graffiti on the wall built by Israel throughout the West Bank and the Jerusalem area. Moreover, a narrative on a direct lineage between Palestinians and the ancient Canaanites, who built the first urban settlement in today's Jerusalem prior to the arrival of the Jewish people and King David, is meant to provide an alternative to Israel's 3000-years-narrative of 'national' rights, which is underpinned materially and legally by Israel through archaeological excavations in Jerusalem, the administrative redrawing of the city's boundaries and urban development projects, house demolitions and the building of the separation barrier/wall. In contrast, framing Israel as an 'outside' (European) colonial power, that has no national links to Jerusalem, plays a central role in parts of Palestinian society, while the notion of Jerusalem as an 'eternally' undivided Jewish city figures equally strong in parts of Israeli society. While claims that deny religious rights to the other side exist at fringes of Israeli (e.g. the Temple Mount Movement) and Palestinian society, even maximalist nationalist narratives tend to acknowledge at least some religious rights for all three major faiths. This brings in memories of the Ottoman Empire insofar, as such policies establish continuity to the eighteenth and nineteenth century Ottoman *firmans* (decrees) that established a so-called status quo with a view to religious claims and rights, a policy largely followed (albeit flexibly interpreted) by British, Jordanian and Israeli authorities. What should be noted here is that with a view to the Muslim holy sites both the King of Jordan as well as the King of Morocco (both claiming to descend from the prophet Muhammad) have some largely religiously defined and symbolic oversight rights with a view to the Muslim holy sites in Jerusalem.

Finally then, memory cultures related to Jerusalem migrate, 'Jerusalem's fate is intertwined with that of the world' (Sarsar, 2002) as they did during the nineteenth century when they found their way into European identity narratives. This migration can be seen on two levels. First, Jerusalem occupies a special place in imaginaries of imperial powers and international organizations. Thus, while since the Peel Plan of 1936 a two-state solution is, in theory, the major point of reference for the international community, Jerusalem sits uneasily here – attesting to the city's special status. The Peel Plan foresaw a division of mandate Palestine, but exempted Jerusalem, which the British hoped to keep. The 1947 UN Partition Plan then suggested to divide mandate Palestine but suggested to transform Jerusalem into an international city under UN-tutelage, a *corpus separatum*. This is an idea not entirely forgotten, as the Geneva Initiative and related proposals make clear. Thus, a widespread solution popular in liberal circles is that Jerusalem should be divided politically between Palestinians and Israelis, while keeping the city 'united' and 'shared' in all forms except formal sovereignty. Often this comes with calls for some international presence and supervision of such a formal division. Moreover, in international law, and notwithstanding the status of all territories captured by Israel in 1967 as occupied Palestinian territory, East Jerusalem has somewhat of a special status, often being mentioned explicitly alongside and in distinction to the adjacent West Bank. The relevance of Jerusalem in US politics – but also elsewhere as in Iran after the Islamic revolution where a leading army branch, the Al-Quds brigades is named after the city – has also been a central feature of relevance to memory cultures. The linkage to Israel and Jerusalem shapes what it means to be American. This can take different forms. For example, US president Clinton emphasized during the 2000 Camp David negotiations, where he suggested a political (but not physical) division of the city that he in the meantime knows every Jerusalem city street by name – while President Donald Trump moved the US embassy to Jerusalem, but closing the US consular mission to the Palestinians at the same time. These examples reflect the degree to which policies on Jerusalem not only contribute to great power politics but also serve a purpose for a strongly polarized domestic political debate in the US and a weakening bipartisan consensus.

4 Conclusion

As mentioned in the introduction, the crucial part of the Ottoman past in the post-Ottoman presence is not the past itself. It is not the sheer existence of history, but the fact that there is an Ottoman past in collective memory. The crucial aspect highlighted in this chapter pertains to the use made of this past. At different times, different actors have utilized the past and its memory for different goals, thereby embedding post-Ottoman memory cultures firmly in key modes of historicity outlined in the introduction, in particular complex temporalities and the significance of power and domination (modes 2 and 5). Certainly, the Kosovo myth is a good example for such dynamics (but requires a need for interpretation as suggested by mode 4): while in the early centuries the function of the myth – apart from entertainment on dark winter evenings – was probably to bolster religious feelings of the Orthodox population and prevent conversions to Islam by stressing the heroism of sacrifice against the Ottomans and promising redemption. In the nineteenth century, the myth played a prominent role in nation-building, in acquiring independence from the Ottomans, perceived as liberation from foreign occupation and in state-building processes. In the twentieth century though the myth was used for Serbia herself establishing control and domination over territories and people, often (as in the Kosovo campaign during the late 1990s) framing this as a defence against imperialist threats. In the case of Jerusalem, resistance to Ottoman rule came first from outside imperial powers – Europeans that 'rediscovered' Jerusalem and fought over geopolitical and symbolic influence. For Arab/Palestinians and Jews/Israelis, Jerusalem also became a central reference point in symbolizing national unity and fostering transnational solidarity with their respective national causes. In both cases, we have also highlighted the degrees to which there is a feedback between local/national actors and the international sphere, with memory cultures revolving around Kosovo and Jerusalem migrating from inside/out and outside/in.

References

Alnaimatt, F. (2017). The Christians of Jerusalem during the British Mandate, 1917–48, *Contemporary Arab Affairs*, 10(1), 118–37.

Anscombe, F. (2006). The Ottoman Empire in Recent International Politics – II: The Case of Kosovo, *The International History Review*, 28(4), 758–93.

Anscombe, F. (2014). *State, Faith, and Nation in Ottoman and Post-Ottoman Lands*, Cambridge: Cambridge University Press.

Bieber, F. (2002). Nationalist Mobilization and Stories of Serb Suffering. The Kosovo Myth from 600th Anniversary to the Present, *Rethinking History*, 6(1), 95–110.

Busse, J. (2021). The Historical and Social Embeddedness of the Post-Ottoman Space in World Society, in P. Kohlenberg & N. Godehardt (eds.). *The Multidimensionality of Regions in World Politics*, London: Routledge, 75–93.

Cohen, P. A. (2014). *History and Popular Memory: The Power of Story in Moments of Crisis*, New York: Columbia University Press.

Djordjević, D. (1991). The Tradition of Kosovo in the Formation of Modern Serbian Statehood in the Nineteenth Century, in W. S. Vucinich & T. A. Emmert (eds.). *Kosovo: Legacy of a Medieval Battle*, Minneapolis: Minnesota University Press.

Djokić, D. (2009). Whose Myth? Which Nation? The Serbian Kosovo Myth Revisited, in J. M. Bak et al. (eds.). *Uses and Abuses of the Middle Ages: 19th–21st Century*, Munich: Wilhelm Fink.

Doumani, B. B. (1992). Rediscovering Ottoman Palestine: Writing Palestinians into History, *Journal of Palestine Studies*, 21(2), 5–28.

Ekmečić, M. (1991). The Emergence of St. Vitus Day as the Principal National Holiday of the Serbs, in W. S. Vucinich & T. A. Emmert (eds.). *Kosovo: Legacy of a Medieval Battle*, Minneapolis: University of Minnesota Modern Greek.

El-Khatib, A. (2001). Jerusalem in the Qur'an, *British Journal of Middle Eastern Studies*, 28(1), 25–53.

Emmert, T. A. (1990). *Serbian Golgotha: Kosovo, 1389*, New York: Columbia University Press.

Erll, A. (2011). *Memory in Culture*, Basingstoke: Palgrave Macmillan.

Fendius, E. M. (2016). *Jerusalem Studies: The State of the Field*, *Israel Studies*, 21(3), 221–41.

Halberstam, D. (2001). *War in a Time of Peace: Bill Clinton and the Generals*, New York and London: Scribner.

Halbwachs, M. (1980). *The Collective Memory*, New York: Harper & Row.

Hammond, A. (2004). The Uses of Balkanism: Representation and Power in British Travel Writing, 1850–1914, *The Slavonic and East European Review*, 82(3), 601–24.

Jacobson, A. (2011). *From Empire to Empire: Jerusalem between Ottoman and British Rule*, New York: Syracuse University Press.

Jung, D. (2014). The 'Ottoman-German *Jihad*': Lessons for the Contemporary 'Area Studies' Controversy, *British Journal of Middle Eastern Studies*, 41(3), 247–65.

Kaplan, R. D. (2005). *Balkan Ghosts: A Journey through History*, London: Picador.

Khalidi, R. (1997). *Palestinian Identity: The Construction of Modern National Consciousness*, New York: Columbia University Press.

Levine, Lee I. (2008). Jerusalem in Jewish History, Tradition, and Memory, in T. Mayer & S. Mourad (eds.). *Jerusalem: Idea and Reality*, London: Routledge.

Malcolm, N. (1998). *Kosovo: A Short History*, New York: Macmillan.

Mayer, T. (2008). Jerusalem In and Out of Focus: The City in Zionist Ideology, in T. Mayer & S. Mourad (eds.). *Jerusalem: Idea and Reality*, London: Routledge.

Mayer, T. & Mourad, S. A. (eds.) (2008). *Jerusalem: Idea and Reality*, London: Routledge.

Mazower, M. (2000). *The Balkans*, London: Modern Library.
Montefiore, S. S. (2011). *Jerusalem: The Biography*, London: Weidenfeld & Nicolsen.
Nasrallah, R. (2016). Future Scenarios for the Old City of Jerusalem, *Palestine-Israel Journal of Politics, Economics and Culture*, 21(4).
Nenadović, P. M. (1893). Memoirs [Serbian], Belgrade: Štamp. Kraljevine Srbije.
Pavković, A. (2001). Kosovo/Kosova: A Land of Conflicting Myths, in M. Waller, K. Drezov & B. Gökay (eds.). *Kosovo: The Politics of Delusion*, London, Routledge.
Said, E. (1979). *Orientalism*, New York: Vintage.
Said, E. (1995). Projecting Jerusalem, *Journal of Palestine Studies*, 25(1), 5–14.
Sarsar, S. (2002). Jerusalem: Between the Local and Global, *Alternatives: Turkish Journal of International Relations*, 1(4), 53–72.
Schwandner-Sievers, S. & Fischer, B. J. (eds.) (2002). *Albanian Identities: Myth and History*, Bloomington: Indianapolis University Press.
Smith, A. (1997). The 'Golden Age' and National Renewal, in G. Hosking & G. Schöpflin (eds.). *Myths and Nationhood*, New York: Routledge.
Todorova, M. (2009). *Imagining the Balkans*, Oxford: Oxford University Press.
Wasserstein, B. (2008). *Divided Jerusalem: The Struggle for the Holy City*, London: Yale University Press.
Wigen, E. (2013). Ottoman Concepts of Empire, *Contributions to the History of Concepts*, 8(1), 44–66.
Zirojević, O. (2000). Kosovo in the Collective Memory, in N. Popov (ed.). *The Road to War in Serbia: Trauma and Catharsis*, Budapest: Central European University Press.

Conclusion

14 Can Historicism Win over IR?

Ayşe Zarakol

1 Introduction

The Presence of the Past makes a compelling case for historicism in International Relations (IR) and the broader social sciences. Historicism has had different meanings and lives in the social sciences,[1] but the editors and contributors here understand historicism in a manner similar to Bevir, who defined it as 'a philosophy that emphasizes the importance of history in understanding, explaining, or evaluating phenomena' (Bevir, 2017: 1). Historicist approaches 'need not study the past' (Bevir, 2017: 1), but they do need to pay attention to how the past shapes the present; as our editors, Klaus Schlichte and Stephan Stetter, also observe in their Introduction to this volume: 'the past is not over'. Historicism thus demands that we approach our analyses from the starting point of 'the unity of past, present and future, mediated and enacted through invocations of specific dimensions of the past, which allow to make sense of the present and conceive of the future' (Editors' Introduction). Schlichte and Stetter also helpfully identify six modes of historicity, which can help guide IR and other social science research: '(1) the role of history in shaping reality, (2) the centrality of complex temporalities, (3) the paramount importance of the temporality of observers, (4) the necessity to interpret contexts, (5) the significance of sedimented forms of power and domination and (6) change through non-linear pathways' (Editors' Introduction). The first understanding of historicity asks us to think about how the past shapes not only the material conditions of the present but the ideational ones as well. The second understanding of historicity asks us to shed (implicit or explicit) teleological understandings of history in our research. The third asks us to consider the historicity of the observer. The fourth points us to the importance of historiography in understanding history. The fifth underlines the significance of power dynamics in historical analysis. And finally, the sixth understanding emphasizes the contingency of historical outcomes.

[1] For more on this cf. Barkawi et al. (forthcoming); cf. Steinmetz (2020).

The other chapters in the book, which draw from IR, Sociology and Global History, also clearly demonstrate what can be gained by adopting a historicist sensibility in IR and other disciplines concerned with the study of world politics. The common thread throughout the chapters is imperialism (or colonialism) and its legacies. In Chapter 2, George Lawson brings a historicist sensibility to the study of international organizations, a subfield in IR that is usually completely devoid of history (which may explain why in recent years it has been international lawyers and historians rather than IR scholarly who have really broken through into the public discourse on this subject). In Chapter 3, Thomas Müller considers the role colonial hierarchies have played in the evolution of collective hegemony from the Concert of Europe to the G7. In Chapter 4, Joël Glasman and Klaus Schlichte bring historicism to the study of statehood in Africa, with focus on Ugandan and Cameroonian welfare services. In Chapter 5, Benjamin de Carvalho and Halvard Leira (re)introduce privateers into the historical narrative about the emergence of the modern international order. In Chapter 6, Iver B. Neumann and Einar Wigen draw out the legacies of Eurasian steppe traditions in today's Eurasia. In Chapter 7, Mathias Albert reads IR through comparative lenses with its past. In Chapter 8, George Steinmetz discusses the difficulties in seeing the presence of the imperial past in disciplines other than IR. In Chapter 9, Teresa Koloma Beck uses a Fanonian approach to understand the colonial dynamics present in conflict settings such as Kabul. In Chapter 10, Julian Go analyses the colonial origins of policing in the US and the UK. In Chapter 10, Tomoko Akami turns the historicist lens onto IR itself, providing an account of colonial dynamics in the formation of IR, with a focus on IR. In Chapter 11, Daniel Speich Chassé provides a historicist genealogy of the concept of the 'Third World'. In Chapter 12, Anna Vlachopoulou and Stephan Stetter discuss post-Ottoman memory cultures and how they are used in contemporary politics.

And via those chapters you have arrived here, to the chapter that is to supposed to serve as a conclusion to it all. I was not part of the original conversation that led to this volume, but my own sympathies about historicism and historicist approaches in IR are already public (cf. e.g. Zarakol, 2011a, 2011b, 2017a, 2017b, 2018, 2022; Barkawi et al., forthcoming). It will therefore come as no surprise when I say that I very much welcome the addition of this book to the growing canon of IR and interdisciplinary works that help advance the cause of having more and better history (and historicism) in our study of world politics, many of which are already discussed by the editors in their Introduction to this volume. When I look at this volume, the now long list of citations in historical IR and the rapid growth of the HIST section at ISA, I am delighted to see how much more space there is in IR for historical and historicist approaches than there used to be back when I was a student, and how this openness to historicism also allow us to converse more (and more productively) with colleagues from other disciplines such as sociology and history.

In this chapter, I would like to interject a note of caution to that optimism, however. I would like to use the opportunity I have been given to move the discussion away from how persuasive historicism is as an approach to social science – as demonstrated by this volume – to the structural constraints historicism faces in IR in particular and the social sciences in general. Because after all, despite all the headway we have made, one could argue that it is a case of too little, too late. We thus need to question what allowed IR to get so thoroughly divorced from history in the first place. In other words, I want to ask (in the specific context of IR) why – if the arguments in favour of historicism are so compelling (and they are) – does historicism have such relative difficulty in gaining a strong foothold, even after decades of the historical turn and the accompanying calls to incorporate more historicism into our approaches? What are the *structural* obstacles that the historicist move faces that cannot be overcome by rhetorical persuasion alone? And what, if anything, can be done about such obstacles beyond producing volumes such as this one with excellent and convincing chapters on the presence of colonial and imperial legacies in the present? The proof may be in the pudding, as they say, but it will not be found if the pudding is not consumed.

There is of course a simple answer to the question of why historicism has not made as much progress as it should have in IR. That simple answer is that IR got divorced from historicism because IR was an 'American social science' and the way the discipline globalized is in many ways a fine example of (academic) imperialism at work. And it remains difficult to remedy this problem because IR remains still in many ways an 'American social science' even as that American influence is decreasing (Hoffman, 1977; Waever, 1998; Maliniak et al., 2011; Maliniak et al., 2012; Maliniak et al., 2014). But of course that is a simple answer that actually begs the more difficult question: why should American IR be necessarily ahistorical and anti-historicist? Moreover, that simple answer is a bit misleading on its own because it suggests that as the discipline became less US centric, it will also easily become more historicist. Unfortunately, there are other obstacles beyond US-centrism to adopting a historicist approach in IR (and other social sciences).

In the remainder of this short chapter, I first discuss why IR's particular American origins as a discipline (as well the continued domination of US standards in the evaluation of IR scholarship globally) makes it difficult for historicist calls such as the one advanced by this volume to resonate in the wider discipline. In other words, I provide a historicist explanation for why historicism faces an uphill battle in IR. I then conclude the chapter by discussing why the problem will not be solved automatically as American influence in the discipline and the world decreases. Unfortunately, many approaches to IR hailing from other parts of the world have their own motivations to reject historicism even as they seem to care more about history than US-based approaches. Historicism is unpalatable to all political projects that require various categories to be given, natural and/or unchanging. American IR is just one version of how that requirement manifests (as scientism). I also speculate briefly on how those of who favour historicist approaches can deal with such resistance.

2 International Relations as an 'American Social Science' and the Roots of Its Anti-historicism

International Relations was famously observed to be an 'American social science' first by Hoffman (1977). Hoffman argued that IR emerged in the US (and as a social science) precisely because the US was a Great Power, and that the discipline could not be developed to the same stature without a national context to exercise real foreign policy power. In other contexts, he argued, 'scholars will not have the motivation ... to turn individual efforts into a genuine scientific enterprise, and will either turn to other fields ... or merely reflect, more or less slavishly, and with some delays, American fashions; or else there will be often brilliant individual contributions, but unconnected and unsupported' (1977: 49). To put another way, when Hoffman labelled IR an 'American social science', he actually meant that the field did not even really exist elsewhere. And at the time he was writing this argument had some plausibility; many people studied world politics outside of the US, but not in the 'disciplined' way that Hoffman was observing about American IR.

Hoffman's (1977) article is especially significant not only for that declaration, however, but also because it makes some interesting observations about the nature of IR as practiced in the US, especially as it pertains to the issue of historicism. To recap briefly, Hoffman first describes the traits he observes in IR which make it a particularly *American* social science: 'the profound conviction ... that all problems can be resolved via the scientific method' (45); the influence of natural sciences and economics (46); presence of immigrant scholars asking big questions (46); the rise of the US and the accompanying interest of policy-makers in IR scholarship (47–49); the institutional arrangements that allowed scholars to join the ranks of policy-makers (49); the presence of foundations and think tanks (50); and the American university system (51). After discussing these factors that give IR its distinctively American flavour, Hoffman also points out some problems the discipline has run into as a result: 'There was the hope of turning a field of inquiry into a science, and the hope that this science would be useful. Both quests have turned out to be frustrating' (51). He also bemoans the fragmentation of the discipline (52–54) and the fact that research which justifies itself with reference to utility is often 'torn between irrelevance and absorption' vis-a-vis the policy world (55). These complaints presciently foreshadow many of our current debates about IR.

For our purposes here, however, the most intriguing section of the article comes at the end, where Hoffman suggests that there are some traits that could be identified as essentially American that the discipline *should* aim to overcome. These traits, according to Hoffman, are: 'the quest for certainty' and what could be called presentism or lack of a historical sense (57). Put another way, Hoffman observed in 1977 that lack of historicism (or even anti-historicism) was baked into the American origins of IR, and went hand-in-hand with the quest for certainty. He also noted that these traits created some serious substantive blind spots in the field: the two examples Hoffman gave for understudied research areas were the relation of domestic politics to international affairs and international hierarchies (58). According to Hoffman, American scholars were not interested in history and did not know how to study it properly even when they were interested in history because the discipline has been organized around the question of 'What should we do?' and not the question of 'What should we know?' In conclusion, Hoffman argues that going forward IR 'needs triple distance: it should move away from the contemporary, toward the past; from the perspective of a superpower ... toward that of the weak and the revolutionary ...; from the glide into policy science, back to the steep ascent toward the peaks which the questions raised by traditional political philosophy represent' (59). In other words, he issues many of the same warnings and calls as the editors of this volume.

Forty years on, international hierarchies (cf. Lake, 2011; Bially Mattern & Zarakol, 2016; Zarakol, 2017a) and the relation of domestic politics to the international have received some attention (see e.g. the Democratic Peace Theory literature). Yet, we would be hard-pressed to argue that American IR, which still occupies a good portion of mainstream IR, has come to care more about the question of 'What should we know?'. It is also difficult to argue that the discipline has left its ahistoricism behind. The ahistoricism was still there (and identified as a major problem) quarter of a century after Hoffman when Buzan and Little

(2001) wrote another famous article on the state of IR: 'Why International Relations has failed as an intellectual project and what to do about it'. And it is still very much here, another two decades later, despite all the aforementioned successes of the historical turn; if it were not, there would be no reason for this volume to exist.

The handmaiden of ahistoricism as identified by Hoffman, that is, the 'quest for certainty' in the search for empirically verifiable generalizations, also persists, and in fact, may have even increased since the time of Hoffman. This is manifest in the shift from inter-paradigmatic debates (the war of -isms) to so-called non-paradigmatic research that is driven primarily by mid-level hypothesis testing and to the rise of experimental methods: 'the field is moving away from developing or carefully employing theories and instead emphasizing ... simplistic hypothesis testing. Theory usually plays a minor role in this enterprise, with most of the effort devoted to collecting data and testing empirical hypotheses' (Mearsheimer & Walt, 2013: 428; cf. Achen, 2002: 424, 443; Braumoeller & Sartori., 2004 – as cited by Mearsheimer and Walt). Mearsheimer and Walt attribute this 'growing emphasis on methods at the expense of theory' (2013: 429) to a number of factors, such as the difficulty of innovating new grand IR theories, availability of data and computer technology (445), the influence of Gary King, Robert Keohane and Sidney Verba's *Designing Social Inquiry* (1994) as well as the democratic peace literature, the proliferation of IR PhD programs (446) and 'the professionalization of academia' (447). These generalizations do not always apply to most non-US IR, where theory-oriented work (though most of it also ahistoricist) is mostly welcome. However, the end result has been a growing fragmentation of the discipline in recent decades, all the while the calls to globalize IR get stronger.

It may be asked why the particular traits in IR as identified by Hoffman should keep manifesting as a trend towards positivism and empiricism; for example, what Mearsheimer and Walt (2013) label as the hegemony of 'simplistic hypothesis testing', or the experimentation fad or the identification revolution of the most recent decade. It is not really because policy-makers demand this: American IR has certainly become more methodologically sophisticated since Hoffman's time, but there is no evidence that such scholarship is more attractive to policy-makers. The gap between IR scholarship and policy-making in the US has arguably even grown since Hoffman's time. In any case, despite their empiricism, it is also a well-documented fact that such approaches in IR often fail to yield concrete empirical results in practice and continue to have issues with replicability. The attraction of such approaches to American IR therefore lie not in their production of 'valuable' empirical findings or their utility to policy-makers, but rather in the theoretical model of the external world that underwrites hypothesis testing (and similar approaches). Understanding this fact is key to understanding why calls to have more historicism in IR are consistently resisted by traditional (American) mainstream of the discipline.

Hypothesis testing (or other positivist approaches to IR) take as their starting point a world wherein the 'quest for certainty' is an achievable goal, if not always achieved. For example, statistics operates on the assumption that social phenomena follow 'natural law' and that 'every event is causally connected with previous events belonging to its own series, but it cannot be modified by contact with events belonging to another series. A "chance" event is a complex due to the concurrence in time or place of events belonging to causally independent series' (Keynes, 1921: 283, as quoted by Collins, 1984: 335). In such a world, it is theoretically possible to arrive at certainty; even 'chance' events can be causally explained if one had perfect access to data. This is why statistics is not *just* a method, but rather 'substantive theory of the world' in its own way (Collins, 1984: 335). And that theory is assumed or believed, rather than proved: 'it is not clear how we can know that the events are not completely unconnected' (Collins, 1984: 335). Hypothesis testing is thus 'more a matter of faith than an ultimate criterion of truth' (Collins, 1984: 335).

Positivist/empiricist approaches in IR could in principle become at least bit more historicist, and show some sensitivity to how things change over time. But this is rarely practiced; for example, datasets in IR have mostly lacked any sense of historicism, largely assuming (even when measuring temporal change) a system static enough across time and space to create commensurable variables. In other words, in this world only the variable varies, everything else – society, people, institutions, concepts, categories, meanings – they are all static, unchanging. Other positivist methods make similar leaps of faith when it comes to the generalizability of the finding beyond the immediate study. Experiments, for instance, assume that studies based on a group of people at one particular moment in time tell us something about people everywhere and always, when we could easily question whether even the same group of people would respond in the same way in the future. Of course, it is not American IR that is dominated by hypothesis testing (and more broadly positivism) but political science and other social sciences in the US as well. Anyone who has seen coverage of US Presidential elections knows that generalizations based on previous voter behaviour – sometimes going back centuries – are treated as having full applicability in the present. Most everyone talking about elections, from journalist to academics, participates in the make-believe that the US has not fundamentally changed since the eighteenth century.

And here we come to the crux of the matter. Historian Dorothy Ross explains the presence of these shared traits across the US social sciences with reference to the 'ideology of American exceptionalism' (1993: 103). In *The Origins of American Social Science*, Ross focuses on the formative years of economics, sociology and political science in the US, between 1870 and 1929, noting that 'what is most striking about American social science is its emulation of natural science and its liberal ideological boundaries' (1993: 100). In the nineteenth century, the nascent social sciences were animated by the desire to alleviate the anxiety caused by novelty in human affairs and the loss of belief in divine purpose (101): [evolutionary positivists] 'were trying to compensate themselves for the loss of an unchanging world by clinging to the belief that change can be foreseen because it is ruled by an unchanging law' (Ross, 1993: 102). In the US, the ideology of American exceptionalism was crucial in the formation of social sciences because it offered a solution to problem of constructing a science of a historical (thus changing) world (1993: 100, 103). Put more simply, the ideology of American exceptionalism helped US social sciences concoct the secular version of the idea that the world was unchanging.

The myth of American exceptionalism, in essence, was the idea that the *US exists outside of history* and not subject to its whims: 'America as an unchanging realm of nature, that had left behind the structured, changing European past; America as the final repository of law and the end of history' (107). Because America was exceptional, it would not be subject to the same crises the Old World faced and vice versa: 'The exceptionalist idea of America quickly became the basis of nationalist ideology ... from their earliest American moments, social science writers took as their central task the maintenance of America's exemption from the fate of modern Europe' (104). This belief underwrites the quest for discovering naturalistic laws akin to those found in natural sciences: 'only science could plumb an ocean that was not part of history, but of the system of nature' (107). Other parts of the world may need history and historicism, but not the US ... America was free from history, and others will inevitably arrive where America is at some point in the future: thus studying patterns in the behaviour of US agents now is all we need to understand how the world works. A version of this faith still animates much of US IR and has been exported[2] around the globe through the hegemony of US approaches in the discipline.

[2] On the other hand, this process of dissemination is never as smooth as it usually assumed to be (cf. Çapan & Zarakol, 2018).

3 Declining US hegemony: More Room for Historicism?

If the American influence on IR is one of the main reasons why calls to historicism such as this volume face an uphill battle, then for historicism to advance one of two things have to happen: either American IR itself has to become more open to historicism or American IR needs to be decentred. We may in fact be in a period where both possibilities are in play, which makes this volume timely. However, we need to temper that optimism with a degree of realism.

Ross (1993) argues that historicism has in the past made inroads into American social science when the belief in American exceptionalism weakened, due to periods of prolonged economic or political crisis. Currently, the outcome of the 2016 Presidential elections and still-looming threat of democratic backsliding has created a crisis of confidence in the US; with many US political scientists arguing perhaps for the first time that US is not exceptional and should be studied via a comparative lens. Admittedly, it is more the study of American and comparative politics that was shaken by the developments of recent years, but some of the questioning has made its way into IR as well, via the crisis of the Liberal International Order debates. There is a worry that the mainstream approaches to IR overlooked some important factors which are now driving this crisis. That opening makes room for historical and historicist approaches in IR (as well as other non-mainstream takes): for example, even positivist American IR is starting to show some interest in how historical hierarchies play out in the present, especially with regards to race (cf. Freeman et al., 2021).

A moment of caution is in order before we start celebrating, however. In the past episodes Ross studied, such periods of opening ended however with exceptionalism and scientism being reasserted in American social science even more vigorously than before, albeit under new guises. But why does this pattern keep repeating itself? As Ross explains it: 'In America … the rise of heterodoxy … brings reaction towards scientism, not only from the right, but from a liberal centre that sees science as an escape from ideological warfare and from some on the left who believe science can be used for their own critical purposes' (110). And I would submit that it is not only through scientism that the chaos of crisis is tamed, but also through insisting on fixity of categories: for example, a historicist move to understand how past shapes the present of race relations in the US can become recaptured by essentialist takes on race relations (both on the left or the right), and arguably this process is already underway in the US. Thus, we should not assume that the current opening for historicism in American IR – such as it is – will always be available.

Another thing we should not assume is that waning US hegemony – in the world and in the discipline – will automatically make room for more historicism in IR. Other academies have their own historical sociological dynamics, and American exceptionalism is not the only national(ist) exceptionalism that has shaped knowledge production around the world. Many other countries have their own narratives of why they are unique. We need to remember that historicism fundamentally presents a threat to all such accounts and any type of essentialist thinking about national(ist) or civilizational identity. Historicism inevitably disturbs the notion that essences are given, unchanging and bounded. Most political projects do not like to be reminded of these possibilities.

For similar reasons, it is also important to not confuse calls for taking history seriously with calls for taking historicism seriously. It may be that American exceptionalism is relatively unique in manifesting as a trend towards scientism and positivism in natural sciences. This may lead us to conclude that just getting away from scientism and having more history in IR as American influence wanes fixes the problem. But unfortunately, there are ways to study history that are not historicist; and in fact, many national narratives around the world are based on such static readings of history and historical grievances. For these reasons, declining US hegemony will not automatically bring historicism into the discipline, even if it creates an opportunity.

At the end of the day, it always bears reiterating that disciplinary conversations in IR (and social sciences) are always implicated in and shaped by the politics of the world that we study. The editors' Introduction also underlines this point, but the same framework that helps us understand why historicism is so important for social science analysis can also help us understand why it has been so strenuously resisted by so many corners of social science. Overcoming that resistance will require more than a scholarly discussion about why historicism is better than its academic alternatives; it requires openly acknowledging the *political* reasons why historicism is not favoured, especially by those in power or at the top of a given hierarchy.

References

Achen, C. H. (2002). Toward a New Political Methodology: Microfoundations and ART, *Annual Review of Political Science*, 5, 423–50.

Barkawi, T., Bell, D. & Zarakol, A. (forthcoming). What Is 'Historicism'?, in S. Goddard, G. Lawson & O. J. Sending (eds.). *Oxford Handbook of International Political Sociology*, Oxford: Oxford University Press.

Bevir, M. (2017). Historicism and the Human Sciences in Victorian Britain, in Mark Bevir (ed.). *Historicism and the Human Sciences in Victorian Britain*, Cambridge: Cambridge University Press.

Bially Mattern, J. & Zarakol, A. (2016). Hierarchies in World Politics, *International Organization*, 70(3), 623–54.

Braumoeller, B. & Sartori, A. E. (2004). The Promise and Perils of Statistics in International Relations, in D. Sprinz & Y. Wolinsky (eds.). *Models, Numbers, and Cases: Methods for Studying International Relations*, Ann Arbor: University of Michigan Press.

Buzan, B. & Little, R. (2001). Why International Relations Has Failed as an Intellectual Project and What to Do about It, *Millennium: Journal of International Studies*, 30(1), 19–39.

Çapan, Z. G. & Zarakol, A. (2018). Between 'East' and 'West': Travelling Theories, Travelling Imaginations, in A. Gofas, I. Hamati-Ataya & N. Onuf (eds.). *The SAGE Handbook of the History, Philosophy and Sociology of International Relations*. London: SAGE Publications.

Collins, R. (1984). Statistics versus Words, *Sociological Theory*, 2: 329–62.

Freeman, B., Kim, D. G. & Lake, D. A. (2022). Race in International Relations: Beyond the 'Norm Against Noticing', *Annual Review of Political Science*, May. https://doi.org/10.1146/annurev-polisci-051820-120746.

Hoffmann, S. (1977). An American Social Science: International Relations, *Daedalus*, 106(3), 41–60.

Keynes, J. M. (1921). *A Treatise on Probability*, London: Macmillan.

King, G., Keohane, R. O. & Verba, S. (1994). *Designing Social Inquiry: Scientific Inference in Qualitative Research*, Princeton: Princeton University Press.

Lake, D. (2011). *Hierarchy in International Relations*, Ithaca: Cornell University Press.

Mearsheimer, J. J. & Walt, S. M. (2013). Leaving Theory Behind: Why Simplistic Hypothesis Testing Is Bad for International Relations, *European Journal of International Relations*, 19(3), 427–57.

Maliniak, D., Oakes, A., Peterson, S. & Tierney, M. J. (2011). International Relations in the US Academy, *International Studies Quarterly*, 55(2), 437–64.

Maliniak, D., Peterson, S., Powers, R. & Tierney, M. J. (2014). *TRIP 2014 Faculty Survey*, Williamsburg: Institute for the Theory and Practice of International Relations. https://trip.wm.edu/charts/

Maliniak, D., Peterson, S. & Tierney, M. J. (2012). *TRIP Around the World: Teaching, Research, and Policy Views of International Relations Faculty in 20 Countries*, Williamsburg: Institute for the Theory and Practice of International Relations.

Ross, D. (1993). *The Origins of American Social Science*, Cambridge: Cambridge University Press.

Steinmetz, G. (2020). Historicism and Positivism in Sociology: From Weimar Germany to the Contemporary United States, in P. Herman & A. van Veldhuizen (eds.). *Historicism: A Travelling Concept*, London: Bloomsbury.

Zarakol, A. (2011a). *After Defeat: How the East Learned to Live with the West*, Cambridge: Cambridge University Press.

Zarakol, A. (2011b). What Makes Terrorism Modern? Terrorism, Legitimacy, and the International System, *Review of International Studies*, 37(5), 2311–36.

Zarakol, A. (2017a). States and Ontological Security: A Historical Rethinking, *Cooperation & Conflict*, 52(1), 48–68.

Zarakol, A. (2017b). *Hierarchies in World Politics*, Cambridge: Cambridge University Press.

Zarakol, A. (2018). Sovereign Equality as Misrecognition, *Review of International Studies*, 44(5), 848–62.

Zarakol, A. (2022). *Before the West: The Rise and Fall of Eastern World Orders*, Cambridge: Cambridge University Press.

Index

CPSIA information can be obtained
at www.ICGtesting.com
Printed in the USA
LVHW011808230723
753220LV00007B/620

9 781009 199056